CW01023203

The Military History of Ancient Israel

Other Books By Richard A. Gabriel

Great Armies of Antiquity (2002)
Sebastian's Cross (2002)
Gods of Our Fathers: The Memory of Egypt in Judaism and Christianity (2001)
Warrior Pharaoh (2001)
Great Captains of Antiquity (2000)
Great Battles of Antiquity (1994)
A Short History of War: Evolution of Warfare and Weapons (1994)
History of Military Medicine: Ancient Times to the Middle Ages (1992)
History of Military Medicine: Renaissance to the Present (1992)
From Sumer to Rome: The Military Capabilities of Ancient Armies (1991)
The Culture of War: Invention and Early Development (1990)
The Painful Field: Psychiatric Dimensions of Modern War (1988)
No More Heroes: Madness and Psychiatry in War (1987)
The Last Centurion (French, 1987)
Military Psychiatry: A Comparative Perspective (1986)
Soviet Military Psychiatry (1986)
Military Incompetence: Why the American Military Doesn't Win (1985)
Operation Peace for Galilee: The Israeli-PLO War in Lebanon (1985)
The Antagonists: An Assessment of the Soviet and American Soldier (1984)
The Mind of the Soviet Fighting Man (1984)
Fighting Armies: NATO and the Warsaw Pact (1983)
Fighting Armies: Antagonists of the Middle East (1983)
Fighting Armies: Armies of the Third World (1983)
To Serve with Honor: A Treatise on Military Ethics (1982)
The New Red Legions: An Attitudinal Portrait of the Soviet Soldier (1980)
The New Red Legions: A Survey Data Sourcebook (1980)
Managers and Gladiators: Directions of Change in the Army (1978)
Crisis in Command: Mismanagement in the Army (1978)
Ethnic Groups in America (1978)
Program Evaluation: A Social Science Approach (1978)
The Ethnic Factor in the Urban Polity (1973)
The Environment: Critical Factors in Strategy Development (1973)

The Military History of Ancient Israel

Richard A. Gabriel

Foreword by Mordechai Gichon

Westport, Connecticut
London

Library of Congress Cataloging-in-Publication Data

Gabriel, Richard A.
The military history of ancient Israel / Richard A. Gabriel ; foreword by Mordechai Gichon.
p. cm.
Includes bibliographical references and index.
ISBN 0–275–97798–6 (alk. paper)
1. Military history of the Bible. 2. Bible. O.T. Pentateuch—History of Biblical events. 3. Bible. O.T. Former prophets—History of Biblical events. 4. Jews—Wars. 5. Military art and science—History—To 500. 6. Palestine—History, Military. I. Title.
BS1197.G32 2003
221.9'5—dc21 2003053022

British Library Cataloguing in Publication Data is available.

Library of Congress Catalog Card Number: 2003053022
ISBN: 0–275–97798–6

First published in 2003

Praeger Publishers, 88 Post Road West, Westport, CT 06881
An imprint of Greenwood Publishing Group, Inc.
www.praeger.com

Printed in the United States of America

The paper used in this book complies with the Permanent Paper Standard issued by the National Information Standards Organization (Z39.48–1984).

10 9 8 7 6 5 4 3 2 1

To Joel and Ann Klein
Whose lives have helped light the earth

and for

Mordechai Gichon, soldier, teacher, scholar,
and Chava, whose gentle eyes calm the storm

Contents

Illustrations

FIGURES

TABLE

Foreword

Once more Professor Richard Gabriel takes us to the ancient Near East to what is to western civilization its most holy center, Palestine, birthplace of Judaism and Christianity. Thus naturally we associate biblical Palestine with the message of peace, the essential core of the Bible's teaching. Both the Old and New Testaments envisage eternal peace at the end of the days as the ultimate goal of divine providence when all people "will beat their swords into plowshares and their spears into pruning hooks. Nation shall not lift up sword against Nation, neither shall they learn war anymore" (Isaiah 2:4). How and when did these ideas crystallize in ancient Israel? There need not have been a logical and immediate outcome of adopting the belief in one god. The Bible explicitly mentions the Almighty as "the Lord of Hosts" (*Adonai Zebaoth*). The ancient Israelites, like all believers until now, were convinced of the Lord's role in war. He was the divine *spiritus movens* that bestowed both victory and defeat on their earthly hosts. They put their trust in God to lead his people to triumph over those pagan nations that were against Israel.

The prayer for ad hoc victory in war was, however, soon paralleled by the overwhelming quest for divinely imposed peace in the conduct of human affairs. The prophets prophesied peace, *shalom*, no less than thirty times in the Bible as it has come down to us. Israel's fondest hope was the time when each and every man will enjoy peace "sitting under his vine and under his fig tree" (Micah 4:4). Military efforts will become unnecessary and redundant. Zechariah proclaims that God himself will "cut off the chariot from Ephraim and the horse from Jerusalem" because "he shall command peace unto the nations . . . from sea even to sea and from river even to the end of the earth" (Zechariah 9:10).

The explanation for this development in the eschatological outlook of the ancient Israelites and its making the Bible the eternal battle cry for peace lies in the geopolitical situation of biblical Palestine. This country's history is one of the most extreme examples of the truth of Napoleon's remark that "[t]he history of any country is in its geography." Geography, of course, includes various aspects. One of these is security, which has a deep imprint not only on life but also on the minds and aspirations of a country's inhabitants. Palestine is the land-bridge between Africa and Eurasia. One of the consequences is that since the beginning of recorded history, it has served as a battlefield and thoroughfare for armies marching from Egypt into Syria and Asia Minor, Mesopotamia and beyond. These were forced to make their way along the narrow belt between the Mediterranean and the edge of the Arabian deserts. I have counted the passage of no less than twenty-eight foreign armies through or into Palestine from the mid-second millennium B.C.E. to the Roman conquest. This means, of course, in both directions, from the south and from the north and northeast, and often both ways. The strategic importance of the land-bridge for commerce and traffic in peace, not less than for movement in war, was such that larger neighbors and the great powers of the day tried for both these reasons to obtain influence or, even better, a foothold in Palestine, which means that a large part of the wars on the land-bridge were waged partly or completely for its domination. The pressure on the land-bridge's population was, of course, immense. The more so since it had to face constantly a further menace from inroads and invasions from the nomad desert fringe tribes. There is no better way to demonstrate the latter menace than to cite Joshua 9:3: "and so it was when Israel had sown, that the Midianites came up and the Amalekites and the children of the east . . . and destroyed the increase of the earth and left no substance of Israel, neither sheep nor ox, nor ass . . . for both they and their camels were without number and they entered the country to destroy it."

Under this all-round pressure, only a people knowing how to make the best of the, by nature, apt for defense Palestine hill country and ready to do so, was able to establish and preserve independence and preserve comprehensive internal autonomy even under foreign domination. Only two nations achieved more than ephemeral rule over all or major parts of the Palestine land-bridge: the Israelites in about the twelfth century B.C.E. for over a half millennium, and then the Crusaders, for up to 200 years, half of them on the coast only. Their distinct religious faith and the firm belief that their defense of the Holy Land was an act of defense of their faith and thus assured of heavenly support are important factors in explaining this phenomenon. In the words of the psalmist: "All nations have compassed me about, but in the name of the Lord, will I destroy them" (Psalms 118:10). On the physical side, it was of course the warlike qualities of the Jews (so named after the Babylonian Exile) and of the Crusaders that enabled them to establish themselves in the Promised Land and keep it.

In this, his latest book, Dr. Gabriel takes us to the genesis of the first Jewish commonwealth and to its highest peak of physical expansion—the reigns of David and Solomon, a situation attained once more only in the eightieth century B.C.E. when the combined efforts of Jeroboam II of Israel and Uzziah of Judah established ancient Israel for thirty-five years as the major power between the Nile and the Euphrates. The subject, among others, has also been dealt with by the writer of this introduction. Professor Gabriel's work has added new vistas and insights to our understanding of the military history of the Bible and relying upon his extensive knowledge of the armies of the ancient East and his expert understanding of military tactics and strategy has provided us with additional colorful detail of biblical armies and wars by drawing penetrating conclusions from the often sparse and laconic information offered by the Bible. *The Military History of Ancient Israel* makes exciting reading for scholar and general reader alike, and, even if I sometimes come to different conclusions from those of the author of the book, I am stimulated in my own thought and work by the new insights, conclusions, and thoroughly original ideas presented by Professor Gabriel in the present volume. A good example is the author's emphasis upon Israel's "Egyptian connection" which he had argued with great acumen in his recently published opus *Gods of Our Fathers: The Memory of Egypt in Judaism and Christianity.*

A fundamental problem faced by any writer on Bible history is his attitude toward the historic veracity of the Bible accounts. Dr. Gabriel has chosen to deal with the Bible narrative, at least in terms of its military elements, as it stands. In providing a clear, lucid, logical, and straightforward story with great detail, he has strengthened the thesis of the writer of these pages; to wit, the tactical and topographical detail of many of the biblical battles from Joshua onward is of such military accuracy that it could not have been invented either by bard or by scribe. Oral tradition or written records, such as the *Book of the Wars of the Lord* mentioned in the Bible but lost, have preserved the true tactical accounts that are in glaring contrast to the heroic epics of antiquity (such as the *Iliad*) in spite of their kernel of truth, or to one of the knightly romances of the Middle Ages, both of which lack this detail completely.

The compelling truthfulness of the tactical detail based on the topographic features led Gabriel to adhere to the Bible narrative, even if not all the exploits attributed to the people mentioned were necessarily really theirs, or if the chronological order of some events may require adjustment. To his great credit, the author deals with these problems openly and with scholarly integrity. Competent scholars have pointed out that Joshua did not capture all of Canaan; others feel that there was much peaceful infiltration. The Bible itself lends evidence to both perspectives. Neither view rules out the fact that these battles were fought by Joshua or by leaders of other, and probably later, waves of conquest unknown to us. Infiltration alone could not have brought about the Israelite lodgment and eventual dominion over Canaan. Infiltration may even have been the cause for armed confrontation with the sophisticated armies of the Canaanite city-states. The Bible hints at all this more than once.

For example, in Joshua 10 it states in these words, "therefore the five kings of the Amorites (Canaanites) . . . gathered themselves together to smite Gibeon, because it had made peace with Joshua and the children of Israel." This, then, was the preliminary to the Battle of Gibeon, an armed confrontation following the peaceful attempt to gain by diplomacy an ally and a foothold in the Judean mountains.

Another basic, formative, and in various ways traumatic event in Israel's history was the famous sojourn in and later exodus from Egypt, taken correctly (in my view) by the author to contain the kernels of a genuine historical event, and very much treated as such, with far-reaching implications for Israel's early military history. Unlike all previous accounts, Gabriel begins the story of Israel's military history not with the battles of Joshua, but with a thorough examination of the military skills, capabilities, tactics, and strategy during the Exodus and without which the success of the Exodus is much more difficult to explain. This is a genuinely innovative and important contribution to ancient military history. Gabriel's work provides new stimulus to Exodus studies and important insights into many facets of Biblical research.

We cannot not mention Gabriel's treatment of the Exodus as history since on the ground of the absence of straightforward evidence a number of scholars tend to deny the historical veracity of the Exodus and transport it into the realm of myth. Without going into the important and itself decisive question of what reason and what stimulus there was for an invention of this kind, I suggest that the argument is baseless. To be sure, the absconding of a small foreign community, estimated by Gabriel and his sources at about 30,000 to 35,000 souls, from the eastern confines of Egypt was certainly not considered by its rulers a major event, and, as such, would only be mentioned, at best, in the border district records which have not been preserved. Throughout all of history concerned parties would only rarely and under very special conditions refer to their own defeats in inscriptions and records destined for the general public. No Egyptian monumental inscription, we may be certain, would have recorded the defeat involved, nor can archaeology come to our rescue. We know nothing of the sojourners' material culture. The more locally assimilated, its nature would have been akin to the contemporary Egyptian, or the less so, it would have resembled one of the plethora of nomad encampments strewn over contemporary Sinai.

This brings us to the same arguments where the period of early Israelite statehood is concerned. Neither Egyptian nor archives from states neighboring to Israel have come to light, nor should we expect commemorative monuments for a period that was largely one of disgrace as far as they were concerned, just because it was a time of Israelite ascendancy. Add to this the highly probable then-existing injunction against the erection of laudatory and votive inscriptions to the God of Israel other than in the Temple of Jerusalem (if at all)—and the spurious arguments *ex silencio* against regarding the biblical narrative as authentic because of the lack of written evidence which may be safely shelved.

There remains the absence of clear archaeological evidence for many events. However, many sites concerned have not been fully excavated. At those that have been excavated, such as biblical Megiddo and Gezer, the excavation was carried out intermittently by a series of scholars, spread over many decades and at times in vestiges already seriously disturbed by former diggers. This makes stratification difficult. In the Late Bronze Age, Early Iron Period, an additional obstacle to clear conclusions is the general deterioration in Canaanite settlement, which causes much confusion with dwellings and defenses of earlier periods. Last, but not least, the habit of definitively dating pottery with a very short margin of error and the disregard of the many ways pottery connected with one people or civilization survive on sites taken over by others, all make dating pottery in the twelfth and eleventh century B.C.E. often questionable. Moreover, biblical tales of complete sack and destruction may not have been different from those records of later times that speak of the total razing of defenses of a captured place when the victors usually made do with substantial breaches and the like.

The present state of archaeological research does not enable us to pronounce a final verdict on the accuracy of Bible history. The accumulated facts, such as we know them, are neither sufficient nor decisive enough. On the other hand, we must bear in mind that the aim of the biblical narrative was not the record of historical facts pure and simple, but the demonstration that abiding by the laws of the Tora was the only way to assure the flourish of the Israelite people. Consequently, assumed or even proven discrepancies between the Bible story and archaeological findings need not trouble the student of military history since all agree that the Bible narrative reflects exactly conditions and the material background of its age.

This said, my colleague's work offers an innovative and insightful analysis of the military elements presented within the biblical narrative, and is a gem of a book that should be used to its fullest extent in reading and studying the subject of warfare in the Bible. I finish with the words of Hillel, the great first century B.C.E. sage who recommended to his students and colleagues *ve ata sil u gmor*—"and now go take up the book and read and study."

Mordechai Gichon
Professor Emeritus of Military History and Archaeology
Tel Aviv University
Fellow of the Society of Antiquities

Preface

The idea for this book originated in a visit I made some years ago to Israel to see old friends. I had been to Israel many times over the last two decades, but my focus had always been on military matters of a more recent kind even though my general interest in ancient military history had, from time to time, brought elements of Israelite military history to my mind. But it was during a visit in 1999 that I was taken on a tour by Mordechai Gichon—one of Israel's most famous military historians—of the Aijalon Valley, the battlefield where Joshua had commanded the sun to stand still. Armed with a copy of the Old Testament in Hebrew, Professor Gichon walked me over the ground in precise historical detail as he explained Joshua's victory over the Canaanites. The experience was overwhelming. A few days later my friend Reuven Gal, director of the Carmel Institute, took me on a tour of the Jezreel Valley. There, from upon the hill where ancient Endor sits, we sat overlooking the valley floor and Mount Gilboa on the far side as my old friend explained the battle of Mount Gilboa where Saul met his death at the hands of the Philistines. Reuven, too, was guided in his explanation by the descriptions contained in his copy of the Old Testament. I had, of course, known for many years through my visits with the Israeli military that the Israeli Defense Force (IDF) sometimes used examples from the Old Testament to instruct their troops and officers in tactical proficiency, often going so far as to require their students to fight the same battles on exactly the same ground! But my experiences in following Reuven and Mordechai over the battlefield terrain described in such detail in the Old Testament afforded me a new respect for and interest in the Old Testament as a documentary source of military history.

I had read several accounts of the battles in the Old Testament written by others and, while generally impressed by these descriptions, I found there existed no genuinely comprehensive analysis of the military history of ancient Israel. By comprehensive I mean an account that uncovers, includes, and analyzes all items and references to military events, including those that were clearly cited in or might reasonably be inferred from the text as relating to logistics, tactics, manpower, fortifications, command and control, weapons and weapons manufacture, troop leadership, and military strategy. I wanted to produce an account that integrated these military references, to the extent possible, with whatever information on Israelite culture, economics, politics, sociology, demography, and psychology could be derived from almost a century of previous research by archaeologists, historians, classicists, and anthropologists. The goal was not to produce merely a description and analysis of Israelite battles in chronological order, but to attempt to discern the military history of ancient Israel as a continuous narrative from the exodus through to the breakup of the imperial state following Solomon's death. The idea was to search the biblical texts for all references to military matters and see if sense could be made of them from a purely military perspective, all others for the moment being disregarded.

A more religious man probably would not have attempted the task, for, as Daniel Boorstin remarked in *The Discoverers*, "the presumption of knowledge is the enemy of discovery." To regard the Bible as a religious text makes it difficult to regard it as a military text, for if one accepts the text as describing miraculous events, one will likely be blinded to the text as military history. So, for example, if Yahweh is seen as leading the Israelites across the Reed Sea by parting the waters, then one is unlikely to see that the account of the crossing of the Reed Sea is an accurate description of a routine tactical maneuver, namely, the night crossing of a water obstacle. It was my intent to read the biblical texts only as military history, nothing more. To my surprise, the texts are starkly revealing of military history when read in this way. For example, it has been customary to regard Israelite military history as beginning with Joshua and the conquest of Canaan. But when the text is read only as military history, it turns out that Exodus contains a wealth of information heretofore not addressed by military historians that sheds considerable light on the military capabilities of the Israelites before the assault on Canaan. It was my idea to read the texts with the military eye of a somewhat experienced infantry soldier and see if they made sense. I believe they do indeed!

I have confined my analysis to the books of Genesis, Exodus, Leviticus, Numbers, Deuteronomy, Joshua, Judges, and I and II Samuel, texts that encompass the time of the Israelite descent into Egypt through to the death of Solomon. It is only after Solomon that our information concerning Israelite military history can begin to be corroborated from other sources outside the biblical texts. The analysis presented herein, then, is confined to the earliest sources of Israelite military history. Of course this raises the difficulties of language, context, and meaning in the Hebrew text. To say that my Hebrew is rusty is to pay me an undeserved compliment, for by no stretch of the imagination could it ever have served me adequately as a research tool. Instead, I was forced to rely upon the most acceptable English translations of the Hebrew text. In this regard I have relied heavily upon the *Anchor Bible* translation as well as the *Tanakh*, the definitive English translation used by most rabbis. To deal with the idioms of the language as well as the various contextual meanings of words in the original Hebrew, I have, like everyone else, relied upon the *Veteris Testamenti Concordantiae Hebraicae Atque Chaldaicae*. But neither of these would have been sufficient without the invaluable assistance provided by my good friend and colleague, Dr. Joel Klein. Professor Klein holds a Ph.D. in Oriental Languages and was a rabbi for 30 years before retiring and obtaining another degree in psychology. He is also an accomplished scholar in the area of Israelite religious history. Dr. Klein served as my teacher and translator of Hebrew words and their meanings in constant reference to the *Concordantiae*. He read every word of the final manuscript for accuracy, meaning, and context and cross-checked every reference in the manuscript against the meaning of the original Hebrew text. It is no exaggeration to say that without the help of my esteemed and dear friend, I could never have written this work.

Nonetheless, only I can be held responsible for any inadvertent mistakes that may have crept into the work. What follows is, I think, a new approach to an old subject, a purely military reading and analysis of the Old Testament's first books with an eye to constructing a consistent historical narrative through which we might come to understand the military history of ancient Israel in greater detail and larger context. Only the reader can judge if I have succeeded.

1

The Land of Israel

From the beginning of military history, perhaps no element of warfare has been of greater importance to the conduct of battle than terrain, the ground that constitutes the tactical or strategic box within which armies have to fight. More than anything it has been terrain that has affected the development of tactics and terrain that has influenced the evolution of military technology, often as a reciprocal influence upon or reflection of tactical innovation itself. It was the broad open desert of Egypt and the Sinai that made it necessary for the Egyptians to develop a light and fast chariot that could cover ground quickly. This design permitted Egyptian chariots to participate in all phases of the battle, including the pursuit. In Anatolia, where the ground was uneven and mountainous and covered with forest glens and defiles, the Hittite chariot developed in response to the specific tactical problem presented by the terrain. The terrain of Anatolia placed a premium upon ambush and the short rush to contact. The Hittite chariot was sturdy, heavy, and carried three- and four-man crews, armed mostly with spears instead of the bow, a machine ideally fit for a quick rush against the enemy launched from ambush. In Canaan, a land of rugged hills and mountains and broad coastal plains and open valleys, armies employed both types of machines depending on the terrain in which the battle took place.[1] From the very beginning of warfare in antiquity, terrain, tactics, and the development of weapons technology have gone hand in hand, just as they continue to do in the modern era.[2]

The land of Israel presented the military commanders of antiquity with complex tactical and strategic problems, just as it does in the present day. Even the most casual student of military history cannot help but notice that many of the military bases of the Israeli Defense Force (IDF) are located in precisely the same places as those of other armies throughout history who "sat" upon the land of Israel. The major trunk roads in modern Israel are but improved and paved versions of the same roads used by the armies of antiquity, as are locations of many of the old fortifications. Two of the Israeli armies main reserve armor depots, one in the Galilee and one in the Negev, are located close to where Solomon positioned his chariot depots. All of this for the same reasons, of course, namely, that nothing compels the conduct of warfare quite as terrain does. The IDF bases are where they are today because they are similar solutions to the same tactical and strategic problems that confronted the commanders of antiquity.

The land of Israel has been witness to war since time immemorial. The first coherent account of war on the Palestinian land-bridge dates from the time of Pharaoh Pepi I (2375–2350 B.C.E.) of Egypt during the Sixth Dynasty, and appears as an inscription in the cenotaph of the Egyptian general, Uni. The inscription tells how, after a series of rebellions by the people of "the land of the Sandwellers" (Palestine), an Egyptian army moved out of Egypt following the coastal road ("the way of Horus" to the Egyptians, later the *via maris* or "way of the sea" to the Romans) that ran from Gaza up the coast under the seamost spur of Mount Carmel and on to the Littani River in Lebanon. As the Egyptian army approached northern Palestine (near modern Haifa), a second army under Uni sailed along the coast in troop transports and "made a landing at the rear of the heights of the mountain range on the north of the land of the Sand Dwellers,"[3] probably the northern end of the coastal plain near Dor. While the army of the Sand Dwellers turned its attention to the Egyptian main force advancing up the coastal road, Uni landed at their backs near the *Antelope's Nose*,[4] probably the seaward spur of Mount Carmel called the *Camel's Nose* by modern residents, and took the enemy by surprise "while a full half his army was still on the road,"[5] and "every backslider among them was slain."[6] Thus from the earliest time in antiquity, long before there was an Exodus or Joshua, and before there were Jews, the Palestinian land-bridge was the cockpit for war and great power conflict. The reasons for this state of affairs were primarily geographic.

A number of geopolitical factors have contributed to making Palestine a central arena of warfare in the Middle East. First, Palestine is the only land-bridge that connects Eurasia with Africa. There is no practical detour between the Mediterranean Sea and the desert. One can choose to pass along the coast of Palestine or through the Jordan Valley, but there is no military or commercial alternative route around the area.[7] As a consequence the security of Egypt began not at the Delta fortresses, but at Joppa and, under Pharaoh Thutmose III, even farther north at Megiddo. For the Mitanni, the Hittites, and the Syrians—and later the Assyrians and Babylonians—Palestine was the soft underbelly through which the most logical routes of invasion from the west passed. At one time or another all these imperial powers sought to control these routes by military occupation or political alliances with the Canaanite city-states. Regardless of who inhabited the land-bridge or which power controlled it at any time in antiquity, all had to live under the constant threat of war and military intervention by the great powers of the day.

A second factor contributing to the geopolitical strategic equation in antiquity was the relative poverty of the country. The amount of arable land within Israel's borders was too small and fragile to support a large population. The size of Israel's population in antiquity was always insufficient to both farm the land and sustain a large standing military force. A small army defending such a strategic land tempted the great powers to become involved in the area again and again with the consequence that Israel was conquered and occupied time and time again by foreign powers. Within the city-states of Israel itself, small armies and the varied terrain placed a premium on infantry and innovative tactical applications that maximized the advantages offered by the terrain. Even after some of these city-states acquired the chariot they maintained sufficient infantry forces, mostly light infantry, to accommodate combat in areas not suitable for chariots.

Third, Israel's long coastline made it relatively easy to invade the country from the sea, and neither the Canaanite city-states nor the national states of David and Solomon ever succeeded in adequately finding a solution to this strategic problem. Time and again the Egyptians came upon the land by sea, often supported by a joint land attack up the coastal road or through the Negev or Jordan Valley. Philistines, and later, Phoenicians, found it easy to gain access to the country by sea. The coastal plain is one of Israel's largest stretches of cultivated land offering a temptation to Israel's enemies. The strategic vulnerability of the coastline was compounded by the fact that Israel's boundaries between arable land and the desert to the south and east were wide open and difficult to defend. The cultivated land on the fringe of the desert was always a tempting prize to the nomadic desert raiders "who do not know grain."[8] Solomon constructed no fewer than 38 strong-points and fortresses in the Negev to protect Israel's southern border from these raiders and other adversaries.[9]

These factors, and others of a mostly tactical and local nature, influenced the conduct of warfare in Israel throughout antiquity. It is difficult to find elsewhere in the West such a small country with so great a diversity of geography and climate. Measured west of the Jordan River, the land of Israel is comprised of only 6,000 square miles of land area. Including the land east of the Jordan, the land of *Eretz Israel* of the Bible and the old colonial holding known as Palestine, it was still only 10,000 square miles. For most of its history, Israel was approximately the size of Vermont.[10] During the time of the Israelite monarchy (1004–926 B.C.E.), the Israelites spoke of their land as running "from Dan even to Beersheba," the area from the southwest foot of snowcapped Mount Hermon in the north to the edge of the southern desert, a distance of only 150 miles. From west to east, from Acco to the shore of the

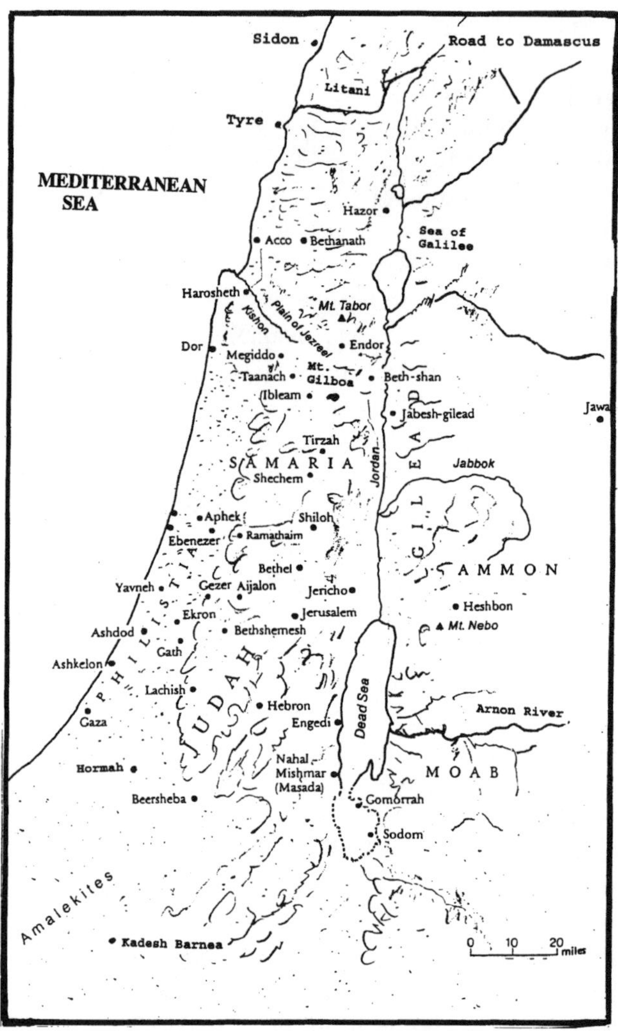

Figure 1.1 The Land of Israel

Sea of Galilee, is only 28 miles as the crow flies. Even at its widest point in the south where the shoreline curves away from the mainland, the distance from Gaza to the Dead Sea is only 54 miles. Within this geostrategic box, terrain, altitude, and climate combine to confront the military mind with an almost infinite variety of militarily relevant conditions under which an army might be forced to fight. The climate on the coastal plain, for example, is relatively mild, averaging 64 degrees year round. To the south and east, temperatures in the Negev are brutally hot, while in the northern mountains (9,100 feet above sea level on Mt. Hermon), the temperature is in the alpine range and there is snow almost year round on the summits. At the Dead Sea, less than 20 miles from temperate Jerusalem, the summer heat is brutally intense and no agriculture is possible. Across the Jordan Valley on the Transjordan Plateau, the climate is temperate and snow falls in the winter. Terrain altitudes range from 9,100 feet in the northern mountains, to the Sea of Galilee, which is 685 feet below sea level, to the Dead Sea, which is 1,275 feet below sea level. In places the altitude drop is precipitous. From Mt. Hermon to Lake Huleh, for example, the drop is almost 8,000 feet in a few miles. From Jerusalem to Jericho, a distance of slightly more than 15 miles, the terrain drops 3,300 feet![11] In geographic terms, Israel can be divided into four main zones: (1) the coastal plain; (2) the central hill country, including the Mount Carmel spur; (3) the cleft of the Jordan Valley; and (4) the plateau of the Jordan Valley.

THE COASTAL PLAIN

The long unbroken plain running from the Mount Carmel spur south to Gaza discouraged Israelite interest in seafaring while presenting Israelite commanders with an unsolvable problem of defending Israel from seaborne invasion. To the north, the Canaanites—later known to the West as Phoenicians[12]—became a seafaring nation because two critical conditions found on the coastal plain in Israel were absent in the north. First, the southern coastal plain is unhindered by mountains, making agriculture comparatively easy while in the north the mountains run very close to the coast leaving only a thin strip of land available for cultivation. Second, the harbors of the north—Sidon and Tyre—are deep and protected from the storms and wind of the Mediterranean. Israel, by contrast, has no good natural harbors. Even Acco was a marginal harbor with no natural windbreaks until the British built its modern seawalls. Dor, the old Canaanite city just below the Camel's Nose of the Mount Carmel spur, offers only a shallow harbor. It is so unprotected as to be little better than the open beach just to the south of the city. Joppa, too, its famous natural rocks notwithstanding, offers no storm-proof harbor. Only Caesaria was a safe harbor in antiquity. But its harbor is an artificial creation with sea walls built from a marvelous new material, hydraulic concrete, invented by Roman engineers. Evidence of how Israel's poor harbors discouraged seafaring is found in the fact that Gaza, the largest and most important trading center of ancient Israel in antiquity, lay three miles inland from the sea; no attempt to provide it with a port has ever succeeded.[13]

The coastal plain is divided into three sections. The northernmost section is the *Plain of Acco*, located on a small bay just north of the Mount Carmel spur running west to east from modern Haifa. This small fertile area is fed by the Kishon River and was the site of many towns during ancient times. The Acco plain connects the Bay of Haifa and the northern road leading to Tyre and Sidon directly to the Jezreel Valley, providing an excellent avenue of advance in both directions for invading armies. The plain connects to the Jezreel at the point where the shortest road from the coast runs against the southern flank of the Carmel spur along the ancient Wadi Melik (Way of the Prince). The junction of the Wadi Melik and the Jezreel is guarded by an ancient Canaanite fortress at Yonqn'eam where it also controls the intersecting north-south road leading to Megiddo and Ta'anach farther south.

The second section is the *Plain of Sharon*. Twelve miles wide at its greatest, this plain stretches between the Camel's Nose and the Yarkon River near Joppa to the south. The northernmost part of the Sharon plain was called the Plain of Dor for its proximity to the old Canaanite town of the same name. Four shallow rivers run down from the central hills into the plain: the Poleg, Alexander, Hader, and Tanninim (Crocodile) rivers.[14] In ancient times the area closest to the coast where these streams struggled to reach the sea was thick, malarial marshlands. Thutmose III, in his campaign against Megiddo, was unable to make his way through the marsh and had to detour overland along the Wadi Ara instead of the more secure Wadi Melik closer to the mountains.[15] A thick line of sand dunes along the coast obstructed the rivers' flow to the sea, forcing the flow to spread over the land and forming an impassable swamp. Roman engineers drained the swamps and constructed an aqueduct leading to the Tanninim River to provide Caesaria with a supply of fresh water, transforming the former swamp into agricultural land. Arab occupation in the seventh century saw the aqueduct fall into disrepair, returning the land to its natural state in which it remained until the Israelis drained the swamps again after the War of Independence in 1948. In antiquity the Sharon Plain was mostly suitable for grazing, and biblical descriptions of "forests" in the area are not to be understood as tall trees, but as low *maquis*-type vegetation still typical of the region.[16] The most important city of the plain of any strategic significance was Aphek, at the mouth of the Yarkon River, which controlled the coastal road. The city had been a Canaanite fortress from at least the Early Bronze Age (3100–2000 B.C.E.). The ruins of a seventeenth-century Turkish fort stand on the site today.

The third section of the coastal zone is the *Philistine Plain* or *Philistia*, literally "land of the Philistines," that runs from Joppa south to Gaza. The area is well watered and generally level with few trees and rich soil making it suitable for cultivation. However, the land is always under threat from drifting sands that often blow from the eastern desert on sirocco winds. This was the site of the Philistine settlement in the tenth century B.C.E. after their defeat at the hands of Ramses III. The Philistines settled along the coastal plain at Ashkelon, Ashdod, Gaza, Gath, and Ekron, where they remained as a threat to Israelite expansion until Nebuchadnezzar of Babylon destroyed and occupied Philistia and deported their rulers in 604 B.C.E. This section of coastal plain was never a center of Israelite strength in antiquity, and the strategic position of Philistine cities butting against the *shephelah* continually threatened Judah, the heartland of Israel itself.

THE HILL COUNTRY

The hill country is part of an almost unbroken chain of hills running south from southern Syria through the center of Israel, forming a spine like that of the skeleton of a fish, before dropping and disappearing into the desert south of Hebron. The northern portion of the chain beginning in the foothills of Mount Hermon and ending in the Jezreel Valley is called Galilee and is divided into Upper and Lower Galilee. Upper Galilee is rugged and mountainous, reaching a height of almost 4,000 feet at the Huleh ridge. Seen from this point, Galilee appears to be a giant wheel with its hub on the Meroam ridge. From this central watershed rains and streams have carved out valleys that run in all directions like spokes from a wheel.[17] Lower Galilee is less hilly and has a milder climate comprising rolling hill lands suitable for agriculture. The southern end of the Galilee is cut through by the Jezreel Valley, which from ancient times was fertile and filled with cities and towns. Watered by the mountain runoff and the river Kishon, the valley runs along two parallel tracks from the base of Mount Carmel southwest to Beth-shean where it joins the Jordan River valley and its wide fertile plain. One track runs between Mount Tabor and the Hill of Moreh and the other between the Hill of Moreh and Mount Gilboa. At the base of Mount Carmel at the valley's western end, the Wadi Ara connects the Jezreel with the coastal road and the sea. Guarded by Megiddo, this track is the shortest route from the coast to the Jezreel and offers the easiest route of invasion. Ten miles north of Megiddo, the Wadi Melik connects the coastal road with the Jezreel at the point where the Plain of Acco meets the Jezreel, offering yet another invasion route. At its most eastern end, the Jezreel meets with the Jordan Valley near Beth-shean, providing the most frequently used route into Israel by desert nomadic raiders. Halfway down the valley near Mount Gilboa, the main road along the Samaria mountains begins, offering hostile armies access to Shechem and Jerusalem itself.

The hills and mountains of Samaria form the geographic center of the country. The mountains run like the spine of a fish all the way from Mount Gilboa in the Jezreel Valley to just south of Hebron where they disappear into the desert. Running along this spine is a major road that connects Mount Gilboa with the Samarian high plateau and from there on to Bethel and Jerusalem. This road passes through the broad Samarian plain between Mount Ebal and Mount Gerizim and is of major military importance. In the center of the mountains is the Plain of Samaria where the well of Jacob sits in the middle of a broad flat plain. From here the road continues south to Jerusalem. Other roads run from this plain to the east and west, making it a key road junction for movement in any direction. It was down this road that Saul led his army to do battle with the Philistines in the Jezreel Valley at the foot of Mount Gilboa.

Judah is the third section of the hill country and is a continuation of the same chain of mountains. They are shortest as one approaches Judah and Jerusalem from Samaria, 2,500 to 2,600 feet, rising to their highest point on the spine near Hebron at 3,370 feet. The mountains trap the rain clouds so that the western side of the plateau is adequate for cultivation. To the east, there is a sheer drop into Jericho and the Jordan Valley through deeply cut wadis and barren hills called the Wilderness of Judah. Judah is the heart of the land of the Bible, an isolated plateau shaped like a long rectangle running 50 miles north to south and 15 or so miles wide, extending from the hills near

Bethel to the north and on to Hebron in the south. The plateau averages 2,500 feet in height. There is a modest dip in the elevation near Jerusalem, forming a natural saddle through which the ancient track from the coast to Jericho passes giving the city its original strategic importance. Seen from east to west, there are four geographic zones in Judah: (1) the Wilderness of Judah, (2) the Judean plateau, (3) the *shephelah*, and (4) the coastal zone, each about 10 to 15 miles wide and about 50 miles long.[18]

The military key to gaining the Judean plateau is the *shephelah*, a fact that explains why it was the scene of so many battles between the Israelites, Canaanites, and Philistines during the period of Israelite settlement. If one imagines the spine of the fishbone running along the Judean ridge, the rib bones extending downward through the *shephelah* (literally, "lowlands") to the coastal plain and the *Via Maris* are alluvial valleys connecting the plateau with the sea. Seen from the sea, four of these valleys point like arrows to avenues of approach for an invading army attempting to reach the plateau and Jerusalem. It is no accident, then, that since ancient times each of these valleys has been guarded by a fortified city to block the path of any invader. So it was that Gezer guarded the approaches to the Aijalon Valley, Beth-shemesh protected the Sorek Valley, Azekah and Socoh covered the approaches through the Elah Valley, and both Maresha and Lachish farther south protected the approaches around Hebron.[19] The strategic importance of the *shephelah* was enhanced by the fact that it was separated from the Judean plateau by a longitudinal valley forming a natural moat between the two features. It is not possible for an invader to climb a low hill in the *shephelah*, gain a ridge, and follow it up to the plateau. Instead, an invader is forced to make his way up the streambeds along one of the four valleys that connect with the plateau. Only at the northernmost edge of the *shephelah*, at the Aijalon Valley, is there a route that runs partially along a ridge. This route, the road to Beth-horon, was the one preferred by attacking armies. But when blocked by fortresses this route, too, becomes unusable.

As difficult as it may be, however, the routes through the wadis can be negotiated by infantry. The way is steep and narrow, twisting here and there, suitable for ambush, and completely unsuited for wheeled vehicles of any kind. Without opposition, however, the lead elements of an advancing army can move through the *shephelah* and gain the plateau in just over six hours' march. And this fact explains why it has always been fought over. The *shephelah* is a strategic and geographic zone of transition. To an army on the coastal plain, it is a staging area for an assault on the plateau. To the defenders of the Judean plateau, the zone is a forward defensive area where the enemy may be engaged at greatest advantage before he gains a foothold on the plateau. To the Philistines as dwellers of the coastal plain, the fortresses guarding the valleys were seen as staging garrisons for offensive military operations against them. From very ancient times, then, the *shephelah* was vital to the defense of Judah, as it was equally vital to any nation that sought to protect its trade or military routes along the coastal road. The Israelites fought the Philistines over it, the Egyptians built Gezer to protect it, and Judah Maccabee defeated the Seleucid army by moving through it. The Crusaders fought for control over the area as Napoleon did in his incursion into Palestine in 1799. In World War I General Allenby's campaign against the Turks captured Jerusalem by moving up an old road that the Romans had built through the *shephelah*, and the Israelis fought for it during their War of Independence in 1948, all for the same tactical or strategic reasons.

At the end of the mountainous fish spine, southward beyond Hebron, lies the Negev, the land-bridge between the southern hill country of Judah and the mountainous wilderness of the Sinai. The Negev of the Bible probably comprised the hill region south of Hebron to Kadesh-Barnea into the Wilderness of Zin. Today it is a much larger area comprising almost half the territory of modern Israel.[20] True to its name, which means "dry" or "parched," the annual rainfall near Beersheba is not more than eight inches and often considerably less, and no agriculture could be sustained here during biblical times.[21] Barren and hot, the Negev nonetheless played an important part in Israel's history. It was Kadesh-Barnea on the outskirts of the Negev from which the Israelites launched their first attempt to conquer Canaan. Numbers 21:1 says, "When the Canaanite king of Arad, who dwelt in the Negev, learned that Israel was coming by way of Atharim, he engaged Israel in battle and took some of them captive." The "way of Atharim" is a main track leading from Kadesh-Barnea to Arad. Other tracks mentioned in the Bible are "the way of Shur" leading through the Sinai to Egypt, the "way to Arava" from Kadesh-Barnea to the Arava Valley, and the "way of the reed sea" along the Arava Valley to Eilat. During Solomon's time, Beersheba was a fortified administrative center with 38 forts and strong-points arrayed in depth to protect Solomon's main port at Ezion-Geber, as well as the trade routes to Egypt. These fortresses were of some concern to Egypt, who saw them as a threat to Egyptian security. Five years after Solomon's death, Pharaoh Shishak (Sheshonq I) attacked Judah, destroying the fortifications of the Negev.[22]

THE JORDAN VALLEY

The Jordan Valley is part of a great geological fault that extends down through Syria where it divides Mount Lebanon from the anti-Lebanon range known in the Bible as Hermon and Amana. The fault continues through Palestine as the Jordan Valley runs ever southward until it forms the Arabah and the Red Sea. Its main watercourse is the Jordan River which has its source at the western side of Mount Hermon, running through Lake Huleh at sea level, and then dropping down into the Sea of Galilee whose surface is 685 feet below sea level. The land around the Sea of Galilee has been under cultivation from antiquity, but the steep mountains across the valley made communication difficult so that for most of history activity around the sea has been oriented westward. The Jordan River leaves the sea as a clear stream, but becomes quickly silted until running into the Dead Sea at 1,275 feet below sea level. The Jordan was sufficient, along with the runoff from the hills across the valley, to sustain a healthy agriculture in the wide Jordan valley from early antiquity. From a military perspective, the Jordan Valley has always tempted nomadic raiders with its agricultural abundance, as well as providing invading armies from Syria an easy route to Jericho and Eilat, just as it provided the Egyptians, and later the Arabs, with a similarly easy south to north route of advance. An army moving up or down the valley can, at Beth-shean, move westward into the Jezreel Valley cutting the country in two and positioning itself for further movement north and south.

THE TRANSJORDAN PLATEAU

Across the Jordan Valley, high above the valley floor, is the Transjordan plateau. The plateau is divided into five sections by four main rivers. From north to south these rivers are the Yarmuk (not mentioned in the Bible), the Jabbok, the Arnon, and the Zered. To the north of the Yarmuk River lay the biblical land of Bashan, the modern day Golan plain where rainfall is abundant and wheat fields and vineyards predominate. From the Yarmuk south to beyond the river Jabbok was the land of Gilead. Full of springs and well watered, Gilead supported a much larger population than Bashan and was often the object of Israelite attention. The Jabbok flows east and north in a semicircle before emptying into the Jordan. In the upper reaches of the river's course lay the land of Ammon, stretching southward to the Arnon, which formed the border between it and the land of Moab. A high and level plateau, it was easily defended and rarely the subject of Israelite intentions. South of the Zered River lay the biblical land of Edom through which Moses and the Israelites passed on their way to Jericho. Edom was frequently the subject of Israelite attention because it controlled the trade routes from the desert to Gaza and also possessed deposits of copper and iron ore in abundance that Israel lacked from which to fabricate agricultural implements and weapons.

The geographic diversity of the land and its mountains enforced a high degree of isolation upon cities and towns that made the formation of a national political, military, or geographic entity very difficult. The land of Canaan was a land of powerful city-states; each city-state was under its own ruler who was vying for control and defense of sufficient land to support and defend itself. Egyptian influence, too, fostered fragmentation by playing off one king against another, a policy later practiced by the Assyrians and, much later, by the Romans. Although each of the Canaanite city-states was independent, when presented with an external threat they were capable of acting in concert militarily. In these instances the entire country became a single strategic and tactical arena. Figure 1.2 offers a portrayal of Israel as a single strategic arena, showing the interrelationships of geography, road nets, natural obstacles, fortifications, and avenues of advance that were militarily significant to the conduct of war in antiquity on the Palestinian land bridge.

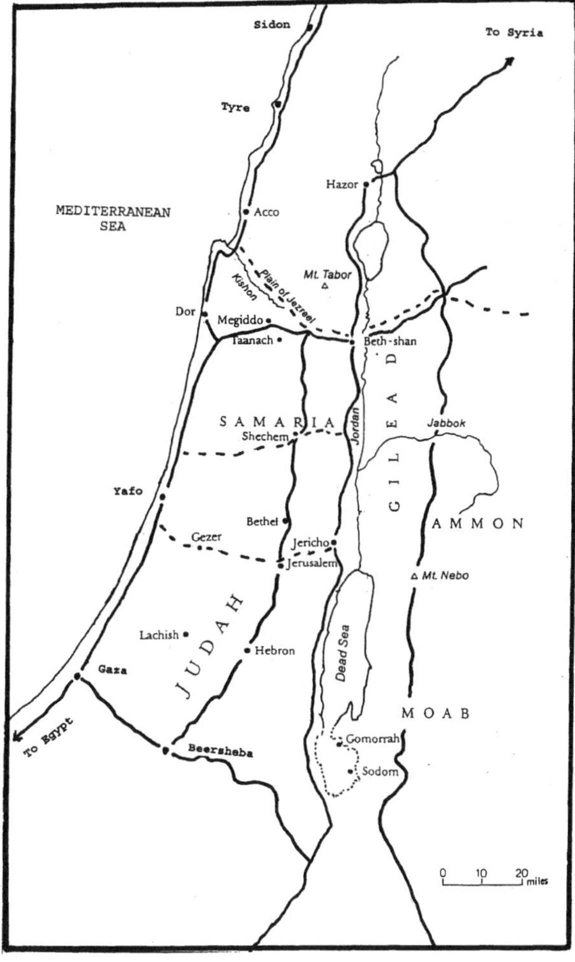

Figure 1.2 Strategic Roads, Passes, and Fortifications

Central to the strategic portrait are the major fortifications and routes of advance critical to successful invasion or defense. From north to south and west to east, six major fortified cities hold the key to Israelite defense strategy: Hazor, Megiddo, Beth-shean, Shechem, Gezer, and Jerusalem. Each of these fortresses sits astride a strategic road or valley or wadi track vital for invasion or defense. In addition, the land was pockmarked with scores of smaller fortified towns and fortresses built by successive local kings and imperial administrators of occupying powers. For example, during the time of the divided monarchy there were no fewer than 19 major fortified strongpoints guarding the approaches to Jerusalem alone.[23]

Hazor (modern Tel-el Kedah) is situated in the upper Galilee on a hill rising above the river where a number of trade routes come together like the spokes of a wheel. The most important of these roads climbs steeply out of the basin of the Sea of Galilee in a series of steep switchbacks until the flat plain is reached at the top. Here for a few miles the ground is level before it drops off through a narrow winding cut in the mountains passing under Hazor's walls before debouching upon a wide plain. This is the main road from Israel to Damascus. Viewed from the other side, it is the main road that connects Damascus to the Syrian and Lebanese ports on the Mediterranean. Originally a Canaanite city, Hazor became an important commercial center with a sprawling city at the base of the fortified hill upon which the fortress itself sits. By the sixteenth century B.C.E., it held as many as 40,000 inhabitants, making it the largest city in Palestine at that time.[24] Hazor was the strategic key to Israel in the north, and it was down this road that Syrian, Assyrian, and Babylonian armies marched on their way to the heart of Palestine.

Megiddo is located south and west of Hazor in the lower Galilee at the place where the spur of the Carmel Mountains drops down and meets the Jezreel plain. The city was originally a Canaanite town built around 3300 B.C.E. and was fortified with high walls from a very early time. With travel up the coastal road blocked or made very difficult by the Sharon swamps or passing under the Camel's Nose made too dangerous by enemy forces, the fastest route into the Jezreel was through the Wadi Ara, a route that meets the Jezreel plain under Megiddo's walls. In addition, the north-south road also passes before the fortress. This road leads north and joins the plain of Acco. From here an army could move easily along the Kishon River up to the bay of Acco and farther northward or move westward along the Wadi Melik and gain the coastal road. To the south lies Ta'anach, a major staging point for the ascent up the gentler side of Mount Gilboa and the main trunk road leading to the Samarian plain.

The west-east road passing under Megiddo's walls at the Wadi Ara continues down the entire length of the Jezreel valley until it joins the Jordan River and the Jordan Valley south of the Sea of Galilee. Here sits *Beth-shean*, another Canaanite city turned into a major Egyptian base by Thutmose III.[25] Beth-shean controls the entrance and exit to both the Jordan and Jezreel Valleys at its easternmost outlet. It was here that the desert nomads tried time and again to invade Israel proper lured by its well-watered and extensive agriculture. Beth-shean also controls the main north-south access to Hazor, as well as the main wadi track leading up the mountains to the Transjordan plateau and a main invasion route to Syria. Beth-shean is the strategic key to northeast Israel as Megiddo is key to the security of the northwest.

Shechem (modern Nablus) is the strategic key to the geographic heartland of Israel. Located in the center of the Samarian plain between Mount Ebal and Mount Gerizim, Shechem sits astride the main road that runs from the Jezreel at Mount Gilboa along the longitudinal spine of the central mountain massif connecting the south with the north of the country. It was a heavily fortified city in 2000 B.C.E. and remains vital to the defense of central Israel and Jerusalem itself. From its position on the Samarian plain Shechem also controls an important east-west route connecting it with the sea to the west and with the Jordan Valley to the east.

On the edge of the coastal road at the foot of the *shephelah* sits mighty *Gezer*, the city that Pharaoh gave Solomon as a wedding present when Solomon married Pharaoh's daughter. A Canaanite town dating from 3000 B.C.E.,[26] Gezer sits at the junction of two important venues of advance. Troops operating from Gezer can easily cut the *Via Maris*. To its back, however, lies the important entrance to the Aijalon Valley, the main and easiest route through the *shephelah* leading to the plateau of Judah and Jerusalem itself. From here troops can stage for an invasion of the plateau or, conversely, Gezer can become a major element in a defensive strategy to protect Jerusalem.

Jerusalem is located in a small saddle along the main spine of the mountains of the central massif controlling the main longitudinal road from Shechem to Hebron to the south and the Negev. Within the Negev itself, Beersheba is the key to controlling the road leading from Gaza on down to Eilat. Jerusalem also sits across the main west-east road that passes in front of Gezer through the Aijalon Valley to the Judah plateau and down again terminating at Jericho to the east and joining the main southern axis through the valley of the Dead Sea. In concert with the four fortified cities guarding the entrances to the valleys through the *shephelah*, the steep mountains of the Wilderness of Judah in the east and the steep terrain to the south of Hebron combine to provide Jerusalem with formidable natural defenses quite apart from the many strong-points built by Canaanites and the Hebrew kings. Jerusalem, then, is both the strategic key to the central part of the country, as well as the psychological heart of the Land of Israel.

All other things equal, the nature of the tactical or strategic terrain over which an army had to maneuver was one of the most important elements of determining the conduct of battle throughout the ages. In this regard it is perhaps wise to recall that before the advent of mechanical transport in war, namely, the railways of the American Civil War, no army could move faster than its feet would carry it. To be sure chariots and cavalry could move more rapidly, but only for short periods and then mostly alone. In any case, no commander of antiquity would have been so foolish as to go into a chariot or cavalry attack without his infantry as direct support or as a platform of maneuver. This, of course, brings us back to the speed of the marching man as the true measure of military mobility and maneuver. Within the tactical and strategic arena of operations that was the Land of Israel in ancient times, the diverse nature of the military geography conferred advantages and disadvantages upon attacker and defender alike. In war, however, all things are rarely equal, and the nature of the armies that fought with one another brought to the battlefield their own special characteristics and capabilities that permitted them to exploit or be exploited by the military topography of the land itself. These armies are the subjects of the next chapter.

NOTES

1. See Richard A. Gabriel, *The Culture of War: Invention and Early Development* (Westport, CT: Greenwood Press, 1990), 40–42, for the development of the chariot

in response to a number of factors, including terrain. For the capability of various types of chariots under combat conditions in antiquity, see Richard A. Gabriel and Donald W. Boose Jr., "Megiddo" and "Kadesh," in *The Great Battles of Antiquity* (Westport, CT: Greenwood Press, 1994).

2. For an excellent analysis of the dynamic relationship between military technology and tactical requirements over time, see Martin Van Creveld, *Technology and War from 2000 B.C.E. to the Present* (New York: Free Press, 1989).

3. James B. Pritchard, *Ancient and Near Eastern Texts Relating to the Old Testament* (Princeton, NJ: Princeton University Press, 1955), 228.

4. Ibid.

5. Ibid.

6. Ibid.

7. Chaim Herzog and Mordechai Gichon, *Battles of the Bible* (Jerusalem: Steimatzky's Agency Ltd., 1978), 12.

8. Ibid., 13.

9. Rudolph Cohen, "The Fortresses King Solomon Built to Protect His Southern Border," *Biblical Archaeology Review* 11 (1985): 65; see also by the same author, "Solomon's Negev Defense Line Contained Three Fewer Fortresses," *Biblical Archaeological Review* 12 (1986): 40–45.

10. *The Westminster Historical Atlas to the Bible* (Philadelphia, PA: Westminster Press, 1945), 17.

11. Ibid., 17–18.

12. The word Canaan literally means "land of the purple" in the Canaanite language and is probably derived from the Canaanite technology of producing purple dye from the murex snail found off the coast of Sidon and Tyre. When the Greeks encountered the Canaanites, they translated the name into their own word for purple, "phoenicia." Ever since the world has known the Canaanites who settled along the Lebanese coast as Phoenicians.

13. Interestingly, one of the major inducements offered to Yassir Arafat by President Clinton at the Camp David talks in 2001 to reach an accommodation with the Israelis on the Palestinian issue was to build a major port facility for the city of Gaza.

14. Oded Borowski, "The Sharon—Symbol of God's Abundance," *Bible Review* 14, no. 2 (April 1988): 40.

15. For Thutmose's route of march to Megiddo, see Gabriel and Boose, "Megiddo," in *The Great Battles of Antiquity*.

16. Borowski, "The Sharon," 40.

17. Herzog and Gichon, 16.

18. Harold Brodsky, "The Shephelah—Guardian of Judea," *Bible Review* 3, no. 4 (winter 1987): 48.

19. Ibid., 50.

20. Oded Borowski, "The Negev—The Southern Stage for Biblical History," *Bible Review* 4, no. 3 (June 1989): 40.

21. Ibid.

22. Cohen, 69.

23. Jacob Liver, ed., *The Military History of the Land of Israel in Biblical Times* (in Hebrew) (Jerusalem: Israel Defense Forces Publishing House, 1964), 417.

24. Michael Grant, *The History of Ancient Israel* (New York: Charles Scribner, 1984), 17.
25. Ibid., 18.
26. Ibid., 18–19.

2

Armies of the Bible

The armies that fought their way into history on the Palestine land-bridge between the thirteenth and sixth century B.C.E. occupy a unique place in military history. Their presence when the Israelites were forging a homeland by force of arms, and the writing of their great national saga that Western civilization came to call the Old Testament, ensured that almost everyone at one time or another came to hear of Canaanites, Philistines, Israelites, Egyptians, and Assyrians and the tales of Joshua, Saul, and David, the great generals of the Israelite armies. The Old Testament provides the military historian with a rich human context through which to study the armies and wars of the Bible, a dimension of human understanding that is all too frequently absent in more modern and technical accounts of warfare. The great national saga of the Israelites was played out against the conflicts of the five major combatants—Canaanites, Philistines, Assyrians, Egyptians, and the Israelites themselves—who often occupied the same land at the same time, struggling with one another for power and influence and presenting the historian with a unique opportunity to compare the armies, tactics, and military technology of each against the others.

CANAANITES

The period between 1800 and 1550 B.C.E. is called the Middle Canaanite period when climatic conditions improved and cultural development flourished, permitting the people of Canaan to rebuild their old fortified cities into powerful new urban centers. During this time the first written documents in Canaanite appear, and it is from this period that Canaan as a recognizable entity with its own culture can be said to have come into being.[1] Egyptian documents from the time of Senusret II (1897–1878 B.C.E.) tell of a previous time when there were a number of independent Canaanite kingdoms ruled by warrior princes who had learned how to fortify their towns, which then grew into city-states that the Egyptians were forced to deal with militarily. During this time Canaanite society was formed around tribes, each ruled by a warrior chieftain (*malek*) who held his position by virtue of being the fiercest warrior in the tribe. These chiefs maintained household guards (*henkhu*) as part of their personal retinues; these guards probably constituted the main combat element in tribal wars.

The name *Canaan* is very old and in antiquity denoted that territory between Gaza in the south and the upper reaches of the Lebanon north to Ugarit. To the east, the land of Canaan ran to the base of the central mountain massif of later Judah and Samaria, northward through the Jezreel to include the Beka up to Kadesh. Later, in the middle period, Canaan was subject to the passage of a group of immigrant tribes originating somewhere in northern Syria that moved slowly over the land-bridge until they entered Egypt itself, settling in the Delta near Avaris and defeating the Egyptians by force of arms. These were the Hyksos. While the origin of the Hyksos remains uncertain, there is no doubt that these sophisticated people introduced their military technology to Canaan[2] where it was adopted by the rival princes of the Canaanite city-states. The origin of this sophisticated technology, like the Hyksos themselves, is uncertain but may lie in the technology of the Hurrian-Mitannians of the upper Euphrates.

The Hyksos, and later Mitanni, military influence thus brought a number of new weapons to Canaan that revolutionized warfare on the land-bridge. It was from the Hyksos that the Canaanites acquired the chariot and the horse as a weapon of war. The composite bow, socket axe, and the sickle-sword also made their appearance in Canaan at this time.[3] Within a century the long dirk or dagger that under the later influence of the Sea Peoples developed into the straight sword was in evidence. The coat of mail came into use at approximately the same time, probably worn only by the armed charioteer. Later, we find Canaanite infantry wearing body armor as well.

The new military sophistication of the Canaanites during this period was reflected in a change in the nature of military fortifications of Canaanite cities. Canaanite princes now constructed their cities atop a new kind of massive rampart: a slanted bank of packed earth called a glacis. The glacis joined an exterior ditch, a fosse, obstructing the most likely avenues of approach. The architecture, of course, was a reaction to the widespread use of the twin technologies of the chariot and the battering ram in Canaanite warfare. During this time Canaan had extensive contacts with the Mitanni-Hurrians, and it is likely that they now became the predominant influence on the Canaanite method of war. The Mitanni influence in the new architecture, for example, is suggested by the fact that two powerful cities in north Syria, Carchemish and Ebla, possess the same fortifications.[4]

The influence of the Mitanni-Hurrian culture was strongly reflected in the transformation of Canaanite society during this period into one based upon the Mitanni model. There now came into existence a feudal warrior caste in Canaan based upon heredity and land possession. As in the land of the Mitanni, these warriors were called *maryannu*, and like their Mitanni cousins, they were an elite group of chariot warriors. This elite ruled over a half-free, Semitic-speaking class of peasants and farmers (*khupshu*) with no middle or merchant class in between.[5] The transformation of Canaanite military technology and social organization produced a society able and willing to fight wars, especially in resistance to the aspirations of the great powers to the south (Egypt) and to the north (Hittites and Mitanni).

With the creation of the Egyptian Empire under the Eighteenth Dynasty, Egypt moved aggressively to strengthen her influence in Canaan, an initiative that met organized resistance from a coalition of Canaanite princes at Megiddo (1479 B.C.E.). In the wake of the Egyptian victory, Egypt established garrisons in the major towns of the country, including Ullaza, Sharuhen, Gaza, and Joppa, the last two being major Egyptian administrative centers. Each Canaanite city of any size had an Egyptian "political officer" (*weputy*) and a small staff to oversee economic and political matters, including the collection of intelligence. Egyptian garrisons stationed in major towns were often established as "allies of the king" and could be used to support the Canaanite prince in his local quarrels. The fiction of allies notwithstanding, Egyptian power and influence were real, a fact demonstrated by the Egyptian practice of referring to Canaanite princes as *khazanu* or headman instead of the more prestigious Canaanite title of *malek*.[6]

The presence of foreign influence did not prohibit the Canaanite princes from fortifying their important cities and towns, and by the twelfth century B.C.E. the entire country was heavily fortified and each city-state was ruled by an independent king. Although there was no Canaanite "high king" to direct it, the countrywide Canaanite fortification design was so well integrated as to suggest at least some degree of cooperation among the princes. The purpose of these fortifications was to protect the lucrative trade routes that crisscrossed the country linking it to Syria and Egypt and to protect Canaan from the predations of migrating nomadic tribes. Taken together, the system of fortifications was designed to permit the Canaanite princes to mount a mobile defense in depth using chariot warriors. Only as a last resort did Canaanites permit themselves to be besieged in their cities.

By the beginning of the thirteenth century and well on into the twelfth century B.C.E., the Canaanite armies reached the apex of their military effectiveness. Each city-state raised and trained its own armed forces, most of which were very similar in weapons and organization. There was no unified "na-

Figure 2.1 Canaanite Charioteer, 1200 B.C.E.

tional" command for there was no "high king" that ruled over all Canaan. But in time of war, the engaged city-states were capable of acting in concert and coordinating the movement and deployment of their forces. This had been true when Thutmose III had confronted a coalition of Canaanite princes at Megiddo. From the Ugarit texts the term *resuti* or "subordinate ally" has come down to us, suggesting that within the military coalitions princes were able to permit their forces to act at the orders of a higher commander as, no doubt, had been the case with the Canaanites at Megiddo. The king of the city-state usually took the field as commander in chief, but it was not unusual for military command to be delegated to trusted generals. Regular, fully equipped troops called *sabu nagib* were clearly distinguished from militia or irregulars. The term was applied to both infantry and chariotry, suggesting that regular infantry units existed. Field commanders were called *muru-u*, but we do not know the size of the units they commanded. It is likely, however, that the decimal system of unit sizing was employed as it was commonly elsewhere. Although Ugarit was among the largest, richest, and most powerful Canaanite states, its military organization was probably typical of the other states.

The primary striking arm of the Canaanite armies, their arm of decision, was the elite chariot corps manned by the social elite of feudal nobles serving as chariot warriors called *maryannu*. Each *maryannu* was a professional soldier who, originally at least, maintained his chariot, horses, grooms, driver, runners, and equipment at his own expense. His wealth was derived from the holding of a fief which, although originally conferred by the king, seems over time to have become hereditary.[7] Among the general warrior cast of *maryannu* were an inner elite of "picked men" or *na'arun*, a term that appears in the Ugarit texts. Apparently these elite units were comprised of infantry as well as chariotry. The chariot corps was commanded by the *akil markabti* or chief of chariotry. A smaller battle guard called the maryannu of the king also existed.

The Canaanite chariot, much like the Mitannian chariot, was heavier than the Egyptian vehicle but lighter than the Hittite machine. Yadin suggests that this was a result of the increased Egyptian influence in Canaanite affairs,[8] but this is unconvincing. The tactical mission of the Egyptian machine as well as the terrain in which it developed were simply different from those that influenced the development of the Canaanite chariot. Canaan offered few smooth

Figure 2.2 Canaanite Chariot, 1250 B.C.E.

plains where the opportunity for wide-ranging maneuvers and speed could provide dividends. The terrain of Canaan was like that of northern Syria (and the land of the Mitanni) characterized by rocky ground, hills and mountains, forests and glens, conditions that put a premium on surprise, ambush, and shock. The Canaanite chariot was heavier than the Egyptian model having a six-spoked wheel with the axle moved to the center of the platform to take the weight off the animals. This permitted a larger carrying platform whose floor could be fashioned of wood for strength. One result, of course, was that the machine lost a good part of its maneuverability at speed, and the endurance of the animals was also compromised to some degree.[9]

The Canaanite charioteer, like his Mitanni counterpart, was heavily protected by a mail coat of scale armor. His horse, too, wore a textile or bronze scale coat. These devices, of course, were designed to protect the horse and crew from enemy arrows as they closed in to engage. There is no hard evidence that the driver wore armor, but given the Mitanni influence on Canaanite chariotry it is quite likely that he did. The primary weapons of the Canaanite charioteer were the composite bow, a heavy spear, and a club, the latter, no doubt, to be used only in the direst emergency should the warrior find himself afoot.[10] Depending on the tactical mission, the Canaanite chariot was capable of carrying a three-man crew, a fact suggested by the portrayal of the machine with javelin cases. The first recorded encounter by Israelite troops with Canaanite chariots is recorded in Joshua 11:5, 7–9 where, having defeated the Canaanites near the Waters of Merom (Huleh Lake), Joshua "burnt their chariots with fire." In another passage, Joshua 17:16–18, the account speaks of the Canaanites possessing "chariots of iron." In fact, it was not until the Assyrians occupied Palestine that chariots had iron tire rims, which might account for the reference in the text. As Robert Drews has noted, it is likely that the description of "iron chariots" is a redactor's invention, for the light wooden frame of the chariots of Joshua's time would simply have collapsed under the weight of bronze or iron plates.[11] Iron weapons at the time of Joshua (1250 B.C.E.?) were still largely curiosities but later were introduced in some numbers by the Philistines.

Canaanite infantry called *hupshu* had both militia and regular units. Most of the infantry were semitrained militia (*khepetj*) or conscripted and corvee peasantry. These units were lightly armed with bows and spears. There was a long Canaanite tradition dating from tribal days that the infantry supplied

Figure 2.3 Canaanite Infantryman, 1200 B.C.E.

their own equipment, but we are uncertain if this tradition persisted into biblical times. The Amarna letters refer to different types of infantry distinguished by their weapons, that is, bows and spears.[12] Canaanite regular infantry were probably well-trained professionals who were heavily armed. These units wore armored corselets for protection, helmets, and carried a sword and shield and, probably, the socket axe. Until the arrival of the Sea Peoples, the Canaanites used a shield of Hittite design. Shaped like a figure eight with a narrow waist, this shield allowed the soldier a greater field of view of his opponent in close combat and permitted a more flexible wielding of the sword. With the coming of the Sea Peoples, the Canaanites adopted the round shield and outfitted their infantry with the spear. At the same time, however, the Canaanite sickle-sword was replaced by the straight sword of the Sea Peoples. Scale armor for the regular infantry now became commonplace as well.[13]

Elite units of heavy infantry called *na'arun* appear to have served as the palace guard of the Canaanite kings. The Ugaritic texts mention these units as an inner elite of the general *maryannu* warrior caste. The term itself means "picked men," that is, warriors chosen by their king for loyalty and bravery. At Kadesh, Ramses II was rescued in the nick of time by a unit of these elite shock troops who fell upon the Hittite flank breaking the Hittite encirclement. These *na'arun* were Canaanite mercenaries in the service of the Egyptians. A relief of the battle portrays the Canaanites attacking in phalanx formation line abreast in ten rows, ten men deep armed with spears and shields,[14] suggesting that they are elite heavy infantry.

The Canaanite kings supplemented their forces with hired freebooters called *apiru*. The *apiru* were a class of outcasts, debtors, outlaws, and restless nomads who formed themselves into wandering groups of raiders who often hired themselves out to princes and kings for military duty. Often called bandits (*habbatu*) or Dusty Ones, these wandering brigands were a serious threat and often had to be brought to heel by the Canaanite princes by force of arms. One of history's greatest generals, David, was an *apiru*. When forced to leave Saul's court for fear of being killed, David returned to his old mercenary occupation by raising a force of 600 "discontented men" and hiring his soldiers out to one of the Philistine kings. The size and military sophistication of these brigand groups could present a considerable threat to public order. A record from Alalakh tells of a band of *apiru* comprised of 1,436 men, 80 of whom were charioteers and 1,006 of whom were *shananu*, probably some kind of archer. Another text records the capture of the town of Allul by a force of 2,000 *apiru*.[15]

Canaanite tactics were similar to those of the Mitanni in that the army relied upon its chariot units to strike their enemies from ambush, catching them while still in column of march or deploying for open battle. This was precisely the Canaanite plan at Megiddo when an ambush was set for Thutmose III's army along the Ta'anach-Aruna road. The strike was to take place as the Egyptian column moved onto the Jezreel plain. If surprise was not possible, Canaanite generals used the chariot to shock and surprise enemy infantry formations. This required that the chariots be accompanied by "chariot runners" or light infantry. The Canaanite charioteer engaged the enemy from close range by firing his bow again and again, relying upon his heavy armor to protect him from enemy fire. In this tactical application, infantry phalanxes of spearmen supported by archers would act in support or, if on the defensive, hold their positions, providing the chariots with a platform of maneuver.

The primary role of the chariot, however, was as a strategic weapon. The Canaanite chariots were mobile, heavy vehicles that could range far from their bases to protect the Canaanite cities from being besieged. Protecting the city itself was at the center of Canaanite strategic thinking, and the chariots were the key element in achieving this goal. Chariots could be used to intercept armies long before they reached the city walls, forcing the enemy to fight on terrain not of its choosing. Chariots were ideal for ambushing enemy patrols, harassing an enemy's route of march, keeping interior lines open, and chasing down hired mercenary *apiru*. No infantry force could achieve such a mix of tactical and strategic flexibility. Chariots, of course, were expensive, and their crews required extensive training and permanent maintenance at royal expense. The expense was worth it, however, for the chariot allowed the Canaanite kings to erect a strategic defense in depth based upon flexible mobile tactics.

The system of mobile defense worked well for more than two centuries, but Canaan's wealth and strategic position made it too tempting a target for the national predators who wished to control the land-bridge. Over time the encroachments, immigrations, settlements, and aggressions of the Egyptians, Arameans, Sea Peoples, and the Israelites and Philistines took their toll with the result that by the time of King David the Canaanites had been deprived of 75 percent of their land area and 90 percent of their grain-growing land.[16] All that remained of these proud warrior people was the central Phoenician coastal strip together with its immediate hinterlands. But the legacy of Canaan lived on in the modern world. It was Canaanites who first performed the extraordinary feat of dissecting the sounds of human speech into thirty basic sounds, giving the world its first true alphabet.[17] And it was the Canaanites who were the first to set their language to music and taught the Hebrews how to set their poetry to music thereby giving the world one of the greatest gifts of civilization.

PHILISTINES

The penetration of Canaan by the Israelites was already underway when another nation began its assault on the Egyptian province of Canaan: the Philistines. The Philistines came from the west by land and sea. They were the Peleset of the Sea Peoples, and their attempt to conquer Egypt was recorded by Ramses III (1192–1160 B.C.E.) on the great reliefs of Medinet Habu. The Philistines, from which we get the name Palestine, were of Aegean stock and related to both the Minoan and Mycenaean peoples of the Mediterranean islands and mainland Greece and thus to the later classical Greeks. They probably originated in Cyprus or Crete. Their language was non-Semitic and written in syllabic speech like Carian, but the characters of their script strongly resemble the script of ancient Mycenaean Greece.[18] The Sea Peoples swept down the shores of the southeastern Mediterranean in swift ships accompanied by overland movement of their entire tribes, and with fire and iron swords attempted to capture new lands for settlement. Pharaoh Merneptah (1213–1203 B.C.E.) fought a battle with them in Canaan, and even before the great battle with Ramses III (1190 B.C.E.), which halted their advance against Egypt, there is evidence to suggest that Philistine elements had already settled in places along the coast of Canaan.

After their defeat by Ramses III, the Philistines settled in significant numbers in the land of Canaan. Whether they settled there with the approval of the Egyptians or were simply too numerous and militarily powerful for the Egyptians to eject them, the Philistines seem to have reached some sort of accommodation with the Egyptians.[19] The Egyptians employed Philistine warriors as mercenaries in what might have been an attempt to check the power of both Canaanite and Israelite influence. The Philistines settled themselves along the southern coastal plain of Canaan, a fertile strip 40 miles long and 15 or so miles wide. They inhabited the fortified cities of Ashkelon, Ashdod, and Gaza on the coast and Gath and Ekron farther inland. As Egyptian power weakened, Philistine influence in Canaan increased, and in a short time they became virtually independent and began to push out from their coastal enclaves toward the interior central mountains which brought them into conflict with the Israelites.

The political structure of the Philistines resembled at least in its broad outlines that of their Greek relatives. Each city was independent and ruled by a prince whose claim to power rested, as in ancient Mycenae, on his royal blood and prowess as a warrior. There was no high king to rule other kings. When the Philistine cities had to act in concert, say to counter a military threat, they met in a council of princes called the *sarney*.[20] Whenever the Philistine city-states took the field in concert, they acted under a unified military command. The armies of the Philistines were comprised mostly of a well-armed professional feudal military caste, and they were the first to employ iron weapons on any scale. Iron weapons had been extant in Palestine in small numbers from the time of Pharaoh Merneptah. An iron sword bearing Merneptah's name has come down to us from Ugarit.[21] Bronze weapons, too, remained in use by the Philistines at this time, but they did their best to deny the secret of iron mongering to both the Canaanites and the Israelites. This monopoly is recorded in I Samuel 13:19–20: "Now there was no smith found throughout all the land of Israel: for the Philistines said, Lest the Hebrews make them swords or spears: but all the Israelites went down to the Philistines to sharpen every man his share, and his coulter, and his axe, and his mattock." The Philistine settlement of Canaan was successful, and in a relatively short time, they assimilated into Canaanite culture so thoroughly that their own language was lost and replaced by a Canaanite dialect. Their gods of Aegean origin had their names changed, and the Philistine army adopted the full panoply of Canaanite weapons and techniques of war.[22] With the settlement of the Philistines in Canaan and their introduction of iron weapons, the iron age of military technology can be said to have begun.[23]

The first portrayal of Philistine weapons comes down to us from Ramses III's memorial reliefs at Medinet Habu of his defeat of the Sea Peoples. The Peleset are easily recognizable by their combat dress and weapons. Their soldiers wear a distinctive helmet with a band of what were originally thought to be feathers on the crown. More recent evidence suggests that these were not feathers but a circlet of reeds, stiffened horsehair, or even leather strips.[24] The leather helmet was secured by a chin strap. Body armor was a corselet of bronze or leather shaped in an inverted V, probably indicative of overlapping plates of either material. Shoulder guards to protect the clavicles are in evidence, although it is not certain if this feature is genuine or merely the artist's rendering of strong shoulders. A short kilt like that worn by the Hittites is shown, an item of equipment that may well have been acquired by the Peleset during their wanderings in Asia Minor. The long straight iron sword was the main armament of the soldier although some Peleset soldiers are portrayed with the short spear similar to the Greek *dory* of a much later period. The Peleset shield was round, probably fashioned of wood covered with leather or bronze with, perhaps, an iron rim to ward off sword blows, and

Figure 2.4 Peleset/Philistine Heavy Infantryman, 1200 B.C.E.

was equipped with a boss. We know nothing of the shield's handgrip, but if it was of Aegean origin it is likely that the shield was held by a collection of tethers that met in the center of the shield. With this grip the shield was difficult to maneuver, required great strength to use effectively, and required a high degree of training. Even when the grip was mastered, the shield could not be used to press against an opponent with much force.[25] All this speaks to the degree of professionalization of the Philistine warrior class, but raises questions about why the round shield was so quickly accepted by Canaanite and especially Israelite armies which were comprised mostly of semitrained infantry militia.[26] The answer lies in the fact that the round shield was smaller and much lighter than the old full-body shield or figure eight shield, permitting the sword-bearing infantryman much greater speed and mobility on the battlefield. The appearance of the straight sword and light javelin at this time reduced the spear-bearing infantry to a secondary role, permitting the light infantryman to move about the battlefield with increased effectiveness. The light round shield, along with the leather body corselet, was his main protection.

The story of David and Goliath offers yet another glimpse into Philistine weaponry, one that is often assumed to affirm the Aegean origins of the Philistine people. As told by Samuel, "And there came out of the camp of the Philistines a champion named Goliath. . . . and he was armed with a coat of mail. . . . And he had greaves of bronze upon his legs. . . . And the shaft of his spear was like a weaver's beam."[27] To some, this is the equipment of the Aegean warrior as described in the *Iliad.* There is no mention of Goliath's shield in Samuel's account, only of his shield bearer, but some suggest there is no reason to doubt that it was other than the round shield. Nor is there mention of Goliath's helmet, but Yadin is probably correct when he suggests that by Saul's time the Philistines had adopted some Canaanite military equipment, including the metal helmet, probably of bronze and not iron, with cheek plates.[28] The narrow-blade socket axe also came into wide use among the Philistines as well as the socketed blade for the javelin. It is interesting to point out that both these weapons were probably of bronze since bronze—rather than iron—could more easily be worked into this complex shape. Goliath's weapon may well have been a spear as Samuel says, but it is just as likely to have been a javelin, incorporating another Aegean innovation, the loop and cord. Philistine javelins had a slip loop that could be slid over the shaft of the weapon. The loop was attached to a strong cord that was tightly wrapped around the javelin's shaft. When throwing the javelin, the soldier held on to the end of the wrapped cord, pulling it toward him as the weapon was launched thereby imparting a rotational spin to the shaft. The spin stabilized the weapon in flight, lending it both greater range and accuracy.[29]

The Philistine way of war as portrayed in the Ramses reliefs originally placed its greatest reliance upon infantry as befits an Aegean people where the war chariot was rarely used in combat. Instead, Greek warriors used chariots as transport, to ride to the battlefield where they dismounted and fought as individual combatants with little in the way of tactical organization. The offer of Goliath's Philistine commander to David that the battle could be decided by combat between two champions, in effect a duel, once more reflects the Aegean attitude toward war as the stage of individual infantry combatants. That having been said, however, once settled in Canaan the Philistines seem to have quickly adopted the primary weapon of Canaanite armies, the war chariot, and transformed some of their warrior caste from heavy infantry into chariot warriors even as the use of Philistine infantry in later battles remained substantial. The first mention of Philistine chariots in the Bible occurs during the time of Saul, more than a century after the Philistines arrived in Canaan, plenty of time to have become acquainted with the Canaanite chariot. At the battle of Michmash, the Bible recounts that "The Philistines also assembled for battle, with three thousand chariots, six thousand horsemen, and foot soldiers as numerous as the sands of the seashore."[30] The reference to horsemen is curious since cavalry at this time was not yet developed. The mention of infantry "as numerous as the sands of the seashore," however, reflects the continued heavy reliance of the Philistines upon trained infantry to a degree much greater than in Canaanite armies. At Mount Gilboa the Bible recounts another example of the Philistine use of chariots: "The battle raged around Saul, and the archers hit him; he was pierced through the abdomen."[31] As Herzog and Gichon have noted, "The outcome of the battle was decided by the Philistine chariots. Saul was forced to retreat up Mount Gilboa. . . . The chariot-mounted archers followed close upon his heels up the easily traversable western slope and subjected the Israelites on the flat plateau to constant and effective fire."[32]

Both these battles, a well as accounts of others in the Old Testament, permit some speculation about Philistine tactics. To a much greater degree than Canaanite armies the Philistines appear to have maintained a large number of heavy infantry of professional quality in contrast to the light infantry of the Israelites. At both Michmash (a Philistine defeat) and Mount Gilboa (a Philistine victory), infantry troops were used in large numbers with the chariots in support. The maintenance of large infantry units made good sense in light of the fact that the main antagonists of the Philistines were Israelites and not the princes of Canaan. As we shall see later, Israelite armies, at least until the time of Solomon, were comprised almost exclusively of light infantry who specialized in surprise and night attack. In addition, the areas of Israelite-Philistine conflict, at least in the early days, were confined mostly to the mountains of the central massif, terrain highly unfavorable to chariots. Under these conditions, the primary tactical emphasis of the Philistines was upon infantry with chariots used in support. At Michmash, for example, the Philistines appear to have used their chariot squadrons to secure the roads leading to and from the battlefield, probably to prevent further reinforcement or retreat of the Israelite armies. At Mount Gilboa, it was Philistine infantry that bore the brunt of Saul's attack, stopping it and driving the Israelites back up the mountain. It was only after the infantry had held its ground that the chariots could maneuver against Saul's flank thereby subjecting him to enfilade fire from their archers. At Ebenezer-Aphek the battle was joined and carried only by Philistine infantry which faced the Israelites in a set-piece battle in open terrain with the result that the Philistines "slew about four thousand men on the battlefield."[33] There is no mention of chariots in the second battle that followed, and once more the Philistines carried the day with their infantry. It appears likely, then, that the armies of the Philistines, while employing a good deal of Canaanite equipment and the war chariot, seem to have stressed infantry far more than did the Canaanites. Whether this was a tactical response to the terrain or to the nature of their infantry-heavy Israelite enemies or whether it was a people maintaining their traditional military heritage with its emphasis on individual infantry combat cannot be answered here.

Conflict between the Israelites and Philistines grew increasingly frequent as the Philistines pushed out from their main coastal bases and sought to establish trade routes and trading stations that cut across the central mountains into Jordan. The Philistines established a number of trading stations deep in Israelite territory with, we may surmise, small military garrisons to protect them. These stations were seen by the Israelites as a prelude to invasion. From the Philistine perspective, Israelite patrols and occasional forays into the coastal lowlands were seen as a burgeoning threat. Circa 1050 B.C.E., the Philistines forced the Israelites into a contest of arms with the result that the Israelites suffered a terrible defeat at the battle of Aphek. To rally Israelite morale, the Ark of the Covenant itself was brought to the battlefield. A short time later the Israelites were defeated once more by the Philistines. This time the Ark was captured and carried off to Ashdod. The defeat set off a tremendous cry among the Israelites for a national leader who could defeat their enemies and lift the Philistine yoke. The result was the rise of Saul, the first king of Israel.

ISRAELITES

The military history of the Israelites during the biblical period begins with the Exodus (1275–1225 B.C.E.), followed by the invasion of Canaan by the tribes of Israel under Joshua (1225–1200 B.C.E.), followed by the period of the Judges (1200–1050 B.C.E.), the period of Saul (1025–1005 B.C.E.) and David (1005–961 B.C.E.), and ends with Solomon (961–921 B.C.E.). The period from Solomon to 587 B.C.E., the period of the Hebrew kings, is verifiable through sources outside the Old Testament. In each of these periods, the army and politico-military structure of the Israelites changed significantly in terms of organization, weapons, and tactics. Evidence from archaeology suggests the first period when the Israelites invaded Canaan was a time of widespread destruction of Canaanite cities and strong-points, including Hazor, that sometimes dovetails with the campaigns of Joshua. Whether this destruction can be attributed to the Israelites seems unlikely however. The battles of Joshua were conflicts against Canaanites properly so called, but also against rival tribal enemies already settled in Canaan. It may be that the original Israelite penetration of Canaan occurred in areas of sparse settlement in the mountains where significant opposition was unlikely. As the Israelites settled in, however, it is probable that they came into conflict with other peoples of Canaan and that some of these disputes were as likely settled by negotiation as by war.[34]

The biblical account of the period of the Judges must also be placed in perspective. The Book of Judges recounts the military victories of 12 national Israelite heroes (*shophetim*) whose acts of military bravery forged a national consciousness. These accounts present a number of difficulties. In the first place, none of the Judges were national leaders at all, but local tribal leaders combating not national enemies but local ones.[35] None of the Judges held any kind of permanent position, but they were men called to arms in an emergency who returned their authority to the tribe when the emergency had passed. None of the wars of the Judges involved more than a handful of Israelite tribes, and there was no national Israelite governmental structure. As to the enemies of the Israelites, only one of the wars of this period, Deborah and Barak's victory over Sisera near the Kishon River, was a war against a Canaanite enemy. All the others were against local tribal elements—Midianites, Amalekites, and the Philistines.[36] The pressure from the Philistine threat forced the Israelites to ignore the Canaanites who, after all, shared much of a common culture with the Israelites. A number of Canaanite towns, cities, and fortified places within Israelite territory went unmolested for years by the Israelites while they dealt with the Philistines. It was only during the periods of Saul and David that these places could be brought under Israelite control.[37] The accounts of the Judges remained an oral tradition until around 600 B.C.E. when, along with much of the Old Testament, they were finally compiled in written form. Probably for reasons of ethnic identity and national pride the compilers endowed the oral versions of these accounts with an artificial framework, sequence, and chronology that turned the oral tradition into a great national saga of a people attempting to preserve their national identity and culture against foreign cultural and military influences.[38]

The first Israelite military formation, including its means for command and control, is described in the Bible as the Israelites prepared to depart from Sinai and travel to the promised land of Canaan.[39] The book of Numbers describes in detail the arrangement of the Israelite camp and how it is to assemble for and conduct the march. Within the camp each tribe was allocated a fixed area that corresponded to a fixed position in the line of march. Tents were pitched around the tent of the tribal commander whose standard was displayed to mark his position. The Ark was positioned in the center of the camp under the watchful eyes of the Levite guard. Command and control over the tribal host in camp and on the march was accomplished by signals blown on two silver trumpets. A single blast from both trumpets was the command for tribal leaders to gather at the central tent for instructions. A special signal called the Alarm signified the movement of each wing. Although not mentioned, it is likely that a special trumpet call was used to turn the formation from line of march toward any direction to meet a surprise attack with the noncombatants falling behind the newly assembled battle line for protection. The Israelite organization portrayed in Numbers offers a graphic example of how it was possible to manage the migration of an entire people over long distances while providing for their defense on the march.

The campaigns of Joshua offer some insight into the nature of the Israelite armies. Israelite armies of this period were comprised of tribal levies of militia configured as light infantry armed with sickle-swords, spears, bows, slings, and daggers. There was no permanent core of professional officers, and units fought under the command of their own leaders with Joshua in overall command. The lack of an institutionalized military command structure paralleled the absence of a centralized political structure. At this point the Israelites had no king over all the tribes. The leader at any given time was the first among equals of the tribal leaders involved in the battle. Moreover, during the period of the Judges few battles involved more than three or four tribes in confederation. Joshua, presumably, could draw upon the entire tribal host for his manpower. An army of light infantry under Joshua made perfect sense. First, light infantry did not require prohibitively expensive armor and helmets. Second, the terrain in which the Israelites were fighting favored light infantry. The terrain of Canaan is varied, comprised of mountains, deserts, hills, forests, and rocky glades, with only a few open plains which, if a commander avoided them, permitted maximum effectiveness of light infantry. Joshua was fighting mostly in the hills and mountains of the central massif where light infantry, if employed with tactical skill, could be decisive.

Enemy chariots were useless in the uneven terrain and even heavy infantry was at a considerable disadvantage, which made fighting in phalanx very difficult. Moreover, the Israelites had not yet reached a level of military sophistication under Joshua that permitted the use of the chariot. In the battle against the king of Hazor as described by the book of Joshua, the Israelites captured some enemy chariots. Joshua "houghed their horses [cut their hamstrings] and burnt their chariots with fire."[40] Some have suggested that this incident reflects the primitive Israelite technology of war at this time. With no knowledge of how to operate or employ the chariots, it is argued that Joshua had little choice but to destroy them. As we shall see, this argument is far from convincing in demonstrating the level of sophistication of Israelite warfare in Joshua's time. Saul's later inability to field chariots at Mount Gilboa cost him his life, and it was not until the end of King David's reign that there is tentative evidence that the Israelite armies possessed even a single squadron of chariots. It fell to Solomon to change the nature of the Israelite army completely by introducing large scale chariot units for the first time. It has been argued, too, that one of the reasons why so many Canaanite cities and towns were left unmolested by the Israelites until the time of David was because the Israelites had no means to successfully attack them. Once more, this is probably incorrect. The refusal of the Israelites to attempt to subdue certain towns in their midst probably had much more to do with political considerations such as the reaction of the Egyptian garrisons on the coastal plain than with any supposed military inability.

The size of Israelite armies remains a matter of some speculation. Deborah, drawing upon only four of the 12 tribes in confederation, put 10,000 men in the field against Sisera if the Bible is to be believed. To relieve the siege of Jabesh-gilead, Saul called upon the entire nation to provide manpower. As was usually the case, tribes far from the area of concern often balked at sending any men at all. To counter this centrifugal tendency, Saul "took a yoke of oxen, and hewed them to pieces, and sent them throughout the coast of Israel . . . saying, Whosoever cometh not forth after Saul and after Samuel, so shall it be done unto his oxen."[41] The population of the Israelite tribes at this time was about 100,000 to 150,000 people.[42] Calculating 25 percent of the entire population as being of military age, the Israelites could field about 25,000 to 30,000 men at maximum effort. Under most circumstances, however, Saul would have been fortunate to be able to deploy half that number for any given battle. Later, under David and Solomon, the establishment of a centralized political structure led to the establishment of a centralized mechanism for conscription that could more efficiently call up larger levies for national defense.

The most significant military weakness of the armies of the Judges was the centrifugal tendencies of a tribal society that made central direction of any military effort problematical. This weakness eventually produced a catastrophic defeat at Ebenezer at the hands of the Philistines in 1050 B.C.E. which resulted in the military occupation of former Israelite territories, the appointment of Philistine governors, disarming of the population, prohibitions against iron working, and the use of punitive search-and-destroy operations to keep the Israelite population in line.[43] The details of Saul's appointment as king of all Israel by Samuel need not concern us here. Suffice it to say the circumstances of Philistine control provided the stimulus for the Israelites to form a centralized monarchy for the first time in their history. Under Saul the tribal leaders relinquished some of their authority to the central government, most particularly the ability of the king to levy conscription requirements upon all 12 tribes for military service. Saul defeated the Philistines with the new army in three great battles, and reformed the Israelite army somewhat along Philistine lines.

The presence of standing enemy forces just beyond the Israelite borders emphasized the need for a similar standing force within Israel itself. Saul selected 3,000 warriors to serve as the core of a permanent standing army. As in the Philistine army, some of these men were mercenaries. David himself came to Saul's court not from the Israelite levy but as a trained soldier. The Israelite army remained a light infantry force under Saul, although it is not beyond possibility that the professionals were equipped with the protection and arms of heavy infantry. There were no chariot units, however. Saul's army was divided into two divisions, with the smaller one of 1,000 men placed under the command of his son, Jonathan.[44] One of Saul's important innovations was the introduction of the fortified camp for prolonged campaigns. These were well-organized, semipermanent base camps broken into special zones for training, ordinance manufacture, and quartermaster. Each of these zones was overseen by details of specialists. Saul's reforms shaped the character of the Israelite armies for the next 15 years or so until King David made other changes. Although Saul's reforms made it possible to place larger Israelite armies in the field, they were still under armed and ill-equipped when compared to Philistine armies. The lack of chariot units, if only for reconnaissance and scouting, was a major disability. The larger size of Israelite armies may have been what tempted Saul to meet the Philistines in open battle near Mount Gilboa with catastrophic results.

King David's reign was marked by a number of important changes in the Israelite army as he shaped it into an instrument for the acquisition and maintenance of an empire. Herzog and Gichon provide an excellent outline of the major campaigns of David in building the first Israelite Empire,[45] which is addressed later in more detail. David's reforms began with establishing firm control over the national tribal levy by requiring military service of every able-bodied male.[46] For tactical purposes the levy was organized into divisions of thousands subdivided into units of hundreds and subunits of 50 and 10, the latter being the smallest unit to have a permanent commander. The recurrence of the number 600 in the Bible with reference to Israelite combat units raises the question of whether this was the standard combat unit or field battalion. The number conveniently divides by four into units of 150 men (the Egyptian system) and by three into units of 200, a system used commonly by other armies of the day. Either or both systems may have been employed by the Israelite armies under David and later Solomon.

David's conscript army was exclusively an infantry force and a light infantry force at that, just as it had been under Joshua and Saul. Although light infantry provided for great flexibility, there remained the problem of how to obtain a proper mix of weapons and other capabilities in sufficient amounts to achieve the overall tactical objective. This was accomplished in the army of David the same way Joshua had done it, by relying upon tribal units who possessed specific military specialties.[47] In I Chronicles, the Bible records some of the special military proficiencies of the tribes. The Benjaminites, for example, were armed with bows and "could use both the right hand and left hand in hurling stones and shooting arrows out of a bow." Gadites were proficient at "shield and buckler . . . and were as swift as the roes upon the mountains." The sons of Judah "bore shield and spear," as did the Naphtali. The Zebulunites may well have been the Israelite equivalent of rangers for "they were expert in war, with all instruments of war . . . and could keep rank." A bit less clear was the skill of the tribe of Issachar which was explained as "understanding of the times, to know what Israel ought to do," a description that might suggest scouting and intelligence gathering. Gichon and Herzog have described the importance of these tribal military specialists when brought together in David's army:

> In short, David could draw upon the tribal contingents to furnish bowmen and slingers, light and heavy lancers—the former good at fighting in individual combat in difficult terrain, the latter (the children of Judah) forming the closely arrayed heavy phalanx. These were assisted by spearmen, who would hurl their spears before charging the foe with drawn swords. Other tribes were less specialized as far as weaponry was concerned, but were trained to fight in rank and file.[48]

The tribal chiefs were responsible for the training of their levies in the use of weapons particular to their clan, as well as for maintenance of weapons. Most important, they were responsible for providing the tribe's manpower quota to the central army. Alongside this tribal levy was another force comprised of 12 monthly nontribal and nonterritorial divisions, each of which came on active duty for one month a year. Permanently officered by a professional cadre, the king was provided with a large, available cadre of soldiers on one-month service duty every year. This force was expected to take the field immediately in case of emergency and purchase sufficient time for the national levy to be mobilized. A similar system is employed by the Israeli Defense Force today.

The core of the Davidic army was two corps of professional regular soldiers. The first of these were the "mighty men" or *gibborim*, two regiments each built upon a group of special soldiers personally loyal to David called the "Thirty." The first "Thirty" group was the band of loyal followers that had fought with David during his exile. This was a group of hardened combat veterans whose tales of courage were the subject of Israelite poems and ballads. The second "Thirty" was a group of David's followers who formed around him after he had been anointed king of Judah. These, too, were trusted advisors and combat veterans who, as was David himself, were highly skilled in unconventional warfare and tactical innovation. From the groups of Thirty, David selected his personal bodyguard and many of his high-ranking civil and military dignitaries. In this sense, the Thirty were very similar to Alexander's *hetairoi* and Charlemagne's *schara*.[49]

The second corps of regulars in David's army was comprised of mercenaries, including Philistine troops. These hardy professionals were tough combat soldiers whose armament was heavier than most Israelite troops and who could be relied upon to fight well, a not insignificant contribution to morale among soldiers who were mostly conscripts. That mercenary troops, even Philistines fighting against their own people, could be reliable is evidenced by the fact that David himself, when driven from Saul's court, commanded a mercenary corps that placed itself in the service of one of the Philistine kings. Later, when Saul faced the Philistines at Mount Gilboa, David's unit reported for service among the Philistine troops preparing to do battle. It was the Philistine commander who refused David's help. But there is no doubt that David was quite prepared to fight against his former king and countryman.

Some of David's many victories were against enemies that deployed chariots against his army in large numbers. The ability to stop charging chariots with infantry alone arrayed on open ground appears to have been one of the Israelite army's talents, one that finds its modern echo in the maxim that the most dangerous enemy of the tank is the individual infantryman. The key to stopping a chariot charge was to engage the machines far forward of the heavy infantry phalanx with light troops using their slings, arrows, and javelins to harass and slow the momentum of the charge until it was no longer sufficient to penetrate the massed heavy infantry phalanx which then engaged it with spears. Once slowed or stopped, the light infantry, either units in reserve or those recovered from the initial engagement, swarmed over the chariots in close combat where their swords had the advantage over the charioteer's bow. Whereas in Canaanite and Philistine armies the chariot was used as the primary element to deliver shock, in the infantry armies of the Israelites this role fell to the heavily armored pikeman, most often regulars or mercenaries, arrayed in phalanx.

Figure 2.5 Israelite Light Infantryman, Davidic Era, 1050 B.C.E.

We have no reliefs or other portrayals of the Israelite infantry soldier at the time of David. But Stillman and Tallis have constructed a portrait of a typical Israelite infantryman from text descriptions. He was called a "valiant man" (*ish hayil*) or a "selected man" (*ish bachur*), or elite troop. Israelite infantry equipment was a mix of Canaanite and Philistine equipment and included a round shield (*magen*), a short thrusting spear (*romah*), iron straight sword (*hereb*), and a bronze helmet (*koba*). Regular troops like the *gibborim* probably wore scale or lamellar armor called a *shiryon* like the Canaanite soldiers. The tribal militia would be even more lightly armed, mostly with javelins, daggers, and slings.[50]

Governing an empire requires trained administrative personnel, and David's court reflected the increased complexity of the Israelite national defense establishment, one that was far larger and more sophisticated than under Saul. David's court had a commandant of the tribal levy (Joab), a commander of mercenary troops (Benaiah), chiefs and high priests of the religious establishment, a superintendent of corvee labor, various high-ranking military staff officers and advisors, a chancellor (Jehoshaphat), and an official scribe, who we might imply from the Egyptian model was chief historian and, perhaps, chief of intelligence as well. The whole arrangement bears a striking similarity to the structure of the Egyptian court, although the superintendent of corvee labor was probably derived from Canaanite practice.[51] David's court and his legitimacy as king rested upon a far more secure foundation than had Saul's. Saul's claim to kingship was based upon Samuel's pronouncement that Saul had been sent by Yahweh. David's claim, however, rested upon no such special claim to grace. David was made king as a consequence of his military victories and the real power he possessed as head of a conquering army. The two claims, one theological and one constitutional, contested with each other after the death of Solomon with opponents of the monarchy, usually the prophets, using the theological claim to undermine the legitimacy of the monarchy itself.

David had created an empire and now it was Solomon's task to maintain it. With David's death the national strategy of the Israelites passed over to the defense. An army configured for conquest is not always well suited for defense. David's defense establishment lacked two important elements: a well-planned system of fortifications and a powerful strategic striking arm, a chariot corps. Solomon immediately turned his attention to these deficiencies. Under Solomon, Israel acquired a chariot corps which transformed the Israelite army from a light infantry force into an army whose chariots were its arm of decision.[52] The tribal levy remained, but more and more the regular standing army was comprised of professional chariot crews, and specialized regular infantry, the "runners," who accompanied the chariots into battle, providing them with strong infantry support in close combat. The regular militia levy probably continued to function as light infantry.[53] The Old Testament gives the size of Solomon's chariot corps at "a thousand and four hundred chariots and twelve thousand horsemen (charioteers)."[54]

Information regarding the type of chariots employed by Solomon's army is completely lacking, but it seems reasonable that Israelite chariots would be of Egyptian, Syrian, or Canaanite design since they were the most commonplace machines of the day. It is unclear, however, why 1,400 chariots would require a force of 12,000 horsemen. One possibility whose logic is militarily compelling is that the Israelites maintained double crews for each vehicle. This would still leave sufficient manpower to provide a mix of chariot types. Some Israelite chariots may have followed the Egyptian example of being light, fast, and maneuverable machines armed with a driver and an archer.

Figure 2.6 Israelite Charioteer and Horse of Solomonic Era, 1000 B.C.E.

Others, following the Syrian and Canaanite example, might have been heavy machines carrying a crew of three, driver, archer, and lancer/spearman, and used to deliver shock and mounted infantry. The Bible describes the Canaanite chariots as "chariots of iron," but there is no reason to believe that even the heavy Israelite chariots were clad in armor of any sort. Even bronze plate would have been so heavy as to collapse the wooden frame. The idea of a "chariot of iron" is technological nonsense.

Solomon equipped Israel with a system of fortifications from which the nation could be defended with a mobile strategic defense in-depth, the same strategic design employed by the Canaanites two centuries earlier. Major fortifications were built or improved at Hazor, Megiddo, Tamar, Gezer, Baalath, Lower Beth-horon, and Tadmor (Palmyra). Each of these "chariot cities" controlled a key road or pass, possessed a good water supply, and offered suitable ground upon which to employ chariots. At Megiddo and Hazor, Solomon replaced the old casement walls with walls of massive stone; this was in reaction to the growing use of effective battering rams by armies of the period. A casement wall could be easily collapsed by breaking a hole in its base with a battering ram, using the weight of its rubble fill to press outward against the wall itself. Walls of solid stone blocks cannot be collapsed in this manner. Solomon positioned his chariot forces and regular infantry units in some of these "chariot cities" from which they could react to an enemy threat. These cities, of course, could also be used as bases from which offensive punitive expeditions could be mounted and from which regular combat or reconnaissance patrols could be staged. The guiding strategic concept was to engage the enemy on ground of one's own choosing and to do so before the enemy reached the cities. Like the Canaanites before them, Israelite commanders would permit themselves to be besieged only as a last resort.

Figure 2.7 Israelite Infantryman, 800 B.C.E.

The general strategic reserve of Solomon's army was kept in Jerusalem, including the strategic reserve of the chariot corps. To position the reserve in this manner implies that there must have been a network of well-guarded and packed-earth roads leading from Jerusalem to all major defensive positions; otherwise Israelite commanders would have been unable to react in sufficient time. This network of roads would have required road stations, watering points, repair shops, and storage depots along its way and must have run fairly close to existing settlements. Such a system would have had to be maintained on a regular basis, as would the entire military system of defense, and brought into existence a governmental structure centered around Solomon's court that was far more complex and articulated as a response to the growing administrative and military burdens that needed to be dealt with.[55]

Solomon's solution to this increasing complexity was to create a number of commercial monopolies from which the state drew exclusive revenues and to place taxation on a uniform basis, providing a continual and relatively stable source of revenue for the court from which the governmental and military expenses of the state could be paid. Solomon then rationalized the military logistics system. The country was divided into 12 administrative districts that were only generally identical with the tribal districts. The size of each district varied considerably and was determined with a view to making them equal in productivity and wealth so that the burden of military supply would not fall too heavily upon any one district. Each district was to supply the food and materials required by the court and military garrisons for one month, thus rotating the burden from district to district while at the same time assuring a continuous and adequate supply of needed materials.[56] Taken together Solomon's reforms and innovations bequeathed Israel a truly "modern" state in terms of its military, economy, political institutions, and infrastructure. With Solomon, the Israelites ceased to be a tribal society and became a national entity for the first time in their history.

EGYPT

The period from 2686 to 2160 B.C.E., the Old Kingdom, was the first time a definable military organization emerged in Egypt. The military organization of this period was shaped by two factors. First, Egypt was protected by formidable natural barriers to her east and west in the form of great deserts. The peoples of these areas, the Sand Peoples of Palestine and the Libyans to the west, were largely nomadic and represented more of a military nuisance than a real threat. Nubia to the south presented a real threat of invasion, but the fortresses and strong points built in 2200 B.C.E. along with the natural barriers presented by the Nile's depth and rapids contained the threat relatively well. To the north the Mediterranean itself presented a barrier to invasion for shipbuilding had not yet reached the point where ships could be used to transport large numbers of troops across an open sea with any degree of safety. For a period of more than 1,000 years, Egypt was under no significant military threat from outside her borders. Second, Egypt's political order was fragmented. Although united in a single kingdom, the local barons or nomarchs remained sufficiently powerful to obstruct pharaonic power. The nomarchs maintained their own military forces and often exercised control over strategic trade routes. The situation was not unlike that of feudal Europe where the high king was dependent on his ability to control local barons. These two factors combined to shape the structure of the Old Kingdom armies.

The impetus for the army came from the need of the central rulers to defend the state and deal with periodic revolts of the nomarchs. Pharaoh's army probably consisted of a small but regular standing force of several thousand troops organized much in the manner of household guards. Egypt introduced conscription during this time, levying one man in a hundred to service each year. The best of the conscripts went to the regular army, which probably did most of the training of conscripts as well. It was during this period that the first military titles appeared. There were titles of rank indicating "general of recruits" that carried with them the rank of general officer. The standing army was augmented by Nubian auxiliaries in the pay of the king.[57] The great bulk of the army was militia units organized under the command of the local nomarchs. These barons were required to make levies of men available to the pharaoh during times of emergency. In normal times, however, the troops were trained and kept at the local level. The political relationship between the king and the local rulers largely determined if and how many troops could be made available for dealing with national problems. A third element of the army was the large body of conscript troops levied under the system of national conscription that did not go to regular military units. These conscripts received some degree of military training and may have been primarily used to garrison the frontier forts and furnish labor for public works projects. It is unknown how long the term of service for conscript soldiers was, but apparently they remained in service with local militia units for some time after their period of national service was completed.

The structure of the army of the Old Kingdom is unknown, but it is clear that some distinctions were made between regular officer appointments and others. There appear a number of military titles, including those of specialists in desert travel and frontier and desert warfare, garrison troops, frontier troops, quartermaster officers, and scribes, who seem to have functioned as senior noncommissioned officers.[58] There are also titles that refer to "overseers of arsenals," "overseers of desert blockhouses and royal fortresses," and caravan leaders.[59] The size of the combined army remains a mystery. Weni, a commander in the army of the Sixth Dynasty (2345 B.C.E.), recorded that his army was "many tens of thousands" strong.[60] A string of 20 mud-brick fortresses was built in approximately 2200 B.C.E. to guard the southern approaches to

Egypt. Each required up to 3,000 men to garrison. This would suggest an army of at least 60,000 in the frontier force alone.[61] With Egypt's population approaching 2 million at this time, these force levels could easily have been achieved.

The Egyptian armies of the Middle Kingdom (2040–1786 B.C.E.) became more evidently structurally articulated as Egypt struggled through periods of anarchy and the weakening of centralized authority leading eventually to its invasion and occupation by the Hyksos in 1720 B.C.E. This period saw a constant tug and pull between the pharaohs and the nomarchs, who still controlled their feudal armies, although the obligation to provide levies to the crown became clearer. The pharaohs retained their standing armies, supported by conscription, and still employed Nubian auxiliaries. A clearer command structure emerged with the pharaoh acting as field commander on major campaigns and with general officers in charge of safeguarding the frontiers and managing logistics. There were clearer distinctions among junior officer ranks and titles.[62] Titles emerged for such ranks as commanders of shock troops, recruits, instructors, and commanders of retainers, the latter being personal guards of the king. The title of assault troop commander appears for the first time. Progression in junior rank seems to have been to move from command of 7 men to a company of 60 men to a command of 100 men.[63]

The administrative mechanisms of the army became more complex with the proliferation of various titles. For the first time there was evidence of a military intelligence service, reflected in the title "Master of the Secrets of the King in the Army."[64] The army seems to have organized troops on the basis of experience and age, and names appear for units of company and regiment, although the size of these units is not known. Terms for bowmen, garrison troops, police patrols, district officers, and military judges make their appearance. On balance the army of the Middle Kingdom appears more clearly articulated as to its structure than was its predecessor. Still, it is difficult to determine to what extent this difference may be a function of the survivability of records and other evidence rather than anything else.

By 1790 B.C.E., the centralized government of Egypt began to lose ground to the rebellious nomarchs, and the army proved insufficient to bring them to heel. Taking advantage of the disarray, the Hyksos invaded Egypt and established themselves for more than a century as the rulers of Upper Egypt. The name Hyksos is probably a Greek rendering of the Egyptian term *hik-khase*, meaning "chiefdom of a foreign hill country" or "shepherd kings." In the Egyptian idiom this term meant bedouin sheikh.[65] The origins of the Hyksos remain obscure, but it may be that they were the seminomadic peoples of what is now Palestine and Jordan. Of Semitic origin, these peoples were wandering tribes and far below the cultural, economic, and military level of the Egyptians. The Egyptians called them "asiatics," a general term of contempt reserved by the Egyptians for nomadic desert peoples.

One of the more intriguing military mysteries of the Hyksos is how was it possible for such a people to conquer an advanced culture like the Egyptians? The answer lies in their employment of very sophisticated military technology, technology unknown in Egypt at the time. The Egyptian army of the seventeenth century B.C.E. was an infantry force organized by function into units of bowmen, spearmen, and axemen. By contrast the Hyksos army was an army of mobility and firepower. The centerpiece of the Hyksos force was the horse-drawn chariot, but they also used the composite bow, sword, and penetrating axe. In addition Hyksos soldiers were equipped with helmets and body armor and carried quivers for their arrows.[66] These weapons conveyed a decisive military advantage. In 1720 B.C.E., the Hyksos established their capital at Avaris (modern Tanis), and in 1674, they captured Memphis. For the next 100 years or so, the Hyksos held control of most of Upper Egypt while Lower Egypt remained in the hands of the Theban princes.[67]

Over time the Theban princes rebuilt their military strength until, after a series of short but bloody clashes, Ahmose I (1570–1546 B.C.E.) drove the asiatics from Avaris and once again unified the country. Under Amenhotep I (1546–1526 B.C.E.), Egypt began the process of establishing a great empire. Amenhotep pushed Egypt's borders beyond those of the Old Kingdom and established an Egyptian presence in Asia. Thutmose I (1525–1512 B.C.E.), one of Amenhotep's generals, pacified the south, and his successor, Thutmose II (1512–1504 B.C.E.), consolidated Egyptian power in Palestine to the Syrian border. His successor, Thutmose III (1504–1450 B.C.E.), became Egypt's greatest warrior pharaoh and established the empire far into Asia, exacting tribute from Babylon, Assyria, and the Hittites. In the process Thutmose III created a first-rate professional army through which Egypt reached its pinnacle as a military power.

The wars of liberation and expansion under the Thutmosids brought about profound changes in Egyptian society. For the first time there came into being a truly professional military caste. Military families were given grants of land to hold for as long as they provided a son for the officer corps.[68] The army rid itself of the local militias, reorganized its structure, and became a genuine national force based in conscription. The local militias continued in existence, but the nomarchs were reduced in power and lost the ability to withhold military levies from the king. Thutmose III completely revamped Egyptian weapons and tactics. He adopted all the major weapons of the Hyksos—the chariot, composite bow, penetrating axe, sickle-sword, helmets, and armor—and made great improvements in both the physical design of the chariot and the tactical doctrines that governed its use on the battlefield. Thutmose mounted his newly composite bow-equipped archers on chariots and produced the most important military revolution in ground warfare yet seen in Egypt.

The national army was raised by conscription, with the levy being one man in ten instead of the traditional one man in 100.[69] The army was centrally trained by professional officers and noncommissioned officers. The pharaoh himself stood as commander in chief and personally led his troops in battle.

The vizier served as minister of war, and there was an Army Council that served as a general staff. The field army was organized into divisions, each of which was a complete combined-arms corps, including infantry and chariots. These divisions contained approximately 6,500 men, including logistics and support personnel, and each was named after one of the principle gods of Egypt. Later Ramses II organized Egypt and the empire into 34 military districts to facilitate conscription, training, and the supply of the army.[70] The administrative structure was also improved, and there were professional schools to train and test officers and scribes in the military arts.

The two major combat arms of the Egyptian army were chariotry and infantry. The chariot corps was organized into squadrons of 25, each commanded by a "charioteer of the residence," equal to a modern company commander. Larger units of 50 and 150 vehicles could be rapidly assembled and employed in concert with other forces.[71] It was common practice to assemble units whose size depended on the nature of the mission and terrain, an example of the modern practice of "tailoring" a unit to specific function. The chariot corps was supported logistically by staffs who recruited and trained horses and by craftsmen whose task it was to repair the machines while the army was in the field. Egyptian divisions also had mobile chariot repair battalions to ensure the operability of the vehicles when the army was on the march. The fact that pharaoh was often portrayed as leading a chariot charge suggests that the chariot forces were the elite striking arm of the field force.

It is wonderfully paradoxical in an age of bronze that the most innovative and destructive weapons of war at this time—the chariot and the composite bow—were made of wood. The Hyksos invasion introduced the chariot to Egypt, and by the fifteenth century B.C.E., the Egyptians had modified the vehicle into the finest fighting vehicle in the ancient world. The Egyptian chariot was constructed of a light wooden frame covered by stretched fabric or hide to reduce weight. Two men could easily carry the vehicle over streams and rough terrain. The platform supporting the rider and archer was made of stretched leather thongs covered with hide and fashioned in the shape of a "D." The cab was one meter wide, three-quarter meters high, and one-half meter deep. Two horses, usually stallions, pulled the vehicle held by a central yoke pole and outer races guided by reins. The Egyptians were the first to move the axle to the far rear of the carrying platform, a development that increased the speed,

Figure 2.8 Egyptian Chariot, New Kingdom, 1400–1150 B.C.E.

stability, and maneuverability of the vehicle.[72] Belly bars and leg straps helped steady the riders at high speed. Bow, arrow, spear quivers, and axe were attached to each side for easy access during battle.[73] These weapons suggest that the chariot acquired new tactical functions under the Egyptians. It could now be used to engage the enemy with arrows at long range while closing to deliver shock in massed formations. Once the enemy was engaged at short range, the axes and javelins were brought to bear. After the enemy force was shattered, the chariot could be used in lethal pursuit to kill, primarily with the bow.[74] The Egyptian chariot combined the innovative dimensions of shock, lethality, and mobility, making the weapon the only one in ancient armies that could participate in all phases of the battle with equal killing power.

Egyptian infantry was organized into 50-man platoons commanded by a "leader of 50." A *Sa*, or company, contained 250 men, five platoons, plus a commander, quartermaster, and scribe, and was identified by the type of weapon it carried. Units were further identified as being comprised of recruits, trained men, or elite shock troops. The next unit in the chain of command was the regiment commanded by a "standard bearer," although we are not certain of the size of this unit. Above regiment was the *Pedjet* or brigade which was comprised of 1,000 men commanded by a "captain of a troop." This rank was also given to a fortress commander and may have been a general officer rank. A typical Egyptian field division was organized into five *Pedjets*, three heavy infantry brigades and two archer brigades. The addition of 500 chariots organic to the field division brought the Egyptian division to approximately 5,500 fighting men with a supporting force of almost 1,000 men—technicians, carpenters, quartermasters, scribes, logisticians, intelligence officers, and so on—for a total of 6,500 men. To place the logistical burden of the chariot corps in perspective, one need only consider that 500 chariots require 1,000 horses with 250 in reserve. Mixing hay and grain in equal proportions, 12,500 pounds of fodder was required to feed the animals for a single day! The division was commanded by a royal prince or important retainer, but it is likely that the day-to-day command and operations of the division were in the hands of a senior general called the "lieutenant commander of the army." The general structure of an Egyptian division is portrayed in Figure 2.9.[75]

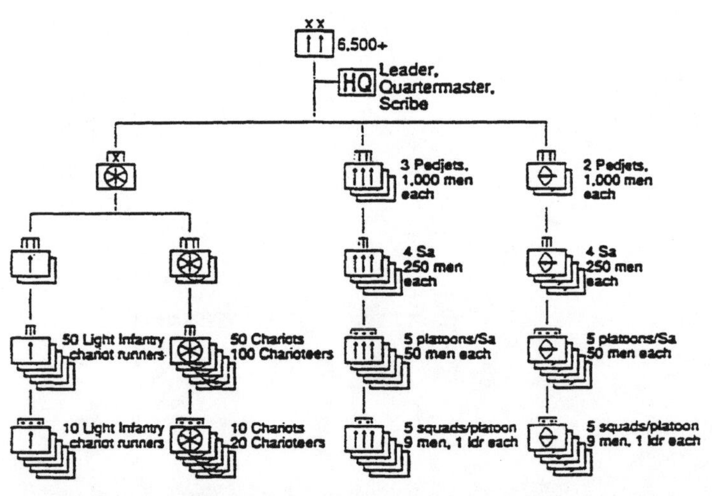

Figure 2.9 Idealized Egyptian Division of the New Kingdom

Egyptian infantry regiments were organized into axemen, archers, clubmen, and spearmen. The latter carried shields and six-foot long spears. Their task was to protect against and disrupt hostile charges aimed at the chariot units. Infantry was the true arm of decision in Egyptian tactical thinking, and usually fought in formations five men deep with a ten-man front in a 50-man platoon. These units could quickly form marching columns ten men wide, providing a degree of flexibility in infantry employment. The roughest and most disciplined of the infantry were the *nakhtu-aa*, or "the strong-arm boys," tough disciplined shock-troops armed with the bull-hide shield; the *dja* or short spear; the *kopesh*, literally "goat's leg" or sickle-sword; the cast-bronze penetrating axe; and the *taagsu* or dagger.[76] The division contained special elite infantry units as well. The *kenyt-nesu* or King's Braves appear to have been the Egyptian equivalent of the U.S. Army Rangers, elite special operations units of heavy infantry used especially for overcoming difficult positions. Thutmose III sent these units through the breaches in the walls at Kadesh. Like modern special operations forces, the Braves were comprised of ordinary soldiers who had distinguished themselves in battle. Hardened infantry veterans all, entry was by merit only. Egyptian light infantry was comprised mostly of mobile archer units called *megau*, literally, "shooters."[77] Egyptian archers and charioteers carried the same bow, an instrument of Hyksos design, constructed of a central wood core with thin strips of horn and leather laminated upon it. The bow was 1.3 meters long, and when drawn to the ear could send a reed-shaft fletched arrow with bronze cast arrowhead through an ingot of copper three fingers thick. The bow was powered by a string of twisted gut, and was a truly formidable weapon in the hands of a trained soldier.[78] Both archers and spearmen wore textile armor and bronze helmets. Elite infantry and charioteers wore body armor fashioned of thin (2 mm) bronze plates sewn in overlapping patterns on a leather jerkin.[79]

Figure 2.10 Egyptian Heavy Infantryman, 1200 B.C.E.

The tactics of the Egyptian army were very well developed and supported by a strong logistical structure. Ramses II introduced the oxcart as the basic form of logistical transport of the Egyptian army at the battle of Kadesh in 1296 B.C.E. The use of the oxcart spread quickly to the other armies of the Near East and remained the basic military logistics vehicle until Philip II of Macedon replaced it with the horse 1,000 years later.[80] Tactical expertise was increased by the presence of a professionally trained officer corps accustomed to maneuvering various types of large units. The Egyptians, by careful and integrated use of field intelligence gathered through patrolling and special collection units (spies, scouts, translators, interrogators, etc.) similar to those found in modern armies, were adept at moving large armies over considerable distances across hostile terrain without being detected. Thutmose III at Megiddo moved an army of more than 20,000 men 300 miles and arrived outside his objective without being detected. In his war against the Mitanni he transported hundreds of raftlike landing craft by wagons over 300 miles to cross the Euphrates and surprise his enemy. Egyptians also used counterintelligence and deception to gain maximum surprise. Prior to the final formulation of battle plans, the Egyptians routinely used the commander's conference in which senior officers were urged to criticize the plan and give frank advice. The result of these practices was sound battle plans that permitted Thutmose III to conduct 17 major campaigns and win them all.

On the battlefield Egyptian forces usually deployed chariot units to act as a screen for infantry and to cover their maneuver during a movement to contact. Engaging the enemy with the long-range composite bow, the chariot archers began killing at a distance as they closed with the enemy. Archer units deployed ahead of the infantry fired on the enemy as it moved to contact. Once the enemy was close, the archer units retired through the infantry ranks or to the flanks and continued to fire into the main body of enemy formations. The infantry now closed at a dead run to maximize shock and a general melee resulted. Chariot units engaged the enemy at any exposed point often dismounting and fighting as infantry once in contact. If the enemy gave ground, chariots in reserve could be committed to exploit the weakness. The mobility of the chariot allowed the use of highly mobile reserves that could be committed at a propitious moment to turn a flank or exploit a breakthrough. It was a military capability that had never before existed in history. If the enemy broke and a rout began, the chariot archers could engage in rapid pursuit with devastating effectiveness. If tactical surprise had been achieved, as at Megiddo, chariot units could engage an enemy not yet fully deployed for battle. If something went wrong, as with Ramses II's battle plan at Kadesh, chariots could be used to rescue a desperate situation.

The Egyptian army lacked only cavalry formations, an innovation that would be introduced 600 years later by the Assyrian army. The failure of the Egyptians to develop cavalry remains curious in light of their knowledge of the horse gained through the Hyksos occupation. It is probable that the horse of that time was simply too small and weak to carry the weight of an armored soldier for very long. In addition, as extensive as the Egyptian Empire was, it never included areas of wide grasslands around the Aral Sea which produced the stronger horses of the later period in sufficient numbers to develop a cavalry force. With the single exception of cavalry, however, the armies of the pharaohs of the Egyptian imperial era were in every respect modern armies capable of conducting military operations in a modern manner and on a modern scale, including the ability to mount seaborne invasions and to use naval forces in conjunction with ground forces for supply and logistics. In its day, the army of imperial Egypt was the largest, best-equipped, and most successful fighting force in the world.

ASSYRIA

Assyria, like the other settlements of the Tigris-Euphrates valley between 1500 and 1200 B.C.E., was a city-state that sat astride important trade routes that the major powers of the day—Egyptians, Hittites, and the Mitanni—sought to control for economic and military reasons. In the twelfth century, Hittite power collapsed and Assyria began a 300-year rise to power under the direction of successive powerful kings that resulted in the establishment of the Assyrian Empire in the ninth century B.C.E. Warfare, conquest, and exploitation of neighboring states became the primary preoccupation of the Assyrian kings. Between 890 and 640 B.C.E., the height of Assyrian power, the Assyrians fought 108 major and minor wars, punitive expeditions, and other significant military operations against neighboring states. During the reign of Sargon II (721–705 B.C.E.), the Assyrians carried out no fewer than ten major wars of conquest or suppression in 16 years. The result was the establishment of an empire that ran from the Persian Gulf to the Mediterranean Sea, from Armenia and northern Persia to the Arabian Desert, and farther west to include parts of the Egyptian Delta. It was the largest military empire in the world, and it was sustained by the largest, best-equipped, and best-trained military organization that the world had ever witnessed.

The economic base of the Assyrian Empire centered on the three major cities of Nimrud, Nineveh, and Ashur, located on the Tigris River in what is now northwestern Iraq. Like Egypt, Assyria was an alluvial state. Unlike the Nile, however, the Tigris is not a friendly or gentle river, and its ever-present threat of violent floods required that major irrigation projects be built and maintained. Building and maintaining these massive irrigation networks required large supplies of manpower which Assyria lacked. Military conquest as a source of slave manpower and the wholesale resettlement of foreign peoples provided the Assyrian solution. As long as Assyria could obtain the raw materials and manpower required to sustain the irrigation system, the Assyrian fields could be made to produce at high levels, and Assyria could sustain an adequate population. But all was dependent on sustaining the irrigation system which, in turn, required large numbers of slaves and prisoners to maintain it.

In most other respects, however, Assyria's economic base was insufficient, especially so for a major power. In an age of iron, Assyria possessed few easily available iron deposits for manufacturing modern iron weapons. It also lacked stone for its building projects, most pointedly for defensive walls and irrigation projects. Except for the weak and thin wood of the palm tree, Assyria had no wood at all. Long, straight wooden beams were required to construct fortifications, public buildings, and temples, and it was wood from which the Assyrian chariots, 40-foot-high siege towers, and vital battering rams were made. In an age of chariot warfare, Assyria had no grasslands on which to breed and train horses. Assyria's geography provided few of the vital strategic materials from which to forge its military strength. The solution was to conquer and occupy the neighboring states to the west, north, and southeast, all of which could provide the raw materials that Assyria required.

Assyria's fragile agricultural infrastructure and lack of military raw materials were aggravated by the country's geographic position on the Tigris, which left it vulnerable to a number of hostile neighboring states whose aggressive designs placed Assyria under constant geopolitical threat. In the early days (1500–1200 B.C.E.), Assyria was the target of Mitannian, Hittite, and Babylonian expansion and vassalage, and, even at the height of Assyrian power, Babylon always had to be watched closely. Southwest of Babylon were the Chaldeans who posed a constant threat to Assyria's southern borders. To the northwest, in the area of modern Armenia, the Urartu posed an even greater threat, as did the Medes in the Zagros Mountains farther to the east. Geography placed Assyria in a vulnerable position, surrounded by hostile powers that commonly raided its trade routes, disrupted its economic supply lines, and attacked it outright whenever Assyria was weak. In the Assyrian view there could be no real security unless these neighboring states were brought to heel.

The Assyrian army was forged in the crucible of 200 years of near constant warfare. The rulers of Assyria during this period proved to be strong and talented men who provided the direction needed to sustain a constant reign of conquest and suppression of revolts. The need to respond to a number of new technologies and strategic needs required that the Assyrian army undergo periods of significant reform, reorganization, and equipment. All these achievements were accomplished by the great warrior kings of the period.

The imperial period witnessed the reigns of six important monarchs, beginning with Assurnasirpal II (883–859 B.C.E.), who was followed by his son Shalmaneser III (858–824 B.C.E.). There then was a period of 80 years in which the archaeological records reveal little about monarchical rule until Tiglath-Pileser III (745–727 B.C.E.) came to power. Six years after his death, the greatest Assyrian ruler and military conqueror, Sargon II (721–705 B.C.E.) ascended the throne. He was succeeded by his son Sennacherib (704–681 B.C.E.) and, 30 years later, by his grandson, Ashurbanipal (668–630 B.C.E.). Under three of these monarchs, Assurnasirpal II, Tiglath-Pileser III, and Sargon II, significant reforms of the Assyrian army were carried out that allowed the development of a powerful and modern military machine.

The Assyrian Empire was no easy empire to govern. In an age of primitive communications, the empire was widely scattered and in some places geographically isolated by mountain ranges and deserts. It was, moreover, comprised of conquered peoples with strong nationalist feelings often tied to local religious, tribal, and blood loyalties. The Assyrians mastered the administration of this state through the use of a highly developed bureaucracy, the establishment of a provincial system of authority, the use of auxiliary armies, deportation, sometimes of whole peoples, and the ruthless use of police and military terror supported by an efficient intelligence system. Within each conquered area a professional civil service ensured that things ran smoothly. Assyrian civil servants were trained in professional schools in a manner similar to the training of Egyptian scribes. The Assyrian civil service numbered about 100,000 functionaries.[81] Behind the civil service stood a police and intelligence apparatus centered in the personal bodyguard of the king, his "troops of the feet," so called because they stood literally at his feet during battle when he fought from his war chariot. These praetorians, about 1,000 in number, had the task of ensuring the loyalty of the civil service and anyone else in a provincial area who might in any way represent a threat to the royal will.[82] The intelligence service employed spies and other agents to accomplish their task, and it was they who enforced the order for recall, interrogation, or termination of provincial officials who had fallen from the favor of the king.

The establishment and maintenance of an empire the size of Assyria's required a military establishment of great size. No accurate figures exist as to the total size of the army, but at the very least the Assyrian army would have to have comprised between 150,000 and 200,000 men.[83] A large part of this force, probably as much as one-third, was composed of auxiliary troops used to garrison the provinces. They were called to actual combat service as the need arose. Probably as much as 20 percent of the total army was comprised of reserve troops that functioned in peacetime as local militia, but could also be called to national service when needed. An Assyrian combat field army numbered 50,000 men with various mixes of infantry, chariots, and cavalry.[84] When arrayed for battle, this force took up an area 2,500 yards across and 100 yards deep,[85] each man occupying a square yard of ground.

An army of this size required considerable manpower, manpower that the Assyrian socioeconomic base could not provide by itself. In the early days of the empire, the army was recruited from the general population by forced conscription. Local provincial vassals sustained feudal militias that the vassals were required to provide to the king in time of war.[86] Tiglath-Pileser III (745–727 B.C.E.) broke the power of the aristocracy and formed the nucleus of a standing professional army centered around an elite royal guard of 1,000 men.[87] Although there are records of the use of auxiliary troops under Assurnasirpal II (883–859 B.C.E.), the practice seems to have been expanded by Tiglath-Pileser. It was formally institutionalized by Sargon II (721–705 B.C.E.), who also expanded the professional army.

Under Sargon II the professional praetorian corps of the army was expanded to several thousand, and an inner elite known as "the companions" or "troops of the feet" formed the spine of the army.[88] Provincial governors were required to raise and support local forces for use in time of war, but the governors were no longer powerful enough to use these forces to resist the king. Yet, local forces were substantial, in at least one instance being comprised of 1,500 cavalry and 20,000 archers.[89] Auxiliary units were thoroughly integrated into the field fighting force but still retained the major function of garrison duty to ensure control of captured populations.

A number of other important reforms increased the fighting power of the army. Assurnasirpal II introduced the first use of cavalry units to the Assyrian army.[90] Indeed, the Assyrians invented cavalry as a new military combat arm. Assurnasirpal was also the first to employ heavy, mobile siege towers and the mobile battering ram. Under his reign there appears the first use of units of wall-breakers who specialized in climbing scaling ladders and weakening defensive walls with axes and levers.[91] Cavalry units were integrated into the force structure and eventually replaced the chariot corps as the elite striking arm. In 854 B.C.E. at the Battle of Karkar, Shalmaneser III fielded a force of 35,000 men comprised of 20,000 infantry, 1,200 chariots, and 12,000 cavalry![92] Even allowing for exaggeration, what is important are the force ratios. At Karkar, there were ten times as many cavalry as chariots.

By Sargon's time the army had been reorganized into a thoroughly integrated fighting force of infantry, chariots, cavalry, siege machinery, and specialized units of scouts, engineers, intelligence officers, and sappers. Sargon also equipped the army entirely with weapons of iron, thereby producing the first iron army of the period.[93] The Assyrian army was also equipped with iron armor and helmets. The production and storage of iron weapons and other metal materials of war became a central feature of the army's logistical base. A single weapons room in Sargon's palace at Dur-Sharrukin (Fort Sargon) contained 200 tons of iron weapons, helmets, and body armor.[94]

The combat forces of the field army were organized in units of ten formed around national and regional formations, each of which specialized in the weapons and tactics at which it excelled. The ten-man squad under the command of a noncommissioned officer was the smallest fighting unit. The normal tactical unit was the company, which could be tailored into units of 50 to 200 men. The company was commanded by a *kirsu* or captain.[95] In battle, infantry units of spearmen deployed in phalanxes with a ten-man front and files 20 deep. These units were highly trained and disciplined in maneuver and represented a main shock force of the Assyrian army.[96]

Assyrian infantry was divided into three types: spearmen, archers, and slingmen. The spearmen deployed in phalanxes to anchor the main line in the center of the battlefield. Each phalanx was comprised of 200 men, ten ranks across and 20 files deep, commanded by a captain. Assyrian spearmen were heavy infantry armed with a long, double-bladed spear and a straight sword for hand-to-hand combat. The sword was secured to a thick belt that ran around a knee-length coat of iron mail armor. The spearman carried a small iron shield and wore a conical iron helmet with a wool or fabric liner which helped to absorb the energy of a blow and dissipate heat.[97] An important Assyrian innovation was the introduction of knee-high leather boots reinforced with iron plates to protect the shins.[98] The combination of weapons and personal protective equipment slowed the movement of the heavy infantry considerably, and the Assyrians continually experimented with various types of lighter shields to reduce the load carried by the soldier in battle.[99]

Units of archers comprised the second type of Assyrian infantry. The Assyrian composite bow seems to have been of a more advanced type than that usually found in the Near East, and bas-reliefs show that it had to be bent with the knee, often requiring two men to string it.[100] Assyrian arrows were iron tipped and had great penetrating power. Some arrows had an iron tan proceeding backward from the shank to which oil-soaked wool was attached. The wool would be set afire and the arrow used as an incendiary device against buildings and wooden gates.

For protection the archer wore a long coat of mail armor, the weight of which considerably reduced his mobility. Before Tiglath-Pileser, a shield bearer carrying a small round shield was employed to protect the archer from counterfire. Later a larger man-sized shield of braided reeds with a slightly bow-backed top was introduced to provide protection from missiles fired from defensive walls. The Assyrian archer also carried a sword for close combat.[101] The Assyrians increased the rate of fire of their archers by introducing an innovation in the arrow quiver. Carried on the back and secured by a shoulder strap, the quiver had a short rod protruding from the bottom front opening to slightly above the shoulder. This innovation allowed the archer to reach back and pull down on the rod, tipping the quiver forward and bringing the arrows within easy and ready reach. Modern archery experts estimate that this type of quiver might well have increased the rate of fire by as much as 40 percent.

The third type of infantry used by the Assyrians was the slingmen. The sling was probably introduced to the Assyrians by mercenaries or conquered peoples, and the Assyrians were slow to adopt it. While some bas-reliefs show slingmen deployed alongside archers in battle on open terrain, the slingmen saw their primary use in siege warfare. Slingers could direct high-angled parabolic fire against the defenders on the wall.

The Assyrian chariot corps constituted the primary striking arm of the army and gradually underwent major design changes over the imperial period. Originally the Assyrian chariot was used in much the same way as the Egyptian and Mitannian chariot, as a mobile platform for archers. But the Assyrian chariot was always a heavier machine with a stiff and heavy front end, a characteristic that made it less maneuverable at high speed.[102] Originally the crew had consisted of a driver and an archer, with the driver armed with a spear and an axe. The archer wore body armor but had little other protection. The mission of the chariot was to attack massed infantry formations, deliver shock, and then, as the Assyrian infantry clashed at close range, to aid in the pursuit.

Figure 2.11 Assyrian Chariot, 800 B.C.E.

Over time the shock role of the chariot increased, bringing with it a need to protect the crew in close combat. The result was the development of an even heavier chariot carrying a crew of three, with the third man acting as a shield bearer to protect the archer and driver. By the time of Ashurbanipal, the Assyrian chariot had evolved into a four-man vehicle with a driver, archer, and two shield-bearers. The weight of the machine now required three and then four horses to pull it, and the wheels became thicker, requiring eight spokes for strength.[103] All crewmen carried a spear, sword, shield, and axe, a development that turned the chariot corps into mounted infantry. The Assyrians maintained a large corps of chariots, but as early as 854 B.C.E. Shalmaneser III had already begun to develop a new combat arm, the cavalry, which eventually eclipsed the chariot corps as the arm of decision of the Assyrian army.

The major advantage of the chariot was that in battles on open terrain it could deliver tremendous shock to massed infantry formations. Its major disadvantage was that in rough terrain its mobility and shock value were severely limited or even lost altogether. As the Assyrian Empire grew, the army was required more and more to traverse difficult terrain and to conduct operations in areas where the terrain was not favorable to the chariot. The need to fight in other than open terrain required another combat arm that could maneuver and was capable of delivering firepower. The solution was cavalry.

The introduction of horses and their growing importance to the Assyrian army required that they be obtained in adequate and safe supply. Since Assyria itself, lacking grasslands, offered few of the conditions necessary to breed these animals in sufficient numbers, the Assyrians developed a remarkable logistical and special organization to ensure an adequate supply of horses for the army. The horse recruitment officers called *musarkisus* were high-level government officials appointed directly by the king. Usually two horse-recruitment officers were assigned to each province. Assisted by a staff of scribes and other officers, they ensured that adequate numbers of horses were assembled and trained for military use.[104]

The *musarkisus* obtained horses on a year-round basis and were responsible for sustaining them in a national system of corrals and stables. Surviving documents indicate that in the city of Nineveh these officers were able to secure 3,000 horses a month arriving on schedules of 100 animals a day! These reports also note that the horses were received from every province of the empire. One report notes that of the 2,911 horses received for a single month, 1,840 were used as yoke horses in the chariot corps, 27 were put to stud, and 787 were riding horses assigned for cavalry use.[105] In addition, the horse-recruitment officers were responsible for securing adequate supplies of mules and camels for use in the logistics train. This efficient logistical apparatus was unknown in any other army of the world at that time.

Originally the Assyrian cavalryman was an ordinary foot soldier equipped with armor, lance, sword, shield, and heavy boots. This great weight severely limited his mobility. Over time the armored coat was reduced to waist length, and the shield made smaller. The Assyrians used a blanket, saddle girth, crupper, and breast straps to stabilize the rider.[106] Later, Assyrian cavalrymen learned to control their mounts with their legs and the heel pressure of their boots (the spur had not yet been invented). This made it possible to place archers on horseback as well and gave birth to the first use of mounted archers in the Near East. Writers of the Old Testament called these cavalry archers "hurricanes on horseback."[107]

There is some debate as to the proportionate strength and role of the cavalry in the Assyrian army. Some analysts suggest that the chariot corps remained the primary fighting arm until the end of the empire, and perhaps so. Yet, as early as the eighth century B.C.E., Shalmaneser III put ten times more cavalrymen than chariots in the field at Karkar. An Assyrian chariot required at least three horses and sometimes four to deploy in battle. It may well have been that the supply system could not provide the numbers of horses required to sustain both large chariot and cavalry forces. The reports cited earlier suggest that for every horse sent to the cavalry, three had to be sent to the chariot corps, and this does not count replacement horses. A field chariot force of 4,000 machines would require 12,000 horses at the very minimum and 16,000 at the maximum, not counting the ready reserve or the horses issued to the forces on garrison duty throughout the empire. Add to this the number required for a small cavalry force of 6,000 and the number of horses that had to be acquired and trained for the army's immediate use in time of war, and it becomes a total of almost 20,000 animals in order to supply a single field army in battle or on the march to the objective.

The Assyrian army was the first army of the Near East to develop an all-weather capability for ground combat. They fought in winter as well as in summer and even conducted siege operations during the winter months.[108] The fact that the army was almost continually at war somewhere in the empire for more than 200 years provided adequate opportunity for developing field techniques by trial and error. When moving through wooded terrain, for example, the infantry proceeded line abreast in separate ranks. Smaller units were sent ahead as point while others provided flank security. If engaged in battle within heavily forested areas, the spear-bearing infantry was used as the primary striking or defensive force as circumstances warranted. In lightly wooded hilly terrain, the mounted archers and spearmen of the cavalry became the primary striking force. While the cavalry usually moved in column, the infantry provided flank security in line formation.[109] As the army deployed in mountainous

Figure 2.12 Assyrian Cavalry Archer-Lancer Team, 800 B.C.E.

terrain, the Assyrians developed the practice of spreading scouts and snipers over wide areas to provide adequate security for the main body. The Assyrians also experimented with mixed units combining infantry, archers, and slingers in a single unit.[110] So adaptable were the Assyrian ground forces that they also fought well in marshlands. Placed aboard light reed boats, they became waterborne marines using fire arrows and torches to burn out the enemy hiding among the bushes and reeds of the swamp.[111]

In open terrain Assyrian tactics were straightforward and relied upon shock, firepower, and discipline. Once the army had been formed for battle, archer and slinger units began firing their missiles from a distance to inflict casualties upon enemy infantry formations. Special archer units were adept at killing chariot horses.[112] Then Assyrian chariots attacked from as many different directions as the terrain would permit, their archers firing as the machines closed with the enemy infantry. The purpose of the attack was to deliver tremendous shock at a number of different points in an effort to shatter the enemy infantry. As the chariots drove into the mass of infantry, their crews dismounted and fought in close combat as infantry. As the enemy mass began to waiver, the phalanxes of Assyrian spearmen, supported by direct fire from archer units, began in disciplined and slow march to close with the enemy. The cavalry, which to this point had been used to pin the enemy flanks, now took up positions to prevent the retreat of the broken enemy, sometimes acting as an anvil against which the infantry and chariot units could drive the fleeing remnants. Once the enemy army broke ranks, the spearmen, archers, charioteers, and cavalry singled out individual targets, rode them down, and killed them.

An army of such size and complexity as Assyria's required a sophisticated logistics apparatus to support and supply it in the field. With few exceptions, such as the recruitment of horses mentioned earlier, little is known about the organization of the logistics system. This being said, however, it is obvious that being forced to fight in so many different climates and types of terrain must have required a high degree of logistical flexibility and planning. The provincial system allowed the Assyrians the advantage of being able to position supplies near their borders in advance of a campaign.

Even when food and water supplies were adequate, there remained the problem of transport. The spine of the supply transport system was the mule and another Assyrian innovation, the military use of the camel. So valuable were these animals that they took high priority as captured loot.[113] In the campaign against Egypt, the Assyrians used camels to cross the Saudi Desert to attack Palestine. The camel served another function as the main transport of the caravan system. As caravan traders themselves, the Assyrians no doubt had maps of every trail, water hole, and oasis of possible military use.

Military power is always slave to political events, and this fact brought about the end of the Assyrian Empire. In 664 B.C.E. the Elamites sacked Babylon only to do it again in 653 B.C.E. In 656 B.C.E. Shamash-shum-ukin, the brother of Ashurbanipal, struck at the Assyrian throne by forming an alliance with Babylon, the Elamites, the Arameans, the Arabs, and the Egyptians against his brother. The result was another costly war that tore the army apart and pitted national and regional forces against one another. While records are sparse, the period between 648 and the death of Ashurbanipal in 630 B.C.E. was marked by periods of civil war provoked by Ashurbanipal's sons fighting over the mantle of power.[114] The weakness at the political center encouraged local governors and generals to pursue their own interests through revolts and corruption. The situation was compounded by a number of large-scale popular uprisings that occurred at the same time.

The end came in 612 B.C.E. when a coalition of Medean and Babylonian armies sacked Nineveh and destroyed what was left of the most powerful empire and army the world had seen until that time. The destruction of Nineveh was complete, and the terror continued for months as the victorious allies subdued one remnant garrison after another. A terrible vengeance was wrought upon the Assyrians, and their cruelty was revenged with even greater cruelty. A biblical commentary captured the sense of terrible vengeance for all history.

> Cursed be the city of blood, full of lies, full of violence. . . . The sound of the whip is heard, the gallop of horses, the rolling of chariots. An infinity of dead, the dead are everywhere! My anger is on thee, Nineveh, saith Yahweh. . . . I will show thy nakedness to the nations and thy shame to the kingdoms. And then it will be said: Nineveh is destroyed! Who will mourn her?[115]

So complete was the destruction of the Assyrian capital that two centuries later Xenophon and his Greek mercenary army of 10,000 men passed the ruins of Nineveh unaware of what they were passing.[116]

NOTES

1. Michael Grant, *The History of Ancient Israel* (New York: Charles Scribner, 1984), 13.

2. Nigel Stillman and Nigel Tallis, *Armies of the Ancient Near East* (Sussex, England: Flexiprint Ltd., 1984), 33.

3. Yigael Yadin, *The Art of Warfare in Biblical Lands in Light of Archaeological Study* (New York: McGraw-Hill, 1964), vol. 1, 79.
4. Grant, 16.
5. Ibid.
6. Stillman and Tallis, 35.
7. Ibid.
8. Yadin, 88.
9. Ibid.
10. Stillman and Tallis, 96.
11. Grant, 19. See Robert Drew, "The 'Chariots of Iron' of Joshua and Judges," *Journal for the Study of the Old Testament* 45 (1989): 15–23.
12. Stillman and Tallis, 35.
13. Yadin, 79–84.
14. Yadin, vol. 2, 108.
15. Stillman and Tallis, 35.
16. Grant, 81.
17. Ibid., 21.
18. Ibid., 67.
19. Chaim Herzog and Mordechai Gichon, *Battles of the Bible* (Jerusalem: Steimatzky's Agency Ltd., 1978), 63.
20. Stillman and Tallis, 38.
21. Yadin, vol. 1, 209.
22. Grant, 68.
23. Yadin, vol. 2, 330.
24. Stillman and Tallis, 149.
25. Richard A. Gabriel and Donald Boose Jr., *The Great Battles of Antiquity: A Strategic and Tactical Guide to the Great Battles That Shaped the Development of War* (Westport, CT: Greenwood Press, 1994), 132.
26. The problem of a grip for the round Greek shield was solved in the seventh century B.C.E. with the introduction of the Argive shield. The new grip consisted of two leather loop straps. The forearm was passed through the first loop strap while the second one was grasped firmly by the hand. This arrangement now made it possible for even the common citizen to learn how to use the shield effectively with the result that a new age of warfare dawned upon classical Greece characterized by the emergence of the citizen hoplite.
27. I Samuel 17:4–7.
28. Yadin, vol. 2, 174.
29. Ibid., 354.
30. I Samuel 13:5.
31. I Samuel 31:3.
32. Herzog and Gichon, 74.
33. I Samuel 4:2.
34. Grant, 55.
35. *Cambridge Ancient History*, vol. 2, pt. 2 (Cambridge: Cambridge University Press, 1973), 539.
36. Ibid., 554.
37. Ibid., 559.
38. Grant, 54.

39. Numbers 10:1–10, 13–27.
40. Joshua 11:7–9.
41. I Samuel 11:7.
42. Herzog and Gichon, 67.
43. *Cambridge Ancient History*, vol. 2, pt. 2, 571.
44. Herzog and Gichon, 68.
45. Ibid., 76.
46. I Samuel 8:11–16.
47. Herzog and Gichon, 85.
48. Ibid.
49. Ibid., 87.
50. Stillman and Tallis, 150.
51. *Cambridge Ancient History*, vol. 2, pt. 2, 584–85.
52. In II Samuel 8:4 the story tells of David capturing a large number of chariots and horses. Keeping only 100 for himself, he destroyed the other chariots and houghed the horses. This is taken by some to be an indication that there may have been a small squadron of chariots in David's army.
53. *Cambridge Ancient History*, vol. 2, pt. 2, 590.
54. I Kings 10:26.
55. *Cambridge Ancient History*, vol. 2, pt. 2, 588.
56. Ibid., 591.
57. Leonard Cottrell, *The Warrior Pharaohs* (New York: Dutton, 1969), 51.
58. Ibid., 18–19.
59. The definitive work on military titles in the army of ancient Egypt is by Alan Richard Schulman, *Military Rank, Title, and Organization in the Egyptian New Kingdom* (Berlin: Bruno Hessling Verlag, 1964).
60. Ibid.
61. Ibid.
62. Cottrell, 51.
63. R. O. Faulkner, "Egyptian Military Organization," *Journal of Egyptian Archaeology* 39 (1953): 39. This article remains the best work on the organizational structure of the Egyptian army even at this late date.
64. Ibid.
65. Ibid.
66. Cottrell, 55–56.
67. *Cambridge Ancient History*, vol. 2, pt. 1, 57.
68. Cottrell, 55–56.
69. *Encyclopedia Britannica*, 15th ed., s.v. "History of Egyptian Civilization."
70. See Schulman.
71. Ibid.
72. Yigael Yadin, *The Art of Warfare in Biblical Lands in Light of Archaeological Discovery* (New York: McGraw-Hill, 1963), vol. 1, 87–89, for a discussion of the design of the Egyptian chariot.
73. Richard A. Gabriel, *Great Captains of Antiquity* (Westport, CT: Greenwood Press, 2000), 28.
74. Richard A. Gabriel and Karen S. Metz, *From Sumer to Rome: The Military Capabilities of Ancient Armies* (Westport, CT: Greenwood Press, 1991), 77.
75. Gabriel and Boose, 49 for Figure 1.

76. Gabriel, 26.

77. Ibid., 27.

78. Ibid.

79. Ibid.

80. Faulkner, 41–47.

81. *Encyclopedia Britannica*, vol. 21 (1985), 930.

82. A. T. Olmstead, *The History of Assyria* (Chicago: University of Chicago Press, 1951), 607.

83. Arther Ferrill, *The Origins of War* (London: Thames and Hudson, 1985), 70. For more accurate figures on the size of the Assyrian army, see Saggs, 145.

84. T. N. Dupuy, *The Evolution of Warfare and Weapons* (New York: Bobbs-Merrill, 1980), 10.

85. Ibid.

86. Olmstead, 603.

87. Robert Laffont, *The Ancient Art of Warfare* (New York: Time-Life Books, 1966), 1:45; see also Conteneau, 142.

88. Olmstead, 603.

89. W. F. Saggs, "Assyrian Warfare in the Sargonid Period," *Iraq* 25, pt. 2 (autumn 1963): 145.

90. *Encyclopedia Britannica*, vol. 21 (1985), 925.

91. Ibid.

92. Laffont; see chart, 40.

93. Ferrill, 67.

94. Laffont, 45.

95. Olmstead, 604.

96. T. N. Dupuy, 10.

97. Yadin, 94–95.

98. On the subject of boots, see Laffont, 45; and Georges Conteneau, *Every Day Life in Babylon and Assyria* (London: Edward Arnold, 1954), 144.

99. I am indebted to Carl Netsch, a blacksmith in Manchester, N.H., who helped calculate the weight of Assyrian iron armor and weapons. Hammered iron an eighth-inch thick weighs 5 pounds per square foot. Accordingly, a soldier in a full suit of Assyrian scale armor, helmet, and iron-shinned boots, armed with a sword and carrying a shield and a spear, would carry a combat load of approximately 60 pounds, or about the same load as carried by a modern soldier.

100. For a description of the Assyrian bow, see Yadin, 295.

101. Conteneau, 61; see also Olmstead, 155.

102. A good analysis of the Assyrian chariot is found in Yadin, 297–300; as regards the subject of maneuverability, see Conteneau, 145.

103. Yadin, 298–99.

104. The definitive work on this subject remains J. N. Postgate, *Taxation and Conscription in the Assyrian Empire* (Rome: Biblical Institute Press, 1974); see also Ferrill, 71–73.

105. Ferrill, 72.

106. Laffont, 48.

107. Ibid.

108. Saggs, 145–46.

109. Yadin, 303.
110. Saggs, 151.
111. Yadin, 303.
112. Saggs, 152.
113. Conteneau, 59.
114. *Encyclopedia Britannica*, vol. 21 (1985), 928–30.
115. Nahum 3:1–7.
116. Laffont, 49.

3

The Exodus

One of the difficulties confronting the historian concerned with the military history of ancient Israel is where to begin. When the subject of Israel's military tradition is addressed, it usually begins with Joshua and the Israelite conquest of Canaan. Just why this should be the case is unclear since even a cursory examination of Exodus reveals more than a few examples of the military art practiced with an expertise quite sufficient to hold the attention of any serious student of strategy and tactics. What is the crossing of the Reed Sea if not a textbook example of how to conduct a night water crossing? Or Joshua's skirmish with the Amalek if not an example of how to fight a rear guard action while protecting the withdrawal of a column? And the desert trek? One can only marvel at the Israelite logistics officers who managed to move large numbers of people through a desert wilderness while keeping them alive until they reached their destination. Many other examples of military expertise and practice could be noted in Exodus, yet the Exodus remains largely unexplored in the search for the origins of the Israelite military tradition.

For the most part, Exodus has been presented to the world not by military historians but by theologians and cultural historians. It has been the theological writers who have taken the lead in portraying Exodus in a manner sometimes ignorant of military matters. The usual source has been Christian translations of the Hebrew Bible wherein the portrayals of the Israelites seem to have been offered to support a particular version of the Exodus saga that is, to be kind, often woefully incorrect and frequently neglectful of the meaning of the original Hebrew text. One notes in this regard the passage in the Christian translation of Exodus 1:13–14. "The Egyptians then dreaded the Israelites and reduced them to cruel slavery, making life bitter for them with hard work in mortar and brick and all kinds of field work. . . . The whole cruel fate of slaves." With this passage began the gross inexactitude that has regarded the Israelites ever since as having been slaves in Egypt.

And, as expected, slaves do not develop military traditions or great warriors. True, from time to time slaves escape. But even if they do, it is in a fearful and unplanned fashion, often surviving by luck or even the grace of God. Not surprisingly, this is precisely the image of the Israelites and their flight from Egypt that has been preserved in the Christian translations. General Sir Richard Gale in his *Great Battles of Biblical History* captures fully the image of Israelites as runaway slaves making their way inexpertly across the desert.

> The long trek over the arid desert was a grim undertaking for a tired and undernourished people. Thousands of them, old and young, men and women, with their children, their sick and the lame, with their goats and their donkeys, their cooking pots and rough black tents must have looked a sorry sight.[1]

Under these circumstances who else, one wonders, but God himself could have rescued such a disorganized lot from themselves?

These images passed easily into the common understanding of the Israelite saga with the consequence that Exodus has been overlooked as a genuine source of the military history and martial tradition of the Israelite people. So the search has usually begun with Joshua and the story of the Israelite conquest of Canaan. The hypothesis of this chapter is that this perspective, as widespread and commonly accepted as it is, is inaccurate. The truth is that Exodus is the saga of a people equipped and familiar with weapons, led by experienced and tactically proficient commanders, who were not Egyptian slaves, and whose military proficiency and operational capability improved greatly during the desert trek until, with remarkable clarity of strategic aim, they were able to achieve their ultimate objective of conquering the land of Canaan. Any claims to the contrary notwithstanding, it is unlikely that a people who were not so equipped and experienced would ever have survived the desert crossing. Thus, it is affirmed here that the military history of ancient Israel ought to begin where it actually began, with the story of The Exodus itself.

THE ISRAELITES IN EGYPT

To comprehend Exodus as military history, it is necessary to understand the sociology of the Israelite tribes during their sojourn in Egypt. For reasons already noted, history has commonly portrayed the Israelites in Egypt as slaves and herd-tending nomads when, in fact, they were neither. Paradoxically the Israelite historical-theological tradition itself has lent credence to the notion of the Israelites as slaves. As S. H. Isserlin notes, the fact that the saga of the Israelites seems to *suggest* that they were slaves is very unusual indeed among the sagas of peoples of the Middle East. All other sagas—Egyptian, Sumerian, Babylonian, Assyrian, Hittite, and so forth—claim that their peoples and kings were descended from or created by gods. Only the Israelites appear to claim that they are descended from slaves, a claim so unusual that it has led theologians and cultural historians to conclude that it was probably true.[2] And, as so often happens with history, once a question has been answered, especially by well-regarded experts, further inquiry ceases and contrary evidence is disregarded.[3] What evidence there is, however, suggests strongly that the Israelites in Egypt were not slaves at all. The Hebrew text of Exodus 1:13–14 offers a significantly different view of the Israelites than is presented in later Christian translations. In the original Hebrew, the text is as follows. "The Egyptians ruthlessly imposed upon the Israelites the various labors that they made them perform. Ruthlessly they made life bitter for them with harsh labor at mortar and bricks and with all sorts of tasks in the field." There is no mention of slavery. The Hebrew term used to describe the Israelites at their labors is *avadim* which in an obscure and irregular usage can connote slaves but which more commonly translates as "workmen" or "workers" or even "servants."[4] The linguistic argument is interesting but is not definitive. More convincing is the historical fact that slavery was never an Egyptian social institution[5] even during the New Kingdom when foreigners lived in the country in large numbers. Slavery did make a brief appearance during the Greek occupation of the third to the first century B.C.E. when the Greeks introduced house slaves. But the practice never caught on among Egyptians themselves.

Three factors worked against the development of slavery in Egypt. First, with a population of 7 to 9 million at the time of the Exodus there was never a shortage of manpower for any military or governmental project. Egypt had a surplus of people to man her army and staff any governmental construction project with ease. Second, Egypt was a highly developed administrative state and possessed the ability to organize and deploy manpower for social tasks on a colossal scale. In this manner Egypt was able to construct and maintain a national irrigation system that ran for 700 miles and to do it for more than 2,000 years! Third, Egyptian religion and law forbade slavery, just as it extended equal legal and religious standing to women and children.[6] As Rostovtzeff notes, Egyptian peasants had legal rights under the law which, when violated, often led to labor strikes. If working conditions on the land or construction project became overly harsh, workers would strike and take refuge in the religious temples where the legal right of sanctuary prohibited employers and police from following.[7] It is somewhat curious, then, that the Israelites should have remembered being enslaved in a country that did not practice slavery on any scale.

If not slavery what, then, did the Israelites experience? The answer is just what the Hebrew text suggests: common physical labor. The Egyptians often employed corvee labor to construct their great temples, government buildings, military forts, and to maintain the irrigation system. Usually this labor was performed by military conscripts who did not meet the standards for assignment to combat units or regular force units, or by the regular agricultural employees on temple and pharaonic estates. This practice survived in the armies of the West until very modern times where it was commonplace for armies to maintain construction battalions that helped bring in the harvest or build roads in the countryside. In the Egyptian army of the New Kingdom, these conscripts would sometimes be supplemented by civilian laborers—the corvee. But these civilian workers were not slaves nor usually impressed against their will. Most government construction in Egypt took place during the inundation, the three-month period of the Nile flood, which began in September and ended in November. Agriculture was impossible during this period, and the land was full of unemployed workers. These temporarily unemployed agricultural workers were hired at local construction projects as a way of keeping them fed. That these workers were not slaves is evident from texts that show military doctors assigned to the construction crews to look after the workers' health and treat their injuries. Considerable attention was paid to the workers' diet to keep them fit and healthy.[8]

Corvee labor had a long tradition in Egypt and was employed to construct the great pyramid tombs. Although it is commonly believed that the pyramids were constructed by thousands of slaves, in fact it was corvee workers who built them and were paid to do so. Moreover, not unlike medieval Christians who willingly worked on building the great European cathedrals as a religious duty, so it was with the corvee workers who built the great pyramids to keep the bodies of their pharaohs, themselves the sons of god, secure. It is likely, then that the Israelites were forced to undertake a period of corvee labor for reasons we examine shortly. In Exodus we find them at forced labor making bricks for pharaoh's new city in the Delta. This period became known in the biblical saga as the Oppression and portrays the Israelites "in bondage" or as slaves. The "enslavement" came to form a central event in the Israelite saga for it was supposedly to escape from it that the Israelites followed Moses into the wilderness and became the chosen people of Yahweh. But if the Israelites in Egypt were not slaves, who were they? And why did they come to regard a temporary period of corvee labor so resentfully? The answer lies in understanding the Israelites not as a tribe of bedouin animal herders, but as a much more complex social entity: the *habiru.*

The discovery of the Amarna Letters introduced the world to a group of people that the Egyptians called *apiru* or, in Akkadian, *habiru,* described as a wandering group of asiatics in Palestine and Syria with whom the Egyptians were familiar.[9] They are portrayed sometimes as brigands, sometimes as fighting against Egyptian troops, sometimes as ethnic units serving within the Egyptian army itself, as tenders of cattle, and as being skilled vintners and stonecutters.[10] The obvious similarity of the words "habiru" and "Hebrew" led some scholars to suggest that the *habiru* might be the Israelites of the Bible appearing for the first time in an historical source outside the Old Testament.[11] Although the *habiru* were indeed an important factor in Egyptian and Israelite history, further research has not completely resolved that they were not the Hebrews.[12]

Habiru was not a designation for an ethnic or racial group, but described a *class* of wandering peoples in Palestine and Syria who came into frequent contact with the Egyptians after the establishment of the New Kingdom. The ethnic mingling so characteristic of the *habiru* seems evident among the Israelites as well. Exodus 12:38 says, "And also many foreigners went up with them, and flock and herd . . . very heavy cattle." The term used for "foreigners" is *erev rav* or "mixed multitude" or "mixture" and is a rare construction. It seems to imply concubines, half-breeds, and other persons who joined the group. It may simply refer to the Egyptian wives, husbands, relatives, and children acquired by the Israelites during their stay in Egypt. Later, in Numbers 11:4 when the people agitated against Moses for lack of food, the term used to describe the non-Israelites among them is *asaphsuph*, or "riff-raff."[13] The ethnically mixed character of the Israelites is reflected even more clearly in the foreign names of the group's leadership. Moses himself, of course, has an Egyptian name. But so do Hophni, Phinehas, Hur, and Merari, the son of Levi.[14] Hur is Moses' sacral assistant, and Phinehas an important priest chosen to guide the army in its war against the Midianites. The Merari clan is one of the Levite subclans who keep the Tabernacle. The fact that such important personages possessed Egyptian names seems to testify to the multiethnic character of the Israelites, which also suggests that it was the welding of this diverse group to the belief in Yahweh, more than ethnic ties, that forged the national identity of the Israelites during the desert trek.

Habiru appears to mean "wanderers," "outcasts," "bandits," or "passers-by."[15] They are described in Egyptian documents as "the miserable stranger. . . . He does not dwell in the same spot, his feet are always wandering. From the days of Horus (from time immemorial) he battles, he does not conquer, and is not conquered."[16] The *habiru* comprised larger groups than bedouin, and their social structure was vastly more complex. Its members were more talented in skills beyond animal husbandry. Gottwald is insistent that the Israelites were not bedouin or simple flock tenders or camel nomads.[17] Rather they were pastoralists comprised of stockbreeders, agriculturalists, soldiers, merchants, construction workers, skilled government employees, and even fishermen.[18] Martin Buber suggests that they were not a tribe in the usual sense of the term, but a group of tribes united in loose confederation so that their name was connected to a common way of life or social interaction rather than an ethnic designation. They were mostly Semites, but not all, a people without a country disassociated from national identity united now and again in common journeys for pasture or plunder. Buber describes them as "semi-nomadic herdsmen who become freebooters if the chance arises."[19] Gottwald suggests that the Israelites possessed the *habiru* quality of being agriculturalists. He notes that during the desert trek the Israelites fondly recall their diet in Egypt as including fish, melons, cucumbers, leeks, onions, and garlic, all of which require at least some agricultural expertise to produce.[20] The Israelites also show expertise in stockbreeding. When Moses asks pharaoh for permission to journey three days into the desert to sacrifice to Yahweh, it suggests that at least some of the Israelite community regularly moved out into the Sinai steppe to herd and pasture their flocks. There is also reasonable evidence to suggest that much of Israelite stockbreeding was neither nomadic nor even quasi-nomadic at all. The many references to large cattle herds as well as to "large cattle," that is, oxen that do not move for seasonal pasturing, imply that some segments of the Israelites were tied to the land by their large bovine herds.[21] This would make sense in light of the fact that Goshen (and pharaoh's Succoth estates nearby) was excellent cattle-raising country. The large store cities (logistics depots) and military garrisons near and in Goshen would have been steady customers for meat and hides, the latter from which to make shields.

As long as life remained good, the *habiru* remained where they were. At times they would remain near a town for a considerable period of time and the best among them rose in the affairs of the town—or even the country as seems to have been the case with Joseph who became pharaoh's vizier—holding governing positions. Some became mercenaries or overseers of public works. This life, Buber notes, required "a peculiar mix of pastoral and military virtues."[22] The *habiru*, then, were much more than seasonal bedouins in search of grasslands for their flocks. They represented an amalgamation of many skills and occupations, including soldiery and governance. Gottwald describes this mix of skills among the Israelites in Egypt in the following way: "They were a people settled in the irrigated region of Goshen, where they gardened, fished, and grazed flocks and herds, their sheep and goats being taken into the steppe during the winter rains."[23] He might have added as well that they were armed to the teeth.

There were other reasons why the *habiru* might remain in an area for long periods, and that was because they had become clients of the host kingdom and performed valuable military service. Most often the *habiru* community had a military arm associated with it so that the line between the *habiru* military and its agriculturalists, herdsmen, or other tradesmen was indistinct, each seeing the others as a part of the same community.[24] In some cases, when *habiru* soldiers were hired by a Canaanite king to protect a certain region, their kinsmen would follow and settle the area. Sometimes *habiru* soldiers might move into an already existing village or town and settle down for a long period intermarrying and becoming leaders of the community. It was "in such settings that early Israel took its rise."[25] Within Canaan, *habiru* military units seem to have been employed in three ways: (1) as mercenaries usually in the role of auxiliary infantry to augment the armies of the Canaanite city-states (as we shall see there is sufficient evidence that such units served in the armies of Egypt during the New Kingdom, as well); (2) as client free-booters to harass the frontiers of rival city-states, a role that required that some form of political legitimacy be extended to them; and (3) as proto-allies where the entire *habiru* group with its wide array of occupations was settled on some land along with the soldiers with the understanding that they protect the land against the client's enemies.[26] The *habiru*, then, "operated as armed groups, semi-independent in the feudal structure, available for hire, as auxiliary troops or resourceful in carrying out freebooting, either on their own or at the instigation of one city-state against another."[27]

Often *habiru* were settled in lands on the borders of a state that were in dispute or where they might come under attack. It was this type of arrangement that seems to have been made between David and his *habiru* freebooters and the Philistine prince when he and his men and their families were settled in the border town of Ziklag in return for agreeing to defend it against the raids of the Amalekites. Under these circumstances the military units of the *habiru* remained independent and under the control of their own leaders, even though they might have received weapons and supplies from the client king. It may have been precisely this kind of arrangement that pharaoh made with Joseph out of gratitude for the latter's service in interpreting the king's dreams and avoiding famine for Egypt. Genesis 47:6 tells us that "Pharaoh spake unto Joseph . . . the land of Egypt is before thee; in the best of the land make thy father and thy brethren to dwell; in the land of Goshen let them dwell." The land of Goshen is a fertile valley in the eastern Delta of Egypt that leads straight from the heart of the Delta to a break in the chain of the modern Bitter Lakes. A major road runs through Goshen (modern Wadi Tumilat) that in ancient times continued through a series of fortifications, the famous Wall of Princes, and the major fortress at Taru called the Gate of the Barbarians. Beyond the fortifications the road joined the ancient caravan trail leading to Beersheba. This axis of advance from the desert to the heart of the Delta cities was the traditional route of invasion from the east, and it was the route used by the Hyksos. Seen in this way, it seems reasonable that the Israelites might have been settled along one of Egypt's most vulnerable and strategic approaches and were expected to use their military capabilities in its defense.

There is no doubt that *habiru* units could be formidable military assets. Their primary skills seem to have been in combat conducted in rough mountainous terrain where they were experts at hit-and-run raids, ambush, and surprise attack. Their reputation was that of tough warriors, solid military professionals the equal of elite units in regular national armies.[28] The Amarna Letters make clear that as Egyptian control in Canaan weakened, *habiru* units were used more frequently by the Canaanite kings to further weaken Egyptian influence. Seti I (1315–1300 B.C.E.), was forced to deal frequently with *habiru* raids on Egyptian outposts in Canaan. In 1310 he sent an army to Beth-shean to deal with the problem, but met with mixed success. That *habiru* units could be of sufficient size and expertise to cause difficulties even for a major power like Egypt is beyond doubt. It will be recalled that David's *habiru* army numbered 600 men. In one list from Alalakh, a similar *habiru* force is listed as comprising 1,436 men, 80 of whom were charioteers. An additional 1,006 soldiers of the same force are described as *shananu*, probably light archers and infantry.[29] Another text recalls that the city of Zallul, north of Carchemish on the Euphrates, was stormed and captured by a *habiru* force of 2,000 men. There is, of course, no indication as to the military strength or capability of the Israelite *habiru* in Egypt. But if, as many scholars suggest, the Israelites were *habiru*, and if they followed the typical pattern of social organization, then it is reasonable to conclude that they possessed a military arm central or at least adjunct to the main social order itself. If the pattern holds as typical of the military arms of other *habiru*, then it is reasonable to expect that the Israelite military arm was comprised of military professionals sufficiently armed and experienced in war to protect the social order from its enemies. Under these circumstances it would have made superb military sense for pharaoh to have settled them across the most likely avenue of advance leading from the desert into the Delta and Egypt's heartland. The area of Goshen and the Wall of Princes were among the most heavily fortified and manned in all Egypt so that any Israelite *habiru* troops stationed in this area would have served as augmented units, a role they traditionally performed in the armies of the Canaanite kings.

It is possible that Israelite troops served an even more important function as a consequence of their close relationship with pharaoh as suggested by the story of Joseph in the Old Testament. The preponderance of scholarship suggests that the Israelites arrived in Egypt most probably during the New Kingdom sometime around the time of Amenhotep III (1417–1378 B.C.E.) during whose reign the Amarna Letters were produced. If so, then the story of Joseph as advisor to pharaoh fits well with the Amarna Age, specifically with the time of Akhenaten himself, so that the "Amarna age would provide a more satisfactory background for it (the story of Joseph) than any other age of which we have knowledge."[30] It was Pharaoh Akhenaten (1378–1359 B.C.E.) who introduced a strict monotheism to Egypt, destroying the old religious establishment and its shrines and temples, causing a degree of social, economic, and political turbulence certainly equal to that caused by the French Revolution.[31] Although it remains a matter for speculation, it is possible that the traditional monotheism of the Israelites and of their leader, Joseph, was one of the factors that might have recommended Joseph and his people to pharaoh. Joseph's ability to interpret dreams and his proven administrative experience notwithstanding, it remains possible that the Israelite belief in a single god may have also served to make the Israelites acceptable to the "god-intoxicated" Egyptian king.

The establishment of the Egyptian Empire had opened up Egypt's borders to foreign visitors far more than ever before, and evidence from reliefs, monuments, and texts suggests a greatly increased presence of Semites in Egyptian governmental and military life. That the Israelites were among these Semites seems probable. Redford supports this view when he notes that even before

Akhenaten there is evidence that many Asiatics had achieved important positions in Egyptian society. Texts and reliefs show Asiatics in the priesthood, police, palace bureaucracy, the military, and the foreign office.[32] In addition to Asiatic soldiers, military units, and charioteers, Buber notes other Semites who rose to high office working for pharaoh. These include the minister of Syrian affairs responsible for granaries there. Another Semite was described as the "highest mouth of the whole land" (a political advisor?), who is shown being awarded the "golden chain" and being driven through the streets in a carriage.[33] It is not unlikely, then, that the story of Joseph may be substantially true, the tale of an Israelite tribal leader who rose to great heights and used his position to help his people. The pharaoh under whom Joseph was most likely to have risen, Rowley asserts, was Akhenaten.[34]

Under these circumstances it would not be unreasonable that Israelite military men might also have risen to important positions within the Egyptian military, more so if Akhenaten had particular use for them. Akhenaten intended to exterminate all traces of the old religious order and replace it with a new god and theology. His campaign of destruction was conducted on such a large scale and so thoroughly accomplished that it could not have been carried out without the support of the army to provide the manpower to deal with the considerable resistance and violence that must have occurred. An inscription on the tomb of Tutankhamen, Akhenaten's successor, describes the destruction as he found it: "The temples of the gods and goddesses were desolated from Elephantine as far as the marshes of the Delta . . . their sanctuaries were like that which has never been, and their houses were foot-worn paths."[35] Every temple from Elephantine to Syria was destroyed and the statues of the gods desecrated. After the initial shock had passed, it was to be expected that the priests would rally the people at their temples and shrines to oppose the defacers. Military units would have been required to surround the temples and control the angry crowds. Violent confrontations and killings must have been commonplace. Although commanded by professional officers, the ranks of the army were comprised of conscripts, and it is likely that their willingness to carry out the murder of their own gods was problematic. Harsh discipline might have been required at times to stiffen the resolve of the troops. More important, there is evidence that special military units of non-Egyptian troops may have been used in the defacement campaign, perhaps to avoid strong resistance among the Egyptian soldiery.

It is in this context that the reliefs found in Akhenaten's new capital need to be understood. These reliefs show the constant presence of the military and portray Akhenaten as a vigorous military commander.[36] In almost every portrayal the king is shown wearing the Blue Crown of war or the Nubian wig, the characteristic military headdress of the New Kingdom.[37] The city itself is an armed camp, complete with watchtowers, within which the king and his soldiers are shown engaged in marching, chariotry, and military exercises.[38] Most interesting is the substantial presence of military detachments comprised

Figure 3.1 Amarna Relief Showing a Unit of Akhenaten's Asiatic and Libyan Mercenaries

of troops whose features suggest Semitic and African origin.[39] Schulman identifies them from their physical features as Nubian, Libyan, and Syro-Palestinian (i.e., Semites).[40] These units may have constituted a foreign legion or even a mercenary praetorian guard that would have shown little hesitation in carrying out pharaoh's campaign against the Egyptian gods. Although these units bear a striking resemblance to *habiru* units, the features of the soldiers in the reliefs are Semitic, the timing with the Joseph story is correct, and the monotheism of the Israelites fits nicely with that of the new pharaoh, there is no conclusive evidence that any of these units were Israelites. The probability that they could have been, however, cannot be entirely excluded and, as we shall see later, might explain a number of events that occurred during the Exodus.

Before proceeding further, it is perhaps valuable to summarize what has been said so far. First, the Israelites in Egypt were neither slaves nor camel nomads, but *habiru,* with a confederation-like form of social organization much more diversified and sociologically complex than that of bedouin, nomads, or seasonal stockbreeding communities. Second, like other *habiru,* the Israelites possessed a military arm comprised of experienced military professionals who often hired out as mercenaries. Third, the settlement of the Israelites in Goshen, a part of Egypt's borderland vulnerable to military attack, in exchange for their military participation in its defense as augmented units to the regular Egyptian units is a typical pattern of *habiru* military employment found elsewhere, most often in Canaan. Fourth, sufficient scholarly evidence places the Israelites in Egypt shortly before or during the reign of Akhenaten and his violent campaign to enforce monotheism upon Egypt. Fifth, special military units comprised of non-Egyptians, including Semites, were used to enforce Akhenaten's program of religious monotheism. The utilization of Israelite *habiru* units in Akhenaten's pogrom, therefore, cannot be completely rejected.

From the death of Joseph to the appearance of Moses, the Bible is silent concerning the activities of the Israelites in Egypt. The death of Tutankhamen had put an end to the bloodline of the Eighteenth Dynasty. Beginning with Ay, Egypt was ruled by a succession of competent military men. Horemheb

(1344–1317 B.C.E.), who succeeded Ay, chose Ramses I as his successor, a soldier from the northeast corner of the Delta who had risen no higher than a "captain of troops" but must have been well known to the king. Ramses I (1317–1315 B.C.E.) was already an old man when he assumed power and died within two years, leaving the throne to his son, Seti I (1315–1300 B.C.E.), also trained as a soldier. Seti passed the scepter to his son, Ramses II (1300–1232 B.C.E.), who ruled for 67 years and was probably the *Meror* of the Bible, who set the Israelites to corvee labor.[41] Ramses' son, Merneptah (1232–1222 B.C.E.), followed him and was probably the pharaoh of the Exodus.[42] The first mention of the Israelites as a people in any source outside the Old Testament occurs in the fifth year of the reign of Merneptah who, after suppressing rebellions in Palestine, erected a stele to his victory which included the following inscription: "Israel is desolated, his seed is not. Palestine has become a widow for Egypt. All lands are united, they are pacified. Everyone that is turbulent is bound by king Merneptah."[43] The hieroglyph used in the text to denote Israel is the hieroglyph denoting a people or tribe, not a settled nation, suggesting that at this time, approximately 1235 B.C.E., the Israelites had moved into Palestine but had yet to conquer it sufficiently to form a stable social order of their own. This fits reasonably well with Albright's conclusion that the approximate date of the Israelite conquest of Canaan, as deduced from the date of the first wave of destruction visited upon Canaanite towns, occurred sometime between 1250 and 1150 B.C.E.[44] The story of the Israelites in Egypt continues when we find them hard at forced labor, making bricks for pharaoh's new city in the Delta. The obvious question is, how did this state of affairs come about? Why was a respected and valued military ally reduced to corvee labor?

The answer seems clear enough from Exodus 1:8–10. "A new king arose over Egypt who did not know Joseph. And he said to his people, "Look, the Israelite people are much too numerous for us. Let us deal shrewdly with them, so that they may not increase; otherwise in the event of war they may join our enemies in fighting against us and rise from the ground." It is probable that this new pharaoh "who did not know Joseph" was Seti I. Almost immediately after he became king, Canaan flared into open revolt, forcing him to lead an army into the area to put it down. He met with only limited success and was barely able to hold onto Beth-shean, Megiddo, and Rehebn. As always, Egypt's enemies were the Canaanite princes, this time assisted by large bands of *habiru* who joined the revolt.[45] It was probably this revolt that prompted Seti to begin construction of a new city and summer capital in the Nile Delta, the great city of Raamses mentioned in the Bible. The city, called the "dwelling of the lion" by the Egyptians, was an important supply base and military strongpoint to protect the main avenue of advance that led from the desert to the Delta cities. Although designed for defense, the city could also be used along with Sharuhen farther east as a springboard for a sudden military strike against Canaan. It was here and at Pithom eight miles away[46] that the Israelites were put to work. Although it was Ramses II who completed the work on the cities and thus gained the title of Pharaoh of the Oppression, it was almost certainly Seti who first set the Israelites to work. But why would Seti oppress the Israelites?

The Bible records clearly enough that the Israelites had become "too numerous." What this might mean in a country of 7 to 9 million people is unclear. It is unlikely that numbers alone were sufficient cause for action against the Israelites. However, their presence in even relatively large numbers in Goshen during the time of Seti's, then Ramses II's, and then Merneptah's troubles with the Canaanite rebels may have led Egypt's kings to see the Israelite *habiru* as a potential fifth column in the midst of a vital military sector. The Canaanite rebels were being openly supported by the *habiru* in the highlands there, sufficient reason to give any military commander cause to doubt the loyalty of their fellow "cousins" in Egypt. Moreover, the location of the Israelites in Goshen might rightly have concerned Seti from a military perspective. The two roads leading from the Palestine-Egyptian border at Oar passed directly through the Wadi Tumilat and Goshen.[47] It was to protect this route that the city of Raamses was constructed. Any military commander with a tactical sense would have been concerned that such an important axis of advance passed through the territory of a people who might have more in common with the enemy than with Egypt.[48] If so, Seti may have forced the Israelites into corvee service to remove them as a factor in the tactical equation.

There may have been yet another reason for Seti's action against the Israelite *habiru*. Seti was a deeply religious man who valued the old gods that Akhenaten had attempted to destroy.[49] Although it had been 57 years since Akhenaten's death, the temples and shrines were still in terrible disrepair. Seti immediately set about rebuilding the holy places and restoring the mutilated inscriptions and statues. He toured the land inspecting the damage, and when he came to Abydos and saw the destruction of Osiris's great shrine, he wept at what the heretics had done.[50] The king's strong reverence for the old gods and his anger at Akhenaten's destruction may have led him to develop a hatred for anything connected with the heretic king. *If* the Israelites had maintained their monotheism after Akhenaten's death, and *if* they had served as praetorians in the king's foreign guard used to destroy the old temples, and *if*, somehow, the Israelites came to Seti's attention, then his own religious fervor might have prompted him to punish the Israelites for the sins of their fathers.

If the Israelites had served in pharaoh's army as mercenaries their officers and any other high-ranking members of the Israelite community would have been exempt from corvee labor. If, under Seti, the military men of the community were now forced to do corvee labor, it would have been regarded as an insult, a deprivation of their former high social status. Under these conditions, it is not unreasonable that they might have come to regard forced manual labor as little better than slavery. Even if the Israelite officers remained exempt, the sight of their families and relatives forced to labor might have been too much to bear quietly. Over time, the military men might have found the condition intolerable and decided to leave Egypt at the first opportunity. The story of Moses surely suggests, albeit under divine guidance, that the Israelites took the initiative in provoking a situation where they would be permitted to leave Egypt. And when they left, the evidence in Exodus suggests there were experienced military men among the group to help guide the Israelites to the Promised Land.

To this point I have argued that there is sufficient reason for questioning the claim that the Israelites in Egypt were slaves or stockbreeding bedouins. I have proposed instead that they were *habiru*, and that as part of that type of community they possessed an experienced and proficient military corps for their own defense. Seen in this light, the adventures of the Israelites as described in Exodus take on new meaning, one that permits a portrayal of the military history of the Israelites commencing much earlier than had been possible heretofore. The rest of this chapter offers an examination of the Exodus from this new perspective and attempts to depict a number of events described therein from the perspective of a soldier hoping to make sense of the tale in military terms. To help the reader see the story with a soldier's eye I thought it useful if, for the moment at least, the reader could be convinced to set aside any reliance upon divine explanations for these events and see them instead as the plans and perspectives of a combat field commander. Whenever I thought it helpful, therefore, I have attributed the commands of Yahweh and Moses as reported in the Hebrew text to the "General." Perhaps this simple literary device will help the reader to see that these commands often make surprisingly good military sense.

THE DEPARTURE FROM EGYPT

The proposition that the Israelites in Egypt possessed a military arm receives strong support from the text of Exodus, which employs a language of military terms and metaphors to describe the departure of the Israelites from Egypt. Exodus 13:19 states clearly that the Israelites were armed when they departed: "Now the Israelites went up armed out of Egypt." The term *hamushim* is used to denote the condition of being armed.[51] The traditional view of the Israelites as slaves does not, of course, accord very well with the use of this term since armed slaves would make no sense. This has led some scholars to interpret *hamushim* as meaning "equipped," in the sense of the Israelites being adequately prepared and provisioned for their journey.[52] But the Exodus text is quite clear that the Israelites were *not* well prepared or well equipped. Thus, in Exodus 12:39 the text tells us that "because they had been expelled from Egypt and could not tarry . . . they had made no provisioning for themselves." The use of *hamushim* to mean "equipped" is, furthermore, an uncommon usage. More commonly, *hamushim* means armed. One student of the subject has noted that while there are any number of roots from which the word might be derived, none make sense in the context of the Exodus text that is not of some implied military meaning. Moreover, the word has come down to us with its original military meaning intact, that is, as armed. As William Propp notes, "the majority rendering, 'well girted, armed, equipped,' fits all attestations well enough and has been adopted into modern Hebrew."[53]

Other terms and metaphors in the Exodus text also suggest a military dimension to the Israelite tribes on the eve of their departure. Exodus 12:37, for example, tells us that "Israel's sons set forth from Raamses to Succoth, about six hundred thousand footmen—the males besides the dependents." The term employed for "footmen" is *ragli*, literally "he of the leg."[54] It is a term that is ordinarily used as a singular collective noun connoting not just *people* on foot, but *soldiers* on foot. In short, *ragli* means infantry.[55] The text goes on to describe how this infantry is organized. Exodus 12:41 describes the infantry units as being formed into brigades: "And it happened at the end of thirty years and four hundred years, and it happened on the bone (body) of this day, all Yahweh's brigades went out from the land of Egypt." The English translation retains this sense of a military formation when it translates the same verse as meaning, "In battle array, the Israelites marched out of Egypt." One interpretation of the Hebrew text is that "in their ranks" the Israelites left Egypt. It seems reasonable, then, that as the Israelite *habiru* prepared to depart from Egypt they did so with their weapons in hand and their military elements formed up in march formations, conditions usually not attributed to slaves.

No sooner had they set their feet upon the road out of Egypt than the presence of a keen military mind is evident in the choice of which route the Israelites would follow. Exodus 13:17–18 reveals the mind of a strategist as he plans his escape. "Now when Pharaoh let the people go, the General (God) did not lead them by way of the land of the Philistines, although it was nearer; for the General said, 'The people may have a change of heart when they see war, and return to Egypt.' So the General led the people roundabout, by way of the wilderness at the Sea of Reeds." The "way of the land of the Philistines" is a reference to the coastal road running from Sinai north to Mount Carmel, known to the Egyptians as the Way of Horus and, later, to the Romans as the *Via Maris*. Its designation in Exodus as passing through the land of the Philistines is a redaction by the text's author, who was writing much later, certainly after the Philistine arrival, to place the route in a context his audience would understand. In any case, the decision to avoid the coastal road was based on important military considerations. The road was well guarded by Egyptian fortresses and strong-points. If, as we shall see, the General was concerned about avoiding the Egyptian authorities, then the coastal road could not be used. Second, the Canaanite towns and cities along the coastal route were also protected by formidable military forces, some including other *habiru* serving as mercenaries to Canaanite kings. These armies would have to be dealt with if the coastal route were chosen, an unacceptable risk to a people whose years of peaceful living in Goshen may have dulled their fighting spirit. The text implies that the Israelites may not have been psychologically prepared for war when it tells us, "The people may have a change of heart when they see war, and return to Egypt." Under these conditions, then, the General's decision to avoid the coastal road and lead the people "roundabout, by way of the wilderness" makes excellent military sense.

But what of the Egyptian authorities? Having received permission to leave Egypt, why would the General be concerned about the Egyptians? Why would the Israelite commander have reason to believe that pharaoh would suddenly change his mind about letting the people go? The reason offered by the text is unconvincing, telling us only that pharaoh changed his mind but not why. Exodus 14:5–6 tells us, "When the king of Egypt was told that the people had fled, Pharaoh and his courtiers had a change of heart about the people and said, 'What is this we have done, releasing Israel from our service.' He ordered his chariot and took his men with him," and gave chase to the Israelites. But could there have been other reasons why pharaoh changed his mind? A clue may lie in the description in Exodus 14:8 that the Israelites were "departing defiantly, boldly." It is important to recall here that the *habiru* were not only mercenaries, but brigands and freebooters as well who could quickly turn from allies to looters if the circumstances required. Exodus 12:39 tells us that the Israelites were forced to leave in a hurry and could not make adequate provisions for their journey. Thus, "because they had been expelled from Egypt and could not tarry . . . they had made no provisions for themselves." To lead the Israelites into the desert without sufficient provisions was to face almost certain death.

No responsible commander could permit such conditions to remain unattended, especially since the Israelites in Goshen were surrounded by the very provisions they required. Both Raamses and Pithom were "store cities," that is major logistics depots for the Egyptian army in the Delta. The route from Goshen to the desert took the Israelites through Succoth, one of pharaoh's largest cattle estates, and the land of Goshen itself was marked by many smaller settlements as well. In short, everything the Israelites needed was there for the taking. It is a reasonable hypothesis that the Israelites might have sacked one of the towns or even the king's estate on the way out of the country to provision themselves for the long desert trek. Exodus 12:35–36 tells the outrageous tale of how Moses proposed to solve the provision shortage by simply asking the Egyptians for them! Thus, "The Israelites had done Moses' bidding and borrowed from the Egyptians objects of silver and gold, and clothing. And the General (the Lord) had disposed the Egyptians favorably toward the people, and they let them have their request; thus they stripped the Egyptians." It is, of course, not plausible that the Egyptians would have provided food, clothing, gold, and silver for the asking. Far more likely is that Israelite brigands took them at the point of the sword. Especially so since it was the General who "disposed" the Egyptians favorably to the idea! Further, the word used to describe what happened to the Egyptians is *nitzeyl*. Although translated as "stripped," it is usually translated as "despoiled," so that the Israelites "despoiled Egypt." Either way, the connotation of the word is that the Egyptians were relieved of the provisions that the Israelites needed at the time against their will.

Relieving the Egyptians of their gold and silver at the same time certainly sounds like a robbery. Later, in the desert, when Yahweh commands that the people construct a tabernacle and tent for him to live in, he orders that it be constructed of gold, silver, precious stones, and other valuable materials. When the General (Moses) asks the people to provide these precious materials and valuable objects for such a sacred purpose, they respond by giving so much gold and silver that the General had to tell them to stop! Perhaps carrying all this heavy, but quite useless, booty through the desert was such a burden that they were glad to be rid of it. In any event, if the news of an Israelite sack of an Egyptian town reached pharaoh's ears, it would surely qualify as the Israelites having departed "defiantly," and perhaps provoked him to try and punish them. Perhaps this is why the General feared the Egyptian authorities and avoided the coastal road.

THE PILLAR OF FIRE AND SMOKE

The Israelites began their march along the well-traveled road leading from Raamses to the edge of the desert. The first day's march, about ten miles, brought them to Succoth. The end of the next day found them in Etham, about eight miles from Succoth. All along the way the Israelites were accompanied by a strange phenomenon, a pillar of cloud and a pillar of fire. Exodus 13:20–22 describes it this way. "They set out from Succoth, and encamped at Etham, at the edge of the wilderness. The General (Lord) went before them in a pillar of cloud by day, to guide them along the way, and in a pillar of fire by night, to give them light, that they might travel day and night. The pillar of cloud by day and the pillar of fire by night did not depart from before the people." Again and again throughout the journey of the Israelites the pillars appear. Miraculous explanations aside for the moment, in Exodus and elsewhere the pillars appear to have two functions. One, as above, is to guide the Israelites as they move over unfamiliar terrain. The second is to signal the Israelites when to camp and when to break camp. And so Exodus 40:36–37 tells us, "When the cloud lifted from the tabernacle, the Israelites would set out on their various journeys; but if the cloud did not lift, they would not set out until such times as it did lift." The text in Numbers 9:17–18 is even more explicit. "And whenever the cloud lifted from the tent, the Israelites set out accordingly; and at the spot where the cloud settled, there the Israelites would make camp. At the command of the General (Lord) the Israelites broke camp, and at the command of the General (Lord) they made camp." What the pillar of cloud and fire appears to be is a signal to the assembled multitude to encamp or break camp, and in that regard is not so much a divine totem but a practical device to improve the General's command and control over his troops.

The same signaling device is found, albeit much later, in the writings of Quintus Curtius, a Roman historian. In his *History of Alexander*, Curtius describes how Alexander, after conquering Egypt and returning to Babylon, prepared his army for movement farther east. These preparations included a number of changes in his regular methods of command and control. As Curtius tells it, "Also in the military discipline handed down by his predecessors Alexander made many changes of the greatest advantage."[56] We may reasonably take from this that whatever changes Alexander made were not to be found in his previous Macedonian military experience. Curtius goes on to describe one of these changes as follows:

> When he (Alexander) wished to move his camp, he used to give the signal with the trumpet, the sound of which was often not readily enough heard amid the noise made by the bustling soldiers; therefore he set up a pole (*perticam*) on top of the general's tent, which could be clearly seen from all sides, and from this lofty signal, visible to all alike, was watched for, (*ignis noctu fumus interdieu*) fire by night, smoke by day.[57]

Until very modern times Arab caravans, including those making their way to the *hajj*, were commonly preceded by a signal brazier of some sort.[58] The Egyptian origins, if any, of this military practice are yet to be examined. Here it is sufficient to note that Alexander adopted a similar device for a purpose as that described in Exodus only after he had spent considerable time in Egypt where, perhaps, he learned of it.

What, then, of the origins of the signal? Is it Egyptian? As with the origins of so many ancient artifacts, the evidence is only partial and thus very tentative indeed. First, we must be clear about what we are searching for. Was there one pillar of cloud and fire or two pillars, one for cloud and one for fire? The expert opinion is that the text implies *two* pillars.[59] The text uses the word *anan* which translates as "cloud" but certainly connotes "smoke" as well.[60] Thus, the pillar of cloud is really, as in the example of Alexander, a pillar of smoke. In any case, we are searching for two pillars or poles, not one. Just such a device seems to be portrayed in the reliefs depicting Ramses II military camp at the battle of Kadesh in the Luxor Temple. A drawing of the lower

Figure 3.2 Ramses II's Military Camp Portrayed at Luxor

left-hand panel is reproduced below. Standing behind Ramses as he sits upon his throne are two figures, each holding a long straight pole. Atop one of the poles appears to be a portrayal of a brazier in full flame. The other figure is holding a second pole atop which sits the bottom half of a brazier partially covered with some sort of top. A brazier partially covered in this manner would dampen the flame and produce smoke. The item atop the second pole closely resembles the hieroglyph for "flame," that is, a clay pot or brazier without a top. The item atop the taller pole is much more problematic since only the bottom is similar to the brazier whereas the top might well represent flames emanating from it. In one of the Amarna reliefs of a marching military unit, a similar item is in evidence. In this one, the flames emanating from the center are much clearer. Nonetheless, the evidence remains inconclusive. Below both poles are two smaller figures of men, each looking up at the tops of the poles. In their hands are narrow fans with which they appear to be fanning air over the flame and brazier. Is this a portrayal of a covered brazier and one in full flame? We cannot be certain. If it is, however, then this might be an Egyptian portrayal of the pillar of smoke and fire signaling device described in Exodus and Numbers.

The portrayals of Ramses II's camp at Kadesh, although they appear in four separate locations, are the only surviving depictions of an Egyptian military camp to come down to us so there are no others where we might search for additional examples of the signal device. There is, however, one more tantalizing clue as to the device's Egyptian origins. When pharaoh's chariots approached the Israelite camp near the Reed Sea they saw the pillar of smoke change into a pillar of fire and shift position (Exodus 14:9). But these "miraculous" events produced no reaction at all on the part of the Egyptian commanders and soldiers, and the Egyptians calmly went into their night encampment and waited for the dawn. This suggests that the Egyptians were observing something that they had often seen before, the enemy commander's signal for his troops to encamp for the night. As we shall see shortly, the Israelite commander depended on pharaoh seeing just that.

THE CROSSING OF THE REED SEA

Perhaps no event in Exodus has captured the religious imagination more than the Israelite crossing of the Reed Sea. Whether portrayed in literature, film, or religious commentary, the event is always portrayed as an example of God's miraculous powers and his willingness to intervene to protect his chosen people. Despite scores of scholarly articles over the last two centuries seeking to prove that this or that location was the site of the event, the event itself has not undergone significant scrutiny from the perspective of military technique. When examined in this manner, however, it is clear that what happened at the Reed Sea was a tactical maneuver known and practiced routinely by ancient and modern troop commanders: a night crossing of a water obstacle. The fact that Israelite commanders could implement this sophisticated tactical maneuver is testament to their military skill and imagination, further evidence of an Israelite military tradition prior to Joshua. Crossing a water obstacle at night is one of the most dangerous and difficult of small-unit tactical maneuvers. The success of the Israelite commanders in executing an operation of this type is substantial proof indeed that the military arm of the Israelite *habiru* had already reached a high level of military operational capability even before they left Egypt.

To understand the crossing of the Reed Sea in military terms it must be recalled that the Israelites had lived in Goshen for a long time and were familiar with the area, including the marshy tract of land where the fertile land met the desert. For years they had taken their herds down the same road they were traveling now to pasture them in the Sinai steppe during the rainy season, a time when the Nile's flood inundated the land of Goshen as it did the rest of Egypt.[61] The main road led directly from the edge of Goshen to a road junction where it joined the old road to Beersheba. It was probably down this road that Moses asked pharaoh for permission to take his people into the desert so that they might sacrifice to Yahweh.[62] As mercenaries serving in Goshen, it is likely that Israelite commanders were well aware of the locations of Egyptian fortresses and strong-points as well as the strength and disposition of Egyptian troop garrisons. These garrisons protected the fords and bridges that made movement through the great salt marsh possible. There were at least four major fortresses on the border,[63] one of which, probably Taru, stood at the junction where the main road met the desert. There were, however, scores of guarded bridges, fords, shallow crossing points, and so on, throughout the area. In describing the location of the Israelites, Exodus 14:2–3 tells us the Israelite camp was located "between Migdol and the sea." The term migdol means tower or fort, and most probably refers to the Egyptian fortress guarding the road junction noted earlier.

It is somewhat pointless to attempt to locate the exact place where the Israelites crossed the Reed Sea. Suffice it to say that the terrain where Goshen met the desert was marshy and wet, deep in places and shallow in others, surely neither sea nor lake for the most part, yet subject to strong tidal flows. The tidal flows of the general area are attested to in antiquity. Strabo seems to be describing them when he notes that "During my stay in Egypt the sea rose so high near Pelusium and Mount Cassius as to overflow the land and to convert the mountain into an island."[64] That the marshy terrain was dangerous to ground troops is clear enough from the description offered by Diodorus Siculus, a first century C.E. Greek historian, who records that during Xerxes' invasion of Egypt in 340 B.C.E., a troop unit of his army drowned in the place.[65] Although Diodorus does not provide further details, it is not difficult to imagine a company of Persian troops walking across a shallow muddy flat only to be trapped and drowned when the tide suddenly came in. And so it may have been that as the military commander marched his people down the road to the desert he had the advantage of knowing the enemy troop dispositions and how to navigate the marshy terrain.

We might imagine that as the General led his people toward the road junction he was mindful of the fact that the column would have to pass directly beneath the Egyptian fortress that guarded the junction. As one of the four major fortresses of the area, the Egyptian garrison would have been large and well armed. The General depended upon a peaceful passage. If he had to fight his way through, the results would be a catastrophe for his people for they were no match for the Egyptian professionals. Perhaps this was when a message reached the General that pharaoh's troops had already left Raamses and were fast closing in on the road behind him, trapping him between them and the Egyptian fortress to his front. If he remained where he was, the General would find himself caught between the classic "hammer and anvil." With the Egyptian garrison to his front and pharaoh's chariots closing from behind, the situation was desperate and in a few hours would be hopeless.

The General assembled his commanders. "Tell the Israelites to turn back and encamp before Pi-hahiroth, between Migdol and the sea, before Baal-Zephon; you shall encamp facing it, by the sea."[66] The order must have struck some of the Israelite commanders as insane, for the General had just instructed the Israelite column to leave the road and head directly into the desert! With no chance of forcing his way through the Egyptian fortress to his front, the General maneuvered to neutralize its tactical significance by moving his people south and west away from the garrison. In a single stroke the Israelites had escaped from between the hammer and anvil and removed the anvil from the strategic equation completely. One can well imagine some headstrong young officer voicing his complaint. "But General, there is no way out of the desert. Pharaoh's chariots can maneuver easily on the flat ground and cut us to pieces. Why, Sir, are we moving farther into the desert?" Exodus 14:3 tells us what was in the General's mind when it explains, "Pharaoh will say of the

Israelites, 'They are astray in the land; the wilderness has closed in on them.' " It is, of course, a basic axiom of war to deceive the enemy as to your intentions, to mislead him into thinking one thing while you prepare to do exactly the opposite. Here Exodus provides us with an example of tactical deception at its best. The General intends to convince pharaoh that the Israelites are lost when, in fact, having lived in Goshen for many years, they know exactly where they are. Indeed, they know the terrain better than the pharaoh and his troops do!

The Israelites turned south and west and marched into the desert. When they had reached a place sufficiently distant from the Egyptian fortress (the *migdol*) and where the firm ground to their front met the watery marsh to their rear, the Israelites encamped and waited for pharaoh and his chariots to arrive. Egyptian units always moved with reconnaissance chariot screens and scouts to their front so it is possible that the Israelite maneuver was observed by these scouts and reported to pharaoh. Probably aware that he was being watched, the General maneuvered to deceive pharaoh once again. Here Exodus 14:19 tells us, "The General (angel of God), who had been going ahead of the Israelite army, now moved and followed behind them; and the pillar of cloud shifted from in front of them and took up a place behind them, and it came between the army of the Egyptians and the army of Israel." The General moved his command tent and its characteristic signal, the pillar of smoke atop a pole, around behind the column to strengthen the impression that the Israelites were facing in a direction of march leading deeper into the desert. The object was to convince pharaoh of what his scouts had already told him, that the Israelites were indeed "astray in the land."

It must have been near dusk when pharaoh and his chariots arrived, for the Egyptians went immediately into camp. From the Egyptian camp it looked exactly like what pharaoh had been led to expect. The Israelites were facing in a direction of march that would take them deeper into the desert. There could be no doubt about this because the Israelite command tent and its signal pillar leading the Israelite column were facing pharaoh. Behind the Israelites lay the tidal salt marsh, cutting off their retreat. To the right and rear of the Israelite camp, at a distance of several miles (two hours march), was the Egyptian fortress. Apparently the Israelites had given up any idea of trying to reach the road to Beersheba. All was as pharaoh's scouts had told him it would be. As dusk gave way to darkness the pillar of smoke atop the Israelite signal standard gave way to bright flame and "the pillar lit up the night, so that the one (camp) could not come near the other all through the night."[67]

The General carried out his plan while pharaoh slept. The bright flame atop the pillar drew the attention of the Egyptian observers completely blocking their ability to see behind it. Modern soldiers are taught when training in night discipline that any bright object at night affects the cones and rods of the eye making the eye physically incapable of seeing in the dark behind the light. Once exposed to a bright light in the darkness, even if the soldier turns his eyes away from it, it can require almost 30 minutes for the eye to readjust. The General could safely maneuver his troops behind the light as long as the direction of movement was to the rear of the Israelite encampment. For all practical purposes, the Egyptians were blind.

Now the *ruah qadim* or forward wind began to blow. It was springtime, the time of the sirocco winds that blew out of the eastern desert with terrific force and terrible noise. Because the Israelites oriented themselves for religious reasons toward the sunrise, the translation of *ruah qadim* as east wind, the forward direction, is correct.[68] The term also realistically translates as "hot desert wind,"[69] or, as I have called it here, a sirocco. As the wind grew stronger, the noise increased until it was difficult to hear. Now the Egyptians were deaf as well. The shallow water covering the sandbar just below the surface began to move as the strong tide flowed out to sea. With the desert wind pushing from the southeast and the tide pulling it northward, the water was gone in a short time, and the ground was dry and hard enough to hold the weight of man and animals. Perhaps the General had been born in Goshen and hunted birds in the marshes or had served as an Israelite auxiliary in the area and had noticed the effect of the sirocco and tide upon the shallow wetlands. If so, like Wellington at Waterloo, perhaps he had kept this piece of ground in his pocket for a long time. The conditions being right, he called his commanders together and ordered the Israelites to withdraw across the marsh during the night and gain the open desert on the other side.

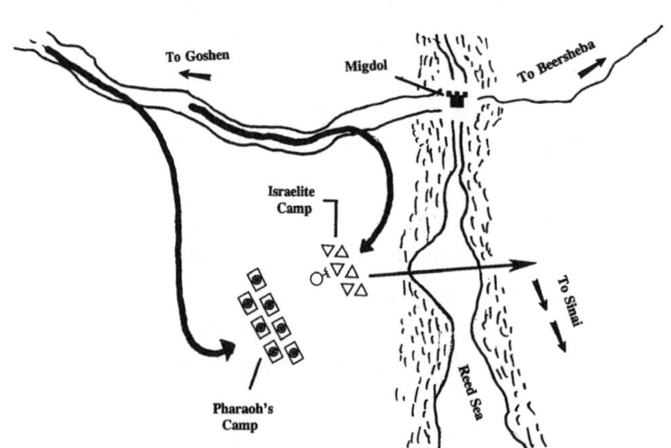

Figure 3.3 Night Crossing of the Reed Sea

As told in Exodus, the tale of the crossing is framed in theological metaphor. "Then Moses held out his arm over the sea and the Lord drove back the sea with a strong east wind all that night, and turned the sea into dry ground. The waters were split, and the Israelites went into the sea on dry ground, the waters forming a wall for them on their right and on their left."[70] Still, as I have suggested, even the theological metaphor contains many of the elements necessary to a more mundane explanation, that is, the execution of a night water crossing. Exodus 14:24 tells us that the Egyptian pursuit began "at the morning watch," or shortly after daybreak. With the Israelites watching safely from the other side of the marsh, the Egyptians appear to have attempted to follow them across the dry bed of the marsh, but the wheels of their chariots became "locked" so "that they moved forward with difficulty."[71] This seems to be nothing more mysterious than chariot wheels caught in the mud. While struggling to free their machines, "the waters turned back and covered the chariots and the horsemen." Perhaps the tide came in and some of the Egyptian troops and horses drowned.

The Israelites had crossed the marsh and gained the desert. But the General knew that they were still in danger. The original plan had been to leave Egypt and return to the land of Canaan. Given the original direction of march, the Israelites had probably intended to cross out of Egypt at the road junction where the old road met Goshen and follow it on up to Beersheba, the road that Jacob had probably taken when he came to Egypt and that remained a well-worn caravan track until modern times,[72] and led directly into Canaan. To return to their original route, however, would have required them to turn north to gain the Beersheba road, a route that would have taken them perilously close to the Egyptian fortress at the junction of the Beersheba-Goshen road, the *migdol* that they had avoided when they turned into the desert. Egyptian reconnaissance chariots, we might reasonably assume, regularly patrolled the area along the road and might easily discover the Israelites in which case they might come under Egyptian chariot attack in open country. Once more the General decided to do the unexpected and turned not toward the land of Canaan but away from it. From Exodus 15:22, "Then the General (Moses) caused Israel to set out from the Sea of Reeds. They went into the wilderness of Shur." And so began the great desert trek of the Israelites in their attempt to return to their promised land.

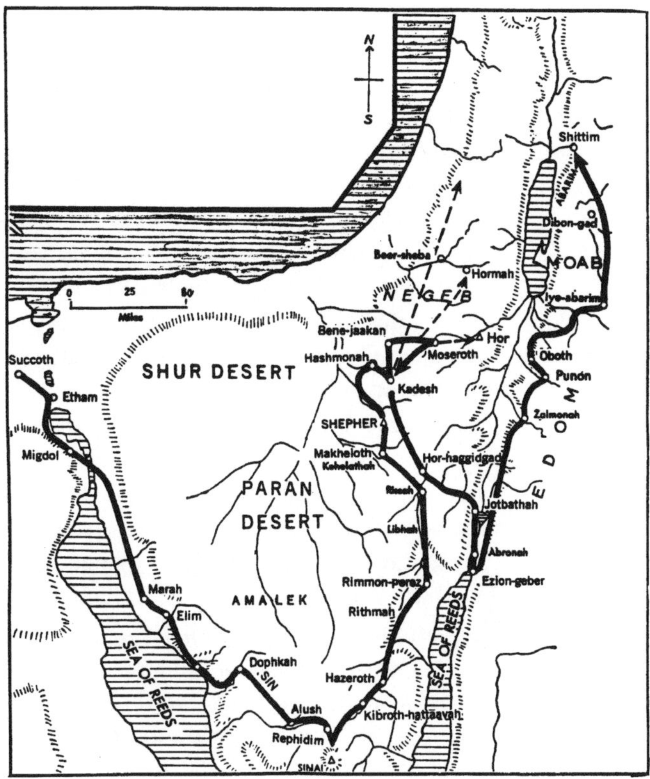

Figure 3.4 Route of the Exodus

JOSHUA AND THE AMALEK

The General's decision to turn south and east into the desert was calculated to take advantage of his knowledge of the hostile terrain over which the Israelites would have to travel. We ought not to believe that the Israelite commander and his people simply "wandered" from one place to another only by fortune (or divine design) to stumble upon Sinai and then Kadesh-Barnea. The texts tell us differently. Moses, for example, spent years among the Midianites tending flocks in the Sinai desert, an occupation that would surely have equipped him with a knowledge of the area and where the all important water sources were located. In addition, the texts inform us that the Israelites were helped by Midianite guides, "who serve as eyes for Israel."[73] These hardy desert bedouins also instructed the Israelites how to "encamp in the wilderness,"[74] that is, how to live off the land. The fact that the Israelites required such instruction, moreover, is further evidence that they were not nomadic desert peoples themselves but *habiru* as I have maintained.[75]

Little more than a month after crossing the Reed Sea, and somewhere in the Sinai near Rephidim, the Israelites were attacked by the Amalekites and forced to fight their first battle. The text suggests an engagement that occurred in two phases. The first was an ambush in which the Amalekites seem to have caught the Israelites in column of march and attacked their rear. Deuteronomy 25:17–19 describes the ambush. "Remember what the Amalek did to you on your journey, after you left Egypt—how, undeterred by fear of god, he surprised you on the march, when you were famished and weary, and cut down all the stragglers in your rear." The Amalekites broke off the attack on the column's rear, probably due to nightfall, and waited to engage them again in the morning. This gave the General time to plan his defense. This time the General placed command of the Israelite fighting men in the hands of a young troop commander named Joshua. "The General (Moses) said to Joshua, 'Pick some men for us, and go out and do battle with Amalek.' "[76] The General explained the plan that was devised during the night. "Tomorrow I will station myself on the top of the hill, with the rod of God in my hand."[77] Here we see the ancient dictum that commanders must be seen by their soldiers to be effective. Egyptian pharaohs were always portrayed as leading their troops in battle, as was Alexander. Caesar, it was said, wore a red cloak so his men could easily identify him during battle, and both George S. Patton (who seriously contemplated wearing a red cloak!) and Irwin Rommel were both known for their presence on the battlefield in plain sight of their soldiers. The text tells us that for the entire day the General stood in plain view on the hill overlooking the battle "until the sun set" while on the battlefield below "Joshua overwhelmed the Amalek with the edge of the sword."[78] And so the Israelites gained their first military victory by force of arms.

What is the historian to make of the account? First, there can be no doubt now that the Israelites are armed, and they are armed, at least, with the sword. This sword, as Yadin and others have noted, is the sickle-sword, the basic second weapon of the Egyptian spear infantryman, called the *khopesh* or "foreleg" of an animal by the Egyptians. The weapon was so completely identified with the Egyptian army, although Canaanites used it as well, that the *khopesh* replaced the mace as the symbol of pharaonic authority.[79] The straight sword had not yet made its appearance in Canaan or Egypt, and would not in any numbers for at least 200 years. Where, then, did the Israelites acquire such weaponry in sufficient numbers if they were not, as the text tells us they were, already possessed of them *before* they left Egypt? Given the expense and difficulty of bronze manufacture, especially so for a people on the move, we may safely rule out the Israelites having manufactured the weapons after they left Egypt.[80] Moreover, the armies of Egypt during the New Kingdom were conscript armies officered by professional officers and supported by a national arms industry. Conscripts were taken into the army, issued weapons, trained and sent to their units. When their duty was over, the weapons and other equipment—shoes, shields, helmets, belts, canteen, and so on—were returned to army supply depots for reuse. If the Israelites at Rephidim were armed with standard-issue Egyptian weapons, this could only be because they were issued them during their mercenary service while in Egypt. When they fell out of favor with pharaoh, there may have been some thought given to disarming them. There is no doubt that the Egyptian army could have been used to accomplish this task but probably at a bloody cost. Perhaps, then, it was simply easier to permit these former mercenaries to leave Egypt and take their weapons with them. Thus it might have been that the Israelites went up out of Egypt armed.

The selection of Joshua to command the troops in battle prompts the question of why he was chosen. He was young, came from no distinguished lineage, and was not shown to have any other special credentials that would qualify him for command. In the absence of other qualifications, it is likely that the choice of Joshua to command may have been based upon his reputation among the Israelite *habiru* mercenaries acquired when he served with pharaoh's armies in Egypt as a competent fighter and commander. In this sense Joshua might have come to the attention of the General because of his already established reputation as a warrior. As Mendenhall points out, this form of "customary military organization" had no permanent command authority nor central political organization that could enforce appointed officers upon troops who did not know them.[81] It is the same form of military organization found in the *Iliad* and, as we shall see, characterized Israelite armies during the period of Joshua and the Judges. Armies like these were put in the field by social groups with no centralized military or political command. As in the *Iliad*, each leader in battle commands troops of his own tribe or clan. Even though their positions may be charismatic, combat leaders are appointed because of their reputations as proven soldiers demonstrated in full view of their peers.[82] This system is regarded as the natural way to fight, since each man knows his peers and social unit from childhood. It was the same system used by the Arab caliphates from the sixth to the eighth century C.E., and, most recently, it is the system of military manning and combat command employed by Afghani warlords.

One might imagine, then, that through skill and good fortune the General had avoided having to set his troops to battle until Rephidim. When, as the text tells us, his column was ambushed from the rear the main body of the column might have taken refuge in narrow terrain with hills on either side. The General remained with the main body and assigned a unit of soldiers under the command of Joshua to take up positions in the rear of the column and prevent further attacks. The General, meanwhile, positioned himself on the top of the hill so his men might see him and take courage. Of course the Amalekites could also see the General, probably giving them pause to wonder whether he commanded additional troops, carefully hidden out of sight, that might outflank or take the ambushers from the rear. The General was once more attempting to deceive his opponent, this time psychologically.

The scenario outlined above, though speculative, has the advantage of playing strongly against the operational capabilities of the Amalekites while reenforcing those of the Israelites. The Amalekites were tribal nomads whose military capability was confined to camel-riding infantry armed with the simple bow. The camel was domesticated sometime around the end of the second millennium B.C.E. and is thought to have been disciplined to military use in the Middle East somewhat later, perhaps even around the time of the Exodus itself.[83] Most of our knowledge of nomadic camel infantry is drawn from accounts written almost a century after the Israelites settled in Canaan.[84] During the time of Judges, Saul, and David, our accounts of the Amalekites as camel infantry are much more substantial, so that it must be said that any discussion of Amalekite military capability is based upon the assumption that it was similar during the Exodus to what was found later. Assuming so, the Amalekite camel infantry at the battle at Rephidim offered speed and mobility, significant assets in open desert country. The camel's well-known ability to travel far on little water also enhanced the animal's military value. Each camel carried a single bowman, although later Assyrian reliefs show two men mounted on a single animal.[85] Camel infantry was well suited to ambush and hit-and-run raids of the type described as having occurred at Rephidim. In uneven or narrow terrain or, in certain circumstances, even in open country, camel infantry was at a severe disadvantage. It could ambush and raid, but it could not effect a strategic decision within a tactical context without having to dismount its riders and have them fight as light infantry. It was precisely this combined ability that made the early (sixth to

Figure 3.5 Amalekite Nomad Camel Infantry, 1200 B.C.E.

eighth centuries) Arab armies so successful. But it was a capability that the Amalekites did not possess.[86]

We might imagine, then, that Joshua took up positions at the rear of the Israelite column while its main body took refuge behind his soldiers in a narrow defile protected by hills on either side. The hills, if only moderately steep, would have prevented any flanking attack or envelopment by the Amalekite camels. Arranged in phalanx, Joshua's spear and shield infantry would have offered an impenetrable wall of spear-points, the first rank at the kneel with its spear-butts stuck in the ground and points elevated at 45 degrees, the second rank, standing, with its spears straight out, blades pointing at the camels' eyes. Behind the heavy spear infantry were Joshua's archers, probably armed with the Egyptian composite bow of greater range and penetrating power than the simple bow of the Amalekites. Behind the archers, perhaps scattered up both sides of the hills to get a better view, were the slingers capable of throwing stone shot the size of a tennis ball 300 yards or more. Although I discuss Israelite weaponry in detail later, if it can be granted for the moment that the weapons described were available to Joshua's men at Rephidim, then his defense as I have described it makes sound tactical sense.

The Amalekites could rush at the wall of spears time and again only to have their camels pull up short, like the horses at Paupen, as long as the Israelite infantry held fast. Every Amalekite attack would be subject to long-range slinger fire before it ever reached the wall of spears and shields. Once in close, Joshua's archers could pick off individual targets. While it cannot be proved, mercenary service in the army of Egypt might well have taught the Israelite archers the tactic of firing at the animals, much as Egyptian archers fired at the horses of enemy charioteers. If so, more animals than men may have died that day. Exodus 17:12–13 tells us that the battle lasted until sunset, and that when it was over "Joshua overwhelmed the people of Amalek with the edge of the sword." It is clear, of course, that from a defensive position Joshua could have done no such thing, since at any time the Amalekites could have broken off the attack on Joshua's fixed position and simply given up the fight. An Israelite infantry force could not have pursued and "overwhelmed" a camel-borne force with any hope of success, although it is possible that if some of the camel-archers had dismounted and attacked as infantry, these units could have been overwhelmed by the Israelites in close combat. What happened then? The text offers us a clue. The word used in the Hebrew text is *chalash* which means "weakened" and also "overcome," but the latter only in the sense of being overcome by weariness or weakness, not by force of arms. The more common meaning of *chalash* is "exhausted," meaning in the current context that Joshua exhausted the Amalekites.[87] This is exactly what we might expect from any cavalry force, horse or camel, as it threw itself again and again against a stubborn wall of disciplined infantry only to expose itself to archer and slinger (small arms) fire as it did so. Sooner or later the enemy commander would have concluded that he could not carry the day. Perhaps he waited until dusk, and turned for home.

Joshua and his men had fought well that day, living up to his reputation as a brave and resourceful warrior. Certainly the General must have been pleased, for from that day forward we find Joshua always at the General's side until the day came when Joshua replaced the General himself and led the Israelites into the Promised Land. As the General's second-in-command, whatever changes in the structure, organization, weapons, and tactics that were made in the Israelite military during the Exodus might well have been accomplished under some influence of Joshua. As we shall see, the Israelite army that emerged from Sinai and then later from Kadesh-Barnea was quite different from the one that left Egypt. And once it had been reformed, it became the instrument in the hands of Joshua that gained the Israelites the land of Canaan.

THE ARMY OF THE EXODUS

To this point I have argued that the Israelite *habiru* who left Egypt and made their way across the desert to Mount Sinai possessed a military arm of some type which they employed in self-defense or as mercenaries in the service of Egyptian kings. While it was possible to offer some reasonable assumptions about the weapons and tactics employed by this force—Joshua's battle with the Amalek—Exodus text tells us nothing about its size, organization, or structure. All this changes after the Israelites arrive at Mount Sinai and encamp there. Much of this time, as we shall see, was spent putting their religious and military house in order. Part of the effort was to create an organized army. Numbers 1:2–4 tells us that the General (the Lord) ordered Moses, "Take ye the sum of the congregation of the children of Israel, after their families, by the house of their father, with the number of their names, every male by their polls; from twenty years old and upward, all that are able to go forth to war in Israel; thou and Aaron shall number them by their armies. And with you there shall be a man of every tribe; everyone head of the house of their fathers." Until now, the professional warriors comprised the Israelite community's military arm in a manner similar to David's band of 600 *habiru* fighters in the service of the Philistine king. In neither case were the soldiers drawn from a tribal or family levy applicable to the entire community. In both cases the soldiers were military professionals, not conscripts. At Sinai the General ordered the Israelite military arm to be completely reformed, introducing for the first time a tribal and lineage levy from which conscripts were to be drawn. The new system surely integrated the professionals within it, most probably selecting the best as troop commanders. The old professional corps lived on in Israelite memory, however. Deuteronomy 2:14 recalls that prior to the assault on the Transjordan 38 years after the Exodus "the whole generation of soldiers had perished from the camp," a reference perhaps to the professional warriors who had led and protected Israel in the early days before the tribal militia. Even though we have no idea as to the size of the Israelite military arm prior to its reconstitution at Sinai, it is certain that the new arrangement expanded the size of the army considerably by making the manpower of the entire community available for military service. It was at Sinai, then, that the modern Israeli Defense Force may find the first evidence of its existence as a citizen army in which all eligible males of the community serve.

The census ordered by the General presents problems for the military historian in that when the numbers of eligible men are listed by tribe, the total number of men comes to 605,550. The second census recorded in Numbers 26 arrives at a figure of 601,730. Both estimates are clearly not possible even for Egypt with its population of almost 10 million. Both estimates are arrived at in the text by examining the census lists which record what appears to be the number of men available from each tribe *multiplied* by the number of units each of which is assumed to mean a unit of 1,000 men strong or an *eleph*.[88] The confusion and numerical inflation results from the use of the term *eleph* to mean 1,000. In fact, it later came to mean exactly that during the time of the monarchy when indeed there were military units of 1,000 men called *alaphim*. However, Mendenhall suggests that the authors of Numbers were writing during or shortly after the time of the monarchy and were familiar with the military system of the monarch and its 1,000 man units. When they reconstructed the census lists in Numbers 1 and 26 they used *eleph* to mean 1,000 thus multiplying the number of units by 1,000 producing extraordinarily high numbers.[89]

Citing Flinders Petrie's early work in 1903, Mendenhall argues that the numbers listed in the census texts are accurate, but miscalculated. Although the term *eleph* surely meant 1,000 during monarchical times, in Exodus times it did not. Instead, it designated a subsection of a tribe. An *eleph*, as understood by the original Exodus census takers, did not mean a military or tactical unit of 1,000 men but a population unit or subsection of the tribe. It was a social unit from which a certain number of fighting men were to be drawn to make up the total number of soldiers required from each tribe.[90] Read this way, the census lists can be adjusted to appear as they do in the table below. If the *number of alaphim* are divided into the total number of men to be levied from each tribe, one arrives at the total strength of the Israelite army in Sinai, or between 5,000 and 5,500 men.[91] This number tallies well with our knowledge of the size of other military forces of the period. Thus, the city of Mari could raise 4,000 troops while Shamsi-Adad of Assyria put 10,000 men in the field and the kingdom of Eshnunna 6,000 men.[92] Here it must be kept in mind that prior to the Iron Age the major limitation on military strength was not usually manpower, but the expense of equipment, especially bronze weapons and chariots which were incredibly costly.[93] The use of the *eleph* for

Table 3.1
Recalculated Size of Israelite Units by Tribe and Estimated Size of Israelite Army

	Numbers 1		*Numbers 26*		*I Chron 12*	
Tribe	Units	Men	Units	Men	Units	Men
Reuben	46	500	43	750[47]	(40)[48]	xxx
Simeon	59	300	22	200	7	100
Gad	45	650	40	500	(40)	xxx
Judah	74	600	76	500	6	800
Issachar	54	400	64	300		200 *rā'šîm* and their men[49]
Zebulun	57	400	60	500	50	xxx
Ephraim	40	500	32	500	20	800
Manasseh (Half-tribe)	32	200	52	700	18 (40)	xxx xxx
Benjamin	35	400	45	600	3	xxx
Dan	62	700	64	400	28	600[50]
Asher	41	500	53	400	40	xxx
Naphtali	53	400	45	400	37	1000 *śārîm*[51]
TOTALS	598	5550	596	5750	329	2300[52]

Source: George E. Mendenhall, "The Census Lists of Numbers 1 and 26," *Journal of Biblical Literature* 77 (1958): 52–66.

military recruitment as well as Moses' division of the people for judicial purposes into units of thousands, hundreds, fifties, and tens point to a major fact: the basis for Israelite political/military organization was not lineage, but territorial organization. Lineage existed, of course, but was of lesser importance since the social organization of early Israel was based on territorial divisions, as was the military draft.[94]

The revised census figures permit an estimate, albeit a highly speculative one, as to the size of the overall Israelite community at Sinai. Israelite men became eligible for military service at age 20, the same age as for military service in Egypt.[95] We do not know until what age soldiers remained in military service, but with the average age of death around 40 years, it was unlikely that one could get more than ten good years, perhaps 15 at the extreme, out of a soldier. If the 5,000 to 5,500 soldiers calculated by the census in Numbers are taken to represent between 20 and 25 percent of the population of the entire community, then the size of the Israelite community during the Exodus was between 20,000 and 25,000 people, far less than the 600,000 or so mentioned in the texts or 100,000 calculated by Lucas.[96] Both larger figures may be safely excluded on the grounds that the logistics of supporting such a large number of people on the march stagger the imagination.

Even the smaller number of 20,000 presents one with difficult, although not impossible, logistical problems in keeping the Israelites alive on their march through Sinai. The logistical tables of modern armies calculate that in the climate of the Middle East a soldier requires 3,402 calories a day and 70 grams of protein to sustain him in *minimal* nutritional condition. The standard military ration of the ancient world of three pounds of wheat per person per day provided only 2,025 calories per day, insufficient to maintain even minimal nutritional requirements for very long.[97] Normal water requirements are five quarts of water per day, but under desert climatic conditions both the U.S. Army and the Israeli Defense Force plan for nine quarts a day as a minimal requirement.[98] Oxen and cattle need to be fed and watered as well. A cow requires 8.3 kilograms of fodder a day and nine liters of water to stay alive.[99] Calculated as a daily logistical burden, then, the Israelite logistical officers would have had to provide 60,000 pounds of wheat, 1,400 kilograms or 3,080 pounds of protein (usually meat), and 140,000 quarts of water a day just to keep 20,000 people alive. The animals would have to graze where they could and, eventually, die or be slaughtered for food.

The Exodus text mentions severe shortages of food and water, implying that the Israelites must have eaten whatever animals they took with them out of Egypt. Even large herds of cattle, sheep, and goats would have been quickly exhausted with limited food and water to keep the animals alive. With no supply train nor anyone from whom to purchase supplies along the route, whatever grain supplies the Israelites carried with them would have been quickly consumed. The biblical tradition itself notes that a whole generation of the original population died in the wilderness, suggesting high losses to thirst and starvation. The text records several outbreaks of disease, during which thousands die each time. Gottwald suggests that the suffering, more than theological disputes or ritual offenses, was what caused the many revolts and power struggles recorded in the text. Often these resulted in large-scale killings of Israelites, further reducing the population. Although biblical tradition attributes the death of Moses to his rejection by Yahweh for a ritual offense, it is at least conceivable that the casualties during the trek were so high, the suffering so great, and the dissatisfaction with his leadership so intense that Moses himself was deposed, banished, or killed by the Israelites and never reached the land of Canaan. A loss rate of 33 percent is not unimaginable under harsh conditions over, say, two years. If the Israelites at Sinai numbered between 20,000 and 25,000, it is possible that the group that left Egypt was between 30,000 and 35,000 people. Given that the death rate on the march would have been highest among the old and sickly, those who survived the trek would have been mostly of an age where they could reproduce another generation at a higher fertility rate than usual. Within the 40 years recorded by the biblical tradition, the Israelites would have mostly regained their population strength and been ready to march on Canaan.

The battle of Rephidim may have brought the question of reorganizing the Israelite military arm to the attention of the General who, it seems, had already decided to install Joshua as his second-in-command. But how might the other experienced officers be used to best advantage? Exodus suggests that the answer was to establish a quasi-military judicial system that guaranteed the officers important social positions and established ethical qualifications for appointment. So began the system of Judges that governed Israelite society for the next 200 years. Exodus 18:25–26 tells us that "The General (Moses) selected men of competence from all Israel and set them heads over the people—rulers of thousands, rulers of hundreds, rulers of fifties, and rulers of tens. And they would judge the people at any time; the difficult matters they would bring to the General (Moses), and all small matters they would judge themselves." Here we find the establishment of the first Israelite judicial system, but it is a system with a decidedly quasi-military caste, one that may have as its first intention the organization of Israelite society along more structured military lines. The later period of the Judges reveals that all the *sophets* were military chiefs first and judicial officers second. The way the Exodus text describes the offices of the system and the men who held them suggests that the General (Moses) may have imposed a quasi-military chain of command upon the judicial system by using military men as judicial officers.[100] The text uses the term *sar* for "rulers" and *sophet* for "judges," and always distinguishes between them. *Sar* is a term most commonly associated with appointed military command and was used later to describe the appointed military commanders of Saul, David, and Solomon, whereas *sophet* connotes only a judicial officer. The text tells us that the appointees were "rulers of thousands, rulers of hundreds, rulers of fifties, and rulers of tens"—that is, military commanders—who also "judge the people at any time."

There is further evidence that the judges were primarily military men. In describing the qualifications of the judges, Exodus 18:21 says, "you shall seek out from among all the people men of competence who fear God, trustworthy men who spurn ill-gotten gain." The term used for "men of competence" is *Is hayil* which commonly connotes a warrior or military commander as well as a rich man or citizen of social influence.[101] Taken along with the term *sar*, it is reasonable to suggest that Israel's first judicial officers were appointed because they were experienced military men of sound character. The linking of sound character to both military command and judicial appointment provides us with the first clear statement in history of the importance of military ethics to leadership, a tradition still evident in the modern Israeli Defense Force's ethical military tradition of *tohar haneshek*.[102]

If the foregoing is correct, then when the Israelites arrived at Sinai the outline of a new civil-military organizational structure had already been put in place so that further reforms could proceed. When the General reorganized the military manpower system by extending military service to the entire community, the military-judicial structure devised previously provided a ready-made command and organizational structure through which the new manpower system could operate. As we shall see, this system persisted through Joshua's conquest of Canaan and the Period of the Judges until Saul reformed it, and, finally, David and Solomon attempted to replace it.

The building of a national army in Sinai may have included a renewed stress on martial spirit and courage, precisely the qualities that need to be instilled in conscripts. We might imagine that when the General (the Lord) addressed the assembled people as recorded in Leviticus 26:36–37, he warned of the terrible punishments he would inflict upon them if they did not obey his rules. One of these punishments was that the Israelites would be known as cowards.

> Those of you who survive in the land of their enemies I will make so fainthearted that, if leaves rustle behind them, they will flee headlong, as if from the sword, though no one pursues them; stumbling over one another as if to escape a weapon, while no one is after them—so helpless will you be to take a stand against your foes!

This is a classic example of the "death rather than dishonor" speech that has been given to new soldiers by commanders ever since armies first crawled upon the land, and one can easily imagine it being given to a group of modern IDF soldiers who are about to begin their conscript military service.

Whoever was in command at Sinai possessed an expert understanding of war and its human dimensions. One element of this human dimension is morale, and Deuteronomy 20:1–4 notes the moral strength that can clearly result from the soldier's faith in God. Be that as it may, troop commanders are very practical men, and it is clear that the Israelite officers possessed a keen understanding of the psychology of war. As in World War II when American divisions about to be sent into combat were repeatedly culled to remove potential psychiatric casualties from the ranks,[103] Israelite military commanders seem to have done the same thing. Deuteronomy 20:5–9 instructs troop commanders to remove certain kinds of people from the fighting ranks precisely because they were not likely to fight well.

> The officials shall address the troops as follows: "Is there anyone who has built a new house but has not dedicated it? Let him go back to his home, lest he die in battle and another dedicate it. Is there anyone who has planted a vineyard but has never harvested it? Let him go back to his home, lest he die in battle and another harvest it. Is there anyone who has paid the bride-price for a wife, but who has not yet married her? Let him go back to his home, lest he die in battle and another marry her." The officials shall go on addressing the troops and say, "Is there anyone afraid and disheartened? Let him go back to his home, lest the courage of his comrades flag like his." When the officials have finished addressing the troops, army commanders shall assume command of the troops.

All of these conditions are the kinds of problems that are likely to affect young men, the conscripts called to war, and not the more seasoned military professionals that comprised the warriors of the old *habiru*. The army of Israel was becoming a national army and now had to deal with problems of morale, fighting spirit, and psychiatric collapse that have afflicted all conscript armies from time immemorial. In requiring troop commanders to examine their troops according to a list of conditions that could reduce troop morale and fighting spirit, the Israelites may have introduced the first practical method of conducting military psychiatric screening.[104]

The practical bent of the Israelite commanders at Sinai is further evident in what appears to be the world's oldest manual on field hygiene, the instructions found in Leviticus and Deuteronomy. Disease and epidemic were the scourge of ancient armies, often causing more deaths and casualties than weapons.[105] The instructions contained in Leviticus and Deuteronomy make clear that the General and his commanders were aware of disease and contagion and prescribed a number of hygienic practices to keep the camp and the army from contracting and spreading disease. Some of the rules, such as those dealing with menstruating women or dietary restrictions, were based on religious requirements. But others have a strong pragmatic effect. The diagnosis and treatment of leprosy, rash, or discharge (infection?) as detailed in Leviticus, for example, require that the afflicted soldier remain outside the camp for seven days to avoid contagion. Even on the march the soldier must remain outside the main column, making do as best he can. To treat or inspect the infected soldier, the priest must go outside the camp, avoiding the risk of contagion if the soldier were to be brought to the priest. The Israelites recognized that disease may also spread through objects such as clothing, blankets, woven material, and even saddles. All these items had to be washed before the recovered soldier was permitted to rejoin the camp. The constant injunctions to wash one's hands before eating or after using the toilet and to wash one's clothes frequently are also excellent military hygienic practices.

Additional hygiene practices were more directly related to military life. Deuteronomy 23:13–14 required sanitary habits that were not practiced by the European armies until World War I! "Further, there shall be an area for you outside the camp, where you may relieve yourself." Separating the latrine from the camp and, most important, the water supply, was frequently not done even during the American Civil War. But separation was not sufficient by itself. "With your gear you shall have a spike (probably a small shovel), and when you have squatted you shall dig a hole with it to cover up your excrement." These two simple practices would have done much to reduce the rate and spread of disease in Israelite armies. Numbers 31:19–24 outlines procedures for dealing with those killed in battle, namely, corpses. Anyone who has killed a man in battle or touched a corpse must remain outside the camp for seven days. While the origin of the corpse taboo may be religious,[106] its practical effect was to reduce contagion by quarantining soldiers who had been exposed to blood, a common disease source. Ancient battles often involved close combat where blood might easily splatter on the soldier.[107] This concern is also reflected in the need to purify any weapons and clothing that have been exposed to blood. Metal weapons—"whatever can stand fire"—were required to be purified by fire. Other equipment, including booty, had to be washed before being brought into the camp.

I have tried to demonstrate that the Israelite army that marched out of Sinai "on the twentieth day of the second month of the second year" since leaving Egypt was a far cry from the original *habiru* force. Nowhere is this more clearly revealed than in the Israelite order of march employed in the departure from Sinai. It is only after the Sinai encampment that the Exodus texts reveal an order of march or military organization at all, forcing us to rely, as I have done, on conjecture and deduction before that. Now, in Numbers 10:11–28, we see clearly the combat organization of the new Israelite national army. Figure 3.6 portrays the Israelite order of march.

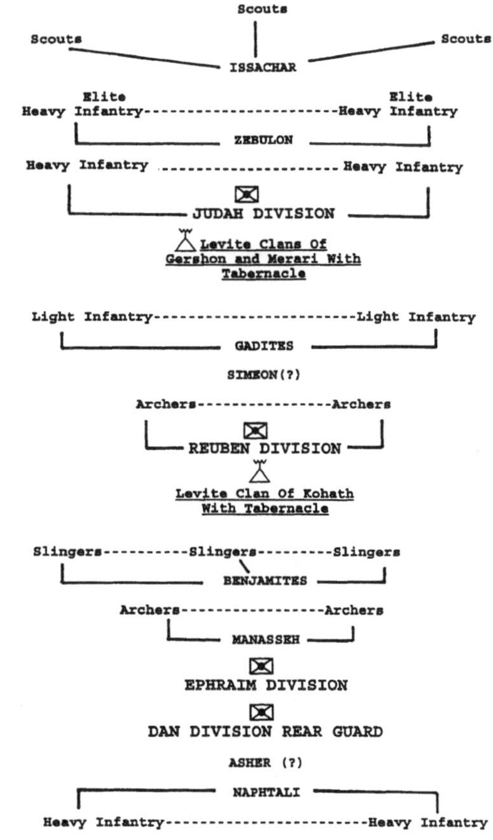

Figure 3.6 Israelite Order of Battle March Leaving Sinai

The column is divided into four divisions, each led by a tribal levy and containing two additional tribal levies within it. Between the Judah division are the clans of Gershon and Merari transporting the dismantled meeting tent while the clan of Kohath carries the sacred objects for the dwelling, presumably the Ark of the Covenant as well, behind the division of Reuben. One is immediately struck by the fact that the division of the column into four sections, each divided into three subdivisions, is the same general order of march found in the Egyptian army of the day.[108] When it is recalled that the military structure with which the Israelites were most familiar was the army of Egypt, it is not beyond reason that the Israelites might have adopted the Egyptian column of march order to their new army.

The combat arms order of the column can also be reconstructed by extrapolation from the military specialties attributed to each tribe in various places in the Old Testament. That tribes developed such combat arms specialties seems probable. The Beni-Hasan mural dating from the nineteenth century B.C.E. depicts a semitic clan entering Egypt and being recorded by pharaoh's officials. The mural depicts the full panoply of tribal arms: spear, sword, and bow. The metalsmith's bellows strapped to the donkey suggest that the tribe had its own craftsmen and armorers.[109] Chaim Herzog and Mordechai Gichon in their *Battles of the Bible* suggest that the development of military specialities during and after the Exodus is almost certain.[110] Moreover, the Israelite experience as mercenaries in the armies of Egypt would, at the very least, have acquainted them with the full range of Egyptian weapons and, as suggested earlier, they may have acquired such weaponry as well. Military specialization, therefore, is not out of the question. However, since the tribal basis of Israelite military organization was not instituted until the Sinai encampment, we may regard its further development as an Israelite innovation. A difficulty arises from the fact that the descriptions of tribal military specialties are *not* contained in the Exodus texts, but are found only in the later texts, making it somewhat uncertain as to whether these specialties also existed during the Exodus. Given that so much of Israelite military structure and practice of the Exodus period survived well into the period of the monarchy, it may well be a reasonable assumption that the military capabilities of the different tribes did so as well. Still, we cannot be certain that this was indeed the case.

Reconstructed in this manner, then, the Israelite column that marched out of Sinai had the Judah Division at its head. Far to the front were the men of Issachar whose special ability was "to know how to interpret the signs of the times, to determine how Israel should act."[111] These were the scouts who excelled at intelligence gathering and interpretation.[112] Behind them at the head of the column's main body were the men of Zebulon, elite heavy spear infantry who fought in phalanx, who "were expert with all instruments of war . . . who could keep rank."[113] Next in the column's van were the troops of Judah "equipped with shield and spear" as regular heavy infantry[114] protecting the disassembled tabernacle. Comprising the second division were the tribes of Reuben, Gad, and Simeon, an entire division of light troops capable of quick response in all directions. The Gadites were light infantry "armed with spear and buckler . . . and were as swift as the gazelles upon the mountains."[115] The troops of Simeon are mentioned only as "valiant men," and were probably light infantry as were the Reubenites skilled with the bow.[116] The Ephraim Division was third in line and was comprised mostly of missile troops, archers (Manasseh) and archer/slingers, the Benjaminites, "who gave support in battle; they were armed with the bow and could use both right and left hand to sling stones and shoot arrows with the bow."[117] There is no description of the combat capability of the Ephraimites. The Dan Division made up the column's rear guard. Aside from knowing that the men of Asher were "ready to man the battle line" (light or heavy infantry), there is no military capability given for Asher and Dan. The last place in the column was occupied by the men of Naphtali armed "with shield and lance," that is, heavy infantry.[118] It will not escape students of ancient armies that the distribution of combat capabilities by unit throughout the column, with the exception of chariot units, is very similar to the combat order of march employed by the Egyptian army. In a movement to contact, the Egyptian army would deploy its scouts, usually chariots, far forward of the main column. Next came the elite heavy infantry, the *nakhtu-aa*, literally, "the strong arm boys."[119] As the enemy approached, light infantry and archers would deploy through the front ranks and engage the enemy at a distance with the bow. As the enemy closed, the light forces withdrew behind the heavy units or retired to the flanks to continue indirect or enfilade fire.[120] As with the Israelites, the Egyptian arm of decision, the fame of its excellent chariot corps notwithstanding, was its infantry. Once more, perhaps, the Israelite experience in pharaoh's army might have made itself felt in the design of the Israelite combat column of march.

The encampment at Sinai was a momentous event in the history of the Israelites for it was there, under the command of a truly expert and experienced military commander of unknown name, that the Israelites formed a national people's army to replace the mercenary corps of the old *habiru* society. Israel was becoming a nation, and it instituted its first tribal levy to raise sufficient manpower for war, producing an army of 5,000 to 5,500 men from a society of 20,000 to 25,000 persons. It was at Sinai that the unknown General instituted the first formal command structure, quasi-judicial in nature, staffed by officers who met strict ethical standards, thus giving the world its first lesson in military ethics. Ceremonies were instituted to instill martial spirit in sometimes reluctant conscripts, as were regulations governing troop selection on psychiatric grounds, and camp hygiene. Last, the Israelite army assumed a combat formation that permitted it to protect itself as it moved from one place to another. The previous Israelite experience as Egyptian mercenaries seems to have been reflected in some of these reforms, although to what extent is uncertain. Two additional Israelite military innovations, however, are almost certain to have been influenced by their Egyptian experience: the Desert Tabernacle and the Levite praetorian guard.

THE DESERT TABERNACLE

In Exodus 25:8–9, the General commands Moses to construct a tent for him to live in, and in Exodus 26–27 and 36–38, he sets forth in great detail how and from what materials the tent is to be made. Indeed, this Desert Tabernacle is described in more detail than any other structure in the Bible, including the Jerusalem Temple itself.[121] What is of great interest is that the Tabernacle is nearly an exact copy of the Egyptian war tent portrayed in the reliefs of the war camp of Ramses II at the battle of Kadesh on the wall of the Great Hall at Abu Simbel.[122] This observation is not new and was first made by the famous Old Testament scholar Hugo Gressmann in 1913.[123] The parallels between the two camps are very strong, and the similarities in dimensions and layout are striking. Ramses' camp forms a rectangular courtyard twice as long as it is wide just as the Desert Tabernacle is rectangular in shape and is 100 cubits long and 50 cubits wide, the same ratio found in Ramses' camp.[124] Ramses' camp is oriented east to west, with the entrance in the eastern wall just as it is in the Desert Tabernacle. The orientation to the east is distinctly Egyptian in that the east is where the sun rises and where, each day, pharaoh greets his father, the sun god. This greeting was expressed in the saying "wak-

Ramses II's Camp

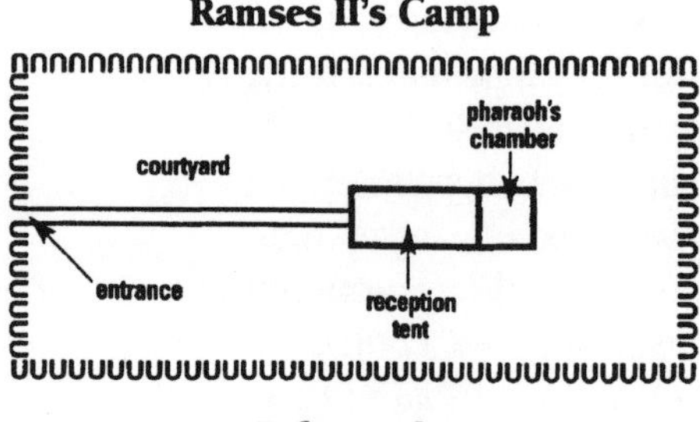

Tabernacle

holy of holies
courtyard
holy tent
entrance

Figure 3.7 Structural Similarity of Israelite Tabernacle with Egyptian Military Camp of Ramses II

ing in life in the tent of pharaoh."[125] All Egyptian monumental architecture is oriented toward the east, and it is probable that the Jewish religious ritual of praying while facing east at the start of a new day or the ancient Christian practice of burying a corpse with its head to the east to greet the sun on resurrection day may have Egyptian origins as well.

The entrance to Ramses' compound and the Desert Tabernacle is, for both, in the middle of the eastern wall with a path leading to the "reception tent" located in the middle of the walled-off compound. Pharaoh's tent is twice as long as it is wide, preserving the same ratio as the compound's outer walls. The "reception tent" of the Tabernacle is also twice as long as its height and width, preserving the same ratio, and in both cases the reception tent leads to a holy of holies that is square, not rectangular, like the reception tent.[126] The sides of each square are equal to the width of the reception tent in both cases. Figure 3.7 portrays the layout and relative dimensions of each structure. In the Egyptian camp the square tent holds pharaoh's golden throne, and it is from here that he holds his meetings with his generals or other important persons. The square tent of the Desert Tabernacle is where the Ark is kept and where Yahweh sits when he communicates with the Israelites.

What is most impressive, however, is the strong similarity of the *interiors* of both square tents, the respective holy of holies. The relief at Abu Simbel, reproduced in Figure 3.8, shows Ramses' cartouche, the Egyptian symbol of the presence of the god that Ramses was regarded to be, flanked on either side by a representation of the falcon god, Horus. The wings of Horus cover pharaoh's golden throne in a symbol of divine protection. The relief is starkly similar to the description of the wings of the two cherubim that cover and protect Yahweh's golden throne in the Tabernacle. Exodus 25:18–22 describes it this way:

> Make two cherubim of gold—make them of hammered work—at the two ends of the cover (of the Ark of the Covenant). . . . The cherubim shall have their wings spread out above, shielding the cover with their wings. They shall confront each other, the faces of the cherubim being turned toward the cover. . . . There I will meet with you, and I will impart to you—from above the cover, from between the cherubim that are on top of the Ark of the Covenant—all that I will command you concerning the Israelite people.

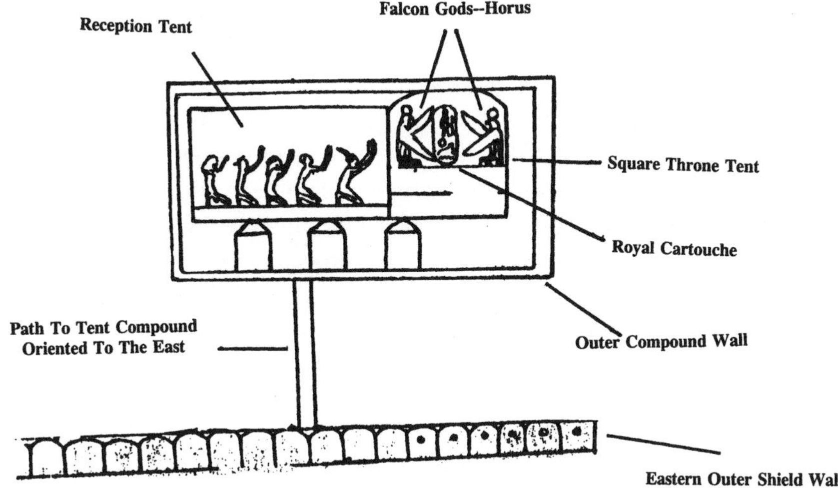

Figure 3.8 Abu Simbel Relief Portraying Ramses II's War Tent at the Battle of Kadesh

It would appear that the holy of holies of pharaoh and Yahweh are similar not only in design, but even in function. For both, it is the place where God speaks to his people.

The similarity between the Desert Tabernacle and Ramses II's war tent has remained a puzzle. One solution has been to suggest that the descriptions were taken from portrayals of Babylonian camps encountered by Israelite writers during the Captivity. Recent archeological research has ruled this out, however, since evidence shows that Babylonian military camps were round or oblong, not rectangular.[127] However, the dilemma remains only if the Israelites in Egypt are regarded as slaves, for as slaves they would have had no opportunity to examine or experience an Egyptian military camp. If, as I have suggested, however, the Israelite *habiru* were mercenaries in pharaoh's army, then surely their officers would have been familiar with an Egyptian camp. If so, when the Israelites first organized their national army at Sinai, the General may have decided that it was time for an appropriate command van as well and ordered that one be constructed along the lines of the model with which he was familiar, the Egyptian command tent. If so, as Homan observes, not only does the physical configuration of the Desert Tabernacle conform to the Egyptian command tent, "but it is also likely that Yahweh's portable tent originally had a military function similar to that of Ramses' camp."[128] Egyptian and Israelite texts describe Yahweh and pharaoh in similar terms as divine military warriors and commanders. Exodus 15:3 refers to Yahweh as "a man of war" and again as one "who fights single-handedly for Israel."[129] The identification of a divine pharaoh with military command is a common Egyptian perception and literary theme so that both pharaoh and Yahweh are often seen as divine warriors. Thus it may have been that like pharaoh's war tent, the Desert Tabernacle may have been regarded as a mobile military headquarters from which Yahweh, traveling with the Israelites, led his people to victory in Canaan.

The explanation offered above solves only part of the puzzle. It is true that service in pharaoh's army by Israelite mercenaries would have made it possible for them to see pharaoh's command tent and compound, but only from the *outside*. The similarities of Yahweh's and pharaoh's *inner chamber* are too detailed not to have been designed by someone who had gained entrance to pharaoh's inner sanctum. How would this have been possible for Israelite officers to achieve? The answer *may* lie in my earlier speculation that some Israelite units *may* have served in pharaoh's, perhaps Akhenaten's, praetorian guard just as the Egyptian reliefs of Semitic special units at Akhenaten strongly suggest. A praetorian guard would have protected the king's person around the clock and have been quite familiar with the inside of pharaoh's command tent where at least some of their guard stations would have been located. If so, perhaps this explains why the General ordered the creation of his own praetorian guard at Sinai.

The Praetorian Guard

The question is immediately raised as to where the Israelites obtained the idea of a praetorian guard since such an institution among a band of *habiru* would have been unlikely. The *habiru* military arm was small, ultimately democratic insofar as position depended on demonstrated military competence and had no territorial or institutional base given the size and relative complexity of *habiru* society. After Sinai, however, Israelite society changed toward a genuine national tribal society with a semipermanent military establishment supported by a quasi-judicial organizational structure around which to raise and organize a national army. Under these changed conditions, a praetorian guard might have appeared possible and even necessary, especially so if the General anticipated some resistance to the new institution of military conscription. While not typical of *habiru* armies, elite military units serving as personal bodyguards to the kings of the Middle East were permanent elements of the military establishments of the major powers of the day. They were known in Egypt and elsewhere as "troops of the feet," literally, those who serve at the king's feet and were charged with protecting his person on and off the battlefield. It was the Levites that would have served as the General's praetorian guard just as, perhaps, some Israelite *habiru* had once served pharaoh.

In the Exodus texts, the Levites are singled out by the General (the Lord) for special status. Unlike the other tribes, they are exempt from military conscription and are given no territorial status with lands of their own. The Levite clans—Gershon, Kohath, and Merari—are given the task of guarding, dismantling, assembling, transporting, and otherwise attending the Desert Tabernacle, the command tent of the General. Numbers 3:12 makes it clear that the Levites are a clan apart, in service only to the General. "I hereby take the Levites from among the Israelites in place of all the first-born, the first issue of the womb among the Israelites: The Levites, therefore, are mine." Like all praetorians, their loyalty to their commander extends even to the use of violence against their kinsmen. That the Levites would do so against their kinsmen is clear enough from the incident recorded in Exodus 32:26–29. The people had created a golden calf while Moses was away atop Mount Sinai. Upon his return, he witnessed this idolatry and flew into a rage. Fearing that the "people were out of control . . . the General [Moses] stood up in the gate of the camp and said, 'Whoever is for the General [Lord], come here!' And all the Levites rallied to him. He said to them . . . 'Each of you put sword on thigh, go back and forth from gate to gate throughout the camp, and slay brother, neighbor, and kin.' The Levites did as the General (Moses) had bidden; and some three thousand of the people fell that day." Then, as if to assuage the conscience of the Levites who had just slaughtered their kinsmen and, perhaps, even family members, the General made them swear an oath of loyalty to him. He said, "Dedicate yourselves to the General (Lord)—for each of you has been against son and brother—that He may bestow a blessing upon you today."[130] If there was an Israelite praetorian guard, it did not survive very long, perhaps because of other incidents like the one at the foot of Mount Sinai. We hear of the Levites as armed police in a few additional instances, but never again after Moses himself dies. Once Joshua assumes command of the Israelite army, the Levites are heard of only as religious guardians of the Ark. There is nothing resembling a special military unit or palace guard until the time of Saul and David. Perhaps the Israelite experience with the institution was a negative one. In any event, if there was an Israelite praetorian guard at Sinai, it apparently did not survive the death of the General who created it.

FROM KADESH TO CANAAN

Having spent much of their time at Sinai reorganizing, replenishing, and, we might reasonably presume, training their new national army, the Israelites set out "in the second year, on the 20th day of the second month"[131] to return to Canaan prepared, if necessary, to fight their way in. After a few days' march, they camped in the desert of Paran. In sound military fashion the General of the Israelites prepared for the invasion by ordering a thorough reconnaissance of his objective. He assembled a task force of 12 men, one from each tribe, and placed the reliable Joshua in command. The General instructed them to "[g]o up there into the Negeb and on into the hill country and see what kind of country it is. Are the people who dwell in it strong or weak, few or many? Is the country in which they dwell good or bad? Are the towns they lie in open or fortified? Is the soil rich or poor? Is it wooded or not? And take pains to bring back some of the fruit of the land."[132] Here is one of the earliest examples in military history of a complete intelligence brief listing all the important operational requirements of the enemy force about which one must have knowledge prior to battle. The emphasis on sound intelligence introduced by the General in the Paran Desert remained strongly integrated into Israelite military thinking, for we find it again and again in the other books of the Old Testament. Joshua's use of scouts and the intelligence provided by the harlot of Jericho is, perhaps, the best example. In modern times the intelligence branches of the Israeli Defense Force enjoy high reputations as being among the best in the world. The General instructed his reconnaissance task force to return within 40 days. In the meantime he moved the main body of the Israelite army up to Kadesh-Barnea, closer to his objective, and there rendezvoused with the returning task force.

The news was not good. The scouts reported a land of difficult terrain, inhabited by fierce and strong people with adequate armies and large fortified cities. Worse, the three main avenues of advance were blocked by powerful enemy armies and fortifications.[133] All the scouts concurred in the report except Joshua and Caleb, probably his aide, who argued that bold action (and faith in God) could carry the day. Here we see the first hints of the self-confidence, courage, daring, and risk that characterized the tactics of Joshua's later campaigns. Napoleon once observed that the commander's instinct was the same as that of a professional gambler. Joshua was willing to risk it all in one bold campaign for Canaan. But Joshua was not yet in command, and the General's calmer head prevailed. There would be no attack. One gathers from the text that the General agreed that the Israelite army was not yet ready for a full-scale campaign against the more militarily sophisticated Canaanite armies. If my earlier analysis concerning the loss rates the Israelites may have suffered on the march to Sinai is correct, it is probable that the Israelite army was still too small when compared with its adversaries in Canaan and, perhaps, comparatively underequipped. And so the Israelites remained at Kadesh-Barnea for a long time, though certainly not 40 years, but perhaps long enough for a new generation to reach military age and increase the size of the army.

At some later time, Deuteronomy 2:14 tells us it was 38 years later, the Israelite army departed Kadesh-Barnea, crossed the Wadi Zered, and entered the Transjordan taking the eastern route toward Canaan. Apparently the Canaanite forces encountered earlier remained sufficiently formidable to convince the General to seek another route. This one also had its risks and took the Israelites through hostile territory. The strategic goal was to reach Canaan, and to accomplish this, the General decided to fight only when he had to, employing negotiation when he could, and taking circuitous routes of march to avoid battle. In attempting passage through Edom and Arad, the Israelite route was blocked by hostile armies. Except for what appear to have been minor skirmishes, the General refused to offer battle, choosing instead to march around the two lands. In Moab, too, he adjusted his route of march to avoid battle. But like Caesar at the Rubicon, once the General and his army crossed the Arnon River, the boundary between Moab and the land of the Ammonites, there was no avoiding a fight. With Moab to their rear, the harsh desert to their right, and the Dead Sea blocking maneuver to the left, there was no choice but to fight. In addition, the land of Ammon was the strategic platform from which the General intended to launch the Israelite invasion of Canaan itself. The two armies met at Jahaz, on the edge of the desert, and here the new Israelite national army gained its first major triumph of arms. The Ammonite army was completely destroyed. As often happened in the ancient world, the defeat of the army left the rest of the country open to conquest and occupation. The Israelites occupied the entire country from the Arnon River in the south to the Jabbok River in the north and east as far as the border.

It was in the Ammonite campaign that the Israelite army seems to have revealed an important new military capability. Not all of the towns surrendered without a fight, and apparently some of them had to be taken by force. Deuteronomy 2:36 tells us of the Israelite storming of these towns: "no city was too well fortified for us to whom the Lord had delivered them." The text also distinguishes clearly between major fortified towns and *bat*, "daughter" towns, the smaller unfortified villages and settlements around them. The same distinction between fortified and unfortified towns/settlements is found again in Numbers 33:41 describing the campaign in Gilead where "we campaigned against the tent villages." After their victory and settlement of Ammon, the Israelites attacked the kingdom of Gilead to the north. Here again we find the Israelite army subduing fortified towns. Deuteronomy 3:3–5 describes the victory over King Og at Edrei. "We defeated him so completely that we left him no survivor. At that time we captured all his cities, none of them eluding our grasp, the whole region of Argob, the kingdom of Og in Bashan: sixty cities in all, to say nothing of the great number of unwalled towns. All the cities were fortified with high walls and gates and bars." It would appear from the textual evidence that the Israelite commanders knew well enough the distinction between genuine fortifications, "tent villages," and unfortified towns and had developed the operational capability to subdue them all. Lacking any evidence of a siege capability (unsupported by the text in any case), the Israelites must have taken these strong-points by storm.

What evidence there is concerning the military capabilities of the armies of Moab, Edom, Ammon, and Gilead suggests that the Israelite account of the battles is fundamentally accurate. It is likely that the old Canaanite cities of these areas had given way, sometime after 1300, to the rise of what Gottwald calls "national states," by which he means a conglomeration of peoples—

Moabites, Ammonites, Edomites, and so on—much like the Israelites who moved into the area and, in the manner of the later Philistines, imposed their rule upon the Canaanites.[134] These kingdoms developed monarchies early on and had a strong central political organization. Much of the population lived in towns,[135] some of them fortified. The fortifications were probably originally built by Canaanites along traditional lines, which means, of course, that they were very substantial indeed. The military organization was probably based upon a small standing army (like the later Philistines) imposed upon a tribal or lineage levy.[136] The armies were primarily infantry, although there is a letter that on one occasion an Ammon king hired chariots from Mesopotamia.[137] Since there is no mention of chariots in the text, we may safely assume that the armies the Israelites defeated were infantry armies.

The textual and archaeological evidence suggests, therefore, that the Israelite army that conquered the Transjordan had become a formidable fighting force indeed. It fought well-organized and disciplined armies and defeated them all. At Jahaz, the terrain forced the battle to occur on an open plain. To fight in the open requires a highly disciplined army, one capable of maintaining formations and tactical maneuver, directed by experienced commanders who could orchestrate the tactical employment of various types of units, heavy infantry, light infantry, archers, and slingers. Moreover, to have won at Jahaz the Israelite army would have had to have been at least close to the size of its adversaries, otherwise it would have been suicide to stand in the open plain against an adversary that had greatly superior numbers. Given that we know the size of other armies of this period to have been around 6,000 to 10,000 men, the earlier estimate of the Israelite army as having been between 5,000 and 5,500 strong (i.e., before any increase at Kadesh-Barnea) might be generally correct. Finally, the Transjordan campaign provides the first evidence that the Israelite army was sufficiently powerful to carry a fortified town by storm, although we are not told how this might have been accomplished.

It was by force of arms, then, that the Israelites had captured the territory from the Arnon River to the foothills of Mount Hermon, comprising all the cities of the plateau and all of Gilead. While some Israelite elements remained in the north, the main body of Israelites settled in the plains of Moab, the lowlands to the northeast of the Dead Sea between Jordan and the foothills below Mount Nebo. Here they remained until another great general, Joshua, led them across the Jordan into Jericho in a military campaign that was to complete the return of the Israelites to Canaan. It was, as I have tried to show, a very different military force that crossed the Wadi Zered than had crossed the Reed Sea. As a consequence of considerable trial and experience, the military arm of the Israelite *habiru* had developed into a genuine national militia army. Its leadership had been transformed from a coterie of mercenaries into an officer corps drawn from among the people on the basis of competence and warrior spirit. Its military formations, hardly evident at all at the Reed Sea, had been transformed into those readily familiar to the army of Egypt, especially so in the column of march formation. The same is probably true as to its mix of weaponry, although the sling never achieved the same importance in the army of Egypt as it did in the army of Israel.

All this seems to have been carried out under the direction of an experienced senior officer whom I have called the General. That the Israelites themselves and, perhaps, even the authors of the Exodus texts may have come to regard such a great commander as somehow possessed of divinity or near divinity is hardly surprising in light of Egypt's belief that their pharaoh, their chief military commander, was also a god, a concept shared by other cultures and armies of the day. What I hope is clear from the preceding analysis, however, is that the Exodus texts reveal the beginning and initial development of an Israelite tradition of arms and, thus, a military history, evident long before Joshua's campaign against Canaan began. In this sense, then, the military history of ancient Israel can be said to have begun much earlier than has commonly been thought to have been the case.

NOTES

1. General Sir Richard Gale, *Great Battles of Biblical History* (New York: John Day Company, 1970), 13.
2. B.S.J. Isserlin, *The Israelites* (London: Thames and Hudson, 1998), 62.
3. The classic work on this phenomenon is still Thomas S. Kuhn, *The Structure of Scientific Revolutions* (Chicago: University of Chicago Press, 1962).
4. I am deeply indebted to Dr. Joel T. Klein, Ph.D. in ancient languages, rabbi, psychologist, and author for helping me translate and understand the roots and derivations of the Hebrew words that appear herein.
5. See Richard A. Gabriel, *Gods of Our Fathers: The Memory of Egypt in Judaism and Christianity* (Westport, CT: Greenwood Press, 2001), 74; M. Rostovtzeff, "The Foundations of Social and Economic Life in Hellenistic Times," *Journal of Egyptian Archaeology* 6 (1920): 176; H. Idris Bell, "Hellenic Culture in Egypt," *Journal of Egyptian Archaeology* 8 (1922): 145.
6. Gabriel, 11.
7. Rostovtzeff, 170.
8. Richard A. Gabriel and Karen S. Metz, "Egypt," chap. 3, in *A History of Military Medicine* (Westport, CT: Greenwood Press, 1992).
9. Perhaps the two best works on the Amarna period are Donald B. Redford, *Akhenaten: The Heretic King* (Princeton, NJ: Princeton University Press, 1984) and Cyril Aldred, *Akhenaten: King of Egypt* (London: Thames and Hudson, 1988).
10. James H. Breasted, *The Dawn of Conscience* (New York: Charles Scribner, 1947), 349.
11. Ibid.; see also Nicolas Grimal, *History of Ancient Egypt* (London: Blackwell Publishers, 1992), 219.

12. H. H. Rowley, *From Joseph to Joshua* (London: Oxford University Press, 1948), 55.

13. Isserlin, 52.

14. Ibid.

15. Karen Armstrong, *A History of God* (New York: Ballantine Books, 1993), 11.

16. Martin Buber, *Moses: The Revelation and the Covenant* (Amherst, NY: Humanity Books, 1998), 25.

17. Norman K. Gottwald, *The Tribes of Yahweh* (Maryknoll, NY: Orbis Books, 1979), 352–59.

18. Ibid.

19. Buber, 24.

20. Gottwald, 454.

21. Ibid., 453.

22. Buber, 24.

23. Gottwald, 454.

24. Ibid., 408.

25. Ibid.

26. Ibid., 397.

27. Ibid., 402.

28. Ibid., 403.

29. Nigel Stillman and Nigel Tallis, *Armies of the Ancient Near East* (Sussex, UK: Flexiprint Ltd., 1984), 83.

30. Rowley, 116.

31. Gabriel, *Gods of Our Fathers*, 54.

32. Redford, 28. So common were Asiatics in Egyptian marketplaces that the hieroglyph "to haggle" literally translates as "to do Syrian business."

33. Buber, 21.

34. Rowley, 116.

35. Breasted, *Dawn of Conscience*, 306.

36. Akhenaten almost certainly suffered from either Frohlich's syndrome or Marfan's disease, either of which would have made any sustained physical effort very difficult if not impossible. The reliefs are almost certainly propaganda portraying the king as physically vigorous when he most probably was not. See Gabriel, *Gods of Our Fathers*, 39–41, for more on Akhenaten's physical condition.

37. A. R. Schulman, "Some Remarks on the Military Background of the Amarna Period, *Journal of the American Research Center in Egypt* 3 (1964): 52.

38. Ibid.

39. Ibid., 58.

40. Ibid., 52.

41. Jonathan Kirsch, *Moses: A Life* (New York: Ballantine Books, 1998), 32.

42. Sir Alan Gardiner, *Egypt of the Pharaohs* (London: Oxford University Press, 1961), 258; Rowley, 132; Grimal, 258.

43 H. M. Wiener, "The Historical Character of the Exodus," *Ancient Egypt* IV (1926): 108.

44. Rowley, 23.

45. Grimal, 248–50.

46. Edouard Naville, "The Geography of the Exodus," *Journal of Egyptian Archaeology* 10 (1924): 19–25, for the geographic locations of the two cities.
47. Ibid.
48. When David and his troops arrived to help the Philistine kings against Saul at the battle of Gilboa, the Philistines feared that David could not be trusted to remain loyal and fight against his own kinsman and so was sent from the battlefield and did not participate in the battle that followed.
49. Peter A. Clayton, *Chronicle of the Pharaohs* (London: Thames and Hudson, 1994), 147.
50. Ibid.
51. William H. C. Propp, *Exodus 1–18: The Anchor Bible* (New York: Doubleday, 1998), 487.
52. Ibid.
53. Ibid., 488.
54. Interestingly, in modern armies the term for unmotorized infantry is "leg infantry."
55. Propp, 414.
56. Quintus Curtius, *History of Alexander*, Book V, ii, 7, trans. John C. Rolfe (Cambridge: Harvard University Press, 1946), 345.
57. Ibid.
58. Propp, 489.
59. Ibid., 549.
60. Ibid.
61. Naville, 24.
62. Exodus 8:22–24.
63. Propp, 490.
64. Chaim Herzog and Mordechai Gichon, *Battles of the Bible* (Jerusalem: Steimatzky's Agency, 1978), 21.
65. Diodorus Siculus I, 30, 4.
66. Exodus 14:2–3.
67. Exodus 14:20.
68. Propp, 499.
69. Ibid.
70. Exodus 14:21–23.
71. Ibid.
72. Naville, 39.
73. Gottwald, 454.
74. Numbers 10:31.
75. The General's Midianite connection may help explain why the first part of the trek aimed at reaching Mount Sinai. The names of Moses' relatives suggest that they might have been Kenites, one translation of which is "metalsmiths." From antiquity, copper has been mined in the Sinai, including the area around Mount Sinai. Copper mines usually have smelters, especially if engaged in bronze manufacture, which give off large plumes of smoke and, at night, a red glow from the fires needed to extract the ore. If such a mine and smelter was located on one of Mount Sinai's ridges high above the desert and if some of Moses' relatives were employed there or even owned it, this might explain why Moses wanted to reach the mountain. Also, to

the Israelites waiting on the open plain, Moses' ascent up Mount Sinai into the smoke and glow from the fire might have indeed appeared miraculous.

76. Exodus 17:9.

77. Ibid.

78. Exodus 17:13.

79. Richard A. Gabriel, *The Culture of War* (Westport, CT: Greenwood Press, 1990), 44; see also Yigael Yadin, *The Art of War in Biblical Lands in Light of Archaeological Discovery* (New York: McGraw-Hill, 1963), 79.

80. Gabriel, *The Culture of War*, 39–40, for the difficulty of bronze manufacture and the impact of iron on the supply of weapons. For greater detail of bronze manufacture, see Clarence H. Long, *Encyclopedia Britannica*, s.v. "metallurgy."

81. George E. Mendenhall, "The Census Lists of Numbers 1 and 26," *Journal of Biblical Literature* 77 (1958): 54.

82. Ibid., 55.

83. Stillman and Tallis, 106.

84. Gottwald, 448.

85. Stillman and Tallis, 221.

86. The difference in combat capability was that the Amalekites were light infantry, mostly bowmen, whereas the later Arab camel infantry were heavy infantry which, when dismounted, could hold their own against rival heavy infantry.

87. I wish to express my sincere gratitude to my old and dear friend Dr. Reuven Gall, president of the Carmel Institute in Israel, for his insight and help concerning the battle of the Amalek.

88. Mendenhall, 59.

89. Ibid.

90. Ibid., 60–62.

91. Ibid.

92. Ibid., 64.

93. For the cost of maintaining chariot forces, see Robert Drews, *The End of the Bronze Age* (Princeton, NJ: Princeton University Press, 1993), 110.

94. Mendenhall, 64–65.

95. T. R. Hobbs, *A Time for War* (Wilmington, DE: Michael Glazier, 1989), 78.

96. A. Lucas, "The Number of Israelites at the Exodus," *Palestine Exploration Quarterly* (1944): 164–68.

97. Richard A. Gabriel and Karen S. Metz, *From Sumer to Rome: The Military Capabilities of Ancient Armies* (Westport, CT: Greenwood Press, 1991), 23.

98. Ibid., 153.

99. Mordechai Gichon, "The Siege of Masada," *Collection du Centre des Etudes Romaines et Gallo-Romaines*, no. 20 (Lyon, 2000): 543.

100. Propp, 632.

101. Ibid.

102. For an analysis of the IDF's doctrine of *tohar haneshek*, see Reuven Gal, chap. 12, in *A Portrait of the Israeli Soldier* (Westport, CT: Greenwood Press, 1986).

103. Richard A. Gabriel, *No More Heroes: Madness and Psychiatry in War* (New York: Hill and Wang, 1987), 87–88.

104. For a history of psychiatric screening in war, see Gabriel, *No More Heroes*, chap. 4.

105. Gabriel and Metz, *From Sumer to Rome*, 99–104.

106. A. S. Yahuda, "The Osiris Cult and the Designation of Osiris Idols in the Bible," *Journal of Near Eastern Studies* 3 (1944): 194–97.

107. For the blood taboo of the Jews, see Morton Smith, *Jesus the Magician* (New York: Barnes and Noble, 1997), 123.

108. See the description of the Egyptian army in chap. 2 of this work.

109. *The Westminster Historical Atlas to the Bible* (Philadelphia: Westminster Press, 1945), 23, for a portrayal of the Ben-Hassan relief.

110. Gichon, 20.

111. I Chronicles 12:33.

112. Gichon, 85.

113. I Chronicles 12:34.

114. I Chronicles 12:25.

115. I Chronicles 12:9.

116. I Chronicles 12:37.

117. I Chronicles 12:1–2.

118. I Chronicles 12:35.

119. See chap. 2 of this work for a description of Egyptian infantry.

120. Richard A. Gabriel and Donald W. Boose Jr., *The Great Battles of Antiquity* (Westport, CT: Greenwood Press), 49–50.

121. Michael M. Homan, "The Divine Warrior in His Tent: A Military Model for Yahweh's Tabernacle," *Bible Review* 16, no. 6 (December, 2000): 22. Homan is a professor at Hebrew University.

122. Ibid., 28.

123. Ibid., 55.

124. Ibid., 30.

125. Ibid.

126. Ibid.

127. Ibid., 55.

128. Ibid., 24.

129. Exodus 14:15.

130. Exodus 32:29.

131. Numbers 10:11.

132. Numbers 13:17–20.

133. Numbers 13:25–31 for the intelligence briefing listing the items to be examined by the reconnaissance task force.

134. Gottwald, 426.

135. Stillman and Tallis, 187.

136. Ibid.

137. Ibid.

4

The Campaigns of Joshua

One cannot read the book of Joshua without coming away convinced that it is a saga of military conquest. Despite the obvious problems of *reflection*—the rewriting of history by authors long after the events themselves—and *telescoping*—portraying disparate events in the order of a single military campaign[1]—there is no doubt that the conquest tradition narrative as transmitted is the story of the land of Israel taken by force of arms. The idea of a group of nomadic fugitive slaves without military tradition or skills overcoming the powerful warrior states of Canaan with their superior military technologies and professional field armies struck many as unbelievable on its face and led to the search for other explanations for the settlement of the Israelite tribes in Palestine. Two hypotheses explaining the emergence of the Israelites were offered. The first held that there had been a gradual and generally peaceful infiltration and settlement of Israelite seminomadic groups into the sparsely occupied hill country distant from the Canaanite urban centers. Although there may have been occasional local conflicts, they did not involve large-scale confrontations with the Canaanite warrior states.[2] A second hypothesis suggested that Canaan experienced the revolt of an oppressed peasant population which gradually coalesced around a newly arrived band of fugitives from Egypt who brought with them a new religion that was egalitarian in orientation. Over time, the disparate groups within Canaan became Yahwehists and adopted the central saga of the Israelites as their own.[3] It is important to note that these hypotheses drew some strength from archaeology or, more correctly, the failure of archaeology to give strong support to the conquest hypothesis. If there had been a military campaign, the argument runs, there would be clear indicators of it. One would expect to find evidence of destroyed settlements, both urban and rustic; new types of settlements and dwellings; changes in weaponry, wares, and ceramic styles; new religious installations; new place and personal names; and evidence from cemeteries. Few of these indicators have been found in Israel to support the conquest hypothesis. But this is the argument from silence, that is, the stones do not speak! As B.S.J. Isserlin has so carefully documented, often the stones remain quiet. Isserlin compared three examples of known military conquests—the Norman conquest of England, the Anglo-Saxon invasion of England, and the Muslim conquest of the Levant—for evidence of the same archeological indicators applied to the Israelite conquest. He found that none of the indicators were decisive in providing sufficient evidence of military conquest in any of the three known cases where we know for certain that it occurred.[4] Accordingly, the case for a military conquest by the Israelites cannot be excluded.

The idea of an Israelite military conquest is sound enough if one examines the assumptions upon which *the case for its rejection* is made. First, the notion of an unsophisticated Israelite military force defeating the warrior states of Canaan over a prolonged campaign seems improbable on the face of it. But why should this be so? Two of the world's most powerful and militarily sophisticated empires, Rome and Byzantium, fell to "barbarian" armies of much less sophistication. It was Germanic horse-borne heavy infantry that defeated the Roman legions and the camel-borne (and later horse-borne) infantries of the Arabs that dealt decisive military defeats to Byzantium. In modern times, the military forces of national liberation movements have repeatedly defeated more powerful and militarily sophisticated colonial armies. Second, the assumption of Israelite military inferiority is based upon the prior assumption that the Israelites were nomadic ex-slaves completely without military tradition, experience, and expertise. As I have attempted to demonstrate in the previous chapter, this was not the case. As we shall see, Joshua's army was hardly the ill-trained, underequipped militia it has often been presumed to have been. Third, the assumption that the Canaanite states were so militarily powerful as to make the possibility of their defeat at the hands of the Israelites unthinkable needs to be examined more closely. The military capability of the Canaanite states at the time of the Israelite invasion was far weaker than it had been only a century before, and this weakness, along with other factors, leveled the field of armed combat considerably.

CANAANITE MILITARY CAPABILITY

The military reputation of the Canaanite warrior states of southern Palestine lived on long after it had ceased to be accurate. The feudal warrior states of Canaan and their powerful armies were the legacy of the Hyksos invasion. The New Kingdom pharaohs drove the Hyksos from the Nile Delta and pursued them through Canaan imposing a colonial regime, complete with military garrisons, upon the country. Egyptian rule waxed and waned over Canaan from 1550 to 1235 B.C.E. when Pharaoh Merneptah imposed virtual military occupation upon the cities of southern Canaan, including Yenoam, Ashkelon, and Gezer, which had been left as autonomous entities during Ramses II's previous attempt to reassert Egyptian control over the region.[5] The Egyptian method of rule was indirect for most of this period, permitting the once-powerful Canaanite states to exist, but weakening all of them by playing them off against each other as it encouraged local conflicts among the rival kings. Sometimes Egyptian forces were used to put down local revolts, and over time the Egyptians seem to have insisted that the military establishments of these city-states be considerably reduced.[6] During the Amarna period (1400–1350 B.C.E.), the 379 documents and letters that have come down to us make it clear that a half-dozen relatively powerful city-states dominated central-southern Palestine: Biridiya of Megiddo, Labayu of Shechem, Milkilu of Gezer, Abudu-Hepa of Jerusalem, Zimdreda of Lachish, and Shuwardata of Keilah.[7]

Over the next 100 years, these Canaanite states, ruled by warrior aristocracies equipped with large chariot armies, fell into decline. At the time of Joshua's invasion, the number of major states in south-central Palestine had increased to nine, thereby reducing the land base of each state. Further fragmentation was evident in the rise of other small cities such as the Hivite cities of Gibeon, Beeroth, Chephirah, and Kirjath-bal, as well as Jericho and Bethel, that competed for the arable land. The amount of land controlled by each city-state was crucial to its military power. The warrior aristocracy was based on feudal land holdings, as was the national treasury on taxes taken from the land. Reduced land meant a smaller chariot warrior class while reduced taxes forced the reduction of paid professional infantries as well. In addition, of course, the size of the urban populations declined, reducing the manpower base that could be called upon to defend the city if attacked. Malamat notes that an analysis of the Amarna letters reveals that the military establishments of these once powerful states had become much smaller.[8] The letters mention Canaanite forces of ten to 50 men while a chariot force of 50 was considered quite extraordinary for the day.[9] In one letter the prince of Lachish asks for a consignment of six bows, three daggers, and three swords, weapons sufficient to equip no more than 12 men.[10] It is a reasonable conclusion, then, that by the time of the Israelite invasion the once powerful chariot armies of the city-states of Canaan were mostly a thing of the past replaced by much smaller forces of infantry and chariots.

This was also the time of considerable in-migration of peoples and the emergence of the *habiru* so that the population of Canaan became ethnically and linguistically mixed. The Bible records the Canaanites as being comprised of seven distinct peoples: Amorites, Jebusites, Hivites, Hittites, Girgashites, and Perizzites. These peoples, some recently arrived, were often at each other's throats over local issues, and we are on safe ground to assume that the peoples of Palestine at the time of the Israelite invasion had developed no single ethnic or national consciousness.[11] One consequence of this state of affairs and the rivalry between city-states was that there was no overarching military or organizational means of creating a united resistance to the Israelite incursion. There was no political cohesion sufficient to forge a united military front against the invaders. Thus it was that no one attempted to stop the Israelites from crossing the Jordan, a major strategic mistake, and even when Israelite intentions were clear after the attack on Jericho, no one came to the city's aid. Only twice do we witness Canaanite states acting in coalition against the Israelites, once when the five southern states joined to oppose Joshua after the Gibeon agreement, and again when Jabin of Hazor assembled a coalition to prevent Joshua's northern advance. The failure to act in concert against the common Israelite threat permitted Joshua to determine the time and pace of engagement picking off his enemies one at a time.

Clausewitz correctly notes that national power is a consequence of military capabilities *and* national will, that is, some direction from the political center as to the ends, ways, and means of national defense is required for success. One without the other is insufficient. From this perspective we have reason to question the assumption by those who hold that a successful Israelite invasion was impossible because the disparity of power between the Canaanite states and the Israelites was so great. In fact, the military establishments of Canaan were much weaker than they had been a century before while any national political will seems to have evaporated entirely. As many a colonial army in the modern period has learned to its regret, the absence of a national political will can put a state at a severe military disadvantage when fighting a highly motivated adversary such as the Israelites appear to have been.

JOSHUA'S ARMY

In the previous chapter, I tried to show that the army of the Exodus was a competent military force, well organized and officered, sufficiently armed, and with significant combat experience at Jahaz and against Sihon of the Ammonites and Og of Bashan. In addition, the Transjordan campaign seems to have required successful attacks against fortified cities, a capability that only a well-trained and sufficiently large military force could accomplish. All this, of course, runs counter to the common conception of the early Israelites as ex-slaves without any military capabilities at all, an impression strongly encouraged by deuteronomic interpretations of the texts wherein the success of military engagements is often attributed to divine intervention. What, then, of Joshua's army at Shittim? What were its operational capabilities? Was this army capable of acquitting itself against the Canaanite armies of the period?

Napoleon once remarked that in war, "quantity conveyed a quality all its own." Given the weapons available to ancient armies, the size of an army often was decisive if only because muscle power was the only way to bring weapons to bear on one's opponent. Killing large numbers of adversaries required large numbers to accomplish. If, as I have suggested, Canaanite armies were shrinking during this time, was the size of Joshua's army sufficient to field adequate numbers to successfully engage the Canaanite armies? To answer this question, we must first arrive at some estimate of the size of the Israelite army at Shittim.

The place to begin is with Mendenhall's estimate of the size of the Israelite army at Sinai as explained in the previous chapter.[12] Mendenhall arrived at a figure of 5,000 to 5,500 fighting men counted in the Sinai census, a figure that implies, as noted previously, a total Israelite population of between 20,000 and 25,000 people. Calculating the loss rate on the march from Egypt to Sinai at about 35 percent, one can calculate the size of the original Exodus population that left Egypt at between 30,000 and 35,000 people. Assuming, then, that 20,000 Israelites survived to reach Kadesh-barnea and that, as the text tells us, they remained there for two generations, about 40 years, how large was the Israelite population from which Joshua's militia army could be drawn when it crossed Wadi Zered and began the march through Transjordan?

To arrive at an answer to this question requires very sophisticated mathematical techniques that are beyond the abilities of the author! I am deeply indebted to Dr. Eric Lufkin whose Ph.D. degree is in mathematical astrophysics and who works as chief statistical analyst for one of the largest financial institutions in the United States. The answer is based on the following assumptions: (1) That 50 percent of the Israelite population was of breeding age when it reached Kadesh-barnea, a reasonable assumption in light of the fact that the rigors of the march to Sinai would have killed mostly the old and the very young; (2) The average age for the onset of first pregnancy was 14 years old, or what it was for Egyptian women at the time; (3) The average age of death was 44 years for men and women (given that the average life span from the Bronze Age to the invention of penicillin in 1923 was about 44 years for both sexes, the assumption seems generally valid); (4) The rate of childhood survival until the military age of 20 years varied between 30 and 40 percent with probabilities being calculated for each of the percentage rates; and (5) The average number of pregnancies over a woman's childbearing age of 30 years varied from six to ten with results calculated for each frequency. It should be noted that if we were to calculate life expectancy and fertility rates for a population in Europe in, say, 1800 or so, these same assumptions would hold as empirically verifiable and correct. The statistical calculations based on these assumptions suggest that if the childhood survival rate were 40 percent, the size of the Israelite population at Kadesh-barnea after 40 years would have been 41,000. If the childhood survival rate is lowered to 30 percent, the population falls to 31,000. We can average the numbers and suggest somewhat conservatively that the Israelite population that crossed the Wadi Zered into the Transjordan was about 35,000 strong. That the population was of some significant size is confirmed by Numbers 22:3–4, which tells us that "Moab was alarmed because that people was so numerous. Moab dreaded the Israelites, and Moab said to the rulers of Midian, 'Now this horde will lick clean all that is about us as an ox licks up the grass of the field.' "

An Israelite population of 35,000 under a militia system of military recruitment accessing all males beginning at age 20 would be able to put between 8,000 and 9,000 fighting men in the field calculated at approximately 25 percent of the gross population. We might conservatively estimate the size of Joshua's army then at at least 8,000 men. So when Joshua 3:13 tells us "that about forty contingents of armed warriors crossed over [the Jordan] before Yahweh for the battle," the strength of these contingents can be estimated to have been 200 men each. These figures can be placed in some perspective by noting the approximate size of the populations of the Canaanite cities during the period of the Israelite invasion. Yigael Yadin suggests that "on the reasonable assumption that there were roughly 240 inhabitants to an urban acre, the population figures of most cities in the ancient Middle East ranged from 1,000 to 3,000, with some cities boasting a population of between 5,000 and 10,000."[13] Given, too, that the population of a city could make about 25 percent of its population available for defense, even if one adds the professional military contingents (severely reduced in size over the previous century) of the larger and wealthier states, the Canaanite city-states that could field 8,000 fighting men was probably relatively few. We arrive, therefore, at a startling conclusion: *in almost every battle between Joshua's Israelite army and the fighting forces of the Canaanites, the numerical advantage was held by the Israelites*, which implies that the citizen army of Israel was indeed capable of undertaking a military invasion of Canaan with at least some chance of success.

If the Israelite army was of sufficient size, how well was it armed and could it also provide itself with sufficient quantities of weapons? With its origins rooted in its Egyptian military service as *habiru* mercenaries, there is no reason to expect that Israelite weapons were much different than those used by the Egyptian and Canaanite armies of the day. Even though Joshua and Judges mention no weapon other than the sword (Exodus mentions the spear), it is not unreasonable that the common weapons of the day were also present in the Israelite army. Judging from the number of times it is mentioned, the sword seems to have been the basic weapon of Israelite infantry. The text uses the term *kidon* to describe Joshua's weapon with which he signaled the ambush at the battle of Ai, a rare and unusual term quite distinct from the more common *hereb* for sword. Keel's research demonstrates that *kidon* is a reference to the sickle-sword,[14] also the basic close-order weapon of the Egyptian and Canaanite infantry. The sickle-sword was of Mesopotamian origin with early models making their appearance around 2500 B.C.E.[15] Brought by the Hyksos to Canaan and Egypt, it quickly became the basic weapon of infantry forces there. Cast of bronze, the earlier models had handles twice as long as the blade, and the handle was attached to the hilt with a rivet. By Joshua's time the complete weapon—blade, hilt, and handle—was cast as a single piece for additional strength and now the striking blade and handle were the same length.[16] The weapon itself was about a half meter (60 cm) long and was usually carried under a waist belt since its design made a sheath impossible. The weapon cut only on the outside convex edge and was a slicing weapon. It could not be used for stabbing—unlike the Roman *gladius*—and lacked the weight and heft to cleave off arms.[17] These limitations made the weapon most useful as a secondary arm for heavy infantry if the spear was lost or broken, but it might have been used as the primary weapon of light infantry as well. If the text is any guide, it was employed as the primary Israelite weapon for dispatching the populations of captured cities once the battle itself had ended.

The basic combat killing weapon of the Israelite heavy infantry was the spear (*romah*). Two or three meters long and held with both hands, the spear was used for stabbing and was not thrown. Shorter spears, a meter or so in length, similar to the later Greek *dory*, were also used. Employed in conjunction with the shield, this short spear was also a stabbing weapon but could be wielded with one hand while the other hand held the shield. This shorter spear is sometimes called a javelin (*hanit*), but this is incorrect. The true javelin is thinner and lighter and meant to be thrown, and was not introduced into Palestine until the invasion of the Sea Peoples a century after Joshua. As we shall see, its effect on infantry warfare against chariots was considerable, but the javelin was not used in Joshua's army.[18] Both spears were in use by Egyptian infantry since pre-Exodus times.

The Beni-Hasan reliefs (1900 B.C.E.) indicate that the Asiatic clans of Canaan possessed the bow (*keshet*) long before the Exodus. While one cannot be certain, the portrayal of the bow in these reliefs appears to indicate a composite bow of the biconcave type, but this is unlikely. By the time of the Exodus, the composite bow was basic equipment in the Egyptian army, and it is reasonable to assume that the Israelite *habiru* were familiar with it. The composite bow was still in use during Joshua's time, but in all likelihood it was replaced in the Israelite armies by the simple bow. The composite bow was the epitome of a high technology weapon for its day. Manufactured from the wood of birch trees, tendons of wild bulls, horns of wild goats, and sinews from the hocks of bulls, it was incredibly expensive to manufacture.[19] Moreover, the difficult layering and lamination of wood, horn, and sinew was completed over long intervals so that a properly aged composite bow might take as much as five years to fabricate.[20] The weapon had to be kept in a special box for transport, was very fragile under combat conditions, and would lose tension under conditions of even moderate humidity. All these factors made it unlikely that the weapon was used by the Israelite army. The simple bow, on the other hand, was cheap, rugged, and easy to manufacture and repair. With a range of 80 to 100 meters (half that of the composite bow), it served well enough under combat conditions. The fact that the Old Testament provides no record of an Israelite archer corps, even though we know from later reliefs that the bow was used in warfare, and the silence of the Joshua and Judges texts on the military use of the bow suggests that while it was certainly employed in war, it may not have been used extensively by the Israelites.[21] Instead, it is possible that its function in war was augmented by the sling, whose range was about the same as the bow.[22] The sling had several things to recommend it over the bow. It was cheaper to manufacture, required little repair, sling stones were abundant and, unlike arrows, required no metal, and it was even deadlier than the bow. The average sling stone was approximately six centimeters in diameter, slightly smaller than a tennis ball.[23] The sling was remarkably accurate and the impact of the sling stone could easily smash a bone, knock a soldier unconscious, or kill outright.

The first mention of shields (*magen*) in the texts appears in 2 Samuel:1–21 in David's lament over the death of Saul: "For there the shield of warriors lay rejected, the shield of Saul, anointed with oil no more." The reference seems to be to the practice of oiling the shield before combat. This makes sense in a hot and dry climate where the wooden frame and hide covering of the shield would dry out and become brittle if it were not kept supple by periodic moistening with some sort of oil, perhaps rendered animal fat. The function of the shield was to protect the infantrymen from other spear-carrying infantry and to protect archers and slingers, who required the use of both hands to wield their weapons, from counterfire. Following the Egyptian and Canaanite models of the day, Joshua's army might well have used two types of shields. The Egyptian-style small oblong shield with a rounded top[24] provided the spear and sword infantry with the usual unsatisfactory compromise between protection and offensive mobility whereas a larger rectangular shield that covered most of the body could be used by slingers and archers. The shield itself was either held by another soldier or planted in the ground while the archers and slingers fired from behind it.[25] The smaller round shield did not appear in Palestine until introduced by the Sea Peoples a century later.

The weapons of Joshua's army—the sickle-sword, long and short spear, simple bow, sling, and shield—were not in any way unusual from the mix of weapons found among the Egyptian and Canaanite armies of the day. Only one infantry weapon, the *garzen* or axe, is missing from the Israelite inventory. Although the axe is mentioned 14 times in the Old Testament, it is always mentioned as a tool for cutting wood and never in a military context.[26] Also not in evidence are armor or helmets, both of which had become commonplace in the major armies. Both items used considerable amounts of bronze in manufacture, which made them very expensive. To equip an army the size of Joshua's with armor and helmets would have been impossible for a people on the move who lacked the land tax base to afford such items. The same is true, of course, of the chariot. The expense of constructing, maintaining, and arming these machines was simply prohibitive. More to the point, the chariot required eight to ten acres of arable grain land to provide sufficient food for a single team of chariot horses for one year,[27] a prohibitive requirement for a people who had yet to settle their own land. As an infantry force, however, Joshua's army was likely equipped with the same array of weapons possessed by its adversaries. Once engaged, the Israelite army gave away nothing to an opponent in terms of weaponry. In open country, of course, the armored charioteer and his machine still held the advantage, one that would not disappear until the coming of the Sea Peoples with their straight iron swords, round maneuverable shields, and light infantry armed with the thrown javelin.

To possess effective weapons is one thing, to possess and manufacturer them in sufficient quantities is quite another. The problem resolves itself to one of metals manufacture since bows, arrows, spears, shields, and slings were easily manufactured from wood and hides—both of which were readily available. That the Israelite clan smiths were capable of this type of weapons manufacture is clear from the Beni-Hasan reliefs. Metals, however, were quite another thing. Spear blades, sickle-swords, arrowheads, and daggers were all fabricated from metal. Unless the Israelites could manufacture and repair metal items, Joshua's army would have had to rely upon whatever it could capture from defeated foes, hardly sufficient to equip an army bent on invasion. How, then, did Joshua's army maintain its supply of weapons?

The weapons of Joshua's day were made of bronze, and despite the fact that the Iron Age is usually dated as having begun around 1200 B.C.E., in fact iron weapons did not replace bronze weapons in any quantity until the tenth century B.C.E. Jane Waldbaum's survey of the 150 pieces of bronze armor and weaponry found in twelfth-century Palestine reveals that 147 were made of bronze and only 3 of iron. Even in the tenth century, when the Iron Age was well underway, there are 53 pieces of iron to 45 pieces of bronze military hardware.[28] Interestingly, these ratios hold for the rest of the eastern Mediterranean region as well, including Greece, Syria, Anatolia, and Egypt. Of the 331 military items found in the eastern Mediterranean, 320 of the twelfth-century items are bronze, and only 11 are iron. For the tenth century, the numbers are 155 iron pieces and 147 bronze.[29] Iron produced in the early days of the Iron Age offered no military advantage. It was soft wrought iron, unusable for weapons. Only after cold tempering, folding, and hammering were introduced to make the metal stronger did iron emerge as a metal useable for war.[30] But this was long after Joshua. In fact, it may have been the unavailability of bronze more than any inherent military advantage in iron that eventually led the armies to equip themselves with iron weapons.[31]

Bronze is made from tin and copper. During Joshua's day much of the copper used in the Levant came from Cyprus, the greatest copper-producing area of the Bronze Age. Other large deposits were found in Ergani Maden in eastern Anatolia and, quite importantly, in Sinai.[32] Tin was by far the rarer metal. Most of it came from the east, perhaps as far away as Afghanistan. The large tin deposits in Brittany, Spain, and Cornwall were exploited only later by Phoenician traders.[33] From 1400 to 1000 B.C.E., the world was stitched together by large empires—Egyptian, Mycenaean, Hittite, Mitannian, and so forth—that made international trade possible and profitable. Just as there was a silk route later, there was an international tin trade that followed the tin route. Tin came from the Iran-Iraq border, to Assur, and on to Mari. Mari seems to have controlled the tin trade to the Levant, and Hazor was a major transshipment point to Palestine. Tin ingots have been found in Haifa harbor, suggesting other sources for the metal as well.[34] The point is that while both tin and copper were expensive materials, they were readily available to be purchased in Canaan.

A clue as to how the Israelites supplied themselves with the materials with which to make weapons is found in Joshua 6:24 which tells us that at Jericho "[t]he city they burned and everything in it. But the silver and gold and objects of copper and iron (probably bronze) were deposited in the treasury of the House of the Lord." It is interesting to say the least that with the same deuteronomic command to slay *kol han-nesama*, literally, "every breathing thing," in those cities given the Israelites as a divine inheritance, the *herem* or ban should require that precious metals were to be saved. Was it, perhaps, because the gold and silver could be used to purchase the expensive copper and tin needed to manufacture weapons? Or that the copper items could be melted down and reused? Bronze, of course, can be remelted and cast repeatedly and would have been particularly valuable to the army's weapons supply. Looked at in this way, the "treasury of Yahweh" was really an arsenal. The importance that Joshua placed on salvaging the metals may well reflect the importance of this source of wealth and materials to keep the army supplied with weapons. After the destruction of Jericho, a soldier, Achan ben Zerah by name, kept 200 shekels weight of silver and a gold bar weighing 50 shekels instead of turning them over to the treasury. The punishment was severe, no doubt as a lesson to others who might keep valuable metals. "Joshua took Achan ben Zerah together with the silver, the cloak, and the gold bar, his sons, his daughters, his ox, his ass, his sheep, his tent, and everything that belonged to him."[35] He took the people (and one presumes even the animals "that breathed") to a place of execution and there "[a]ll Israel stoned him. They burned them and stoned them."[36] Presumably Achan, his wife, sons, and daughters were burned alive!

Bronze casting in the ancient world was not a common skill. Even if the Israelites obtained the materials they needed, who would make them into weapons? The answer appears to be the Kenites, none other than Moses' relatives! Zipporah was the daughter of "Hobab the Kenite" who lived in the land of Midian, an area close to the Sinai copper mines which was known for its metalworkers.[37] The term Kenite is derived from the Hebrew *qayin*, which in its cognate form means metalworker or smith.[38] In the ancient world metal-working was often linked to magic, and some peoples, mostly nomadic peoples, feared and loathed smiths and kept them isolated as outsiders by forbidding intermarriage and even enslaving them.[39] Agricultural peoples, by contrast, usually treated smiths much more kindly, often settling them as permanent members of the community and encouraging intermarriage.[40] Both Forbes and Gottwald agree that the relationship between the Sinai Kenites and the Israelites was particularly close and friendly, and "they seem to have intermarried freely . . . and were thoroughly integrated early."[41] Indeed, the Kenites may have been among the original six clans of Judah where they assimilated and entered Canaan with them.[42] It seems likely, then, that some Kenites of Midian intermarried with the Israelites at least in Exodus times, if not before, and became an integral part of the Israelite community. They were most certainly at Kadesh-barnea. This latter point is of some significance for Kadesh-barnea is close to the Sinai copper mines. Assuming that some way could have been found to purchase tin, it is entirely possible that the new army formed at Sinai and now encamped at Kadesh-barnea was furnished with metal weapons made by the Kenites. Moreover, the amount of tin required for bronze is only a small percentage of the total, less than 10 percent of the amount of copper required.[43] This would go some way in explaining how the now expanded Israelite army came to be equipped with sufficient weapons with which to carry out its successful invasion of the Transjordan. To press the matter further, a subclan of the Kenites at Kadesh-barnea were the Rechabites who may have specialized in chariot making.[44] They were specialists in crafting items from wood and hides, perhaps including shields, spear shafts, arrows, bows, and slings. Although there is no textual reference to the Kenites making weapons for the Israelites, "it is a reasonable hypothesis that their skill in metallurgy was important in supplying Israel with copper tools and weapons."[45] The Kenites then may well have been the armorers for the Israelite army beginning at Kadesh-barnea and continuing until the time of the monarchy, when the Philistines, realizing the military importance of these smiths, may have deported or otherwise removed them from the midst of the Israelite territories so that as I Samuel 13:19 tells us, "no smith was found throughout all the land of Israel."

Not all Kenites settled among agricultural communities. Like Tinkers, some preferred to travel from place to place selling their skills as they went, remaining on good terms with all the combatants and working for any of them as the opportunity presented itself. Smiths were essentially noncombatant technocrats. In exchange for their skills, they received food, a place to live, and the protection of the community, even in Canaanite cities. It was the fact that "there was peace between Heber the Kenite and his wife Jael and Hazor" that may have tempted Sisera to seek refuge in Heber's tent after the debacle at the Kishon River. For whatever reason, Jael drove a metal-tipped tent peg through Sisera's temple as he lay asleep! Evidence of the itinerant nature of some of these smiths is found in the fact that while few metal mines have been found in Palestine, there are scores of ancient smelting furnaces scattered throughout the country.[46]

The presence of Kenite weaponeers in the Israelite army also explains why Joshua established his logistics base at Gilgal, somewhere between the Jordan and Jericho, where he installed the Ark upon a platform of stones taken from the Jordan. There the Israelites were secure from surprise attack even when the army was away on operations. From there the produce of the countryside on both sides of the Jordan could be exploited for food and other supplies.[47] But there was, perhaps, another reason, and that was that Gilgal was the location of the Israelite weapons arsenal, where the Kenite smiths fabricated and repaired weapons. The fact that Gilgal offered a short and secure supply line to the copper deposits of the Sinai, the material required in the greatest quantity to make bronze, provided a major advantage. Forbes, citing Livy, Dionysius, and Cicero, has calculated that a Roman army of eight legions (approximately 40,000 men) required 1,600 smiths and craftsmen (*fabri*) to keep it prepared for battle.[48] Calculated proportionally, Joshua's army of 8,000 would have needed 320 smiths and wood craftsmen to fabricate and repair its weapons and keep it fit for battle. If only 100 or so of these *fabri* were metalsmiths, then scores of furnaces were spread over an area of several acres as hundreds of laborers kept the furnaces supplied with wood and copper ore. The operation was large and complex and could not be easily moved. Here, then, might be one reason why Joshua's army always returned to Gilgal after a campaign. An army at war loses and breaks many weapons, and it was at Gilgal that these weapons were replaced and repaired to maintain the army in fighting trim. After the covenant at Shechem, when the Israelite coalition expanded, there may have been an even greater need for the production of weapons to supply the new manpower.

If we can believe that Joshua's army at Shittim was already a large, well-equipped, experienced military force when it crossed into the Transjordan and won its first victories, perhaps we can now explain how it was that Joshua was able to reduce the fortified cities of Bashan and Sihon described at the end of the previous chapter. Yigael Yadin has noted that there are five ways to subdue a city: (1) penetration from above, i.e., assault over the walls by scaling ladders or hooks; (2) penetration through the barrier walls, i.e., the use of battering rams and siege machinery to knock the walls down; (3) penetration from below, i.e., mining or tunneling; (4) siege; and (5) penetration by ruse, i.e., entrance gained by some unguarded passageway or, as Malamat notes, enticing the enemy out of the gates by deception.[49] The usual method of attack was the first one, over the walls using scaling ladders. The archers and slingers kept up a steady fire against the defenders on top of the wall to keep their heads down and disrupt their efforts at defense. Under this suppressive fire assault, teams rushed the wall with ladders at several points and tried to make their way over the top. If the Israelites followed the common practice of the day, their soldiers would have slung their rectangular shields over their backs holding them in place with shoulder straps. This protected the soldier's back from defensive fire much like a turtle's shell and left both hands free with which to climb the wall.[50]

This method required strength and courage on the part of the attacking soldiers, but its outcome was usually successful for the defenders usually could not muster sufficient manpower to check simultaneous assaults at widely spaced points on the wall. The proportion of fighters—professionals and dragooned civilians—averaged about 25 percent of the city's population "so that small cities had about 300 fighting men, the medium sized cities about 1,000 to 2,000, and the large cities several thousand." The defenders had to man every meter of wall while the attackers could strike at several places at once, and "even a city of average size had a perimeter of 700 meters, and in the big cities it was often several kilometers."[51] Under these conditions the advantage lay with the attacker. Given the size of Joshua's army on its march across the Transjordan as between 8,000 and 9,000 men, using the simplest of methods the Israelites would have been able to easily subdue the fortified cities of Bashan and Sihon.

Jericho is a case in point. The city itself enclosed 8.5 square acres,[52] so that Jericho's defenders had to defend 1,400 meters of perimeter wall. Using Yadin's estimate of 240 people per urban acre, the size of the city's population was approximately 2,000 people of which 25 percent or 500 could be used to defend the wall, or one man every 2.74 meters. Attacking Jericho was an army of 8,000 to 9,000 men. An army this size could encircle the entire perimeter wall with one man every meter, six men deep! Under these circumstances, or similar ones in the cities of the Transjordan, the size of the Israelite army provided it with the means to subdue the cities of its opponents with little difficulty.

Weapons and fighting men are but the raw material of armies that must still be turned into operational capabilities if the army is to fight well. How well this is accomplished depends on the quality of its commanders and the discipline and training of its troops. The tactical organization of Joshua's army is uncertain due to few textual references. In preparing to cross the Jordan, the troops are arranged in *hamusim* or "battle array"[53] and "about forty contingents of armed warriors crossed over."[54] The use of *eleph* to designate "contingents" in the text[55] again raises the problem of the word's meaning addressed earlier. In the present context, however, the *eleph* seems to imply a unit of constant size, although not yet 1,000 men as under the monarchy. For example, it is used to describe the number of *enemy* casualties inflicted on the defenders of Ai: "The casualties on that day, both men and women, were twelve contingents—all the inhabitants of The Ruin,"[56] a use that would make no sense unless the Israelites understood the *eleph* or contingent of Joshua's time to have a certain number of men. Based on the statistical analysis offered earlier in this chapter, the strength of these contingents may have been approximately 200 men. That the contingent may also have been a tactical unit seems likely as well. When the reconnaissance scouts briefed Joshua on the strength of the garrison at Ai, they recommended that Joshua "not deploy all the people (meaning the entire army), for about two or three contingents can go up and defeat The Ruin."[57] At 200 men, the Israelite contingent is about the same size as a combat company in the modern Israeli Defense Force.

The military organization of the combat units was probably the same during Joshua's time as for the later period of the Judges. Judges provides two terms that hint at the military organization of the Israelite army. The first is *mehoqeqim* or commander,[58] quite different from the term *sar* used during the monarchy. The later term implies a troop commander appointed from a central authority while *mehoqeqim* seems to imply a different source of authority, perhaps one based on an officer's reputation for military prowess. Another term associated with military organization is *moshekim beshevet sopher* that literally means "wielders of the scribal staff."[59] A looser translation is "musterers," perhaps "men who can gather other men around them." This could imply that they were recruiters, but this is unlikely since in a militia system based on *alaphim* recruiters would be unneeded. Men who gather other men around them can, however, reasonably be seen to imply some sort of small unit tactical commander.

The qualities required of a combat commander during Joshua's time were understandably different from the managerial and interpersonal skills often cited as being necessary to the modern military commander. Modern armies are highly structured authoritatively so that authority flows from position and not personality. Personal qualities may become important in any given case, but in no case are they the *source* of command legitimacy. Joshua's army was a *premodern* organization in that it was loosely articulated authoritatively and highly personal in terms of the selection of combat commanders. Thus personal qualities become the *source* of command legitimacy. Hobbs has identified some of the qualities of a successful combat commander in ancient armies[60] that are useful in assessing Joshua's leadership qualities. It must be kept in mind, too, that Joshua was the only soldier remaining from the original Exodus and had been a soldier all his life.[61] As second-in-command under Moses, he had helped shape the new Israelite army and, as Moses grew old, was probably the person most responsible for its equipment, training, and discipline over the long period at Kadesh-barnea. It was also likely to have been Joshua who commanded the successful armies of the Transjordan campaign in the field and may have selected other officers for combat command. Avigdor Kahalani, one of modern Israel's most decorated field commanders, once noted that to be effective an army must become the instrument of its commander's will.[62] It is important to keep in mind that the Israelite army was in fact the creation of a single field commander, Joshua himself, and that we might reasonably expect that he would look for the same qualities in his unit commanders that he himself possessed. If so, then the army of Israel may have been very well led indeed at the tactical level.

The Bible refers to the Israelite soldier as *gibbor chayil* or "the man of valor." Among the important qualities of a warrior in ancient times were physical abilities like stamina, physical dexterity, and strength. Although in his midsixties, Joshua is portrayed as leading his men in uphill night marches and pursuing the enemy into the Aijalon Valley without stopping to rest. Joshua also established himself as a combat leader willing to risk his own life. In every battle Joshua "leads from the front," exposing himself to the same risk as his men. Charisma must have attended Joshua as well, for he was the last of the "old ones" who had come out of Egypt, who knew Moses, and who attended him at the Tent of Meeting and on Mount Sinai. As Hobbs notes, a leader must also live by community standards,[63] and Joshua always took pains to take care of the Ark and to assuage the priesthood. He often attributed his victories to specific tactical advice provided by Yahweh himself showing himself attentive to the basic beliefs of the Israelite people. But the most important mark of the warrior in ancient times was his willingness and ability to kill. This quality was central to the reputation of Saul and David and sparked the most contentious dispute between them. So it was that Saul killed his thousands, but David killed ten times that number. And here Joshua was ruthless. Time and again he ordered the extermination of city populations and personally executed some of the rival commanders he captured. Like Saul and David after him, Joshua became a blood-soaked warrior, and like them he was admired for it. If Joshua selected them, it is likely that his unit commanders displayed many of the same qualities as their commander in chief.

The fighting spirit and unit cohesion of Joshua's army must have been high. The army was a militia force whose men fought with their own clans and with comrades they had known from childhood. Led by well-respected tactical commanders with reputations for bravery, the Israelite army was fighting for a cause it believed was divinely inspired. The proximity of their children and families to the battlefield encouraged every soldier to fight well, for defeat risked the death or enslavement of their kin. In addition Israelite commanders made every effort to remove those men who possessed characteristics that might provoke their collapse or flight in battle from the fighting ranks. Joshua's army must have been an army of lions willing to kill on command and fight to the death in defense of their people. It is interesting that the same list of factors that motivated Joshua's soldiers—militia primary groups, local units, good commanders, religious ideals, and the belief that defeat would result in the destruction of their homes and families—are seen by today's Israeli Defense Force commanders as having similar beneficial effects on the motivation of the modern Israeli soldier.

Whenever we read of Egyptian armies, as in the Papyrus Lansing, there is clear evidence of harsh discipline—beatings, disciplinary confinement, back-breaking labor, and so on—routinely inflicted upon the conscript soldier.[64] Similar descriptions can be found for other armies of the period. There is no evidence of such systematic mistreatment of the militia soldiers in Joshua's army. To be sure the story of Achan and his family having been stoned and burned for a breach of military discipline is evidence that Israelite officers could deal severely with such cases. But the absence of other descriptions in the texts leads one to suspect that they were relatively rare.

Among the most striking characteristics of Joshua's army was its high level of combat training as reflected in their ability to conduct sophisticated tactical maneuvers on the battlefield. The Israelite army was comprised of *melumedey milchamah* or soldiers "trained for war." The range of tactical maneuvers and operational capabilities of Joshua's army is truly impressive, as we shall see when we analyze Joshua's battles in the following section. These included the systematic use of tactical reconnaissance, forced marches at night over rugged terrain, ambush, tactical surprise, the concentration of forces at the *Schwerpunkt*, enticement, decoys, deception, coordination of divided forces, tactical communication, indirect approaches, feints, diversionary movements, lethal pursuit, and the storming of fortified cities. As regards Israelite tactical ability, Malamat says that "throughout the literature of the ancient Near East . . . the books of Joshua and Judges remain unique in the number and variety of battle schemes gathered."[65]

It is sometimes thought, although incorrectly, that the training of irregular forces is much easier to accomplish than that of formal armies. In fact the reverse is often true since the articulated command structure and established war-fighting doctrines of professional armies simplify tactical thinking and application, albeit at great risk when confronting irregular forces. In fighting the Roman Army, for example, Hannibal could always anticipate that its formations, tactics, and manner of fighting would be about the same, applications that had been successful for the armies of Rome for centuries. Hannibal's brilliance lay in his ability to devise tactical applications that took advantage of Roman predictability. Scipio Africanus realized this and rearranged the shape of the Roman legion, changed its armament, added good cavalry, and changed its tactical array, all to Hannibal's deficit and defeat. Joshua's army can be said to have been an "irregular force" only in the sense that it was comprised of militia soldiers instead of the professionals characteristic of his Canaanite adversaries. In terms of discipline, training, morale, quality of leadership, and operational capability, however, it was certainly as professional as any army of the day.

This professional quality was evident in another area besides tactical proficiency and that was the ability of the Israelite militia soldier to kill on command regardless of the horror it entailed. The American Civil War general, William Tecumseh Sherman, remarked that "the very business of war is to produce results by death and slaughter." In modern times when combat death is often inflicted from a distance, it is sometimes forgotten (although rarely by infantrymen!) that in the ancient world death was dealt one's adversary closely and personally so that pain, suffering, fear, and gore were readily apparent to the slayer. Joshua was fighting a war of conquest in which the objective was not the killing of enemy soldiers but driving settled peoples off the land and out of the cities. To accomplish this required the application of strategic brutality, for nothing works so well in this regard as the fear of death lest it be death itself. To achieve his strategic goal Joshua's army had to be trained to carry out the wholesale slaughter of combatants and noncombatants when ordered to do so, in the fashion of other professional armies of antiquity for whom the slaughter of noncombatants was not unusual. This is very nasty business indeed, and it often sickens even the hardiest of professional soldiers. The fact that Israelite commanders were able to order their men to do it again and again and have their orders carried out is sad but telling testimony to the high degree of discipline in Joshua's army.

Contrary to popular belief, then, the Israelite army that gathered at Shittim in preparation for the invasion of Canaan was not a ragtag rabble of fugitive ex-slaves who were poorly armed and without military experience, conditions that would certainly have required divine intervention if the Israelites were to succeed. Although the evidence is incomplete, it can be reasonably argued that the Israelite army at Shittim was a relatively large force, well equipped with the usual infantry weapons found in Egyptian and Canaanite armies and structurally articulated into company-sized tactical units led by experienced commanders drawn from the clans and families of the militia soldiers which they led, circumstances that produce highly cohesive and spirited fighting units. The Israelite army had been highly trained and was capable of executing a wide array of complex tactical maneuvers. Using the tribal host as its logistical base, it was capable of supplying itself in the field when on campaign and providing itself with sufficient quantities of weapons. Its commander in chief was a charismatic experienced general who had been a soldier all his life and labored for years to forge the army into an instrument of his strong will. Motivated by a belief that he was carrying out God's plan, Joshua undertook his war of conquest and settlement with the single-minded determination required of all successful field commanders. He had served his God long and well, and now the time had come for the promise to be fulfilled. Joshua gathered his army at Shittim and prepared to invade the land of Canaan.

INVASION: CROSSING THE JORDAN

Having been ordered by Yahweh to begin the invasion of Canaan, "Joshua gave the order to the officers of the people: Go throughout the camp and give the order to the people, 'Prepare supplies for yourself, for within three days you will cross this Jordan to enter and possess the land that Yahweh, god of your ancestors, is giving to you as a possession.' "[66] The phrase "officers of the people" makes it clear that the military was in charge of the operation, and not the judicial officers that Moses had set over the people at Sinai.[67] Unlike their Exodus from Egypt, this time the Israelites were logistically prepared for the march with three days' rations. Joshua had calculated that the crossing of the Jordan would take three days. Once over the river, the Israelites intended to live off the land of Canaan. Joshua's divine exhortation that God is the ultimate commander of the operation was common in ancient times, especially in Egypt where pharaoh was considered a god. Thus, prior to the attack on Megiddo, Thutmose III instructed his troops, "Prepare ye! Make your weapons ready, since Pharaoh will engage in combat with the wretched enemy in the morning."[68] Joshua reminded the tribes of Reuben, Gad, and half-Manasseh of their promise to Moses to help their Israelite kinsmen conquer Canaan and placed them in the van. "But you shall cross over in battle array before your kinsmen—all you burly warriors—and help them."[69] This is curious since heavy infantry in the van would have made more tactical sense whereas the Gadites were light infantry and the men of Reuben and Manasseh were archers/slingers. Why only soldiers from these three tribes are mentioned by tribal association in the warfare sections of the book of Joshua is also puzzling.[70] Perhaps despite their light weapons they had a reputation for reliability or ferocity, but this is uncertain.

Before committing the army to crossing the Jordan, Joshua sent two spies from his base at Shittim to conduct a reconnaissance of the objective. Joshua instructed his spies to "Go, have a look at the land—and Jericho."[71] The broad mission brief implies that the spies are to do more than scout the defenses of the city itself, no doubt reconnoitering the proposed route of march, location of the river fords, and the avenues of approach that might be used in the attack. Once over the river Joshua planned to feed the Israelites from the land of Canaan, a plan that required an assessment of the size and quality of the spring harvest of the Canaanite farms around Jericho. Although the text emphasizes the reconnaissance of the city, it is likely that the scouts' mission brief was far more extensive. Once inside Jericho, the scouts "rested" at the house of a prostitute named Rahab. The choice of a whorehouse or, as has been argued, an inn as a base of operations was sound tradecraft. Not only are such places sources of loose talk, but they are one of the few locations in a small city where strangers could appear without raising questions. The Israelite spies, however, were not so fortunate, and the king's counterintelligence agents detected their presence almost immediately, indeed the same night they arrived! "So the king of Jericho sent word to Rahab. 'Bring out the men who came to you, who entered your house this very night. For they came to explore the whole land!' "[72] The text implies that the king was aware of the Israelite presence less than 30 kilometers away and their intentions. If so, his decision not to engage them at the Jordan using the river as a tactical obstacle was a major strategic mistake. Rahab misled the king's agents, telling them that the Israelites had left the city around dusk when in fact she had hidden them on her roof. She provided the Israelite scouts with the important information that the city's inhabitants and its defenders were already psychologically defeated. The stories of the Israelite victories over Sihon and Og just across the Jordan and their slaughter at the hands of the Israelites had reached Jericho. "When we heard about it, we lost heart, and no man had any more spirit left because of you."[73] This also explains why the king of Jericho's intelligence service was alert to the possibility of a penetration by Israelite scouts. In return for her cooperation and helping the scouts escape, the Israelites agree to spare Rahab and her family.

Rahab's house, in the Hebrew phrase, was *beqir ha-homah e shevah*, or "in the wall of the wall" of the city.[74] Jericho's fortifications were of the casement type in which parallel walls—the inner and outer walls—were divided by cross walls into chambers that could be filled with rubble for strength or left unfilled and used for houses, storage rooms, and stables. Casement construction had been employed since the early Bronze Age (third millennium B.C.E.). The Israelites instructed Rahab "to tie the length of crimson cord to the window through which you let us down"[75] so that the Israelites attacking the town will know that Rahab's house and its occupants are to be spared the slaughter. Then Rahab "let them down by a rope through the window—for her dwelling was at the outer side of the city wall and she lived in the actual wall."[76] The Israelite scouts returned to Shittim and informed Joshua of the low state of morale in Jericho, telling him that "all the land's rulers grow faint because of us."[77] Now convinced that he possessed the psychological advantage, Joshua ordered the army to march toward the Jordan River and prepare to cross.

The march to the Jordan from Shittim required only one day. The Israelites encamped on the river's banks for that night. It was three days later before Joshua gave the order to attempt the crossing.[78] He ordered the Ark and the priests to lead the people to the riverbank. Moses, of course, was dead, and the pillars of smoke and fire that attended his command van are heard of no longer. Instead, the Ark of the Covenant had become the new Israelite palladium of war, the sign of Yahweh's presence on the battlefield. Once at the riverbank, the priests touched the water with their feet, and "the water coming down from above stood still. It arose in one heap a great distance from Adam the city which is beside Zarethan. And the stream going down toward the Arabah Sea was entirely cut off. The people crossed opposite Jericho."[79] More miraculous still was that "[t]he priests carrying Yahweh's Covenant-Ark stood firmly on dry ground in the middle of the Jordan; and all the Bene Israel crossed on dry ground until finally the entire nation had crossed over."[80] The Jordan typically overflows its banks with the late winter and early spring rains. The river's flow is at its fullest in early spring when the rains are joined by the melting in the anti-Lebanon range. Even at full flood, however, the Jordan is little more than a wide stream, never more than 90 to 100 feet across, with its channel, usually no more than ten feet, meandering in zigzag fashion from bank to bank which sometimes leaves the midstream the shallowest. There are any number of fords that might be construed to be "opposite Jericho" as the text suggests, and even at full flood some of these fords are less than three feet deep.[81] When in flood, however, the Jordan can possess a current strong enough to sweep a man off his feet. Indeed, the current was likely to have been more of a problem than the river's depth.

The text explains the crossing of the Jordan as a miraculous event expressed in deuteronomic terms. The river "rose in one great heap," stopping its flow, and the "Bene Israel crossed on dry ground." This event has been explained less miraculously in geologic terms. The banks of the Jordan are comprised of soft limestone, which, if collapsed by an earth tremor, might tumble into the river and temporarily block its flow, providing a dry land-bridge upon which the Israelites could cross. Something like this seems to have actually happened in 1267, 1906, and in 1927, the last instance preceded by an earthquake.[82] In addition, the area leading from Jericho to the Dead Sea's southern terminus is certainly a zone of geologic instability. Even so, the explanation that an earthquake caused a land-bridge over which the Israelites crossed defies credibility. No general, and certainly not one with the tactical genius of Joshua, could plan an invasion around the *chance* that an earthquake *might* somehow occur at the precise time and place at which his army was to cross a river! More likely there is some more reasonable explanation.

The clue lies in Joshua's planning. The Israelite army had been camped at Shittim less than a day's march from the Jordan for some time. It is simply inconceivable that the locations of the Jordan's shallowest fords were not known to Joshua in advance or that the line of march was not directly toward the ford already selected. No competent officer would attempt a river crossing without a reconnaissance, and if the shallow fords were not already known, it is certain that one of the primary elements of information to be gathered by the Israelite scouts sent to Jericho would have been to locate the most suitable fords for crossing the river. Indeed, where did the scouts cross on the way to the city? Given a suitably shallow ford, the problem would have remained the river's current. Even a strong but shallow current can be reduced relatively easily by breaking its strength a few yards upstream from the crossing point. Military commanders in India often accomplished this by positioning a file of elephants a few yards upstream and using the bulk of their legs to break the current's direction and speed. In the American West, wagon trains often used their cattle herds or their wagons to break the current while the people crossed a short distance downstream. Even so simple a device as placing a line of large stones upstream will work. During the British Mandate of Palestine in the first quarter of the last century, Irish engineers in the British army developed a clever method for breaching wadis with bridges that would survive the spring floods and permit vehicles to cross even at flood. The device was called an Irish bridge, and they remain in common use all over Palestine. Although often fabricated of concrete, an Irish bridge can easily be constructed of stone. The idea is to construct a platform of rocks along the river's bottom under the water's surface by piling one stone atop another in several layers until the platform is both wide and long enough to cross the ford. Caesar used this same device several times in crossing the flooded Rhine. In streams with a zigzag current where the shallowest depths are in the middle of the stream, laying, say, four layers of stones across the river's width might well result in a section of the bridge actually being above the water at its shallowest point, that is, in the center of the stream, so that "the priests who bore the Ark of the Lord's Covenant stood on dry land exactly in the middle of the Jordan . . . until all of the people had finished crossing the Jordan."[83]

That something like the piling of stones to break the current occurred is suggested by the fact that prior to leaving Shittim Joshua equipped the Israelites with rations to last three days. These were consumed when the Israelites encamped on the east bank of the river before crossing into Canaan. There appears no sound military reason for the three-day encampment. Indeed, such a delay would only serve to provide the king of Jericho with more time to gather his forces, time for allies to arrive, and time to deploy his army along the Jordan using the river as a tactical obstacle. But if Joshua knew the fords were in flood and planned to cross anyway, he may have reasoned that some sort of bridge or current barrier would have to be constructed to effect the crossing and that three days was a reasonable amount of time to accomplish the task. The text suggests curiously that Joshua was concerned about stones. After the crossing, he instructed one man from each of the 12 tribes to go to the point where the priests stood on dry land in the middle of the Jordan and carry 12 of the stones to the next place of encampment, presumably Gilgal, where he placed them in a sacred circle. Other men were sent back to the river to gather more stones from which a platform was constructed within the circle upon which the Ark was placed.[84] Religious explanations aside, Joshua's order to remove the stones may have been intended as something quite different: to destroy the crossing point into Canaan. If Joshua wished to convey the message that the die was cast, that there was no turning back, the destruction of the crossing point, albeit for ritualistic reasons, would certainly have accomplished that end. Joshua knew that soldiers fight more courageously when there is no possibility of surrender or retreat. Joshua was pulling up his bridges behind him for sound military reasons.

With the army gathered at Gilgal, Joshua ordered all adult males of military age to be circumcised. The reasons for this command are unclear. The text notes that all of the males of *military age* who had come out of Egypt had been circumcised, but all had died by this time. None of those born on the trek and now of *military age* had been circumcised.[85] The original significance of circumcision among the Israelites is elusive for the Bible is clearly opposed to every practice of scarification and mutilation of the body, including tattooing, on the grounds of pagan idolatry.[86] Moreover, circumcision was a well-established Egyptian practice and not, as sometimes believed, a Mesopotamian practice.[87] Much of the evidence points to the Israelites having acquired the practice in Egypt.[88] Egyptian circumcision was performed on 13- to 14-year-old males to mark their passage into adulthood, but does not seem to have been universally practiced by all classes. To some degree it seems to have been a mark of high social status. The Egyptian procedure was performed publicly, and reliefs show boys with one hand on their hip and the other placed upon the head of the physician performing the operation while kneeling before the patient. It was expected that the patient would endure the pain in silence and with dignity, thus reinforcing the association between the ceremony and personal courage.

Joshua probably had opportunity to witness such displays while in Egypt and may have adopted the ceremony for the Israelite army—for only males of *military age* were circumcised at Gilgal—as a rite of passage and, perhaps, a means of testing the courage of new recruits. If so, then when the text reads, "and it was these that Joshua circumcised" it may mean exactly that, namely, that Joshua himself officiated at the circumcision of the troops, thereby endowing the ceremony with a distinctly military character. In Egypt and Israel, then, the ceremony was associated with individual courage and military service and in Israel also with a covenant between the soldier and Yahweh. The Gilgal circumcision represents a covenant with the Divine Warrior,[89] and Joshua may have introduced it as a way of separating the warriors from the rest of the people by bestowing a special status upon them. On the other hand, there were risks. Genesis 34:25 records that when Simon and Levi avenged the rape of Dinah they killed the recently circumcised males "on the third day, when they were still in pain." Modern physicians estimate that it would take a circumcised male at least ten to 14 days to recover from the surgery and be able to return to his duties as a soldier. At Gilgal, then, the Israelites were defenseless for more than two weeks while the soldiers recovered. To put his army at such risk made little sense unless Joshua reasoned that the psychological benefit to be gained, expressed as increased unit cohesion, status, and self-esteem, was worth it. The Greek general Xenophon remarked in this regard that "the strength of an army resides not in its weapons, but in its soul." Joshua seems to have been an early believer in the idea that the "soul" of the soldier is the most important element in why he fights.

On the eve of the attack against Jericho, Joshua encountered an angel who was *sar tseba Adonai*, or a "commander of Yahweh's army," a story no doubt designed to emphasize that Yahweh was to be present at the battle. The encounter "happened while Joshua was near Jericho"[90] and not, as some have supposed, at Gilgal which was "on the eastern border of Jericho."[91] What was Joshua doing near Jericho the night before the battle? It had been almost three weeks since the last reconnaissance of Jericho (a day's march from Shittim, three days encampment to build the ford, and ten days for the troops to recover from the circumcision), and, like any good commander, Joshua was making his own final reconnaissance on the night before the battle.[92] Yahweh himself revealed the plan of attack to Joshua. The army was to form a column with an armed guard marching before and behind the priests carrying the Ark and to "march around the city, all the fighting men going around the city once,"[93] doing so in complete silence. The silent march was to be repeated for six consecutive days. At daybreak on the seventh day, the column assembled and began its now familiar march. This time, however, they marched around the city seven times. On the seventh circuit, "The priests blew the trumpets. When the people heard the sound of the trumpets, the people gave a tremendous shout. The wall collapsed on the spot. The people went up into the city, every man straight ahead, and took the city."[94]

Jericho is yet another story told in deuteronomic terms. If the tale is analyzed from a military perspective, however, we find evidence of Joshua's tactical imagination once more. The text employs the Hebrew term *sabbotem* to describe the movement of the column at Jericho. Taken in context the term does not mean "to march around" but more precisely "to encircle."[95] Thus it is by no means clear if the column marched around the city or if the city was simply encircled by the Israelite army. As noted earlier, Jericho was fortified by 1,400 meters of perimeter wall. If the Israelite army of 8,000 men encircled Jericho, it did so in a formation where each man occupied a meter of ground in a phalanx six men deep. Why did Joshua order the army to appear each day and encircle the city in silence presumably standing silently in place for hours only to withdraw to their camps without attacking? The answer may be that Joshua was attempting to weaken the will of the enemy by increasing the fear and uncertainty that Rahab the prostitute and the Israelite scouts had detected earlier. Joshua knew that Jericho's army did not engage him at the Jordan when they would have had the advantage. Nor did it attack when he was encamped at Gilgal. And when Joshua moved into position to attack the city, he found that "Jericho was shut up tight because of the Bene Israel."[96] Whoever the enemy commander was, he had already shown himself to be timid and unaggressive. Joshua's repeated encirclement at Jericho was probably designed to increase the enemy commander's uncertainty even as it heightened the fear within the garrison.

In the end, of course, the city still had to be taken by force. If we do not take the text too literally that "the walls collapsed on the spot," and understand it to mean that the resistance suddenly collapsed, then we can inquire as to what Joshua did to make the resistance collapse so suddenly. An army of this size assaulting a small city of only 500 defenders could easily have overcome the walls with scaling ladders at any time during the six days. Why, then, did Joshua wait until the seventh day? Part of the answer may have been an attempt to weaken the resolve of the defenders. Another reason may have to do with Rahab the prostitute. Rahab's "dwelling was at the outer side of the city wall and she lived in the actual wall."[97] When the Israelite scouts left, they instructed Rahab to "tie this length of crimson cord to the window through which you let us down."[98] Fashioned in this manner, the crimson cord would only be visible from *outside* the city wall, making it useless as an indicator of Rahab's house by Israelite soldiers ravaging the city from the *inside*. That is why the Israelite scouts told Rahab to keep herself and her family inside the house during the attack, warning that "if anyone ventures outside the doors of your house, his blood will be on his head."[99] What, then, was the purpose of the crimson cord?

The answer might be that the crimson cord marked the window through which Israelite elite troops could enter the city. The dust and confusion caused by the Israelite army as it assembled and marched around the city (if they did march) was sufficient distraction for small numbers of Israelite troops to enter the city through Rahab's window. Indeed, Rahab already had a rope to assist them, the same one she had used previously to let the Israelite scouts down from her window. The idea was to infiltrate a few men at a time into Rahab's house, using the army's activities outside the wall as a distraction. At, say, five or six men a day, the Israelites would have placed 35 to 40 men inside the house when the great noise arose from the army outside the walls signaling the start of the attack. The infiltrators could then have been used in two ways to bring about the sudden collapse of resistance. The text does not tell us the location of Rahab's house relative to the city's main gate, but hints that it might have been fairly close by. When Rahab was questioned by the king's intelligence agents about the Israelite scouts, she told them that "when at dusk the gate was about to close, the men (the Israelite scouts) went out,"[100] suggesting that she might have been able to see them leave from her window. If this was the case, then the main gate was nearby, and we might imagine that the infiltrators emerged from their hiding place, attacked the main gate from the inside, overpowered the guard, and threw it open to the sudden rush of the attacking army. Or, if Rahab's house was some distance from the gate, the infiltrators may have rushed from their hiding place to overpower the nearest defenders on the wall. In short order they would have cleared a section of the wall making it easy for the men below to use their scaling ladders. With similar attacks occurring all along the perimeter wall, a considerable number of troops could have successfully scaled the wall in a matter of minutes, especially so if the defenders were suffering from low morale. In either scenario the defense would have collapsed quite quickly, perhaps tempting the text's author to employ the metaphor that "the walls collapsed on the spot."

Jericho was the first Israelite objective in Canaan, and Joshua put the city to the sword: "They put everything in the city under ban—man and woman, young and old, ox and sheep and ass—at the mouth of the sword. . . . The city they burned, with everything in it."[101] The deuteronomic explanation aside once more, was there any valid military reason to destroy Jericho? The answer is concealed in the more fundamental question, Why attack Jericho at all? It is not quite accurate to say that Jericho commanded the approaches to the central Judean ridge. In fact there are several approaches, north and south of the city, that Joshua could have used. With its modest size and small garrison, Jericho would have presented no significant military threat to the Israelite rear if it had been bypassed. Moreover, why go through the trouble of attacking a city that was not going to be used for Israelite resettlement? This was, after all, a war of conquest and resettlement, a fact that might explain why, except for Hazor and the northern royal towns, Joshua did not usually burn the other cities captured in his campaign. Finally, in ancient times Jericho already had a reputation for being an unhealthy place to live.[102] Jericho's water supply depended on a single well, Elisha's Well, located below the city, a location that lends itself to contamination. Archaeological investigations have uncovered evidence of the shells of *bulinus truncatus*, the tiny snail that carries the parasite for *schistosomiasis* or "snail fever," still endemic to Egypt and Iraq.[103] The disease produces genitourinary discharge (which, given Rahab's profession, she might have been aware of!), lethargy, weakness, low fertility, and high rates of miscarriage.[104] Indeed, these very circumstances may have been what prompted Joshua to place a curse on the city and whoever attempted to rebuild it. But if Joshua knew that Jericho was a pesthole, then why attack it at all?

The reason might have been psychological. Joshua's war was a war of extermination, and Jericho was destroyed with utter ruthlessness to strike fear in the minds of the rulers of other cities that Joshua planned to attack. It was a technique used occasionally by the Romans in their war with Hannibal and, much later, almost routinely by the Mongols. It was said of the Mongols that their army was preceded by an army of fear. Jericho was by any military calculation a "soft" target, and it was attacked and destroyed as part of Joshua's campaign of psychological warfare to frighten his enemies. It is instructive in this regard that after the Israelites suffered a minor setback at Ai, Joshua was most concerned with the effect of the defeat on the reputation of his troops in the minds of the Canaanites. Jericho was the first battle to be fought on the soil of Canaan, and perhaps Joshua wanted to make certain that the first combat in the Promised Land was a success, for nothing so excites an army as a successful bloodletting. In all these respects Joshua demonstrated his understanding of that most crucial element of war, the psychological mindset of the soldier.

THE BATTLE OF AI/BETHEL

With Jericho in flames and the reputation of the Israelite army spreading over Canaan, Joshua moved quickly. The strategic objective was to gain a foothold in the Judean highlands before the Canaanites could react in concert to block the Israelite advance. From the Israelite camp at Gilgal the route to the ridge ran uphill along one of the branches of the Wadi Muheisin where it gained the ridge in front of the stronghold of Ai, the terminus for several routes of approach leading to the top of the watershed. Ai was not far from the Gibeonite city of Beeroth (near Ramallah) and was almost in the midst of the group of Gibeonite towns, including Beeroth, Chephirah, and Qiryath-Yearim. Any future alliance with the Gibeonites would require the removal of Ai, a Bethelite town, from their midst. A successful attack on Ai might offer political benefits, as well as military advantages. Ai itself had been a strongly fortified town more than 1,000 years before, but during Joshua's time it was probably little more than a large urban ruin.[105] Still, its location was strategically important, and Gichon's suggestion that the Bethelites had refortified it in anticipation of an Israelite attack seems sound.[106] Ai stood on the edge of the ascent to the Judean ridge, a location that offered the advantage to the defense by forcing the attackers to fight uphill. Second, combat in an urban ruin is difficult because intact combat units cannot be brought to bear effectively. The broken ground shapes the battle into one of close combat where individual, and not unit, fighting ability has the advantage. Under these conditions the Israelite numerical advantage could not be directly brought to bear. The Bethelites were likely aware of the size of the Israelite army and understood that a defense of Bethel itself some four kilometers away from Ai was unlikely to succeed against such numbers. But if a significant force could be placed forward in the ruins of Ai where the arena favored the defenders, and the Israelites would be made to suffer high casualties, then, perhaps, the Israelites would withdraw. It was a risky plan, but one based on sound tactical thinking.

Joshua's first move was to send out spies to reconnoiter the objective. "They returned to Joshua and reported to him, 'Not all the troops need go up. Let two or three contingents go and attack Ai; do not trouble all the troops to go up there, for the people there are few.' "[107] The proper role of tactical intelligence units is to gather information, not to make operational recommendations, which is the proper province of the commander. Here Joshua committed a fundamental error. He accepted the operational recommendations without further analysis. Unlike the crossing of the Jordan or the attack on Jericho, this time Joshua did not undertake his own reconnaissance before formulating his operational plan. "So there went up thither, from the people, exactly three contingents. But they ran away in defeat before the men of Ai! The men of Ai struck down six of their men, whom they chased from in front of the gate as far as the Quarries, striking them down at the descent."[108] Perhaps the Israelite unit that reconnoitered Ai had been spotted prompting the Bethelites to strongly reinforce the garrison there so that when the three Israelite contingents, about 600 men, approached, they may have done so incautiously, perhaps, as the text implies, even directly at the main gate, only to be taken by surprise and mauled by the larger Bethelite force now occupying the ruin.

The effect of the defeat on Israelite morale is somewhat more difficult to explain. The text tells us that "the hearts of the troops sank in utter dismay."[109] If the Israelite force of 600 men suffered "thirty-six of their men" dead, a loss rate of approximately 5 percent, one would not expect the defeat to have had such a negative effect on morale. However, if the 36 dead were from a single unit say, to use the Egyptian example, a "platoon" of 50 men (four platoons to a company contingent), then 36 dead becomes understandably more terrifying in the minds of the Israelite soldiers. Perhaps a single platoon was sent into the ruins as an advanced probe only to be trapped in the rubble, surrounded, and slaughtered. Or perhaps it approached the main gate expecting no resistance and was exposed to murderous fire from the walls and a counterattack through the gate, killing two-thirds of the platoon in full view of their comrades. Surprised and frightened at the unexpected horror, the Israelite force turned and ran. Offering their backs to the enemy, they suffered additional casualties "at the descent" until gaining the safety of the Israelite camp.

When told of the rout, Joshua's reaction was to worry about the effect of news of the defeat on the psychology of his adversaries. Having destroyed Jericho precisely to strike fear in the minds of his enemies, Joshua had to reckon with the fact that news of the defeat would quickly spread and reduce the psychological advantage that Jericho had given him.[110] The objective effect of the defeat on the army was negligible, for it was still intact and capable of fighting, that is, unless demoralization was permitted to spread through its ranks. To prevent this and preserve what was left of his psychological advantage, Joshua attacked quickly. This time he would not be drawn into the ruin. "So Joshua and all the fighting force rose (prepared) to go up to Ai. Joshua chose thirty, a man from each contingent (the burly warriors) and sent them out at night."[111] This was the ambush force, and Joshua moved them into position west of the city under cover of darkness. The size of the force is uncertain. A force of 30 men would have been far too small to be effective and the translation of *eleph* as "thousand," albeit incorrectly, would produce a force of 3,000, far too large to conceal. Perhaps the reference to "the burly warriors" implies that the men were from the tribes of Gad, Reuben, and half-Manasseh in which case a contingent from each would produce a unit of about 600 men or, as we shall see, about the right size for its twofold mission. Joshua spent that night with the main force at Gilgal preparing for the next day's march to the objective.

Early the next morning, Joshua mustered his troops and marched them up the steep track leading to the small plateau atop the ascent, a march of six to eight hours, probably arriving late in the afternoon near dusk. "All the fighting force that was with him advanced near the city and encamped to the north of Ai, with a hollow [shallow saddle?] between them and Ai."[112] During the night

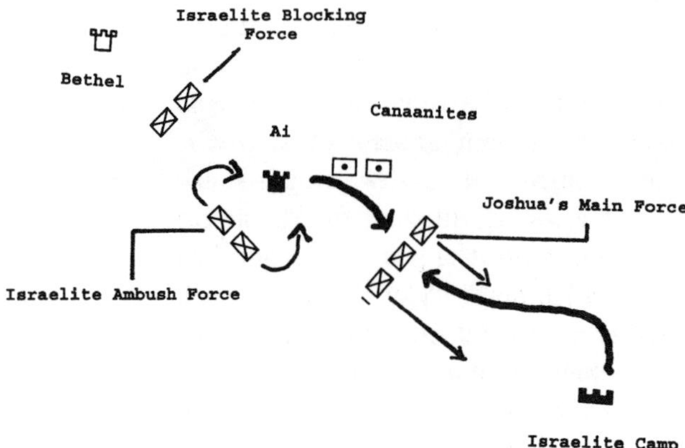

Figure 4.1 Battle of Ai, Phase 1

Joshua assembled a force of "exactly five contingents and stationed them in ambush between Bethel and Ai."[113] This was a second ambush force placed between the two cities to prevent reinforcements from Bethel from reaching the ruin. At five contingents, the blocking force was 1,000 men strong. Figure 4.1 portrays the relative positions of the two forces on the eve of the battle. Then "Joshua went out that night into the valley." Not repeating the mistake he had made earlier, Joshua conducted his own reconnaissance before the battle to make certain that all was in order and, if possible, to determine the size of the enemy force he was facing at Ai. The only hint of the size of the enemy force comes after the battle when the text tells us "The casualties that day . . . were twelve contingents—all the inhabitants of Ai."[114] Thus the enemy force in the ruin may have numbered between 1,800 and 2,400 men, or the entire army of Bethel. That the king was in personal command of his troops is evident from the text that tells us that the king was captured and hanged from a tree by the Israelites.[115] There is no evidence that any chariots were involved in the battle, so we must imagine the ferocity of an infantry battle between two large armies, one fighting for possession of the land, the other for its life.

The next morning Joshua led the main force across the shallow saddle that separated the Israelite camp from the enemy position and arranged the army in battle formation before the ruin in full view of its defenders. The Ai garrison relinquished its defensive advantage and left their positions to attack the Israelites in force. Why the enemy commander chose to attack is unclear. It is possible, however, that he remembered how easily the Israelites had been put to flight a few days earlier. But if Joshua had deployed his entire main force on the plateau, it would have been apparent to the enemy commander that he was seriously outnumbered and that a frontal attack risked failure. Perhaps Joshua had left a sizable segment of his army behind the rise created by the saddle and positioned out of sight of the defenders between the rise and the edge of the descent. If so, the enemy commander would only have seen an Israelite force of considerably smaller size and been tempted to attack out of his positions. In any case, Joshua and his men feigned a panicked retreat—"Joshua and all Israel let themselves be routed before them and fled into the wilderness"[116]—that is, across the shallow saddle and over the small rise. Sensing another easy victory, the defenders of Ai came completely out of their positions in the ruin so "there was not a man left in the ruin, or even the sanctuary, who did not go after Israel."[117] Having set the bait and watched the enemy take it, Joshua now sprang the trap.

From somewhere atop the small rise formed by the far ridge of the saddle, Joshua turned and "pointed the kidon (sickle-sword) in his hand toward the city. The ambush rose swiftly from its position and ran (toward the city) while he stretched out his hand,"[118] perhaps using the reflection from the side of the blade flashing in the sun as a signal. The Israelite troops set in ambush rushed the defenseless fortifications and set them ablaze. Now the fleeing Israelites turned around and faced the enemy at their backs. One might imagine that the Israelites fled over the small rise and joined the remainder of the army lying in wait. As the enemy came over the rise in hot pursuit, they were met by a much larger force than had originally assembled on the plateau. The enemy units had lost cohesion in the pursuit so when the Israelites closed quickly with them "they were unable to flee either backward or forward . . . so that they were in the very midst of Israel, scattered hither and thither."[119] Caught suddenly in a maelstrom of violence, the men of Ai were cut down "on the open plateau, in the hills by the descent, and wherever they pursued them until they were wiped out and all had fallen to the sword."[120] It must have been over fairly quickly, and the entire enemy army died that day. And when its body moved no more, it was left to rot where it had fallen. Joshua turned his attention to the survivors in the ruin and had them all executed along with the king who was hanged from a tree until sunset when his body was cut down and his corpse thrown in the dust at the foot of the city gate. With the victory at Ai, the Israelites had gained a foothold on the Judean ridge from where they could attack the major Canaanite cities that controlled the spine of the central massif. The Canaanite states were powerful enemies with large armies comprised of professional warriors, and if they should decide to act in concert, Joshua's army would be at a severe disadvantage. It was, perhaps, to deal with such a possibility that Joshua journeyed to Shechem.

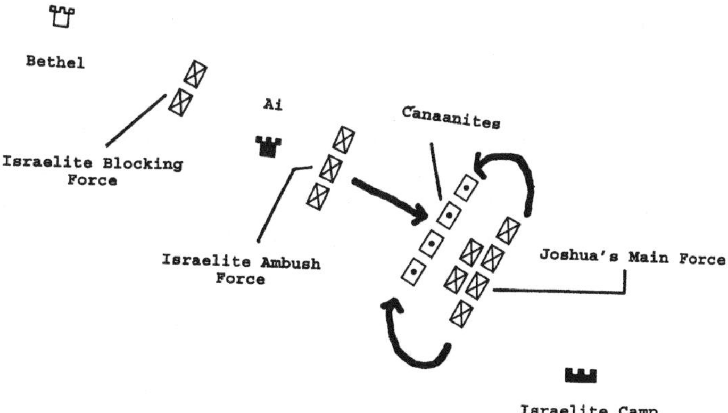

Figure 4.2 Battle of Ai, Phase 2

THE SHECHEM COVENANT

The conquest tradition narrative speaks of three phases of military operations through which the conquest of the land of Canaan was accomplished. The first was the conquest of the Transjordan between Bashan and the Arnon River by Moses, the second was Joshua's conquest of the central hill country, and the third his conquest of Galilee and the north country. Curiously there is no mention of the land in between, the area of central Palestine from just north of Jerusalem to where Mount Gilboa touches the Jezreel. During the time of Joshua the capital of this region, Shechem, was no longer the powerful Canaanite state it had been 100 years earlier but had become an important cult center for local worship.[121] There Mount Ebal is the higher of the two mountains flanking the important east-west pass through the north central hill country opposite Mount Gerizim. Whoever controls this pass controls the upper spine of the central ridge leading to the Jezreel. During Joshua's time the area was settled by militarized *habiru* groups living outside the control of the Canaanite cities.[122] It was to Shechem and the *habiru* that Joshua journeyed in search of military allies.

The text tells us, "Then it was that Joshua built an altar for Yahweh the God of Israel near Mount Ebal. . . . And there he wrote on the stones a copy of the Treaty-Teaching of Moses which he recorded in the presence of the Israelites. . . . There was not a word of all that Moses had commanded which Joshua did not read before the general assembly of the Bene-Israel: the men, women, youngsters, and aliens who journeyed in their midst."[123] It is interesting that Joshua performed the covenant ceremony in the presence of the *ger* or "resident aliens" and the *ezrah*, or "aborigines."[124] Who were these people? Scholars of the Shechem incident suggest that the resident aliens may have been the descendants of other Hebrew tribes—perhaps the Leah tribes—who had established themselves in the area during the time of the Patriarchs and had never descended into Egypt.[125] The Jericho conquest may have been carried out by them long before Joshua and the story later incorporated in the narrative. The aborigines or native peoples of the area were probably other *habiru* with no lineal or historical connection to the Israelites.[126] The events at Shechem suggest a treaty between the Israelites and other *habiru* residents of the central hill country, one that implies some degree of religious conversion.[127] As Boling and Wright explain, "the events at Shechem must have involved religious reformation and conversion on a large scale, of such proportions in fact as to be worthy of being called a "mutation" in the evolution of the world's religions. The Shechem covenant was the reconstitution of Israel in Canaan, following the pattern of Mosaic Yahwehism."[128] Such a treaty would support Mendenhall's thesis that the Israelites began as a *religious* community, not a lineal or ethnic one, drawing to itself from the earliest days various ethno-social elements who were admitted as long as they accepted Yahweh as their deity.[129] It is clear that fertility rates alone could not explain the increase in the Israelite population sufficient to conquer and settle all of Canaan. Rather, it was mostly through accretion that the Israelite movement grew so rapidly. It is likely, then, that Gottwald is correct when he says the fighting tradition of the Exodus Yahwehists combined with a tested and experienced military force among the underclass Canaanites (*habiru*) and that military cooperation gradually came to include an infusion of Yahwehistic cultic practices and ideology, so that "the Exodus Yahwehists became a powerful catalyst in energizing and guiding a broad coalition of underclass Canaanites."[130]

The *habiru*-Israelite alliance at Shechem provided Joshua with freedom of movement all along the central spine of the Judean ridge blocked in the south by Jerusalem and in the north by the obvious risks of venturing upon the open plain of the Jezreel. It also expanded the Israelite logistics base increasing the area upon which it could draw for food and materials. Most important from a military perspective, however, is that the alliance probably increased the manpower base upon which Joshua could draw to sustain and increase his army. We do not know if the covenant occurred before or after the attack on Ai, but the text suggests after. If so, it might have been that Joshua was able to draw upon the manpower of his new allies for his campaign against the five Canaanite kings and, later, his southern campaign in the *shephelah*. As we shall see, it is also difficult to imagine that Joshua would have been able to defeat the northern Canaanite alliance without additional military manpower provided, perhaps, by his new allies. And here we see Joshua's brilliant strategic mind at work as he utilized skilled diplomacy and religious ideology to increase Israelite military power, sufficient proof, even in ancient times, of the accuracy of Clausewitz's dictum that "diplomacy is the conduct of war by other means."

JOSHUA'S WAR WITH THE CANAANITE KINGS

Joshua's destruction of the Bethelite army at Ai seems to have had the desired effect of striking fear in the heart of his adversaries, prompting the leaders of Gibeon and its daughter towns to seek an alliance with the Israelites. The text reveals the Gibeonite fear of Joshua's army when it tells us that "they don't even hide their fear"[131] and then again when the Gibeonites themselves tell Joshua, "We feared greatly for our lives, because of you."[132] From Joshua's perspective, however, the treaty was based on cold military calculations. Gibeon was the largest of four small cities that sat astride the east-west and north-south axes of the Judean ridge's central spine, controlling movement in both directions. Gibeon was located about eight miles from Jerusalem at the east-west crossroads on the road running from Jericho over the ridge continuing on to descend westward to the coastal plain through the Beth-Horon pass and the Aijalon Valley. Its daughter towns—Chephirah (meaning "lioness") located six miles west of Gibeon, Beeroth, perhaps the modern city of Ramallah, and Qiryath-Yearim (literally, "Woodsville") near the border where the tribal lands of Judah, Benjamin and Dan converged—all possessed military significance in geographic terms. The Israelite-Gibeonite treaty was a form of mutual assistance pact among unequals common in Hittite and Egyptian diplomatic practice—"a pact with a protege"—and bound both parties to its terms, including military defense.[133]

Moreover, if the text is accurate, then Gibeon also possessed significant military forces that were now at Joshua's disposal, "for it was known that Gibeon was a town as powerful as one of the royal towns, and it was larger than Ai, and that all its men were knights!"[134] If Joshua was also drawing upon the military resources and manpower of his new allies at Shechem, then he appears to have been assembling an enormous military force capable not only of defending Gibeon or the previously conquered areas, but of effecting a *strategic* military decision against the remaining Canaanite city-states located along the Judean ridge. The treaty with Gibeon was a master strategic stroke for it uncovered the northern flank of the kingdom of Jerusalem to Israelite influence and military movement, and Joshua must have calculated that it would produce an immediate military response. Having secured his military manpower base through skilled diplomacy at Gibeon and Shechem, Joshua now had the military resources to deal with a concerted Canaanite armed response. All that was left to do was to provoke it.

And the response was not long in coming. "Wherefore Adonizedek, king of Jerusalem sent unto Hoham king of Hebron, and unto Piram king of Jarmuth, and unto Japhia king of Lachish, and unto Debir king of Eglon, saying, 'Come up unto me and help me, that we may smite Gibeon: for it hath made peace with Joshua and with the children of Israel.' Therefore the five kings of the Amorites . . . gathered themselves together, and went up, they and all their hosts, and encamped before Gibeon, and made war against it."[135] Figure 4.3 shows the location of these cities, as well as the routes employed to assemble the Canaan-

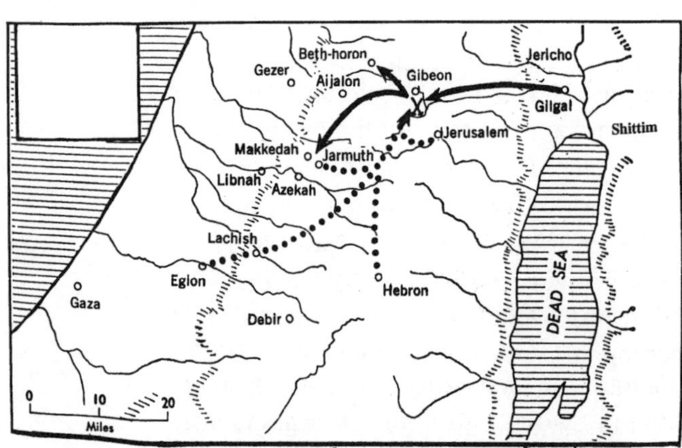

Figure 4.3 Joshua's War against the Five Kings

ite armies at Gibeon. The leaders of Gibeon invoked their treaty with Joshua who moved immediately to engage the Canaanite armies.

The Canaanite armies laid siege to Gibeon and seem to have ignored the Israelites completely. Even in their reduced state, these armies possessed highly trained heavy infantry and chariots, the latter now rendered useless as the Canaanites engaged in static warfare against a fixed fortification. There is, too, no evidence that the Canaanites undertook routine patrols to discern the position and strength of the Israelite force, thereby rendering themselves vulnerable to surprise attack. Joshua moved quickly to take advantage of these lapses. The text tells us that Joshua assembled his army and "marched all night from Gilgal."[136] Mordechai Gichon notes that this is a difficult and twisting climb of about 18 to 20 miles over an elevation of more than 1,000 meters.[137] One imagines Joshua's men almost exhausted as they reached the assembly point somewhere above Gibeon where Joshua permitted them some time to rest before going over to the attack. Although not mentioned in the text, it is likely that Joshua conducted a final reconnaissance before committing to the attack. Gibeon was built on a low rise in the middle of a valley surrounded by ridges. The Canaanites were probably camped somewhere near the several springs and wells in the valley.[138] There were no pickets or patrols. Joshua, ever the imaginative tactician, had achieved complete surprise.

The text does not describe the battle, but it is reasonable to suppose that the Israelites attacked at first light when the sun was at their backs, as it rose over Gibeon in the east, shining in the eyes of the Canaanites, the moon still in the sky to the west over the Aijalon Valley. Malamat suggests that it is this poetic description of the dawn attack that was enshrined in the famous poem in which it is said that the sun and moon stood still until Joshua had defeated his enemies in the Aijalon.[139] The Israelites had the advantage of the terrain in attacking downhill and must have caught the Canaanite armies still in their tents or at breakfast. The shock of the assault shattered the enemy and they took flight. The size of the battle was considerable. Joshua's Israelite contingent was at full strength and may even have been augmented as it almost certainly was later for the southern campaign by some units from his Shechem allies. The Canaanite armies represented some of the most powerful states of southern Palestine and might well have put between 2,000 and 2,500 men each in the field, or an overall force of 10,000 to 15,000 men. Shattered by the sudden attack, the Canaanite army took to its heels with part of the force fleeing to the northwest and others to the south toward Maqqedah.

Following the dictum of Napoleon, Joshua kept the sabre in the enemy's back never losing contact with the fleeing Canaanites. "He pursued them by way of the Beth-Horan ascent. He struck them down as far away as Azekah and Maqqedah"[140] and beyond through the Aijalon Valley itself where even the weather turned against the enemy. "While they (the Canaanites) were in the Beth-Horan descent, Yahweh threw down big stones (hailstones) upon them from the sky—as far off as Azekah—and they died. Many more died because of the hailstones than the Israelites put to the sword."[141] One imagines that some of the Canaanite soldiers had thrown away their shields in the flight and thus had little protection from the hail, although it is unlikely that the midsummer cloudburst killed many of them. Still the pursuit continued even to the gates of Azekah, a Canaanite stronghold with ties to Egypt recently renewed by Ramses II's campaign to restore Egyptian influence in southern Palestine. Because of its alliance with Egypt[142] and, perhaps, even the presence of an Egyptian garrison Joshua broke off the pursuit here and did not attack Azekah during his later southern campaign. Elsewhere, however, the ruthless pursuit of the Canaanite remnants continued unabated. When some of Joshua's units trapped the enemy commanders in a cave at Maqqedah, he told them to seal up the cave, "but do not stay there. Go after your enemies and cut off their retreat! Do not let them enter their towns."[143] Joshua wanted to destroy the Canaanite armies while he had the chance. His reasons were strategic: With their armies crippled by defeat, the Canaanite cities would fall easily to the next stage of the Israelite campaign. Joshua intended to remove the Canaanite presence from the central Judean ridge and resettle it with Israelites.

If ever there was evidence of the fighting quality, leadership, cohesion, and discipline of Joshua's army, it was clearly on display at the battle of Gibeon. The army undertook an 18-mile forced march at night over terrain that rose more than a 1,000 meters in the distance covered arriving at the final assembly point in the dark and undetected. Permitted to rest for a short while, the army still was not allowed to light fires and cook breakfast, going into battle on empty stomachs. They engaged in battle at dawn, and then conducted a fierce pursuit of the enemy for the entire next day resting somewhat at night only to continue the pursuit the next morning toward Azekah 11 miles from the Aijalon Valley. Mordechai Gichon has calculated that "altogether the Israelite warriors had traversed about 30 miles in forty-five to forty-eight hours, two-thirds or more of the time under battle conditions,"[144] a feat only a disciplined and well-trained army could have performed.

JOSHUA'S SOUTHERN CAMPAIGN

With the Canaanite armies scattered, Joshua struck quickly at their cities and others that were of importance to the defense of the Judean ridge and the routes of approach leading from the *shephelah*. Joshua took Maqqedah during the initial battle and then turned his army against Libnah, which fell in a single day. Lachish required two days to subdue. Then a strange event occurred. Horam, king of Gezer, who did not join the original Canaanite coalition, sent an army against Joshua. The text tells us that "Joshua struck against him and his force until he left no survivor for him,"[145] which implies a battle in the open and not an attack against Gezer itself. What makes Horam's attack curious is that at this time Gezer was closely tied to Egypt as a consequence of Ramses II's initiative to reestablish Egyptian control of southern Palestine. Egyptian control, complete with military garrisons, now ran uninterrupted from Gaza to Azekah, and Gezer and Ashkelon were the last remaining semiautonomous Canaanite states there. Gezer was the most important city in the south in that it controlled the coastal road as well as the axis of advance up the Judean ridge to Jerusalem and down to the Jordan and to Beth-shean. It was only a short while later that Pharaoh Merneptah rescinded Gezer's autonomy and occupied it with a strong Egyptian garrison. It is possible that the clash with Horam of Gezer may have been instigated by the Egyptians to limit the Israelite campaign in the *shephelah*, and it is surprising that the text makes so little of such an important military encounter. Gezer remained an Egyptian base until it passed into Israelite hands as a wedding gift from pharaoh to Solomon who married pharaoh's daughter.

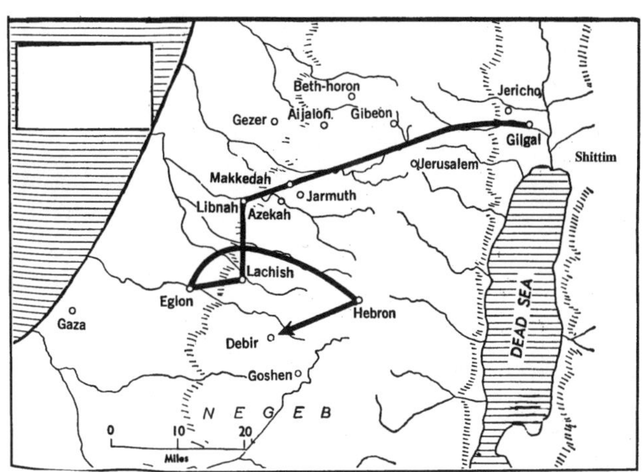

Figure 4.4 Joshua's Southern Campaign

Figure 4.4 portrays Joshua's southern campaign, including his attacks against Eglon, Hebron, and Debir. The campaign makes excellent strategic sense. Having driven the Canaanite armies from the Judean ridge and subdued their cities, Joshua moved to occupy all the cities and towns that sat at the entrances of the various routes leading from the coastal plain up to the Judean ridge. But why did Joshua make no attempt to attack and occupy Jerusalem? Given that it led the Canaanite coalition and held a strategic position across the vital road from the coast to the Jordan its continued independence represented a threat to Israelite control of the Judean ridge. The answer is the Egyptians. It is likely that Ramses II and Merneptah maintained close relationships with the rulers of Jerusalem for obvious strategic reasons. It was no accident that Gezer controlled the only avenue of advance leading up the Judean ridge that was not in Israelite hands, a route that Egyptian troops could easily traverse to come to Jerusalem's aid if circumstances required. The road over the ridge to the Jordan and along the central spine was simply too important strategically to permit the Israelites to control it. There is some evidence that Merneptah may have sent troops to stop an Israelite advance in the area some time later and that this incident may be what he recorded on the famous Israel stele.[146] It was not until David's time, after Egypt had withdrawn completely from southern Palestine, that an Israelite army finally entered Jerusalem. Except for this, Joshua's southern campaign was very successful indeed. Behind the army came the settlers, and soon the Canaanite cities and towns were resettled by Israelites. But in the mind of a field general like Joshua there was still much to be done. He turned his eyes to the north.

JOSHUA'S NORTHERN CAMPAIGN

Joshua's victories in the south sounded the tocsin for the northern Canaanite kings. They correctly assessed that Joshua's covenant with the *habiru* at Shechem made it possible for him to turn the entire central massif into a strategic platform for an invasion of the Galilee by guaranteeing sufficient manpower to prosecute the war and freedom of movement to the edge of the Jezreel Valley. Jabin, king of Hazor, took the initiative and gathered a coalition of northern kings and their armies. "They came forth in their armies accompanying them—an enormous force, as numerous as grains of sand along the seashore—with a multitude of horses and chariots. All these kings rendezvoused and pitched camp together—by the Waters of Merom—to fight against Israel."[147] Merom is probably the modern Meron.[148] But the only "waters" in Meron are in a small brook running down a deep, narrow wadi that is too steep, rugged, and small to have been a place to gather an army of perhaps 10,000 men, horses, and chariots. The most likely location that could accommodate such a force is a large pond located 4 to 5 kilometers northeast of Meron itself called Kirket el-Jish or *Agam Dalton*. The pond sits on a small plateau to the north of the modern village of Jebal Jermaq.[149] At the time of the battle the name Merom may not have been a place name at all but used to mean "elevated" or "exalted," thus implying a location somewhere in the mountains. Figure 4.5 portrays the locations of the Canaanite coalition cities relative to the point of concentration at the Waters of Merom. The coalition cities included Madon, Shimrom, Chinnereth, Achshaph, Arabah, Naphath-Dor, Hermon, Mitzpah, and although not mentioned, probably Megiddo. Troop

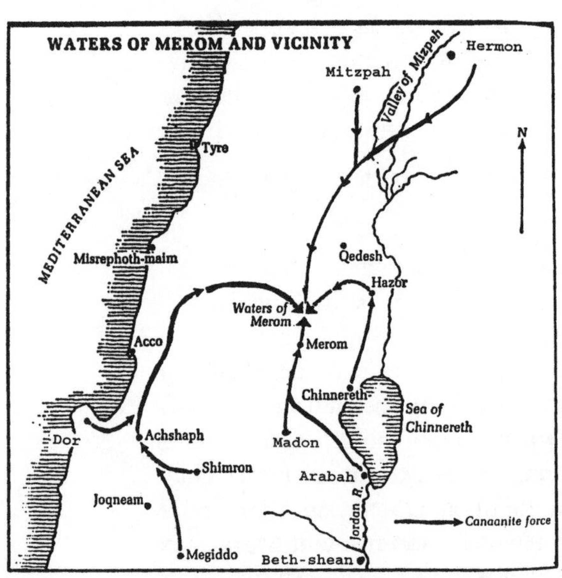

Figure 4.5 Phase 1, Concentration of Canaanite Armies at Merom

units were provided as well by the Hittites, Perizzites, Jebusites, and Hivites scattered in villages and walled towns in the mountains and the lower Galilee.

It has been argued that the choice of the Waters of Merom as a staging area made sound tactical sense insofar as the major avenues of communication in the upper Galilee converged on the central ridge below Mount Hermon and radiated outward in a compass arc of 360 degrees, permitting the gathered forces to move quickly in any direction to engage Joshua.[150] While this is true, there are still sufficient reasons to question that choice of Merom as a staging area for the Canaanite armies. First, the Canaanite armies were a chariot-heavy force, and the ground around the staging area is hilly, steep, and uneven. There are only a few places where a chariot battle could be fought and even then the ground conditions are less than ideal. Why assemble a chariot army in an area where the ground risks trapping it if forced to battle? Second, except for Hazor, Mitzpah, and Hermon, all the other cities of the coalition are located in or very close to the Jezreel. Requiring the armies to assemble at Merom left the Jezreel and the Galilee completely uncovered to an enemy force positioned in the mountains of the central spine, that is, around Shechem or Mount Gilboa, precisely the area where Joshua's armies would assemble in preparation for a thrust into the north. Third, surely the Canaanite commander knew that Joshua was nowhere near Merom but was in control of the central hill country and the *shephelah*, more than 40 kilometers distant from Merom. If the Canaanite plan was to meet Joshua on the open plain of the Jezreel, or even to carry the battle to him by gaining access to the central ridge at, say, Gina (modern Jenin), then almost any assembly point on the northern edge of the Jezreel or at one of the coalition cities within the valley itself would have made more tactical sense than assembling at Merom.

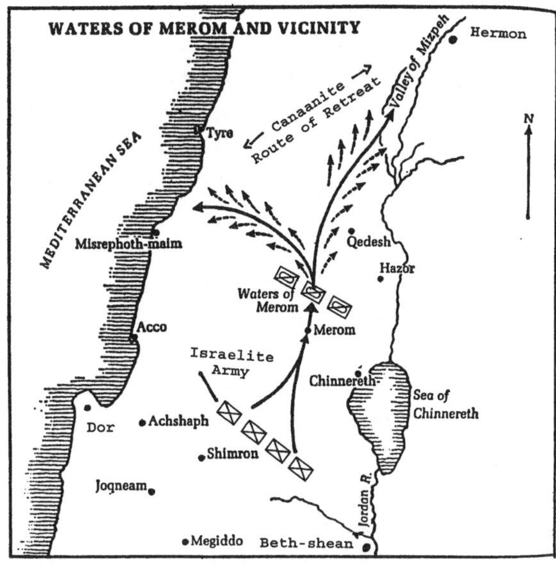

Figure 4.6 Phase 2, Israelite Attack and Canaanite Route of Retreat

The text tells us that "Joshua and his entire fighting force with him took them by surprise at the Waters of Merom and fell upon them from the mountain."[151] The plan was to disable the chariots by houghing (slicing) the hamstrings of the horses just prior to a surprise attack at first light. The key was to prevent the chariot teams from mounting and engaging the attackers. Presumably, for the text is silent, small units would have crept close to the horse corrals in the predawn darkness, knives ready to slash the animals' leg tendons. As the main force came rushing down the mountain to fall upon the Canaanites still in their tents, the small units entered the corrals and carried out their bloody work. It might also be reasonably supposed that some designated lead elements of the main force also headed for the corrals to make certain few animals escaped. The main attack was so ferocious that the Canaanites broke and ran. The Israelites "pressed the attack and gave chase. Toward the Greater Sidon and Misrephoth-maim! Toward Mizpeh Valley to the east! They kept up the attack until he left no survivor for them. Joshua did to them as Yahweh had told him: He hamstrung their horses and burned their chariots."[152] Once more Joshua had taken the enemy by surprise.

The description of the battle, however, raises questions about whether it was really fought at the Waters of Merom. As already noted, to assemble the Canaanite army there offered the Canaanites no advantages at all. Moreover, given that Joshua's army was probably larger than the 8,000 or so he employed before the Shechem covenant, to take the Canaanites by surprise Joshua would have had to move this large army across the open ground of the Jezreel Valley before he could gain even the thin cover of the lower Galilee hills and do so under the very noses of the patrols of the coalition cities located in the Jezreel! Even if the crossing of the Jezreel could have been accomplished without detection, Joshua's army would have to had move up the steep terrain of the lower Galilee for at least two days before it was able to position itself for a night attack. But the text suggests that the towns of the lower Galilee had sent troop contingents to the coalition army and, we may assume, would act as lookouts for any suspicious troop movements through the area. Did Joshua move only at night and hide during the day to escape detection? Could this have been accomplished successfully with so large a force? Even if Joshua maneuvered his army into position without detection, the text tells us he "fell upon them from the mountain." But from what mountain? The lake at Merom is located on a small raised plateau, suggesting that Joshua would have had to cross the open country around the lake to reach the Canaanite forces. Given the small area of the plateau and the enemy force already occupying it, Joshua's attack would have had to have been uphill across open country. If the battle occurred the way the text suggests, including the surprise attack down a mountain, then it might have occurred somewhere else. But where?

It might be that the author of the Joshua text confused the Waters of Merom with the Waters of Megiddo, mentioned in later Israelite texts without, however, identifying its location as near Ta'anach. There are only two water sources near Megiddo: the Qina Brook just below the city itself and the Harod Spring at the foot of Mount Gilboa.[153] Both locations would have made more sense as an assembly point for the Canaanite armies than Merom. Both were closer to most of the coalition cities than Merom, provided ample area in which to assemble a large army and water and graze its horses, offered an ideal field of battle for chariots, denied the Israelites movement across the Jezreel by blocking the route to the north, and were closer to Joshua's army by 40 kilometers. If the Canaanites failed to draw the Israelites into open battle, from either location the Canaanites could have attempted to gain the ridge around Gina (Jenin) exploding across the central mountain plain of Shechem and take the fight to Joshua. A Canaanite assembly at Megiddo or Harod would also explain how Joshua was able to assemble such a large army so close to the enemy without being detected. He would simply have had to move his army to the top of Mount Gilboa or to the southern slope of the hills overlooking the Wadi Ara and the Qina brook at Megiddo. From these positions, Joshua's army could easily have carried out a surprise attack in force at dawn as the text tells us he did.

Wherever the battle occurred, with his victory over the northern Canaanite coalition Joshua completely shattered Canaanite power over Upper and Lower Galilee. He moved quickly to consolidate his position. "They put to the mouth of the sword all persons there. They carried out the ban. Not anything that breathed was left. And Hazor they burned! All those royal towns and all their kings Joshua captured and put to the sword. . . . But all the towns standing on mounds Israel did not burn. . . . All the loot of these towns, including cattle, the Israelites plundered for themselves. But all the human beings they put to the sword, until they wiped them out. They left nothing that breathed."[154] Sometime later, following the great victory and as commanded by Yahweh, Joshua apportioned the land to the tribes of Israel. And like Cincinnatus and Scipio Africanus after him, the great general retired from public life being drawn back only once to deliver a farewell warning to the people of Israel before his death. Elie Wiesel has noted that only the *midrashic* tradition has inquired into Joshua's personality and private life. According to this tradition Joshua married later, but all his children were females and no son was left to follow in his father's footsteps. Joshua died alone and was buried in a place called *Thimnath serah* which is in *Har gaash*, which means an angry mountain. It was said that although Israel was at peace and prospering, no one took the trouble to come to Joshua's funeral. In war, he had been their great general and hero. In peace, he was no longer needed. And it was said that no one came to pay final respects, an honor to which all men are entitled.[155]

NOTES

1. Abraham Malamat, "Israelite Conduct of War in the Conquest of Canaan According to the Biblical Tradition," in *Symposium Celebrating the 75th Anniversary of the Founding of the American Schools of Oriental Research*, edited by F. M. Cross (Cambridge, MA: American Schools of Oriental Research, 1979), 37.

2. For a good overview of these hypotheses, see B.S.J. Isserlin, "The Israelite Conquest of Canaan: A Comparative View of the Arguments Applicable," *Palestine Exploration Quarterly* 115 (1983): 85–94.

3. George E. Mendenhall, "The Hebrew Conquest of Palestine," *Biblical Archaeologist* 25 (1962): 66–87; see also Norman K. Gottwald, *The Tribes of Yahweh* (Maryknoll, NY: Orbis Books, 1979), for a more complete presentation of the argument.

4. Isserlin, 87–94.

5. See *The Westminster Historical Atlas to the Bible* (Philadelphia, PA: Westminster Press, 1945), 15; see also Itamar Singer, "Merneptah's Campaign to Canaan and the Egyptian Occupation of the Southern Coastal Plain in the Ramesside Period," *Bulletin of the American Schools of Oriental Research* 269 (1988): 3–4.

6. Malamat, 40.

7. Robert G. Boling and G. Ernest Wright, *Joshua: The Anchor Bible* (New York: Doubleday, 1982), 165. From here on, this source will be quoted as *Anchor Bible*.

8. Malamat, 40.

9. Ibid.

10. Ibid.

11. Gottwald, 499.

12. George E. Mendenhall, "The Census Lists of Numbers 1 and 26," *Journal of Biblical Literature* 77 (1958): 52–66, for the original calculations as to the size of the Israelite army at Sinai.

13. Yigael Yadin, *The Art of Warfare in Biblical Lands in Light of Archaeological Discovery* 1 (New York: McGraw-Hill, 1964), 19.

14. Othmar Keel, *Wirkmachtige Siegeszeichen im Alten Testament*, 11–82, cited in *Anchor Bible*, 240.

15. Richard A. Gabriel and Karen S. Metz, *From Sumer to Rome: The Military Capabilities of Ancient Armies* (Westport, CT: Greenwood Press, 1991), 63–64.

16. Yehuda Margowsky, "War and Warfare," *Encyclopaedia Judaica*, vol. 16 (Jerusalem: Macmillan Company, 1975), 268.

17. Robert Drew, *The End of the Bronze Age: Changes in Warfare and the Catastrophe ca. 1200 B.C.* (Princeton, NJ: Princeton University Press, 1993), 196.

18. For the history and use of the javelin in Palestine at this time, see Drew, 180–185.

19. Margowsky, 268. The materials of the composite bow are listed in Aqhat A, tablet 6, lines 20–23; Pritchard texts, 151.

20. Wallace McLeod, "An Unpublished Egyptian Composite Bow in the Brooklyn Museum," *American Journal of Archaeology* 62 (1958): 400.

21. T. R. Hobbs, *A Time for War* (Wilmington, DE: Michael Glazier, 1989), 121.

22. Ibid., 120.

23. Ibid., 124.

24. Margowsky, 269.

25. Drew, 178.

26. Hobbs, 110. Since the purpose of the combat axe was to penetrate armor and the helmet, its design was radically different from a common wood axe. As such, although the wood axe is mentioned in the texts, it would not have been of very much use as a combat weapon against the routinely armored troops of the Canaanite armies.

27. Stuart Piggott, "Horse and Chariot: The Price of Prestige," in *Proceedings of*

the Seventh International Conference of Celtic Studies in 1983 (Oxford, England: 1986), 27.

28. Jane C. Waldbaum, "From Bronze to Iron: The Transition from the Bronze Age to the Iron Age in the Eastern Mediterranean," in *Studies in Mediterranean Archaeology* 54 (Goteborg, 1978), 39, Table IV.1.

29. Ibid.

30. Hobbs, 138.

31. John Strange, "The Transition from the Bronze Age to the Iron Age in the Eastern Mediterranean and the Emergence of the Israelite State," *Scandinavian Journal of the Old Testament* 1 (1987): 17. The first ancient army to be fully equipped with iron weapons was the iron army of Assyria under Sargon II (721–705 B.C.E.), almost three centuries after the first introduction of iron weapons in the eastern Mediterranean. See Richard A. Gabriel, *The Culture of War: Invention and Early Development* (Westport, CT: Greenwood Press, 1990), 60; see also Arthur Ferrill, *The Origins of War* (London: Thames and Hudson, 1985), 67.

32. Ibid., 13.

33. Ibid.

34. Ibid., 35.

35. Joshua 7:24.

36. Joshua 7:26.

37. R. J. Forbes, *Studies in Ancient Technology* (Leiden: E. J. Brill, 1964), 37.

38. Gottwald, 578. The description of the Kenites as metalsmiths is found in Genesis 4:22 which identifies the father of the Kenite tribe as Tuban Qayin who was "a forger of brass and iron."

39. Forbes, 92.

40. Ibid.

41. See Forbes, 92, and Gottwald, 321, on this point.

42. Gottwald, 321.

43. Strange, 13.

44. Gottwald, 577.

45. Ibid., 321.

46. Hobbs, 138.

47. Malamat, 43.

48. Forbes, 96; see also Livy, I.43; Dionysius 7.59; and Cicero, *de Republica* II.39.

49. Yigael Yadin, vol. 2, 16; see also Malamat, 50.

50. Yadin, vol. 2, 20.

51. Ibid., 19.

52. *Anchor Bible*, 205.

53. Ibid., 127; Joshua 1:14.

54. Joshua 3:13.

55. *Anchor Bible*, 176.

56. Joshua 8:26.

57. Joshua 7:3.

58. Gottwald, 507.

59. Ibid.

60. Hobbs, 90.

61. Caleb, of course, survived as well, but we have no evidence of his role as a soldier until Judges, where the capture of Hebron is attributed to him.

62. Personal conversation with General Kahalani, March, 1983.

63. Hobbs, 94.

64. Ibid., 101.

65. Malamat, 46.

66. Joshua 1:10–11.

67. The term "all the people" refers only to the army and is distinguished from "the Bene-Israel" which means the entire Israelite people. See *Anchor Bible*, 206.

68. *Anchor Bible*, 126, citing Yadin.

69. Joshua 1:14.

70. *Anchor Bible*, 126.

71. Joshua 2:1.

72. Joshua 3:3.

73. Joshua 2:11.

74. *Anchor Bible*, 148.

75. Joshua 2:18.

76. Joshua 2:15.

77. Joshua 2:24.

78. Joshua 3:1–3.

79. Joshua 3:16.

80. Joshua 3:17.

81. *Anchor Bible*, 170; one of these shallow fords is still used today and is located 12 kilometers southeast of Jericho and is called al Maghtas by the Arabs.

82. Ibid., 168.

83. Joshua 3:17.

84. Joshua 4:4–9.

85. Joshua 5:4–6.

86. *Anchor Bible*, 193.

87. E. A. Wallis Budge, *Osiris and the Egyptian Resurrection* (New York: Dover Publications, 1973), 219–24, for origins of circumcision and its Egyptian connection.

88. Ibid.; Richard A. Gabriel, *Gods of Our Fathers: The Memory of Egypt in Judaism and Christianity* (Westport, CT: Greenwood Press, 2001), 73–74; see also James H. Breasted, *The Dawn of Conscience* (New York: Charles Scribner, 1947), 353–354.

89. Eric Isaac, "Circumcision as Covenant Rite," *Anthropos* 59 (1965): 444; see also *Anchor Bible*, 194, "Moreover, in early Israel it is in covenant with the Divine Warrior that circumcision became important." Exodus 15:3 describes Yahweh as a Divine Warrior.

90. Joshua 5:1. Professor Joel Klein suggests that the angel's description as *sar tseba Adonai* suggests a connection between Joshua and the "commander" based in a common membership in the Egyptian Atenist religion. In his *Through the Name of God* (Westport, CT: Greenwood Press, 2001), Klein argues that the term Adonai is really an interpretive spelling of Aten, the god of Akhenaten's Egypt. Joshua, whose name *bin Nun* suggests that he was of Egyptian origin, may be meeting with a member

of the same cult resident in Jericho who appears, therefore, to be telling Joshua that there is a fifth column inside Jericho that will help the Israelites in their attack. Joshua's removal of his shoes and bowing before the stranger also suggests an Egyptian ritual.

91. *Anchor Bible*, 196.

92. The text is generally understood to mean that Joshua made his reconnaissance the night before the battle. See *Anchor Bible*, 198.

93. Joshua 6:3.

94. Joshua 6:20–21.

95. *Anchor Bible*, 206.

96. Joshua 6:1.

97. Joshua 2:15.

98. Joshua 2:19.

99. Joshua 2:19.

100. Joshua 2.5.

101. Joshua 6:21, 24.

102. E. V. Hulse, "Joshua's Curse and the Abandonment of Ancient Jericho: Schistosomiasis as a Possible Medical Explanation," *Medical History* 15 (1971): 376.

103. Ibid.

104. Ibid.

105. J. Maxwell Miller, "Archaeology and the Israelite Conquest of Canaan: Some Methodological Observations," *Palestine Exploration Quarterly* 109 (1977): 87–93.

106. Chaim Herzog and Mordechai Gichon, *Battles of the Bible* (Jerusalem: Steimatzky's Agency Ltd., 1978), 31.

107. Joshua 7:3.

108. Joshua 7:4–5.

109. Joshua 7:5.

110. Joshua 7:9, for his reaction to the rout at Ai.

111. Joshua 8:4.

112. Joshua 8:11.

113. Ibid.

114. Joshua 8:25.

115. Joshua 8:29.

116. Joshua 8:15.

117. Joshua 8:17.

118. Joshua 8:19. The analogy with Moses at Rephidim is obviously intended by the author.

119. Joshua 8:22.

120. Joshua 8:24.

121. *Anchor Bible*, 247.

122. Gottwald, 494.

123. Joshua 8:30, 32, 35.

124. Joshua 8:33.

125. *Anchor Bible*, 247–48.

126. Ibid.

127. For a good overview of the Shechem event, see Milt Machlin, *Joshua's Altar: The Dig at Mount Ebal* (New York: William Morrow, 1991).

128. Robert G. Boling and G. Ernest Wright, *Joshua* (New York: Anchor Bible, 1982), 271.

129. George E. Mendenhall, "The Hebrew Conquest of Palestine," *Biblical Archaeologist*, 25 (1962): 86.

130. Gottwald, 495.

131. Joshua 9:3.

132. Joshua 9:24.

133. *Anchor Bible*, 271.

134. Joshua 10:2.

135. Joshua 10:3–4.

136. Joshua 10:9.

137. See Herzog and Gichon, 35; Malamat 52–53. Gilgal is 250 meters below sea level, and Gibeon is 840 meters above sea level.

138. Herzog and Gichon, 35.

139. Malamat, 53.

140. Joshua 10:9.

141. Joshua 10:11.

142. See Itmar Singer, cited earlier.

143. Joshua 10:18.

144. Herzog and Gichon, 36.

145. Joshua 10:33.

146. For an excellent treatment of Merneptah's Canaan campaign and the importance of the Israel Stelle, see Frank Yurco, "Merneptah's Canaanite Campaign," *Journal of the American Research Center in Egypt* 23 (1986): 189–215.

147. Joshua 11:4–5.

148. *Anchor Bible*, 307.

149. Ibid.

150. Herzog and Gichon, 39.

151. Joshua 11:7.

152. Joshua 11:8–9.

153. The notion that the battle at the "waters of Merom" may have been fought elsewhere receives some support in Drew, *The End of the Bronze Age*, 211–12. As to the location of the "Waters of Megiddo," the *Westminster Historical Atlas of the Bible*, 44, suggests that it was the Kishon River where Deborah defeated Sisera. While the Kishon is indeed overlooked by a mountain, Mount Carmel, that could have hidden Joshua's large army, getting the army there undetected would have required its movement under the very walls of Megiddo itself, something very risky indeed. For these reasons, the Qina Brook and the Harod Spring seem to me to present more tactically sound locations.

154. Joshua 11:11–14.

155. Elie Wiesel, "Joshua: Silent at the Tent Door," *Bible Review* 14 no. 6 (December 1998): 21.

5

Wars of the Judges

The book of Judges was put into final form sometime around Judah's exile in Babylon, circa 587 B.C.E.,[1] almost 600 years after the events described in it occurred. The arrangement of the stories in the text is artificial, the product of the later redactor's intention, perhaps, to justify Israel's then present need for a strong monarchy, so that the connections between the stories are unreliable as history. As T. R. Hobbs has observed, trying to understand Judges as coherent history is "comparable . . . to the task of writing a modern history of the Hundred Year's War with only the barest of outlines, and the memories of eyewitnesses passed on by word of mouth over six centuries!"[2] These difficulties notwithstanding, Judges contains substantial information of interest to the military historian and there is much that can be gleaned about the period between 1220 and 1040 B.C.E. from other historical and archeological sources, permitting some observations about the military history of the Israelites during this time. Some of the stories, the civil war between the Israelites and the tribe of Benjamin, Deborah's battle against Sisera, and Gideon's campaign against the Midianites are rich in military information. Others, such as the victory of Othniel over Cushan Rishathaim, Ehud's assassination of the king of Moab, Shamgar (a Hurrian or, perhaps, one of the Sea Peoples; not an Israelite) who "struck down a Philistine brigade single handedly, using an oxgoad,"[3] the exploits of Samson, or the attempt by Abimelech, Gideon's son, to establish an Israelite monarchy at Shechem, offer little in the way of information interesting to the military historian. Not surprisingly, then, this chapter focuses upon the exploits of Deborah and Gideon, as well as the tale of the Israelite civil war against Benjamin.

Judges continues the story of the Israelite settlement of the land of Canaan and the difficulties it involved. Joshua's victories established the Israelites in

Canaan, and his assignment of the land by tribes was only the beginning of a process of settlement that continued for at least another two centuries until the establishment of the monarchy under Saul and David finally gave possession of most of the country to the Israelites. Between 1200 and 1100 B.C.E., the hill country became dotted with new settlements and towns indicating an increase in population concurrent with the settlement of the Israelites.[4] Contrary to the high culture of the Canaanite and Philistine cities, the Israelites appear to have lived poorly. Everywhere there are signs of poverty and a low standard of living. House construction was crude and the settlements ill planned. What fortifications were evident were poorly constructed and not very effective in resisting attack. There is also no evidence of Israelite trade with other peoples.[5] The first passages of Judges make it clear that the Israelites were by no means in control of Palestine and that much of the land was still in the hands of Canaanites. The text tells of the tribe of Judah attacking the Perizzites and Canaanites at Bezek, moving on into the *shephelah*, the Negev, Debir, Hebron, Gaza, and Zephath while the tribe of Joseph captured Bethel.[6] Most of these victories, if they occurred at all and are not redactor propaganda designed to emphasize the importance of the principal tribe of Judah in later Israelite history, did not endure very long, for later in I Samuel we read that some of these places still remained in the hands of the Philistines.

Other Israelite tribes had no more success in assuming possession of the lands allotted to them by Joshua. Thus Manasseh "did not dispossess" Beth-shean, Ta'anach, Dor, or Megiddo, while Ephraim failed to drive the Canaanites from Gezer. Zebulun failed to take Qitron or Nahalal where the Canaanites "continued to live in their midst." The tribe of Asher failed to subdue Acco or Sidon, and Naphtali did not dispossess the inhabitants of Beth-shemesh or Beth-anath; "rather they settled down in the midst of the Canaanites."[7] Many of the Canaanite cities remained outside Israelite control for the entire period of the Judges and were not subdued and occupied until much later. Jerusalem and Beth-shean were not taken until David's time, and Gezer remained an Egyptian protectorate until the time of Solomon. It is clear, as well, that Hazor, Ibleam, Megiddo, and Ta'anach remained outside Israelite hands until the very end of the period.

The death of Joshua had left the Israelites leaderless, at least insofar as there was no appointed successor who could impose a sense of national direction on the Israelite tribes. Military leadership passed not to an individual, but to the *tribe* of Judah at the command of Yahweh,[8] which was another way of saying that leadership of the Israelites reverted to the traditional tribal assembly, the *qahal*, a representative body comprised of military age males from each of the tribes.[9] The *qahal* had existed during the Exodus and Joshua's time, but the strong personalities of Moses and Joshua had been able to curb its centrifugal tendencies. In the absence of strong leadership, the tribal assembly was a weak institution, especially so in dealing with matters of national defense. It met only in times of threat, was hobbled by endless deliberations, each tribe held a veto over its own troops, and the assembly could only muster the army for war and could not, by itself, declare war. That decision remained with Yahweh and was determined by divination (Gideon) or by the oracles of the priests (Samuel). For the two centuries that comprise the period of the Judges, Israel had no permanent and effective national governmental or defense institutions and no national leader to give the loose Israelite tribal confederation direction and form. Over time the confederation became less and less cohesive, dulled by purely local responses to local problems, until it was held together only by common tradition and the Yahwehist covenant.[10] One consequence was a growing accommodation with the local Canaanites, including intermarriage and religious worship. "But the Israelites settled down amidst the Canaanites . . . [and] they took their daughters for themselves as wives and their own daughters they gave to their sons. And they served their gods!"[11] In short, large segments of the Israelite population were assimilating both ethnically and religiously into the Canaanite culture surrounding them.

Under these circumstances, local threats and conflicts had to be dealt with by individual tribes requiring local responses. Thus it is that with the exception of the Benjaminite civil war, there is not a single example of the Israelite national army being mustered to deal with a major military threat. Deborah's call for national mobilization resulted in only four tribes rallying to the colors—so, too, in the case of Gideon. Judges recounts the exploits of military leaders who arose to deal with local military threats with little or no help from the national militia. While the text makes clear that Yahweh himself "selected" the judges, in fact this is but a poetic rendering of the traditional tribal assembly's ability to select its own military commanders in time of need. The textual notion that the judge becomes a judge only when "Yahweh's spirit" fills him, is a further poetic expression of the traditional Israelite idea that before battle Yahweh's decision (*mishpat*) had to be sought by the priests. We might imagine, then, the priests consulting Yahweh as they sought to determine if the commander chosen by the tribal assembly was an acceptable choice. It was in this manner that the Israelite tribes defended themselves in the absence of any national governing or military authority capable of concerted national action.

The military threats to Israelite independence are portrayed in Judges as a series of defensive wars and clearly reflected their limited and local nature insofar as none of Israel's enemies were sufficiently powerful to achieve anything but regional control. Accepting the order of the text for the moment, the first "oppressor" of Israel arose as an eight-year occupation by Cushan Rishathaim who came from the land of Aram Naharaim in Syria.[12] Malamat has argued that Cushan Rishathaim conquered Israel on his way to attack Egypt sometime between 1205 and 1200 B.C.E. when Egyptian records tell of a foreign ruler occupying the Delta.[13] Cushan Rishathaim is known as Irsu in the Egyptian records, which also tell of his defeat and expulsion by Pharaoh

Set-nakht around 1200–1198, a period that fits well with the story of Othniel's victory over the Syrian prince in Palestine.[14] Ramses III (1198–1166) counterattacked through Palestine pursuing the Syrians to their homeland, and it is likely that it was this campaign that permitted Othniel his victory, perhaps in some skirmish against a local garrison or even as mercenaries fighting with the Egyptians, although there is no evidence for this.

Ehud the Benjaminite fought against a coalition of Moabites, Ammonites, and Amalekites who defeated the Israelites and occupied Palm City (Jericho). In the course of delivering tribute to the Moabite king, Ehud killed him with "a short-sword (it was double-edged)" concealed under his clothes on his right thigh.[15] The incident is interesting for what it reveals about Israelite weapons of the period. The short-sword is really a dagger, and the fact that it was double-edged suggests that it was made of iron, not bronze. It may be the first mention in the Bible of an iron weapon in the possession of an Israelite soldier.[16] As to military technique, the text tells us that Ehud was "a man restricted in his right hand,"[17] or left-handed, a trait commonly attributed to the tribe of Benjamin whose left-handed slingers were renowned for their skill. In Ehud's case, being left-handed gave him a critical advantage in concealing the weapon from the Moabite bodyguards. Most soldiers were right-handed and wore their weapons on the left side for easy reach. Concealed as it was on Ehud's right thigh, the dagger was in a place not likely to be noticed or searched by the king's guards. Given, too, that Ehud was left-handed, the use of the dagger from the right side would have been natural for him, giving him plenty of strength with which to plunge the dagger so deeply into the king's body.

Shamgar, the Anathite, is remembered in Judges for having struck down an entire Philistine brigade single-handedly.[18] Here the enemy is the Philistines who had begun to arrive in Palestine as part of the second wave of Sea Peoples sometime around 1195, after their defeat by Ramses III on the banks of the Nile. Shamgar is a non-Israelite name and may be of Hurrian derivation,[19] and his presence in Palestine at the same time that the Hittite Empire was collapsing setting many of its polyglot peoples in motion suggests he may have been part of the pre-Philistine invasion of the Sea Peoples.[20] The description of Shamgar as "the Anathite" implies a military designation involving the name of the famous warrior goddess and consort of Baal, Anath,[21] suggesting that Shamgar may have been a mercenary in the hire of the Israelites. If so, it is further evidence of the inability of the Israelite tribes during the period of the Judges to manage their own military affairs effectively.

The great battle between Sisera and Deborah and Barak are dealt with in detail later. Suffice it to say here that the enemy was a Canaanite army centered around a city of the Jezreel Valley, evidence of the fact that the Israelites were settled within the midst of the peoples of Canaan. Gideon's war against the Midianites, however, represents a new kind of enemy. Midian is the name of a desert confederation of nomadic tribes that had long been intertwined with Israelite history. Although some of the Midian tribes, Kenites and Rechabites, for example, had intermarried with the Israelites, there were periods of open warfare between the two peoples reaching back at least to the Exodus.[22] But the Midianites of Gideon's time were probably the remnants of new waves of immigration from eastern Anatolia and northern Syria set in motion by the Hittite collapse. These desert raiders brought with them a fearsome new weapon, the domesticated camel, presenting a completely changed military configuration to which Gideon and the Israelites had to adjust. Jephthah's defeat of the Ammonites presented no new military challenges since the Israelite and Ammonite methods of war were similar. The Ammonite advantages in military organization first encountered by the Israelites in their engagements in the Transjordan during the Exodus had been offset by Gideon's time by the military experiences of the Israelites during Joshua's time. Samson's enemies are, of course, the Philistines, but his portrayal in Judges as an "elite fighting man" harassing the Philistine border towns with his companions reveals little of Israelite or Philistine warfare.

One of the reasons why Judges does not seem to present an account of a coherent historical period as does Exodus and Joshua is due to some extent to the redactor's arrangement of the stories in an order that does not correspond to what we now believe to have been the historical order of events. If the individual stories are rearranged in proper historical order, Judges makes a bit more sense. At least such an arrangement makes possible the partial discernment of the historical context in which the battles and events seem to have occurred. In this way, perhaps, the military elements of the text can be more accurately addressed, although it must be added that one is always on shaky ground in dealing with almost any aspect of the military history of the period. The following rearrangement of the Judges stories is suggested: (1) 1225 B.C.E.: Joshua and the conquest of Canaan, (2) 1195 B.C.E.: Othniel, (3) 1190–85 B.C.E.: the Gibeah Outrage, (4) 1150 B.C.E.: Gideon/Abimelech, (5) 1150–35 B.C.E.: Samson, (6) 1130–20 B.C.E.: the Danite migration, (7) 1125–1050 B.C.E.: Deborah and Barak.[23]

The two most important changes to the original order are the placement of the Gibeah incident near the beginning of the period and Deborah's battle with Sisera at the very end. The evidence for this arrangement seems adequate. It has long been recognized that the Gibeah incident that provoked the civil war between the Israelite confederation and the tribe of Benjamin actually belongs to the earlier part of the period, close to the events recounted in the story of Othniel.[24] Some support is found in Malamat's research that established Othniel as contemporaneous with the story of Irsu in Egyptian records or sometime around 1195 B.C.E. Moreover, the placement of the Gibeah incident at the end of Judges was probably deliberate redactor propaganda designed to demonstrate the need for a strong monarch at the time of rewriting. Thus, the argument is made at the end of Judges referring to the Gibeah incident that "In those days there was no king in Israel; every man did what was right as he saw it."[25] Finally, placing the Gibeah incident somewhere close to 1200 B.C.E. instead of two centuries later makes archaeological sense. Albright (1933) and Lapp (1965) have both noted that the evidence from archaeology suggests that Gibeah was destroyed by fire around early 1200 B.C.E. and then abandoned or only partially occupied during the Philistine period until Saul restored it as his rural headquarters around 1020.[26] It seems reasonable, then, that the Benjaminite civil war must have occurred at the beginning of the period and not, as the text suggests, at the end.

Dating Deborah's battle with Sisera is only somewhat less difficult insofar as it has long been held that the battle occurred somewhere around 1125 B.C.E. or, perhaps, even as late as 1050 B.C.E. despite its placement in Judges in the first half of the text.[27] The argument rests on the notion that in the *Song of Deborah* the battle with Sisera takes place "at Ta'anach by the waters of Megiddo," implying that Megiddo was unoccupied at the time. Otherwise one would have expected that the battle would have been located by reference to Megiddo rather than Ta'anach. Knowing that Megiddo was unoccupied during the first quarter of the twelfth century, the implication is that Deborah's battle took place during that time. Convincing or not, the consensus of scholarly opinion is that the battle with Sisera occurred sometime between 1125 and 1050 B.C.E., much later than the text of Judges implies. By accepting the chronology offered earlier if only as a heuristic artifice the military history of Judges can be made more comprehensible. Even so, history requires context, and it is to the historical context of the period of the Judges that we now turn.

THE PERIOD OF THE JUDGES

The two centuries encompassing the period of the Judges were a time of great and traumatic change in Palestine and the ancient world of the eastern Mediterranean. The international order produced by the great empires that had reached their peak around 1400 B.C.E. was in decline, and by the beginning of the period of the Judges all of the great imperial states were near collapse. Of the great empires only Egypt survived, and she, too, only narrowly avoiding what Robert Drew has called the Catastrophe.[28] The extent of the social, political, cultural, military, and economic dislocations that occurred during this period was little short of astounding. Every major civilization in the eastern Mediterranean—the Mycenaean Greeks, Hittites, Assyrians, Syrians, Egyptians—was racked by traumatic events, including widespread revolts, famine, drought, war, invasion, population die-offs, and the migrations of peoples once settled within the old imperial borders. During this period the cultural unity of Mycenaean Greece came to an end, and some parts of the country suffered a decline in population of as much as 75 percent. Even writing came to an end in Greece, and the period came to be known to later Classical Greeks as the Dark Age.[29] In 1212 B.C.E., Pharaoh Merneptah sent grain ships to alleviate the famine that was devastating the Hittite Empire. We hear of revolts of the peoples of Ionia against their masters and invasions of the capital, Hattusus, itself. Hittite records fall silent when Hattusus was destroyed shortly thereafter along with Troy, Miletus, Tarsus, Alaca Hoyuk, Alishar Hoyuk, Carchemish, Alalakh, Ugarit, Qatna, Qadesh, and other cities of the once powerful Hittite Empire.[30] At the same time, military campaigns ceased completely in Assyria, and revolts broke out throughout the country. An Assyrian chronicle of 1082 B.C.E. states that "a famine [so severe] occurred [that] people ate one another's flesh."[31] In the Sumerian heartland near modern Basra, archaeological surveys suggest that the population declined by almost 25 percent while further north, in parts of Assyria, the decline approached 75 percent![32] The widespread destruction of cities during this period seems to have occurred as a result of deliberate military action in which most were burned. Figure 5.1 graphically portrays the extent of the urban destruction of the period.

In Palestine the destruction was just as terrible as elsewhere. Succoth and Lachish were destroyed around 1190 B.C.E. Most of the cities along the coastal road, including Ashkelon, Ashdod, Gaza, Jaffa, and Acco, were also destroyed, as were Bethel, Beth-shemesh, Debir, and Lachish.[33] Megiddo and Beth-shean seem to have held out the longest, but they, too, had both succumbed by 1150 B.C.E. And, "as everywhere else, these cities were burned, the destruction being either total or so extensive that archaeologists assume that virtually the entire city was destroyed."[34] There is no reason to expect that the drought, hunger, and population mobility witnessed elsewhere did not occur in Palestine as well, and it is clear that some of the "oppressors" mentioned in Judges were the predations of migrating peoples seeking relief from the disruption. Although it has been criticized, Sir Flinders Petrie's description of the

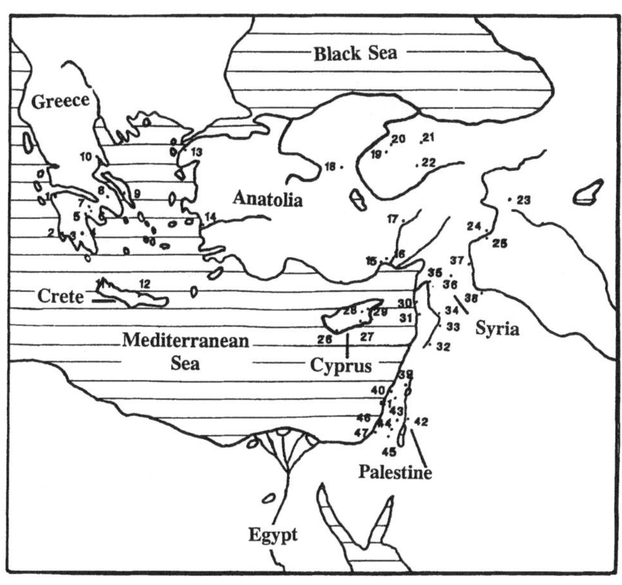

Figure 5.1 Major Cities Destroyed in the Catastrophe, circa 1200 B.C.E.

GREECE: 1. Teichos Dymaion 2. Pylos 3. Nichoria 4. The Menelaion 5. Tiryns 6. Midea 7. Mycenae 8. Thebes 9. Lefkandi 10. Iolkos; CRETE: 11. Kydonia 12. Knossos; ANATOLIA: 13. Troy 14. Miletus 15. Mersin 16. Tarsus 17. Fraktin 18. Karaoglan 19. Hattusas 20. Alaca Höyük 21. Maşat 22. Alishar Höyük 23. Norşuntepe 24. Tille Höyük 25. Lidar Höyük; CYPRUS: 26. Palaeokastro 27. Kition 28. Sinda 29. Enkomi; SYRIA: 30. Ugarit 31. Tell Sukas 32. Kadesh 33. Qatna 34. Hamath 35. Alalakh 36. Aleppo 37. Carchemish 38. Emar; SOUTHERN LEVANT: 39. Hazor 40. Akko 41. Megiddo 42. Deir 'Alla 43. Bethel 44. Beth Shemesh 45. Lachish 46. Ashdod 47. Ashkelon.

period of the Judges offered at the beginning of the twentieth century may not have been far off the mark.

> The period of the judges was a terribly barbaric age; its fragmentary record speaks of savage retaliations, and fierce struggles of disorganized tribes. Judge after judge arises out of a mist of warfare, only to disappear and leave a confusion as black as before. [The judges] with their bloody record . . . leave no trace of peaceful arts; not even the arts of civilized warfare.[35]

It was during this time that the Philistines first appeared in Canaan and eventually settled along the southern coast. The Philistines were one of a number of Sea Peoples who ravaged the coasts of Anatolia, Cilicia, Syria, and Palestine for more than half a century bringing with them a new technology of war and the introduction of iron. Most probably of Aegean origin, they had settled in the area of Ionia for sufficient time to acquire an affinity for Hittite culture and military technology only to be driven on by the disruption of the Catastrophe to seek new homes. We first hear of the Sea Peoples in Egyptian records when Merneptah defeated a coalition of Libyans and Sea Peoples attacking Egypt from the west. Merneptah's victory stele (not the Israel stele) describes these Sea Peoples as "roaming the land and fighting to fill their bellies daily; they have come to the land of Egypt to seek food for their mouths."[36] The Egyptian records tell of several different peoples involved in the enemy coalition. They included the *Akawasha*, probably the Achaeans, an element of the Mycenaean Greeks; the *Tursha*, perhaps the *Tyrsenoi* mentioned by Herodotus, who came from Lydia and were the forebears of the Etruscans; the *Lukki*, known from the Amarna archives as living in Asia Minor; the *Sherden*, also mentioned in the Amarna records, who were hired by the Egyptians as mercenaries and are mentioned as fighting in the army of Ramses II at the battle of Kadesh, and later settled in Corsica and Sardinia; and the *Sheklesh*, a people of unknown origin who eventually settled Sicily and gave the island its name.[37] After the defeat by Merneptah, nothing more is heard of these peoples for almost a decade when once again they attempted an invasion of Egypt.

This time the attack came from the east. Having overrun Anatolia and Cilicia, the Sea Peoples turned south and attacked Syria, laying waste the coast and turning Ammaru into a strategic platform for an invasion of Palestine and Egypt. Seeking to preempt the attack, Ramses III moved an army north in his fifth regnal year (circa 1194 B.C.E.) and defeated the enemy coalition somewhere in Syria. Three years later, the Sea Peoples had recovered from the defeat and launched another invasion attempt. This time one army attacked overland through Palestine while another traveled by boat along the Canaanite coast. In the wake of the armies were the families, livestock, and wagons of the invaders. They had come to stay. The coalition was led by the Philistines whose origin is thought to have been in Illyria or Crete, the Tjekker from Asia Minor, the Denyen of the Amarna letters (perhaps the *Danaoi* of Greek legend), and the Washasha, an unknown people. Ramses met and defeated the land army probably near Sharuhen on the Palestine border. He then defeated the naval force by placing his archers on boats and bringing the invaders under withering fire while they were still aboard ship. Egyptian infantry mounted aboard ship then closed with the shipboard enemy and defeated them in hand-to-hand combat. Having beaten the enemy, Ramses wasted no time in turning his victory to greater strategic advantage. For more than 20 years, Egypt had sought to strengthen its hold on Palestine, and both Merneptah and Ramses had taken steps to increase the Egyptian garrisons in the coastal towns of Canaan. From time immemorial Palestine had been vital to Egyptian defense, serving as a strategic buffer against invasion when Egypt was weak and as a strategic platform for projecting Egyptian power northward when strong. For years the growing menace of the *habiru* and the newly settled hill peoples (Israelites?) in Palestine had been of concern. Now Ramses solved the problem by settling the Sea Peoples in Canaan itself, first in the Egyptian garrison towns of Gaza, Ashkelon, and Ashdod, which were occupied by the Philistines. Later, additional garrison towns, Ekron and Gath, were constructed. To the north, the Tjekker were settled in Dor.[38] Over time Egyptian power weakened, and the Philistines became a powerful independent coalition of warrior kings, a development that set the stage for the conflict between them and the Israelites recorded in the Bible.

The widespread social disruption and migrations of the period seem to have been set in motion by dramatic climatic changes between 1300 and 1100 B.C.E. that produced higher than average temperatures, prolonged drought, crop failures, and famine. These in turn led to social disorder and the movement of peoples seeking better lives. It is wise to remember in this connection that the agriculture of the ancient world was far more fragile and dependent upon favorable weather than in the modern age. Even a single season of low rainfall was often sufficient to produce death by hunger. Greater demands of the cities for more food to feed their populations in hard times only made matters worse, presenting the agricultural population with the choice of starving where they were or moving in search of better land and pasture for their flocks. Under these circumstances, the feudal social orders of the day collapsed precipitously and social disorder became widespread.

The evidence for climatic change during this period is convincing. Tree logs from 1200 B.C.E. reveal periods of narrow growth, an indication of prolonged drought. Geological records indicate that lakes and glaciers shrank, indicating a drier and warmer than normal period. The monsoon rains in the Indus Valley were below normal, and the water level of the Nile dropped drastically after 1300, reaching its lowest point between 1200 and 1100 B.C.E. The water levels of the Tigris and Euphrates also dropped during this period. In Palestine the evidence suggests that drought and heat conditions may have been even worse. Analyses of wood charcoal remains from sites north of the Negev reveal a changing pattern of vegetation in which the usual Mediterranean flora were replaced by species more common to the Saharan regions.[39]

Against this background of climatic change and social disruption, Robert Drew has suggested that a revolutionary change in military technology caused the widespread destruction of the cities during this period. For the first time in two centuries, new military techniques made it possible for militia-levied infantries to defeat the chariot armies of the old order.[40] It might be noted, too, that these changes provided the militia armies with a significant advantage over the heavily armored spear-bearing infantries of the old system. Already weakened by climatic and social disruption, the old imperial feudal orders had been forced to reduce their expensive standing armies only to face the improved military capabilities of their adversaries. It was probably this set of circumstances that permitted the Aegean peoples in league with the other peoples of Ionia to destroy the chariot and heavy infantry armies of the Hittite Empire. The new military technologies were (1) the round shield, (2) the javelin, (3) the infantry corselet, (4) the leg and arm greave, and (5) the iron straight sword.[41]

The infantry corselet, originally made of expensive bronze but now fashioned of inexpensive leather, provided the light infantry with its first affordable body armor making combat with the heavily armored charioteers and spear infantry more survivable. This was also true of the greave, most particularly the arm greave that protected the forelimb during close sword combat. The round shield was smaller and lighter than the old figure eight, oblong, or square shields used by the feudal armies affording the infantryman a greater degree of mobility on the battlefield. When this mobility was coupled with a new infantry weapon, the javelin, the days of the chariot armies were numbered. Swarms of infantry could now attack the chariots at close range, where the composite bows of the charioteers were of less use, employing their light shields for protection while attacking both charioteer and horse with thrown javelins, two or three of which could be carried by a single soldier. Once the chariot charge had been slowed or stopped completely, the infantry could engage with the new iron sword or extended dagger that was making its appearance at this time. The old feudal armies had been expensive and highly trained. The new military technologies and tactics could be readily employed by less trained militia levies that were far less expensive to equip. It was at this time that iron weapons were introduced as the technology of iron making, first put to practical military use by the Hittites, was being spread by the Sea Peoples throughout the eastern Mediterranean. It was the Philistines who introduced iron to Palestine shortly after 1200 B.C.E.[42]

Throughout the Bronze Age, metalsmiths had known how to make iron, but the technique was difficult to master. As long as the stability of the international system permitted adequate supplies of tin and copper, it was easier to manufacture bronze. Iron was made in the same way and in the same kind of furnaces as bronze and copper, but it was not possible to raise the temperature of the smelting furnaces above 1,200 degrees—sufficient to melt copper and tin, but below the 1,537 degrees required to melt iron. Unlike copper and tin, heated iron ore does not produce molten metal suitable for casting into molds. Instead, it produces a sponge or bloom consisting of iron mixed with slag and cinders. If the bloom is reheated to 1,100 degrees, it becomes possible to separate the metal from the slag by hammering. The finished product, however, is wrought iron and much too soft to make weapons. To be an effective weapons material, iron has to be heated in proximity to charcoal and carbon monoxide so as to produce a steel surface. A mere 0.5 percent of coal (carbon) makes the steel harder than bronze, and if it is hammered while cooling off its hardness is doubled. The secrets of quenching and tempering were discovered only much later.[43] As noted in the previous chapter, it required two centuries after the Philistine arrival in Palestine before iron weapons became common enough to replace bronze.

The iron weapons introduced during this period were most significant not for any militarily important technological advantage they provided over bronze weapons, but for the fact that whereas bronze weapons had been very expensive and, therefore, could be made only in limited quantities, iron ore was commonly available. Once the secret of iron making was mastered, it spread quickly, making it possible to equip large infantry militia armies with iron weapons at a greatly reduced cost. Thus it was that the period of the Judges witnessed a military revolution that made it possible for the new militia armies to destroy the old Canaanite feudal order with the result that, at the end of the period, an Israelite monarchy dependent on the new military technologies and tactics finally began to emerge.

THE GIBEAH INCIDENT

The description of the "outrage" that caused the bloody civil war between the Israelite confederation and the tribe of Benjamin is found in Judges 19: 21–25. Its value to the military historian is that the Gibeah story offers a revealing glimpse into Israelite political and military institutions of the time.[44] If our earlier argument is correct that the Gibeah incident occurred at the beginning of the period of the Judges, about the same time as the story of Othniel, then it occurred about 30 years after Joshua's death, or about 1190–80 B.C.E. This accords well with the text itself, which tells us that the period begins after the death of Joshua and after "Joshua had discharged the troops and each one of the Israelites had gone to his own plot to take possession of the land. . . . Finally, all of that generation were gathered to their fathers, and after them there arose another generation who knew neither Yahweh nor the work that he had done on behalf of Israel!"[45] The Gibeah incident reveals an Israelite military system still intact and functioning fairly well a generation after Joshua in marked contrast to later descriptions of military events in Judges which suggest that the Israelite military system had almost completely collapsed.

The Gibeah incident began with the attempts of a Levite living in Ephraim to retrieve his concubine from her father's house in Bethlehem. While returning to his home, the Levite stopped and spent the night in the Benjaminite town of Gibeah in the house of a kind townsman who had offered him accommodations. During the evening a group of local "hell-raisers" surrounded the house demanding the Levite come out so that "we would get to know him."[46] Instead, the Levite forced his concubine out the door where the locals "got to know her. They vilely mistreated her all night long." In the morning, the concubine was found dead on the doorstep. The Levite gathered her body on his donkey and returned home. There, "he took the knife, got a firm hold on his concubine, and systematically dismembered her, cutting twelve pieces; he sent her throughout all the Israelite territory." An envoy carried a piece of the concubine's body to each of the Israelite tribes with the request that the national tribal assembly "take counsel and speak." The great assembly gathered at Mizpah and voted to require the tribe of Benjamin to hand over the offenders. Benjamin refused. The assembly then consulted Yahweh at Bethel and declared war on the Benjaminites. The Benjaminites mobilized their forces. "On that day the Benjaminites mustered out of their cities 26 sword-bearing contingents. . . . From all this people there were 700 elite soldiers, each restricted in his right hand; (i.e. left-handed) and each one could sling a stone at the hair without missing!"[47] Apparently Benjaminite slingers were trained to fire their missiles at the heads of their targets.

The fighting men of Benjamin are mentioned in Judges as always being "restricted in the right hand." This is interesting in light of the fact that the name of the tribe is *bin yameen*, those "of the right hand" or more literally, "of the south." The ancient Israelites referenced all directions from the east, the direction out of which the sun rose. Facing east, one's right hand points to the south, thereby designating the right hand as being from the south. Just why a tribe whose name implied being right-handed should have so many left-handed soldiers within it is curious, and implies some deliberate effort to use the left hand in war or, what is the same thing perhaps, not to use the right hand for certain tasks. It might have been that the use of the right hand was originally for cultic reasons. If, as I have suggested in chapter 3, that some of the Israelites of the Exodus had once been followers of Pharaoh Akhenaten's god, Aten, whose right arm possessed special powers, then perhaps the early Benjaminites served at the "right hand" of Aten in some ritualistic capacity and preserved this memory by not using the sacred right hand and arm in war. This is, however, speculative and unsupported by any evidence.

The Israelite confederation "mustered 400 sword-bearing contingents, all of them warriors."[48] After two unsuccessful frontal attacks that ended in defeat, the Israelites employed the same tactic that Joshua had used against Ai. An ambush force was placed behind the city of Gibeah while the main force mounted another frontal assault. When the Benjaminites came out to meet the assault, the Israelites fled in feigned panic, and the Benjaminites gave chase. The ambush force then attacked the city and set it afire. When the Benjaminites saw the smoke, they lost heart. The Israelites stopped their flight, turned around, and attacked the Benjaminites. "The total of Benjaminites who fell that day was 25 sword-bearing contingents, all of them prosperous men. . . . So the men of Israel returned to the Benjaminites and put them to the sword—from each city, men and beasts and all that were found. And all the cities that were implicated they destroyed by fire."[49] The rest of the tale wherein the tribe of Benjamin is finally reconciled with their Israelite brethren is of no military relevance and need not concern us here.

The Gibeah story reveals much about the condition of Israelite military and political institutions a generation after Joshua. It is clear, for example, that the national army could still be called to war as a unified body under a central command as it could under Joshua. The mustering of the national army for the Benjaminite civil war is the only place in Judges where it was accomplished successfully. None of the later Judges were able to muster even a majority of the tribes in their wars, a fact that speaks to a decline in the organization and, perhaps, even the existence of a national army. The national political assembly, the *qayam*, that provided the social machinery for mustering the army and selecting its commanders was also still functioning a generation after Joshua. It is not evident in later Judges and disappears completely as a functioning institution under the monarchy. The tradition that only Yahweh, and not the assembly, could declare war was still alive at Gibeah when, once the decision to go to war had been considered, the assembly moved to Bethel, the seat of the central Israelite sanctuary and the location of the Ark of the Covenant, to seek *mishpat* or Yahweh's divine will. Here we see the traditional joining of military and religious office governing the conduct of secular affairs first encountered with Moses in Exodus. The union remained throughout the monarchy where no king of Israel could declare war without the advice and ultimate approval of the priests who sought to divine Yahweh's will on the matter. All these traditional institutions evident during Joshua's time were still functioning a generation later. Shortly thereafter, however, they seem to have fallen into disuse.

The confederation army was still a large force, although the evidence of Gibeah suggests that it was already declining. The text tells us that the Benjaminites could muster 26 sword-bearing contingents while the confederation army put 400 similar contingents in the field.[50] Leaving aside the question of how many men comprised a contingent, it seems clear that the *number of contingents* that could be raised was smaller than during Joshua's time. The original census of the Israelite army that appears in Numbers 1 and 26 indicates that the Israelite tribes could muster 598 and 596 contingents, respectively. At Gibeah, the confederation could field only 400 contingents, or a decline of approximately 30 percent in its manpower strength. The same ratio holds for the tribe of Benjamin. The Numbers census allots 35 and 45 contingents, respectively, to the tribe of Benjamin. At Gibeah in what we might well assume was a maximum effort at self-defense, Benjamin could muster only 26 contingents, also a decline of 30 percent.[51]

Curiously, the decline in Israelite military manpower strength occurred at a time when the Israelite population was, perhaps, at least twice as large as it was during Joshua's time. Archaeology tells us that the population of Palestine around this time was about 200,000, including non-Israelites.[52] Stager's survey of the period shows that the population of the hill country, which we might reasonably assume was mostly Israelite, doubled from Iron I to Iron II from 40,000 to 80,000. Assuming some settlement of Israelite tribes beyond the hill country as clearly implied by the text, a reasonable estimate of the *Israelite* population in Palestine might be about 100,000 people. Such growth in a single generation cannot be explained by fertility alone. Rather, as Joshua demonstrated at Shechem, a large part of Israelite population growth (if only inferred from settlement patterns) must have come from the accretion of other groups to the Yahwehist cause. A population of 100,000 could potentially field about 25,000 soldiers at maximum effort or approximately 2,000 warriors per tribe. Of course, the manpower pools were not equal for all tribes so that the number offered here is merely an approximation. One can, however, arrive at an approximate size for the contingents at Gibeah. At 2,000 soldiers for the tribe of Benjamin, its 26 contingents would have each comprised about 75 men per unit. For the confederacy as a whole, its 23,000 troops were divided into 400 contingents or 60 men per contingent. Even so, the Gibeah incident reveals a situation in which the number of men available for military service a generation after Joshua was *proportionally* smaller than it was during Joshua's time even though the Israelite population was considerably larger. From this point forward, whenever we encounter manpower levels for the wars described in Judges, both the number and proportion of warriors is always smaller than found at Gibeah, an indication, perhaps, that the centrifugal tendencies of the decentralized tribal social structure had taken a toll on Israelite military capabilities.

The logistical preparations for the Benjaminite war show that the efficient logistics system that Joshua put in place was still functioning. Judges 20:10 implies this when it tells us that "We will take ten of every hundred men of all the Israelite tribes (and a hundred of every thousand, and a thousand of every ten thousand) to supply provisions to the troops." Moreover, the references to the army bearing swords and the Benjaminites possessing swords and slings suggests that the army was still well equipped with weapons. This stands in marked contrast to the complaints of other commanders in Judges that the forces under their commands were always insufficiently supplied or completely without weapons, and raises the question of how it came to be that the Israelite armies of the later period were so poorly supplied with the implements of war.

A clue lies in Judges 20:26 which records that before the battle with the Benjaminites the Israelites went up to Bethel to consult with Yahweh. Under Joshua the main cultic sanctuary had been at Gilgal, which also served as the main logistics base and weapons manufacturing center for the period of the conquest. It was here that the Kenites had their furnaces for making bronze weapons and the Rechabites their workshops for making spears, shields, and other weapons. Sometime later in the period Joshua 24 tells how the Ark of the Covenant was transferred to Shechem. By the time of the Judges, the sanctuary had moved again, this time to Bethel where it remained until Samuel's time, when it was moved to Shiloh where it was captured by the Philistines after the battle of Ebenezer-Aphek around 1040 B.C.E.[53] There is no mention of what happened to the weapons makers when the sanctuary moved from Gilgal, but it is a reasonable assumption that they did not move with it to the new location. There is, moreover, no textual evidence that the arsenal at Gilgal was reconstructed at any of these locations. Within a generation of Joshua's death, the international order that had made the copper and tin trade possible was in collapse, bringing the trade in tin to a halt and severely reducing the trade in copper. The raw materials from which to manufacture bronze weapons disappeared. Without them, the Kenite metalsmiths had no way to earn a living. Moreover, with the exception of the burning of Gibeah and, perhaps, Lish by the Danites, the practice of the *herem* had disappeared in the period of the Judges, and with it, we may reasonably presume, the source of money to support the weaponeer's trade. It may also have been that with the decentralization of the Israelite national defense establishment as a consequence of the tribal land disbursement and the disbanding of the army by Joshua there was simply no provision made for sustaining the weapons industry.

There is some evidence that with the metals manufacturing industry declining the Kenite smiths pulled up stakes and did what they had always done when times were difficult, they returned to their traditional way of life as itinerant smiths. As we have noted, some of the Kenite clans had long since settled among the Israelites. But with no way of earning a living, even the settled Kenites had nothing to exchange with their kinsman agriculturalists in return for food and shelter. Under these circumstances, many of the metalsmiths took to the road or even returned to their traditional home in the desert, perhaps to make a living turning the copper deposits of Sinai into household wares and farm implements. Robert Boling has suggested that in Judges the Kenites "acquired a reputation for unilateral action," that is, for picking up and moving, and are portrayed "as the polar opposites of Judah . . . as conquering Israelites."[54] The text of Judges 1:16 also tells us that "[t]he descendants of the Kenite, the father-in-law of Moses, had gone up from Palm City with the Judahites to the plain south of Judah, going down from Arad . . . and they went and lived among the Amalekites!" Palm City or Jericho is very close to Gilgal, the site of Joshua's arsenal. The text suggests that the metalsmiths were leaving their homes among the Israelites and heading southward—"going down from Arad"—returning to their traditional roots in the Midian desert near the Sinai copper deposits. To emphasize the magnitude and importance of the Kenite movement, the text's author points out for emphasis, "And they [the Kenites] went and lived among the Amalekites!" Given the historical animosity between Israelites and Amalekites, such an accusation is striking indeed. Additional textual evidence for Kenite movement is found in Judges 4:11 in Deborah's war against Sisera. The text says that "Heber the Kenite had separated from the other Kenites, descendants of Hobab, father-in-law of Moses, and had pitched his tent at Elon-bezaanannim, which is near Kadesh." Here is a description of an itinerant metalsmith trying to make a living by plying his trade alone rather than among a settled group of smiths such as those who had resided at Gilgal. If the Israelite weapons industry had indeed collapsed, then it explains why the later text of Judges testifies to the poor quality and meager numbers of weapons available to Israelite commanders. Indeed, a list of the weapons described in these later texts is evidence of the low state to which the Israelite military art had fallen. The following weapons are mentioned in Judges: the double-edged dagger of Ehud (specially fashioned and not a common weapon of the Israelite soldier), ox-goad, tent peg and hammer, trumpets, jars, torches, thorns, briars, a sword (presumably still the bronze sickle-sword), an upper millstone, bare hands, the fresh jawbone of an ass, and sling stones,[55] a far cry from the weapons of the army of Joshua!

In one respect, however, the Israelite army at Gibeah seems the same, and that is in the area of tactical proficiency. The same difficult tactical maneuvers that Joshua employed in the battle of Ai were employed by Israelite commanders at Gibeah, including the difficult tactic of feigning withdrawal only to turn and reengage on command while another part of the army rose from ambush to attack the city proper. It might be added, importantly, that the Israelite commanders at Gibeah were the regular unit commanders selected by the individual tribes. Unlike later battles, there was no need for great heroes or Yahweh-inspired judges to lead the army to victory at Gibeah. It seems that the old cadre of unit commanders who had won their spurs under Joshua had succeeded in transmitting their military expertise to the next generation, which performed admirably at Gibeah. But soon these combat commanders were no more in evidence as the stories of Judges make clear, forcing the Israelites to rely upon Yahweh and a new Israelite military institution, the personal warrior band.

Judges 9:4 records the appearance of Israelite warrior bands serving in the armed forces comprised of men personally loyal to their war chiefs. "Abimelech hired some worthless and reckless fellows" who went with him and killed his brothers. In Judges 11:3, "Men of low character gathered about Jephthah and went out raiding with him." These bands are reminiscent of the *habiru* mercenaries of earlier times, but we have heard nothing of them since the constitution of the Israelite army at Sinai. There is no mention of a personal warrior retinue around Moses or Joshua who, after Sinai, were always portrayed as leaders of a national army. The war bands noted in Judges became a permanent part of the Israelite army and we find them later under Saul (I Samuel 14:52) and David (I Samuel 22:1–2). The combination of a permanent force of professional mercenaries dependent on the king and tribal levies called to service to meet emergencies became a basic feature of Israelite military organization under the monarchy. The characterization of these warrior bands as comprised of people of low character persisted even into David's time where they are described as "Every man in difficulties and every man sought by a creditor, and every man with a bitter spirit."[56] These bands probably included some Sea People warriors and Philistines as well. These social outcasts became legitimate, however, once David was made king. Then the warrior bands were redesignated as *gibborim*, the "mighty men" who protected the person of the king.

There was, however, another social element within these bands that merits discussion. These were the *na'ar* or young unmarried men who had not yet become head of a household or come into their landed inheritance. Others, the second and third sons, had no prospect of inheriting the land at all under the Israelite practice of primogeniture. Some of these young men sought adventure and careers in military service and the priesthood.[57] These were David's *ne'arim* or "young men" who served as knights in his army. In Egypt we hear of them as the *na'aruna*, the "youths" who led the attack at Kadesh. A similar socio-military institution is found in medieval Europe where young aristocrats took up military careers as soldiers of fortune until they married or could claim their lands. Often these warriors collected around a wealthy vassal who retained them in return for military service.[58] The violence of which these young headstrong warriors were capable is evident in the story of Gibeon's pool in II Samuel 2:14–16. One of Saul's warrior bands commanded by Abner, Saul's first cousin, encountered one of David's bands commanded by Joab, David's nephew, at the pool of Gibeon. The two commanders agreed to a contest among their respective *ne'arim*. Abner said to Joab, "Let the young men arise and play before us." When it was over, all 24 of these young elite soldiers had been killed in deadly hand-to-hand combat!

Given that these military retinues were not in evidence between the constitution of the Israelite national army at Sinai and the end of the conquest period under Joshua, what accounted for their emergence during the time of the Judges? The answer probably lies in the fact that the collapse of the Israelite national defense structure, including the weapons industry, had reached a point where tribal military commanders could no longer rely upon the national levy for help in dealing with military threats. Judges records again and again that some tribes refused to come to the aid of others or, when they did, arrived too late to be of much use. Under these conditions, recruiting bands of mercenaries who were always ready to fight made sound sense. Thus we may conclude that the emergence of personal warrior bands during the period of the Judges was a reflection of the low state to which the national Israelite defense establishment had fallen. In this regard, the story of Abimelech makes sense as well. Portrayed in Judges as an usurper, Abimelech's attempt to form a central Israelite government by force can be legitimately construed as the act of a person who recognized the poor condition of the Israelite army and understood that it could only be remedied by establishing a strong central monarchy, supported by a standing retinue of professional warriors, who could force the tribes to meet their manpower levies and other responsibilities for national defense. If the chronology offered earlier is correct, Abimelech's attempt at reform occurred around 1150 B.C.E., more than 50 years after Joshua's death, well into the period when the old national army had already reached an advanced state of decay. The soundness of these reforms was fully justified by the fact that they were finally instituted under Saul and David with great success in rebuilding the Israelite national army.

GIDEON AND THE MIDIANITES

Gideon's war against the Midianites is further evidence that the national security situation within Israel during the time of the Judges had deteriorated. Nomadic raids from the eastern desert were an old story in Israel, but during Gideon's time one finds no mention of Canaanite resistance to the raids. Where are, one might ask, the armies of the Canaanite city-states? Why was there no resistance from Hazor or Beth-shean under whose very walls the raiders would have been forced to pass to reach the Jezreel? Judges 6:4 suggests a clue when it tells us that the Midianites would "destroy the land's produce all the way to the neighborhood of Gaza." Moreover, the raids seemed to have occurred on a fairly regular basis, so much so that Israelites had to abandon some of their settlements and hide from the raiders in "the dens which are in the mountains, and the caves and strongholds."[59] Both references imply that not only has the authority of the Canaanite city-states collapsed by Gideon's time (circa 1150 B.C.E.), but the raids on the territory near Gaza suggest that Egyptian authority has collapsed as well. Gideon was the son of Joash of the clan of Abiezer of the tribe of Manasseh living in the territory of Issachar. The territory of Manasseh lay directly in the path of the Midianite invaders. Thus Gideon's war falls into the typical pattern throughout Judges of a local warrior chieftain responding to a localized or regional threat.

The nomadic raids carried out from the eastern desert during Gideon's time seem to have been of a greater magnitude than previously. These raids seem to have involved several nomadic tribes acting in concert. It was not unusual for a completely nomadic tribe to attach itself temporarily to a regular nation that was going to war in order to share in the spoils.[60] In Gideon's case the nomadic coalition included the Midianites, the Amalekites, and "the people of the East."[61] The latter were probably peoples formerly resident in Anatolia and Syria in the Hittite Empire that had been set in motion with the empire's collapse. It was probably these "easterners" who brought with them the domesticated camel and used it as an instrument of warfare. The social organization of these tribal coalitions varied greatly, but Malamat suggests that the Midianites of Gideon's day were ruled by five kings.[62] The text mentions only two kings, Zebah and Zalmunna, and two field generals, Oreb and Zeeb, which might mean that the raiders were the advanced guard for a larger invasion or, more likely, that only part of the Midianite confederation was involved at all.

The raiders crossed the Jordan near the Beth-shean plain aiming at the unprotected fertile fields of the Jezreel. The attacks came in summer, close to harvest time, as the Midianites searched for food for their people and pasture for their flocks and camels. It is likely that the hunger and general desperation caused by the terrible social conditions of the period contributed as well. The text accurately records the impact of these raids on the Israelite settlements in the area. "They would encamp . . . and destroy the land's produce all the way to the neighborhood of Gaza; they would leave no means of livelihood—sheep, ox, or donkey. They and their cattle would come up, and their tents they would bring—as numerous as locusts. They and their camels were too many to count! They would enter the land to devastate it. So Israel became utterly destitute because of Midian."[63] To meet the threat, Gideon first called out his own Abiezerite clan, including his two brothers, and then called for the troops of his Manasseh tribe to rally to him. He sent envoys to the tribes of Asher, Zebulun, and Naphtali and put them on alert. Although the Midianites had camped in the middle of the Jezreel, at Endor, well within the territory of Issachar, Gideon made no attempt to bring Issachar under arms. To do so would have immediately alerted the enemy. Gideon seems to have chosen to forego the additional manpower to preserve the element of surprise in mobilizing his army.

Gideon's men assembled on the northwestern slopes of Mount Gilboa, above the well of Harod, looking down on the Midianite camp at Endor across the narrow valley and below the Hill of Moreh in the northern extension of the Jezreel. With only his clan and Manasseh assembled at Gilboa, Gideon's force amounted to 32 contingents[64] or, if our earlier estimates of 60 men per contingent are correct, then Gideon's army at Gilboa numbered about 2,000 men assuming a maximum effort by Manasseh. Interestingly, the census lists of Numbers 1 and 26 assign Manasseh 32 clan units, precisely the number mobilized by Manasseh for Gideon. The text tells us that "Midian and Amaleq—all the Easterners—lay along the valley, as numerous as locusts!

Their camels were too many to count, as numerous as grains of sand on the seashore."[65] The Midianite horde also included women, children, and men past military age, as well as soldiers. We have no way to estimate the size of its combatant arm, but it must have been significant for the sight of the enemy caused great fear among Gideon's troops. Following the practice of psychiatric troop screening cited earlier in Deuteronomy 20:8, Gideon ordered those men who "are afraid and have lost heart" *(hayare verakh halebab)* to "decamp from Mount Fearful . . . [and] 22 units went home and 10 units were left."[66] Gideon was left with 600 men. Given Gideon's plan, however, the force was too large.

Gideon devised an ingenious method of selecting his best warriors for the attack. Presumably he put the entire 600-man force through some exercise, perhaps marching or running them down Mount Gilboa in the midday heat arriving at the spring of Harod at the foot of the mountain. He watched the hot and thirsty soldiers drink their fill. He then chose his best soldiers in the following manner: "Everyone that lappeth of the water with his tongue, like a dog lappeth, [making noise!] him shalt thou set by himself; likewise everyone that goes down on his knees to drink the water [those that set their weapons aside and didn't remain vigilant] set aside by himself." Gideon chose only the men "that lapped putting their hand to their mouth," that is, the men who drank silently and remained vigilant with their weapons at the ready.[67] The British General, Lord Wavell, noted in his book that a modern commander would find the selection process a sound one.

> The majority of his men, parched by the heat on the bare rocky hills, flung themselves down full length by the stream when their opportunity came and drank heedlessly and carelessly. Only the seasoned warrior with experience of snipers and ambushes, kept his weapon in one hand and his eyes toward his foes, while he dipped the other hand in the water and lapped from it, ready for action at the slightest danger.[68]

With his elite force selected, Gideon prepared to carry out his plan.

All this activity would have taken several days to accomplish during which time one would have expected that the Midianites would have continued their movement westward as befits proper nomads. But the text tells us that the Midianite camp was still where it was several days earlier. Why had the Midianites not moved? Herzog and Gichon suggest the answer lies in Judges 8:18–19 when, after having captured the enemy kings, Gideon asks them, "What manner of men were they whom you slew at Tabor? . . . They were my brethren, even the sons of my mother."[69] The enemy had killed Gideon's brothers near Mount Tabor. Now the first rule of battle is to force the enemy to fight on terrain of your choosing. Gideon had chosen the terrain, but he had to find some way to stop the enemy's westward movement long enough to assemble his army and carry out the attack. Gideon's brothers may have been killed stopping the Midianite westward advance. Mordechai Gichon's original insight that a small force sent into the narrow valley between Mount Tabor and the Hill of Moreh could have blocked the exit from the valley seems perfectly correct. Perhaps Gideon's brothers were lost in the battle to slow the Midianite movement, a high price with which to purchase sufficient time to assemble and deploy the main force.[70] The text seems to support this conclusion. When Gideon conducted a reconnaissance of the Midianite camp the night before the battle, he overheard a man describing a dream to his friend that the man interpreted as an attack against the Midianite camp. What is curious is that the dreamer identified the attacker by name, "this can be nothing other than the sword of Gideon ben Joash, the Israelite!"[71] If the Midianites had captured and killed Gideon's brothers in a previous skirmish near Mount Tabor, they might well have learned of Gideon during their interrogation of his brothers who might have exaggerated the military reputation of their older brother as a way of warning off the Midianites against further movement. In any case, the Midianites remained encamped at Endor long enough for Gideon to assemble the army and carry out his plan of attack.

Gideon divided his 300 warriors into three companies of 100 men each, taking personal command of one of the companies. The commanders of the other companies were instructed to synchronize their movements with Gideon's, to "look on me and do likewise." The night before Gideon and his adjutant, Purah, conducted a reconnaissance of the enemy camp probably determining the best avenues of approach for a night attack. The attack was set for "the beginning of the middle watch," close to midnight and just after the changing of the guard "had newly set the watch,"[72] when the new sentries would not yet be fully awake or their eyes fully accustomed to the night environment. The previous hours of darkness had been used by Gideon to move his troops into position. It is 12 kilometers from the foot of Mount Gilboa to Endor, most of it across open and flat terrain, and would have taken Gideon's men about four hours to complete the approach march. One is surprised at the absence of Midianite patrols, especially so given the likelihood of a previous skirmish with Gideon's brothers. Gideon's men moved into position "on every side of all the camp." Since with only 300 men Gideon could not have hoped to overcome the enemy force, it would have made no sense to surround the camp completely. More likely the camp was surrounded on only three sides leaving an exit to the southeast through which Gideon hoped to drive the frightened Midianites.

Gideon's men carried trumpets and lighted torches in clay pitchers to conceal the flame inside, which raises the question of whether they carried weapons as well. A sickle-sword could easily have been carried in a waist belt and, perhaps, a short spear carried in the same hand along with the trumpet. There is, however, no mention of any weapons, although it is difficult to imagine that any field commander would take troops into battle completely unarmed, no matter how brilliant the plan! On signal, Gideon's men rose from their positions and broke the jars containing the torches making a great noise. Waving their torches and blowing the trumpets, the attackers created panic within the Midian camp so that "the entire force awoke with a start. They yelled and they fled." One imagines that Gideon's men set some of the tents on fire and cut the tethers of the camels sending them stampeding down the valley. Some Midian soldiers attempted to resist, but in the darkness "Yahweh set each man's sword against his own ally throughout the whole camp," and some were struck down by their own comrades. This, of course, would have been a perfect opportunity for Gideon's force to fall upon some of the Midianites, but the text does not record that they did so or that any combat between the two forces took place. As curious as this inaction may appear, it made sound tactical sense. The attack fell shortly after midnight. Its objective was not only to frighten the Midianites, but also to scatter them in a specific direction, to the southeast where Gideon's larger forces could engage and destroy them. To accomplish this required that once the Midianites had been set in motion by the initial attack the noisy pursuit had to continue for as long as possible to keep the frightened enemy on the move. That is why Gideon chose midnight to attack, to leave himself several hours of darkness to exploit the pandemonious pursuit while the night concealed the small size of his force from the enemy. By dawn, one imagines the Midianites scattered across the Jezreel trying to round up their camels and regroup into some sort of order. Figure 5.2 shows the conduct of Gideon's battle against the Midianites in phases. Phase 1 included the movement into position, the attack on the Midianite camp, and the nighttime pursuit.

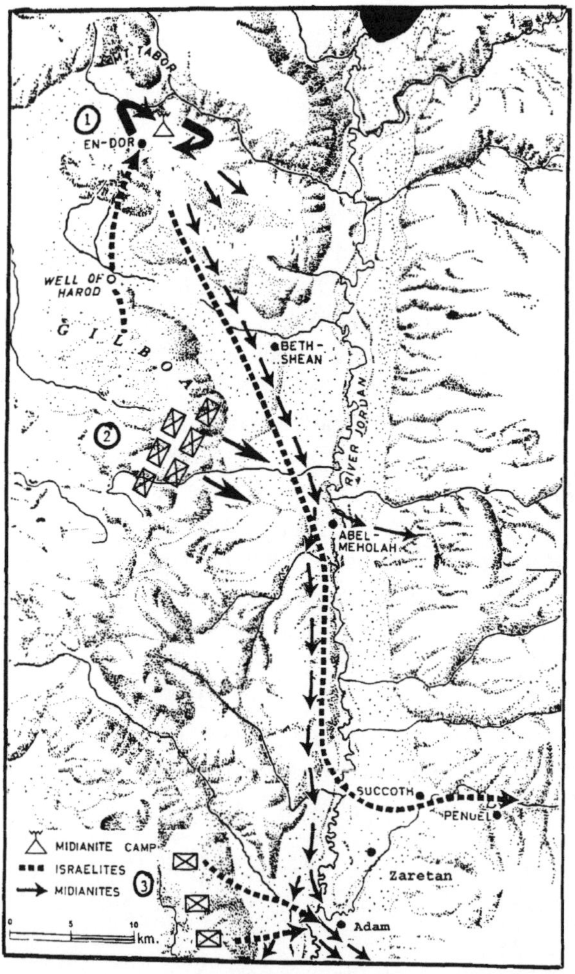

Figure 5.2 Gideon's Campaign against the Midianites

It had been several days since Gideon had called the tribes of Asher, Zebulun, and Naphtali to the colors so that by now they were assembled in position somewhere along the Samarian ridge overlooking the Midianite route of retreat. If all three tribes mustered their full strength, a main force of 6,000 men lay in ambush for the Midianites. By now, of course, the Midianite column would have regained some semblance of military order and was making its way down the valley along the Jordan River seeking to reach the ford at Abel-meholah and cross to safety. Behind them Gideon followed within sighting distance, probably joined now by the 300 or so men who had failed the test at Harod spring and waited in the Israelite camp. As the Midianite column approached the crossing at Abel-meholah, it was struck in the flank by a massive Israelite attack launched from the Samarian ridge. (See Figure 5.2, Phase 2.) The text is silent on the subject of casualties, but it is a safe assumption that a good number of Midianites were killed in the assault while others fled across the Jordan. When the Israelite attack struck the middle of the column, the lead elements, including the Midianite kings and their two generals, were able to escape by galloping straight down the valley seeking another crossing point further south.

But now the full scope of Gideon's plan became clear. He had no intention of driving the Midianites only from the Jezreel or even only from the land of Israel itself. The Midianites had killed his brothers at Tabor, and Gideon was determined to take his revenge by killing the Midianite kings. In short, the goal had been strategic from the start, to destroy the Midianite nomads once and for all and kill their political and military leaders. To this end, Gideon had sent envoys to the Ephraimites in the Samarian hill country ordering them to "Come down against the Midianites and capture the watering places from them as far as Beth-barah and also the Jordan. . . . So all the Ephraimites rallied, and they captured the watering places."[73] Gideon was not only denying the enemy access to the fresh water wells, he was cutting off their retreat by blocking the fords across the Jordan. Now the Ephraimites attacked the Midianite column (Figure 5.2, Phase 3), capturing the two generals, Oreb and Zeeb. The two were summarily executed and their heads presented to Gideon. For all practical purposes the Midianite army was destroyed, and along with it, no doubt, most of its attendant civilians.

Gideon was now a blood-soaked warrior. Even so, it was not enough. The Midian kings had killed his brothers, and for Gideon the war had become one of bloody revenge. Leaving the rest of the army behind (they may have refused to go regarding Gideon as exceeding his authority in undertaking a personal blood feud), "Gideon arrived at the Jordan and went on the prowl, he and the 300 men who were with him wearily giving chase."[74] At Succoth and Penuel, both towns within the Israelite confederation, he asked for food for his men. Both refused, and Gideon swore revenge. Perhaps news of Gideon's renegade feud had reached the town fathers who thought it illegitimate. Or, more probably, both towns were located in proximity to Midian, and the town fathers did not want to make enemies of their powerful neighbors. Gideon pressed on in pursuit of his brothers' murderers.

He caught up with the two Midianite kings, Zebah and Zalmunna, at Qarqor. No doubt thinking they were safe beyond the Jordan, they left the camp undefended even though they had 15 contingents of soldiers with them. Gideon caught them by surprise in a daylight attack and the kings' soldiers panicked and ran. The two kings were captured. Gideon brought them back to Succoth and Penuel, the towns that had refused to help him. There he flailed the town leaders of Succoth with "desert thorns and thistles," and revenged himself on Penuel by destroying its tower and killing the townsmen. In an act that says much about the merciless cruelty of the period of the Judges, Gideon had the two kings brought before him. He then called for Jether, his eldest son. "And to Jether his eldest child he said, 'Take a stand and slay them!' But the boy would not draw his sword, because he was afraid, being still a youth."[75] So Gideon avenged his brothers "and slew Zebah and Zalmunna and took the crescents which adorned the necks of their camels."

One must be impressed by the degree of tactical sophistication and political skill with which Gideon carried out his war against the Midianites. Despite the low state to which the Israelite national army had fallen, Gideon was able to muster sufficient forces to accomplish his military objectives and, we must presume, bring to bear sufficient weaponry to defeat a numerically superior enemy. By launching a surprise attack and conducting a relentless pursuit, Gideon, in modern-day military argot, "was inside the enemy's decision cycle," which is to say the enemy was always reacting to Gideon's initiatives and not the reverse. Gideon's political skill was apparent in his decision to keep his ultimate goal of avenging his brothers to himself, concealing it from his allied contingents until events proved irreversible and their objections had no effect on the outcome in the field. In this sense Gideon reflects the traits of other great generals in history who understood that war is always fought within some political context. The trick is to acknowledge that context and become its master. Gideon was a successful military commander because he clearly understood this often neglected relationship.

DEBORAH AND SISERA

Of all the wars of the Judges, the battle between Deborah and Barak and Sisera, the commander of the Canaanite king's army, is, perhaps, the most problematic for the military historian. The story of Deborah occurs early in Judges, but as already noted, the consensus of scholarly opinion places the battle very late in the period.[76] Moreover, the exact location of the battle remains in doubt. Some scholars have argued that the reference in the *Song of Deborah* (Judges 5:19) to the battle "at Ta'anach by the waters of Megiddo" suggests that the battle must have occurred at a time when Megiddo was unoccupied, otherwise the battle would have been referenced by the more important city of Megiddo instead of the less significant Ta'anach. Archaeological evidence has shown that the decisive break in the occupation of Megiddo probably occurred sometime between 1150 and 1075 B.C.E. If Megiddo was uninhabited during this time, then the reference to Ta'anach instead of Megiddo might make sense.[77] Thus the conclusion is that the battle probably occurred around 1125 B.C.E. However, one can neither infer nor preclude Megiddo's being occupied at that time based on archaeological evidence alone, and neither the *Song of Deborah* nor the Judges text can be seen to imply reasonably anything at all about the occupation of Megiddo. Therefore, archaeology adds nothing to determining the date of the battle between Deborah and Sisera, and there exist no datable historical allusions in the *Song of Deborah* that would enable us to determine the precise historical context in which it occurred.

The location of the battle is also in question. Judges 4 suggests a battle at the foot of Mount Tabor that raged across the swollen Kishon River a few miles away while the *Song* clearly states "Then fought the kings of Canaan at Ta'anach by Megiddo's waters." But in verse 21 the *Song of Deborah* asserts that "The wadi Kishon swept them away, the wadi overwhelmed them—the wadi Kishon." This has led some historians to suggest that there was one battle fought in two phases, one at Ta'anach and the other on the banks of the Kishon.[78] The texts are also contradictory regarding who participated in the battle. Judges 5 records only the tribes of Zebulun and Naphtali as having been involved while the *Song of Deborah* is clear that Issachar and Manasseh also participated. The identification of the enemy is also uncertain. Judges 5 notes that Sisera was the commander of the army of Jabin, "king of Canaan who reigned in Hazor," while the *Song of Deborah* mentions only Sisera without any mention of Jabin. We are forced to admit, therefore, that one of the most famous and oft-retold stories of the Bible stands in isolation. The text says nothing about the causes of the war and nothing of its effects on the circumstances of the Israelite position in Palestine. We remain ignorant of the conditions that led up to the war as well as the conditions that resulted from it.

Little wonder, then, that any analysis of the battle between Deborah and Sisera is likely to be incomplete and, depending upon one's emphasis, controversial. The following analysis is based upon the information in Judges 4 incorporating whatever information found in the *Song of Deborah* that does not contradict the main text. Whoever Jabin, king of the Canaanites was, both texts clearly imply that the king did not take the field. Instead, operational control of the military operation lay with the army commander, Sisera, who lived in Harosheth-hagoiim, a town located in the eastern end of the Acco plain not far from Yonqn'eam. Sisera is a non-Semitic name and probably belongs to one of the Sea Peoples who entered the land of Palestine with the Philistines about 75 years earlier.[79] Perhaps Harosheth-hagoiim was a Tjekker settlement or the home of some other group of Sea Peoples serving as mercenaries for the Canaanite king. Or, since Jabin is not mentioned in the *Song of Deborah*, the battle may have been fought between the Israelites and the Sea Peoples themselves, an occurrence, if it happened at all, that was likely to attract the attention of the Philistines. Whoever the combatants were, the location of the battle and home bases of the combatants suggest that what was at stake was control over the western Jezreel and Acco plains, a long sought goal of the Israelites confined to the hill country and resisted by the traditional Canaanite inhabitants of the area and, now, the newly arrived Sea Peoples.

Sisera's troop strength, the text tells us, included "900 chariots of iron,"[80] a number that Herzog and Gichon have pointed out was fairly close to the 924 chariots captured from the Canaanite coalition by Thutmose III at the battle of Megiddo.[81] But the battle of Megiddo had been fought more than 300 years before, at a time when the great Canaanite city-states were at the zenith of their military power. They had been in decline for more than two centuries by the time of Deborah's battle with Sisera, and it is unlikely that such a large number of machines could have been put in the field by any single Canaanite city-state or even a coalition of states at this late date. More likely the number of chariots under Sisera's command was much smaller. However many chariots took the field, we can reasonably assume that they were supported by units of Canaanite heavy infantry although here, too, we must note that the number and size of these units had also been declining over the previous two centuries.

The number of Israelite troops that took the field under Barak ben Abinoam, the seasoned commander from "Qedesh in Naphtali" in southeastern Galilee, is also uncertain. Judges 4:6 tells us that Deborah ordered Barak, "Go, deploy the troops at Mount Tabor; take with you ten contingents from the Naphtalites and Zebulunites." Ten contingents would amount to only 600 to 700 troops from both tribes, far below that 3,000 to 4,000 both tribes could muster at maximum effort and far too few to deal with Sisera's army. This suggests that the troop list in the *Song of Deborah*, which includes Manasseh and Issachar among the tribes that answered the muster along with Zebulun and Naphtali, might well be correct. Together the four tribes could muster almost 8,000 men among them. If each tribe contributed only ten contingents, the muster would produce 2,400 to 3,000 men, or about what a customary 30 percent levy would yield.[82] Even if Sisera's army possessed 900 chariots (very unlikely), this would equal only 1,800 men. Assume another 1,000 to 1,500 or so for supporting infantry, and the size of Sisera's army comes very close to the 3,000 man Israelite army commanded by Barak.

Deborah was a prophetess who was "judging Israel at that time . . . in the Ephraimite hill country, when the Israelites went to her for the judgment."[83] The text implies that some tribal assembly had decided to mobilize for war, and, in the traditional practice of the Israelites since Exodus, representatives of the assembly approached the judge for the *mishpat*, or divine sanction of Yahweh. The text is silent as to which tribe or tribes might have made the request, but it may have been one of the other tribes, Issachar or Manasseh, that are not mentioned in the Judges text but are noted in the *Song of Deborah* as taking part in the war. Issachar would be the most likely candidate since the battle itself took place on its territory. The fact that the assembly was able to muster only four tribes speaks to the inability of a weak Israelite national politico-military establishment to carry out any coherent national defense policy. Local tribal interests had by now completely overwhelmed any sense of shared national interest that the tribes were willing to place above their parochial interests. Even those tribes that answered Deborah's call were pursuing their local interests. Zebulun and Naphtali, settled north and west of the Kishon River, were concerned about containing Canaanite influence as far east and south as possible. Issachar had the most to lose since the Canaanite towns were sitting upon the very land Issachar had claimed for itself. Manasseh, too, feared the expansion of Canaanite power to the southwest, squeezing it between the Canaanites and the Philistines. These four tribes came to the battlefield to protect their respective tribal interests, not to support any national cause.

The *Song of Deborah* can be read as giving voice to the frustration of this lack of Israelite national awareness. The tribes that did not answer the mobilization are described in derisive terms. Thus it is that "Reuben's divisions are command-minded chieftains. Why then did you squat between hearths harking to pastoral pipings" while "Asher squatted at the seashore!" Gilead remained safe beyond the Jordan while "Dan took service on ships."[84] The Ephraimites "have taken root in Amalek" while Benjamin remains "behind you . . . with your troops." Judah is so far removed from meeting its national obligations that it is not mentioned at all. The refusal of so many tribes to rally to the colors must have been a problem of some magnitude to merit the observation that, "Neither shield nor spear was to be seen among the forty contingents in Israel." Deborah's respect for those who did come is clear: "My heart is with the commanders of Israel. Those presenting themselves with the troops—give thanks to Yahweh!"[85]

Deborah summoned Barak to her in Ephraim and gave him command of the troops. Barak assembled ten contingents of troops at Qedesh and from there moved to take up positions on Mount Tabor. Mount Tabor offered several advantages as a base of operations. First, it provided a commanding position from which Barak could observe the entire Jezreel plain in all directions. Second, its heavily forested slopes concealed the location and strength of the Israelite force from Sisera's agents. Third, the steeply wooded slopes were impossible for enemy chariots to negotiate either in the attack or as reconnaissance patrols. Fourth, when the time came to attack, the momentum of the assault would be increased by its movement downhill.[86] Once in position Barak conspired to draw Sisera to him and maneuver him onto favorable ground. This was accomplished by having Heber the Kenite, a traveling metalsmith who may have at some time lived among the Israelites, betray the Israelite position to Sisera with the result that "Sisera called out all his chariots—nine hundred iron chariots—and all the force who were with him, [probably a reference to infantry] *from Harosheth-hagoiim, to the river Kishon*."[87] Just where Sisera took up positions is unclear from the text, but Malamat argues that it was the narrow secondary valley, the Valley of Chesulloth, where Sisera concentrated his forces.[88] The valley was too narrow to permit full combat deployment of any sizable chariot force, and Sisera's presence there may have been primarily an encampment or laager. The text implies that both forces remained in place for several days. Perhaps it was raining or Deborah was waiting for a rainstorm. At some point Deborah said to Barak, "Up! This is the day in which Yahweh has put Sisera in your power! . . . And Barak descended from Mount Tabor, with ten units following him."[89] The Israelite attack shattered the enemy chariot force which seem to have been taken by surprise and broke into a rout, "all the chariotry and fighting force before Barak." Sisera jumped down from his chariot and attempted to flee on foot. The Israelites pursued the fleeing army, "[a]nd Barak chased the chariotry and fighting force all the way to Harosheth-hagoiim. Sisera's entire force fell to the sword; not one was left."[90] Sisera was later slain by Jael, the wife of Heber the Kenite, who drove a tent peg through Sisera's brain as he tried to conceal himself from the Israelite pursuit by hiding in the Kenite's tent.

The meaning of the text seems clear enough until one attempts to reconcile it with two verses that appear in the *Song of Deborah*. Verse 21 tells us that "The Wadi Kishon swept them away. The wadi overwhelmed them—the Wadi Kishon." Attempts to explain this verse have produced the most common interpretation of the battle, namely, that Sisera's chariots became stuck in the mud of the swollen Kishon River and were overwhelmed by the Israelite infantry. Sisera, his own machine stuck fast, abandoned it and fled on foot. The mainstream of the Kishon River is about four kilometers from the foot of Mount Tabor. However, a number of smaller trickle streams reach out from both riverbanks, at least two of which reach into the Chesulloth Valley. A few days of heavy rain would have turned the Jezreel Valley floor along the river into a quagmire. It would also have softened the ground near Sisera's chariot laager. If the Israelite attack took the Canaanites by surprise, forcing them to flee in their chariots as the text suggests, the Israelites would only have had to pursue for perhaps a kilometer or so before the saturated ground began to have its effect on slowing the chariots, well within the operational capability of Israelite infantry. At which point the Israelite infantry would have easily caught and overwhelmed them. The closer the chariots came to the Kishon's sodden plain which lay between Sisera's camp and the city of Harosheth-hagoiim, the softer the ground became trapping the chariots further. Under these conditions Sisera's men might have abandoned their machines and fled on foot. Some might have attempted to swim the Kishon to reach the safety of Megiddo a few kilometers away and might have been "swept away" and drowned.

The whole story swings on the claim that the chariots became stuck in the mud. How likely, then, was it that Sisera's "iron chariots" became mired in the mud? To answer this question we must remember that the very idea of an iron chariot is technological nonsense. Chariot frames were fashioned of light woods and leather. Any attempt to attach iron plates to the cab would easily collapse the frame.[91] Nonetheless, the use of the phrase "iron chariots" by the text's author is certainly deliberate, to convey the impression of heavy machines which might easily be imagined to have become mired in the mud. Like the rest of Judges, the account of Deborah's battle was written down much later, during the period of either Assyrian or Persian occupation of Palestine. The Assyrians had large chariots with iron-rimmed wheels whereas the Persians had chariots equipped with iron scythes on their wheel hubs. Either one might easily qualify in the mind of the redactor as iron chariots so that in assembling the text he might have described the chariots of Deborah's day in terms familiar to him, that is, as "iron chariots."[92]

This aside, how heavy were the chariots of Deborah's time? Egyptian texts record that an Egyptian chariot could easily be carried by two men and, indeed, in Thutmose III's approach march along the Carmel ridge toward Megiddo, Egyptian chariots were carried overland. Making allowance for the fact that Canaanite chariots were somewhat heavier than Egyptian models, a typical chariot weighed about 80 pounds. Two men in bronze armor brought the load to 450 pounds. Two good horses could move the load over hard ground, but not at very high speed and not for long, the weight quickly exhausting the animals.[93] On soft ground, the weight of the chariot and the increased strength required by the animals to overcome the increased friction of the mud would quickly have exhausted the horses. It is quite plausible, then, that Sisera's chariots became mired or at least sufficiently slowed to permit their being overtaken and destroyed by Barak's infantry.

The version of Deborah's victory over Sisera offered above is the simplest explanation of how the battle may have been fought consistent with most of the evidence from both texts. It does not, however, take into account verse 19 in the *Song of Deborah* that suggests another battle also took place "at Ta'anach by Megiddo's waters." Mordechai Gichon's brilliant analysis of the battle takes into account the implications of verse 19 and suggests that there were two Israelite forces involved, one under Barak at Mount Tabor, and a second, originally raised by Deborah on the Gilboa ridge and placed under the command of an unnamed captain when Deborah accompanied Barak to Mount Tabor. This second force, Gichon argues, was coming to the aid of Barak's army when it stumbled into a Canaanite force around Ta'anach. A battle ensued that drew Sisera's attention to his rear whereupon he dispatched a segment of his force to join the fight. When Barak attacked down the mountain he caught Sisera's blocking force by surprise and put it to rout. His pursuit caught Sisera's main force in the rear as it was attempting to cross the flooded Kishon to relieve the Canaanite force at Ta'anach. The Israelite force at Ta'anach by this time had overcome the Canaanite opposition and attacked across the Jezreel catching Sisera's army as it struggled to free itself from the wet ground. Caught between both wings of the Israelite army, Sisera panicked and fled abandoning his troops to their fate.[94]

However Deborah and Barak out-generaled Sisera may be of less importance than the fact that she had led a coalition of Israelite tribes to victory over a Canaanite army at all, the only military victory over the Canaanites recorded in Judges, and did so at a time when the Philistine city-states to the south had already shaken off their Egyptian shackles and become a powerful military confederacy in their own right. Deborah's victory would have made it possible for the Israelites to forge a geographically contiguous zone of influence comprising the territories of Manasseh, Zebulun, Naphtali, and Issachar which included all of the Galilee from the Kineret through the Jezreel and the Acco plain to the sea. This zone would have joined the Israelite settlements in the Samarian hill country at the foot of Mount Gilboa and, most important, touched on the northern border of the Philistine confederacy itself at the border of Manasseh. If Sisera was not a Canaanite but one of the Sea Peoples, perhaps even a Philistine, his command of an army based at Harosheth-hagoiim suggests that the Philistine's Sea People allies may have already largely displaced the Canaanites as the major influence in the western Jezreel. The defeat of Sisera and the establishment of Israelite military influence in an area on the periphery of the Philistine confederacy itself could not reasonably go unnoticed by the Philistines who might have reacted quickly to reverse it.

The period of the Judges ended in a catastrophic military defeat for the Israelites at the hands of the Philistines at the battle of Ebenezer-Aphek, which occurred close to the end of the twelfth century or, perhaps, as late as 1050 B.C.E.[95] In seeking to establish the historical context of Deborah's victory, Mayes suggests that Deborah's war occurred fairly close to the battle of Ebenezer-Aphek, and that it was her victory over Sisera that provoked the Philistines into military action against the Israelites. The Philistines had consolidated their position in southern Palestine throughout the period of the Judges. Except for the sporadic border raids of renegades like Samson, no major military actions appear to have occurred between them and the Israelites, and no effort was made by the Philistines to occupy the central hill country. Deborah's victory changed the military equation, however, forcing the Philistines to attempt to preempt any further increase in the Israelite military strategic position.

The key to the argument, as Mayes observes, lies in the location of the battle of Ebenezer-Aphek. The battle took place at Aphek, 15 miles *north* of Gath, the most northerly of the Philistine city-states.[96] If the Philistines were interested only in expanding their influence over the Israelites, it would have made more sense to strike at some location more directly east of the main Philistine settlements, that is, at the Judean hill country. The Philistine attack to the north of its main position might be explainable, therefore, by a desire to strike at Deborah's assembled coalition which, after defeating Sisera, now controlled the western Jezreel. The text (I Samuel 4:12) indicates that the Benjaminites were involved in the battle, and we might reasonably presume, since Aphek was in Ephraimite territory, that they, too, took the field. If Deborah's original coalition was still intact, this brought the number of Israelite tribes at Aphek to six, the largest Israelite coalition assembled against a common enemy during the entire period of the Judges.[97] I Samuel 4 puts the number of Israelite dead in both engagements at 34,000 men. Even allowing for exaggeration, the text clearly conveys the impression of a large number of Israelite dead suggesting that the Israelite army that fought at Aphek was very large, indeed probably larger than any assembled before during the period of the Judges.

The defeat at Ebenezer-Aphek and the destruction of the sanctuary at Shiloh where the Ark of the Covenant fell into Philistine hands was a prelude to more difficult times for the Israelites. Despite occasional victories like that won by Samuel at the second battle of Ebenezer, Philistine power proved unstoppable and expanded at Israelite expense. After Aphek, the power of Deborah's coalition was broken and Philistine influence expanded westward to include Beth-shean. In addition, the Israelites may have lost control of some gateway cities protecting the invasion routes from the *shephelah* to the Judean ridge. A permanent Philistine garrison was stationed in the stronghold of Gibeah, and the Philistines appear to have established some degree of control over Judah, at least to the extent that they could enforce the embargo on iron making. As was so often the case during the period of the Judges, Israelite political and military institutions had shown themselves inadequate to the task of national defense. Deborah's victory over Sisera and the Israelite attempt to consolidate its gains at the battle of Ebenezer-Aphek were the last great efforts to make the old institutions work successfully. And once more the attempt failed, this time with disastrous consequences for Israelite independence.

NOTES

1. Robert G. Boling, *Judges: The Anchor Bible* (New York: Doubleday, 1975), 18. From here on in this chapter, this source will be referred to as *Anchor Bible*. See also T. R. Hobbs, *A Time for War* (Wilmington, DE: Michael Glazier, 1989), 28.
2. Hobbs, 28.
3. Judges 3:31.

4. *The Westminster Historical Atlas of the Bible* (Philadelphia, PA: Westminster Press, 1945), 45.
5. Ibid., 25.
6. Judges 1:4–22.
7. Judges 1:27–33.
8. Judges 1:1–2.
9. Hobbs, 34.
10. Ibid., 36. The term for a loose confederation of separate groups for religious or political purposes is amphictyony.
11. Judges 3:5–6.
12. Judges 3:7–9.
13. A. Malamat, "Cushan Rishathaim and the Decline of the Near East," *Journal of Near Eastern Studies* 13 (1954): 233–34.
14. Ibid.
15. Judges 3:16.
16. For an analysis of the weapons mentioned in Judges, see J. Moyer, "Weapons and Warfare in the Book of Judges," *Discovering the Bible*, edited by T. Dowley (Grand Rapids, MI: Erdmans, 1986), 43–50.
17. Judges 3:15.
18. Judges 3:31.
19. Benjamin Maisler, "Shamgar: A Hurrian Name?" *Palestine Exploration Quarterly* 66 (1934): 192–94.
20. *Anchor Bible*, 90.
21. P. C. Craigie, "Anath," *Journal of Biblical Literature* 91 (1972): 239–40.
22. For Israelite relations with the Midian tribes, see Exodus 2:15, 4:31, and 18: 1–27. For warfare between the two peoples, see Numbers 25 and 31.
23. *Anchor Bible*, xxi; see also A.D.H. Mayes, "The Historical Context of the Battle against Sisera," *Vetus Testamentum* 19 (1951): 253–360, for dates of the battle.
24. *Anchor Bible*, 279.
25. Judges 21:25.
26. W. F. Albright, "A New Campaign of Excavation at Gibeah of Saul," *Bulletin of the American Schools of Oriental Research* 52 (December 1933): 6–12; see also Paul W. Lapp, "Tel el-Ful," *Biblical Archaeologist* 28 (1965): 1–13.
27. Mayes, 353.
28. Robert Drews, *The End of the Bronze Age: Changes in Warfare and the Catastrophe, ca. 1200 B.C.E.* (Princeton, NJ: Princeton University Press), 1993.
29. William H. Stiebing Jr., "Did the Weather Make Israel's Emergence Possible?" *Bible Review* 10 (August 1994): 20.
30. Ibid.; Drew, 9.
31. Stiebing, 22.
32. Ibid., 23.
33. Drew, 9, 15–16. The data portrayed in Figure 5.1 are also drawn from Drew.
34. Ibid., 16–17.
35. *Anchor Bible*, 9.
36. Stiebing, 23.
37. John Strange, "The Transition from the Bronze Age to the Iron Age in the

Eastern Mediterranean and the Emergence of the Israelite State," *Scandinavian Journal of the Old Testament* 1 (1987): 8–9.

38. Itamar Singer, "Merneptah's Campaign to Canaan and the Egyptian Occupation of the Southern Coastal Plain of Palestine in the Ramesside Period," *Bulletin of the American Schools of Oriental Research* 269 (1988): 6.
39. Stiebing, 25.
40. Drew, chap. 13, for the argument on the impact of new military technologies.
41. Ibid.
42. Strange, 17.
43. Ibid., 16.
44. *Anchor Bible*, 278.
45. Judges 2:6, 10.
46. The sexual reference here is apparently deliberate.
47. Judges 20:16.
48. Judges 20:17.
49. Judges 20:46, 48.
50. Judges 20:15, 17.
51. *Anchor Bible*, 285.
52. Lawrence E. Stager, "The Archaeology of the Family in Ancient Israel," *American Schools of Oriental Research* 260 (1985): 25; B.S.J. Isserlin, *The Israelites* (London: Thames and Hudson, 1998), 192; *Anchor Bible*, 17; and Edward F. Campell Jr., "The Population of Ancient Israel," *Biblical Archaeologist* 23 (1960): 21, in support of the population estimate made here.
53. *Anchor Bible*, 184.
54. Boling, 65.
55. Moyer, 43.
56. I Samuel 22:2.
57. Stager, 25.
58. Ibid., 26.
59. Judges 6:2.
60. A. Malamat, "The Period of the Judges," *World History of the Jewish People*, vol. III (Philadelphia, PA: Jewish Publications Society, 1979), 141.
61. Judges 6:3.
62. Malamat, 142.
63. Judges 6:4–6.
64. Judges 7:3.
65. Judges 7:12.
66. Judges 7:3.
67. Judges 7:5–6.
68. A. Malamat, "The War of Gideon and Midian—A Military Approach," *Palestine Exploration Quarterly* 85 (1953): 68.
69. Chaim Herzog and Mordechai Gichon, *Battles of the Bible* (Jerusalem: Steimatzky's Agency Ltd., 1978), 61. The use of the phrase *"sons of my mother"* makes it clear that these were indeed Gideon's blood brothers and not just his *"brethren,"* a term used to connote half brothers and other kinsmen.
70. Ibid.

71. Judges 7:14.

72. Judges 7:19. It is uncertain by how many "watches" the day was calculated. The rabbinical tradition holds to three watches while Mark 13:35 tells us that the nighttime could be divided into four watches—evening, midnight, cockcrow, and morning. See *Anchor Bible*, 147.

73. Judges 7:24.

74. Judges 8:4.

75. Judges 8:20.

76. *Anchor Bible*, xxi; Mayes, 353, 358.

77. W. F. Albright, "Further Light on the History of Israel from Lachish and Megiddo," *Bulletin of the American Schools of Oriental Research* 68 (1937): 25; see also Mayes, 353.

78. Herzog and Gichon, 48–54.

79. Mayes, 358.

80. Judges 4:3.

81. Herzog and Gichon, 49.

82. *Anchor Bible*, 285.

83. Judges 4:5 On the requirement to seek the *mishpat* prior to going to war, see H. C. Thomson, "Shophet and Mishpat in the Book of Judges," in *Transactions of the Glasgow University Oriental Society* (Leiden: E. J. Brill, 1961–62), 74–85.

84. Mayes, 355. The meaning of this phrase is the subject of debate. One interpretation is that Dan was already living near Lake Huleh. The other interpretation notes that the use of the term *yagur* indicates that the ships Dan was serving on were foreign ones implying they were in fact hiring themselves out as sailors. This would suggest, of course, that the Danites had not yet left their original home near the coast.

85. All quotes in this section are from the *Song of Deborah and Barak*, Judges 5.

86. Malamat, *World History of the Jewish People*, 139.

87. Judges 4:13.

88. Malamat, *World History of the Jewish People*, 139.

89. Judges 4:14.

90. Judges 4:15–16.

91. Robert Drews, "The Chariots of Iron of Joshua and Judges," *Journal for the Study of the Old Testament* 45 (1989): 14.

92. Ibid., 15.

93. Ibid., 18.

94. Herzog and Gichon, 48–54.

95. Mayes, 358.

96. Ibid.

97. With, of course, the exception of the Benjaminite civil war which was not against a foreign enemy.

6

Saul's Wars

The period between 1050 and 1000 B.C.E. was an important time in the military history of ancient Israel. Beginning with the battle of Aphek-Ebenezer, Philistine military control of Israelite territory reached its peak and continued unchallenged for almost 40 years. The power of Philistine control convinced the Israelite tribal elders that the old system of sporadic military organization characteristic of the period of the Judges was no longer adequate, with the result that Israel anointed its first king, Saul of Kish, changing forever its traditional sociopolitical order and ushering in a permanent governmental structure and standing army. Under Saul's leadership the Israelites were able to throw off the Philistine yoke and extend their control to the south and into the Transjordan. For almost five years Saul warred against the Philistines with success only to meet his death at the battle of Gilboa where the Philistine army crushed the Israelites and once more reestablished their preeminence in Canaan. It fell to a later king, David of Judah, to deal with the Philistines and remove the last remaining obstacle to Israelite control of the Promise Land.

The period is rich in military history, and the Bible records a number of important battles: the battle of Aphek-Ebenezer, the second battle of Ebenezer, the battle of Jabesh-gilead, the battle of Michmash Pass, the war against the Amalekites, the contest in the Vale of Terebinth, and the death of Saul at the battle of Mount Gilboa. It is possible to affix dates to these battles with some confidence, although caution is always to be exercised in such endeavors. If, as argued earlier, the battle of Aphek-Ebenezer occurred circa 1050 B.C.E., then it may be used as a baseline from which to calculate the dates of the others. I Samuel 7:2 records that the second battle of Ebenezer occurred twenty years "from the day the ark began to reside in Kiriath-jearim," where it had been established after being returned by the Philistines a few months after they captured it at the battle of Aphek-Ebenezer. Thus we may place the second battle of Ebenezer around 1030 B.C.E. It was shortly after this that Samuel secretly anointed Saul as king. The text makes clear that Saul was still a young man living at home and without a wife or children. He was, however, an adult of military age, at least 20 years old and, perhaps, a few years older. When Saul was officially anointed king by the tribal lottery, he was immediately challenged to respond to the Ammonite attack on Jabesh-gilead. The text presents the challenge as the "proving of Saul," from which it may reasonably be implied that it occurred only a short time after his election. Thus the battle at Jabesh-gilead probably occurred sometime around 1032–1035 B.C.E. When next we hear of Saul, it is at the battle of Michmash Pass, and he is possessed of a full-grown son, a warrior of military age. Indeed, it was Saul's son, Jonathan, who assassinated the Philistine prefect in Gibeah precipitating the clash with the Philistines. Jonathan was at least 20 years old at the time, the age of military service in Israel. If he was born shortly after Saul became king, then the battle of Michmash Pass may have been fought sometime around 1010 B.C.E. By 1005 B.C.E., Saul was dead and David had established himself as his likely successor, making it possible to date the battle of Mount Gilboa at about 1006 B.C.E. If the text is to be believed, the wars with Moab, Edom, the Ammonites, and Zobah also occurred between 1010 and 1006 B.C.E., although as we shall see, this is doubtful.

Two further observations may be offered. The first is that Saul grew to manhood during the Philistine occupation of the Israelite hill country. After the Philistine victory at Aphek-Ebenezer, the Philistines constructed a military garrison in the town of Gibe'at Elohim and stationed troops there. These Philistine troops were still there 40 years later when Jonathan assassinated the Philistine prefect. Gibe'at Elohim is the town of Gibeah, where Saul was born and grew to manhood.[1] Until the Philistines were driven from the town after the battle of Michmash Pass, Saul and Jonathan had lived all their lives under Philistine military occupation, a fact that may explain what might have been an act of spontaneous rage on Jonathan's part when he attacked and killed the Philistine prefect. Second, if the chronology is correct, then with the exception of Saul's relief of Jabesh-gilead, all of Saul's wars, those against the Philistines *and* the other peoples of Canaan, were all fought between 1010 B.C.E. (Michmash Pass) and 1005 B.C.E. (Saul's death on Mount Gilboa). At least this is the conclusion implied by the order of the battles presented in the text.

It is worth considering, however, that, as in Judges, the arrangement of the stories in I Samuel may in some cases be artificial and historically incorrect. Given the power of the Philistine army, it is unlikely that a man of Saul's military disposition would have chosen to fight the Philistines *and* the peoples of Moab, Ammon, Zobah, and Amalek all at the same time on such widely separated fronts. More likely, the wars with Israel's non-Philistine enemies may have occurred during the 20-year period between Saul's anointing and the battle of Michmash Pass when he opened hostilities against the Philistines.

None of Saul's victories prior to Michmash Pass, if, indeed, they did occur in this earlier period, threatened Philistine interests nor did any of them appreciably increase the Israelite geostrategic position and, thus, required no Philistine response. These small wars might, however, have provided Saul and the Israelite army with valuable combat experience and the opportunity to acquire arms in sufficient numbers. Eventually this situation might have come to the attention of the Philistines who then may have taken steps to stop it. Only when at Michmash does the text tell us that, "There was no smith to be found in all the land of Israel, for the Philistines had said to themselves, 'The Hebrews might make swords or spears!' "[2] There is no mention of this restriction in all of the 40 years spanning the Philistine occupation prior to the battle of Michmash Pass, suggesting, perhaps, that the ban on iron making may have been imposed only recently and may have been brought about by heightened Philistine concerns about the improved combat capabilities of the Israelite army.

Before moving on to an analysis of the battles of this period, it is important to note that the strategic equation existing in Canaan during Saul's time was quite different from what it had been during the time of Judges and for centuries before that. Until Saul's time the Israelite saga had been played out against the background of great power conflicts occurring within Palestine itself. All the great empires had at one time or another coveted Palestine and all had made their influence felt on its domestic circumstances. By 1050 B.C.E., the great powers were no longer able to influence events in Palestine. Egypt had been weakened by domestic upheavals caused by dynastic rivalries and a series of civil wars between rival principalities. The central government collapsed and was replaced by a sacerdotal regime controlled by the priests of Amun unconcerned with foreign affairs even as the Libyans and Nubians mounted one invasion attempt after another.[3] The Hittite Empire had disappeared completely, destroyed by foreign invasion, famine, and migration. Babylon was now subject to Assyria, while Assyria itself was only beginning its rise to the status of a world power. For the time, however, Assyria's commercial and security interests were satisfied by its attention to Syria and Lebanon. It wasn't until the middle of the ninth century B.C.E. that any Assyrian king would be concerned with events in Palestine. During Saul's time, the fates of the Israelites and Philistines were completely in their own hands without any threat of outside interference by the great powers.

THE BATTLE OF APHEK-EBENEZER

The battle of Aphek-Ebenezer appears to have been a consequence of Philistine fear that the Israelites had forged a military coalition sufficiently large to threaten Philistine trade routes through the Jezreel Valley and even the northern periphery of Philistia itself. The text confirms Mayes's observation, noted earlier, that it was the Philistines who sought the confrontation,[4] and that the choice of Aphek as their point of concentration drew the tribes of Ephraim and Benjamin into the larger coalition of Naphtali, Zebulun, Issachar, and Manasseh that had previously fought under Deborah and Barak. It is curious that in recording one of the most important battles in Israelite history the biblical texts should remain silent as to the identity of the commander of the Israelite forces at Aphek-Ebenezer. The institution of the judge as military commander, although about to disappear in a few decades, was very much alive at the time of the battle. The account of the defeat at Aphek was apparently written by a seer-priest and judge who, like Samuel, probably opposed the institution of the monarchy on the grounds that the old system of judge-commanders worked well enough. The Philistine oppression began in earnest as a consequence of the Israelite defeat at Aphek and leaving the name of the judge in command of the Israelite army unrecorded was, perhaps, a way of minimizing the failure of the judges system per se. Samuel was quick to claim credit for the victory at the second battle of Ebenezer, even if it was hardly more than a skirmish. The omission of the judge-commander's identity at the battle of Aphek-Ebenezer is the only military encounter in both Judges and Samuel in which the name of the Israelite commander remains unknown.

Whoever the Israelite commander was, he seems to have lacked a sound tactical sense. I Samuel 4:1–2 tells us, "In those days the Philistines gathered to make war against Israel. Israel marched out to meet them in battle and made camp at Ebenezer. The Philistines were encamped at Aphek. They drew up their forces to engage Israel, and the battle lines were deployed." The text confirms that it was the Philistines who sought the battle, lending support to the theory that they were reacting to Deborah's victory and the shift in the balance of power in the western Jezreel Valley. Second, there is evidence of a much-improved Israelite military organization than that usually encountered throughout Judges. At Ebenezer the Israelite armies assembled in request to a national muster, concentrated for battle, and encamped in anticipation of the fight. But it is the phrase "and the battle lines were deployed" that suggests a tactical blunder of the first magnitude by implying that the battle occurred in the open plain between the two camps. A battle between Israelite militia and Philistine professionals on the open plain would have been tactical suicide. Open ground conceded a major advantage to the Philistine chariots, although they are not mentioned in the text, as well as offering the disciplined sword and spear infantry of the Philistines a considerable advantage. Any Israelite advantage would have lain in surprise and the mobility of its light troops, both of which were impossible in a battle on open terrain with the almost predictable result that the Israelites "were routed by the advance of the Philistines, four thousands being slain."[5]

The Israelites withdrew to their camp. Here we encounter what may be evidence of either a divided command or a dispute over what to do next. Whoever was in command was rebuked by the tribal elders for the army's poor battlefield performance. "Why has Yahweh routed us today before the Philistines?" the elders inquired of the commander.[6] The question was really an accusation for the military prowess of a judge was intimately connected to his acceptance by Yahweh. The question implies that the judge had somehow done something, perhaps committed a ritual sin or some personal immorality that caused Yahweh to abandon him and the Israelites. Having defined the problem as one of theology rather than tactics, the elders suggested a theological solution: to send for the Ark of the Covenant that resided at the sanctuary in Shiloh, "so the army sent word to Shiloh to carry over from there the Ark of Yahweh."[7] It is noteworthy that it was not the judge-commander who gave the order, but the elders, which might suggest that the judge-commander had been removed from command.

Although theological solutions to tactical problems are always likely to be problematic, the military significance of sending for the Ark of Yahweh ought not to be overlooked. The presence of the Ark on the battlefield was tantamount to the participation in the battle of Yahweh himself. In this regard, the removal of the judge-commander made sense insofar as Yahweh, the Divine Warrior, was now in command. And the arrival of Yahweh upon the field of battle was not without its anticipated physical influences on the battle. When the Ark arrived, the troops let out a great roar, the *teru'a* or ritual war cry, which, along with Yahweh's presence, was designed to spread a *mehuma*, or general sense of panic inflicted by the deity, through the enemy ranks.[8] One ought, therefore, to see the Israelite use of the Ark for what it was, the application of a theological weapons system employed to affect the outcome of the battle.

The belief that theological factors determine the outcome of war was widespread in the ancient world, and no less so among the Philistines. It comes as no surprise, then, that the Israelite employment of the *teru'a* and *mehuma* had the desired effect upon the Philistines. I Samuel 4:7–8 describes the Philistine reaction as one of near panic. "Gods have come into the camp! Alas for us! . . . who will rescue us from the clutches of these mighty gods? These are the gods who struck Egypt with every kind of scourge and pestilence." But the Philistines were professional warriors, not conscript militia soldiers, and their officers quickly controlled the panic and calmed their men by the age-old device of appealing to their manhood and sense of honor. "Fortify yourselves and be men, you Philistines! Be men and fight!"[9] It is precisely under these conditions that training and experience pay large dividends, as they did for the Philistines that day. The army found its courage, "And they did fight; and Israel was routed and fled, every man to his own tent. The slaughter was very great: there fell from Israel thirty thousands of infantry."[10]

The Israelites suffered a defeat of catastrophic proportions. The text's description of the Israelites as having fled "every man to his own tent" is militarily significant. The phrase is used differently in different contexts. For example, in Judges 20:8 when the army was assembling for battle the men vowed not to return "every man to his own tent" until victory was achieved. When the army is mustering out, as in I Samuel 13:2, "every man to his own tent is sent," that is, dismissed from active military duty. When used to describe the flight after the defeat at Aphek, it means to abandon military service altogether,[11] to have no chance to fight again. The description is of a defeat so total that whatever degree of military unification had been achieved by Deborah and had carried over to the fight at Aphek was now completely destroyed. As indeed it remained for the next 30 years or so while the Philistines remained in effective control of the central hill country and the Jezreel Valley and no Israelite lifted a weapon to resist them.

The casualty figure of 30,000 dead is out of the question as being factual. Earlier I estimated the population of Israel between Iron 1 and Iron 2 at about 100,00 to 150,000, permitting an army of 25,000 or so at maximum effort, or approximately 2,000 soldiers per tribe *as an average*. If there were six tribes assembled for the battle, then the size of the Israelite army was around 12,000 to 15,000 men. As noted earlier the text's use of the term *eleph* is not to be translated as "thousands" but recognized as a unit of military manpower strength which we have earlier calculated to be between 65 to 70 men per *eleph*. So when the text records that 34 *alaphim* of infantry were killed, it means that about 2,200 to 2,500 men died at Aphek-Ebenezer. That was almost 20 percent of the combat force. When taken together with a conservative estimate of two wounded for every man killed,[12] some 4,400 men were wounded or otherwise rendered combat ineffective. The Israeli losses at Ebenezer-Aphek, therefore, amounted to more than 6,000 men or 50 percent of the force, more than sufficient to justify the memory of Aphek-Ebenezer as a military catastrophe in the Israelite national consciousness.

The defeat exposed all of the Israelite hill country and parts of the Jezreel Valley to Philistine conquest and occupation, and the Philistines moved quickly to consolidate their gains. Military governors were appointed in important towns (including Gibeah) and a system of systematic tax and tribute collection was instituted. The important cities of Beth-shean and Megiddo, both controlling major caravan trade routes, were occupied and turned into thriving commercial centers. The text is unclear as to when and to what extent it was instituted, but the Philistines seem to have made some effort to control the manufacture of iron so as to prohibit the Israelites from acquiring iron weapons. This may have entailed some attempt to disarm the Israelites as well, but the degree to which it was successful remains uncertain.[13]

Of considerable interest was the creation of special military units called *hamashhith*, "a professional military unit able to repress any attempt at revolt."[14] These were the raiding parties or search-and-destroy columns mentioned in the text. It is interesting to speculate as to what these *hamashhith* might have looked like.[15] As noted in chapter 2, the Philistines employed several chariot designs depending upon the nature of the tactical problem. One of these was a heavy chariot similar to the Hittite model with six-spoked wheels, four horses, and a crew of three or even four men armed with composite bow, spears, and thrown javelins. Once in contact, the crew could dismount and fight as infantry. These heavy chariots could make their way along the main roads of the central hill country, but if employed alone would have been vulnerable to infantry attack. Most probably they were accompanied by Philistine light infantry arranged in squads of four, each soldier armed with the straight iron sword, a pair of thrown javelins, and a round shield.[16] With two or three squads assigned to each chariot as "runners" (supporting infantry), the Philistine *hamashhith* were highly flexible combat units capable of responding quickly and pursuing Israelite infantry over the rugged terrain that they had heretofore used to great advantage. Being able to pursue the rebels into "their caves and dens" made these special search-and-destroy teams a new and effective weapon for keeping the Israelite population under control.

After the Israelites were driven from the field at Aphek-Ebenezer, the Philistines carried off the Ark of Yahweh and installed it in their own pantheon at Ashdod. In ancient times, all armies carried their national gods with them on campaign, and it was a common practice to capture the gods of the enemy.[17] The biblical text portrays the capture of the Ark by the Philistines as a national disaster, almost sacrilegious in nature, while to the Philistines it was no such thing. It is often believed that the religions of the ancient world routinely distinguished between their own true gods and the false gods of others as modern religions do. In fact, this was not the case. In the ancient world polytheism functioned as a vehicle of *cultural translation* and drew no distinctions among deities with regard to their being true or false. Polytheism's contribution to the ancient world was to overcome the earlier ethnocentric loyalties of tribal "enclave" religions by distinguishing many deities by name, form, and function. Names and forms of these gods varied from culture to culture, but their functions as recognizable cosmic deities were interchangeable.[18] Accordingly, the sun god or fertility goddess of one culture was readily equated with a similar deity in another. This made it possible for deities of both cultures to be seen as the same gods manifested in different forms. While the cultures of tribes and nations were different, their religions provided them with a functional common ground and served as mechanisms of *intercultural transmissibility*.[19] Different peoples worshiped different gods, but nobody contested either the reality of the foreign gods or the legitimacy of foreign forms of worship. When cultures came into contact, they identified foreign gods as simply different forms of their own gods and often incorporated them into their pantheons. This syncretism was a near universal practice among the more complex countries of the ancient Near East until the time of Moses, whose introduction of monotheism asserted that only the god of the Israelites was genuine and all other gods were false, an idea that led directly to the condemnation of the worship of other gods as idolatry.

The installation of the Ark in the pantheon at Ashdod was accompanied by a curious event. The text tells us that Yahweh, "ravaged them [the Philistines] and afflicted them with tumors—both Ashdod and its environs. He brought mice upon them, and they swarmed in their ships. Then mice went up into their land, and there was mortal panic in the city."[20] The text uses the word *opalim*, which means mound, hill, or swelling, to describe the tumors that afflicted the Philistines.[21] The combination of a swarm of shipboard rats and of people suffering from tumors or swelling suggests the clinical indicators of bubonic plague. It was shipboard rats on a boat from the Black Sea that caused the first outbreak of the Great Plague in Italy in the thirteenth century. The swelling of the body's lymphatic nodes breaking through the skin produced the "buboes" described by French physicians as the characteristic symptom of the disease. Ashdod, too, was a port where foreign ships frequently called. If the diagnosis offered here is correct, then I Samuel 5:6 provides one of the oldest descriptions of bubonic plague in the ancient world. If not, then another meaning of the term *opalim* might offer a clue. *Opel* can also mean buttocks in the sense that the buttocks protrude from the body as, perhaps, a swelling. This has led some to suggest that it was not bubonic plague that struck the Philistines but a severe outbreak of hemorrhoids![22]

THE PHILISTINE THREAT

While I and II Samuel are full of references to the Philistines, nowhere does the biblical text offer an explanation of the causes of the general hostility between them and the Israelites that goes beyond theological reasons. Even here, there is no evidence of any Philistine attempt to force their worship of Canaanite gods upon the Israelites. Any apostasy recorded in the text is always laid at the feet of the Israelites themselves, not the coercive efforts of another people to convert the Israelites. Moreover, the number of Philistines in Canaan was far fewer than that of Israelites, perhaps not more than 20,000 or 30,000 original settlers. So few were their numbers that they very quickly adopted the language and gods of the Canaanites even as they imposed their military aristocracy upon them.[23] Gottwald suggests that their numbers were so small that they always remained an elite governmental and military minority who relied upon Canaanite officials and hired mercenaries to govern and to fight their wars.[24] What, then, was the nature of the Philistine threat that made it so fearful to the Israelites?

The degree of Israelite suppression under the Philistines was potentially far greater than it had been under the Egyptians or ever could have been under a single Canaanite state or even a coalition of Canaanite states. First, Egyptian influence had always been required to operate from a base separated from

Canaan by a considerable distance. Also, Egypt was a great power with far-flung interests that often distracted and compromised Egyptian social and economic concerns in Canaan. Not so for the Philistines for whom Canaan was their home and their paramount national interest. Second, Egyptian power was exercised through small garrisons spread thinly throughout Canaan and more so in the central hill country of the Israelites. Little or no attempt was made by the Egyptians to govern or control the country on a day-to-day basis, leaving local affairs and problems to their Canaanite vassals. The Philistines, by contrast, were concentrated in large, well-provisioned, fortified, strategically defensible garrisons from which they could sally forth and exercise regular control over the country. Third, the Philistine odyssey beginning first as an Indo-European people settling in Illyria before moving on to Anatolia and, finally, settling in Canaan[25] had forced them to develop a strong organizational ability that manifested itself in a high degree of political and military cooperation. They were far more organized and coordinated in their activities than any of the Canaanite authorities that had come before them. Their use of a common strategic and, at times, a tactical high command to govern their forces in the field and their habit of political coordination on a regular basis made them a formidable threat. Fourth, Philistine military power was considerably more effective than that of previous powers. The Philistines arrived in Canaan as a light and heavy infantry force and acquired the use of the chariot in Canaan, precisely the reverse of the Canaanite experience before them. Whereas previous Canaanite armies always seemed to be short on infantry, the Philistines used the chariot as an adjunct to their infantry elements. They always retained sufficient quantities of light and heavy infantry that could penetrate the thick woods and mountains that had been the refuge of the Israelites against Canaanite and Egyptian armies. Their ability to tailor their forces to the tactical situation, mixing infantry with appropriate types of chariots, for example, permitted the Philistines to employ a far wider and more diversified array of forces against the Israelites.[26]

The Philistines presented a remarkable convergence of a number of mutually reinforcing factors against the Israelites that no Canaanite state, coalition of states, or even Egypt was able to present. Their unified military and political organization, a secure base within easy striking distance of the enemy, a flexible military field force that could reach within the once secure tactical and strategic zones of the Israelites, and the staying power—strategic endurance—that resulted from a people who saw themselves as fighting for their homeland rather than as foreign occupiers all combined to produce a powerful threat to Israelite independence. But all this speaks only to military capability and not the reasons for employing that capability. Why, then, did the Philistines war against the Israelites? We can immediately exclude two reasons. First, there is no evidence of population pressure that might have caused the Philistines to require more land upon which to accommodate their people.[27] Until the very end, the Philistines remained a minority in Canaan. Second, the Philistine wars were not defensive. Safe behind their walled cities and fortified garrisons, they could have easily kept the Israelites at bay. It was other Philistine interests that caused them to attempt to subdue and subjugate the Israelites.

Among the most important Philistine interests was the need to protect their trading empire. They already held strong positions on the coast north of Philistia proper, in the Jezreel Valley, and in the Jordan Valley. Israelite control of the central hill country and the lands in the Transjordan threatened the caravan routes that passed through or near these areas. As Albright has observed, "The conquest of Israel by the Philistines about the middle of the eleventh century was perhaps dictated mainly by the increasing need of protection for the caravans from the desert."[28] As Gottwald observes, while there is no evidence from biblical texts to support it, "it is likely that the Israelites raided these caravans much as they had raided the Canaanite caravans."[29] It is important in understanding Philistine motives to remember that they were primarily traders and warriors, not agriculturalists. The feudal sociopolitical order adopted from the Canaanites made them no less dependent on landed fiefs for their agriculture and, more important, their military system centered around landed warrior aristocrats. Agricultural taxes provided the wealth to sustain the chariot corps, as well as the surpluses to trade for more exotic products that came into the country by overland commerce. Israelite land holdings and agricultural surpluses were extensive, and would have added considerable wealth to the Philistines. Third, in all ancient societies manpower was important. Conquest of the Israelites would have opened up significant new sources of slaves, corvee labor for building projects, and, not to be overlooked, auxiliary military forces to serve within the army. I Samuel 14:21 notes that during the Philistine occupation of Saul's time Israelite auxiliary units were conscripted from the local population and forced to serve in the Philistine army.[30]

The pursuit of these objectives by the Philistines represented a serious threat to the Israelite way of life. The Israelites had long been a free people loosely organized under a democratic form of decentralized government. The attainment of the Philistine objectives would have required the complete integration of the Israelites into the Philistine version of the old Canaanite feudal socioeconomic order. Such integration would, in a symbolic sense, have meant a return to a set of circumstances not unlike the Israelite bondage in Egypt, and was a grave threat to Israelite national existence. The Philistine preoccupation with the Israelites was good news for the remaining Canaanite cities, however, who also feared being brought under Philistine influence. There is no evidence of any Canaanite-Israelite alliance during this time, but there is some indication that the historical animosity between the two may have come to a halt. I Samuel 7:14 tells us that after the second battle of Ebenezer "there was peace, too, between Israel and the Amorites," for whom one ought to read Canaanites. Later, of course, David incorporated the old Canaanite cities into his kingdom, perhaps in some cases without opposition. The Israelite problem, of course, was how to overcome the Philistine advantages in political and military organization in order to preserve their national autonomy.

THE SECOND BATTLE OF EBENEZER

With the destruction of the sanctuary at Shiloh, Samuel and his band of Levite attendants took to the roads of Israel, plying their trade as seer-priests along with dozens of other "wild bands" of similar *nebi'im*. The term *nabi* comes down to us through the Greek as *prophetes*, and thus our word "prophet." But Samuel and the other wandering prophesiers were not prophets in the strict sense of the word, but seer-priests or *ro'eim*.[31] The prophets, properly called, were a peculiarly Israelite phenomenon that came into existence only after the establishment of the monarchy and the reign of Hosea.[32] These genuine prophets were solitary figures who traveled the land falling into fits of ecstasy while railing against the sins of the Israelites as seen through the eyes of Yahweh. The seer-priests, by contrast, belonged to guilds with rules requiring apprenticeship and ritual training. Seer-priests used specific techniques, often the music of the *halil* or clarinet commonly associated with fits of extreme emotionalism,[33] to bring about states of ecstasy, unlike the prophet who did not deliberately induce these altered states. The seer was a craftsman, like a physician, who did things like predict the future, tell one's fortune, consult the gods, and drive out evil spirits. He was the person to whom people came for advice because he was thought to possess special access to God (*ish ha-Elohim*), thus the practice of consulting the seer-priest for *mishpat* before battle.[34] Unlike the solitary prophet, the more powerful seer-priests conducted business from a fixed shrine, as did Eli and Samuel at the sanctuary of Shiloh. Thus Samuel is not to be understood as a prophet, but a seer-priest who occupied a powerful social position encompassing his roles as priest, seer, warrior, judge, and governor.[35]

The seer-priest's monopoly in the field of religion, especially as head of a powerful sanctuary, gave him a great deal of political and social authority, and like everyone else he had a vested interest in the preservation of the social, religious, and political order that legitimized his authority. When the sanctuary at Shiloh was destroyed and the Ark carried off only to be resettled elsewhere at Kiriath-jearim in the care of another seer-priest called Abinadab, Samuel and his Levite assistants took to traveling throughout the country, trying to recoup their previous social position by holding public meetings in which they railed against the Philistine occupation and called for the people to return to Yahweh's ways. In their view, the Philistine yoke was the punishment of a sinful people who could throw off the oppression only after they returned to strict observance of Yahweh's laws. These meetings seem always to have been held at sanctified sites and on some regular schedule. Thus, "He [Samuel] would go in a circuit year by year to Bethel, Gilgal, and Mizpah, judging Israel in these places."[36] One ought not to gain the impression that Samuel and other seer-priests were revolutionaries. Far from it, for they sought the reestablishment of the old order that had given them social position and power. Moreover, these meetings provided ample opportunity for the seer-priest and his assistants to offer their other services to the assembled crowds and, no doubt, make a good living. Still, their importance in keeping the idea of Israelite national identity alive for more than four decades during the Philistine occupation ought not to be diminished. As Robinson notes, "It is to them that we must ascribe one of the strongest impulses to independence in the days of the Philistine occupation."[37]

The Second Battle of Ebenezer was an accidental consequence of one of these meetings. The text suggests that the meeting might have been unusually large. "Let all Israel assemble at Mizpah," said Samuel, "and I shall pray to Yahweh on your behalf."[38] The meeting was held at Mizpah, the exact location of which is uncertain. It was probably one of the two high peaks either five miles northwest of Jerusalem or five miles north of Jerusalem. Either location afforded a commanding view of an important north-south road. Its strategic location is testified to by the fact that it was an important Judite fortress under Asa in the ninth century. During the Exile, Mizpah was a Babylonian provincial capital.[39] An unusually large number of Israelites assembled at a strategic location to hear a major personality speak on nationalist themes probably attracted the attention of Philistine intelligence officers who may have dispatched their special mobile units to disperse the crowd and, perhaps, arrest Samuel and his wild band of partisans.

The text provides us with some details of the "battle" that ensued. "The Philistines heard that the Israelites had assembled at Mizpah, and the lords of the Philistines went up against Israel. When the Israelites heard, they were afraid of the Philistines."[40] The impression of the text is that we are witnessing a major military engagement. As the Philistines approached, "he [Samuel] cried out to Yahweh on Israel's behalf, and Yahweh answered him."[41] There can be no doubt as to whom is to be credited with bringing Yahweh into the fight, that is, Samuel himself. And when "the Philistines had drawn near to attack Israel . . . Yahweh thundered in a loud voice against the Philistines that day and so confounded them that they were routed before the Israelites. The men of Israel sallied forth from Mizpah in pursuit of the Philistines, harrying them as far as a point below Beth-car."[42] Later, Samuel erected a stele and called it Ebenezer, literally, "the Stone of Help."

The second battle of Ebenezer, then, was hardly more than a skirmish, and Samuel's designation of the engagement as "Ebenezer" may have been a deliberate attempt at propaganda with a double-edged purpose. First, the object may have been to convince the Israelites that the catastrophe of first Ebenezer had been avenged and superceded by victory. Second, while the judge-commander of first Ebenezer remains unknown, the judge-commander of second Ebenezer is clearly Samuel who, in his opposition to the monarchy, argued that the victory at Ebenezer was proof that the old system of judge-commanders still worked well enough and, therefore, that there was no need for a monarchy. In the hands of a skilled propagandist, the skirmish at Mizpah became the great battle of Ebenezer deliberately named after the location of the first battle even though Mizpah was nowhere near the original battlefield.[43]

The text offers some clues as to what really happened at Mizpah. The text tells us that "Yahweh thundered in a loud voice" against the Philistines that day. When used elsewhere in the texts, the phrase usually was employed to mean that Yahweh was speaking in the form of a great storm accompanied by thunder and lightning.[44] The interpretation is consistent with the claim that Yahweh "confounded" the Philistines. The term employed is *wayhummem*, meaning to throw into a panic or confusion. Here, too, however, when the term is used in conjunction with the storm analogy it is taken to mean "Yahweh's arrows" or lightning.[45] One imagines, therefore, that a unit of Philistine chariots approached Mizpah to disrupt the meeting only to have a fierce thunder and lightning storm break out. The sound of thunder and flashes of lightning might have thrown the horses into a panic. Caught on a hilltop as they were, the lightning may have frightened the charioteers who turned and fled back down the road to escape the exposure of the heights. The storm frightened the Israelites as well who also fled down the road seeking less exposure to the lightning, only to have their flight recorded as a fierce pursuit of the enemy in battle! That Samuel's tale of the great battle is propaganda is clear from Samuel's claim that after the battle the Philistines "did not cross the border of Israel again. . . . [and] the cities the Philistines had taken from Israel were restored to Israel . . . and Israel also recovered the environs of these cities from Philistine control."[46] In fact, Philistine control of Israel lasted at least another 30 years, causing the tribal elders to insist on a king "to judge [govern] us in the manner of all the other nations" only a few years after the "victory" at Ebenezer. The old system of judge-commanders had produced military defeat, humiliation, and foreign occupation, and the tribal elders now sought to be rid of it and replace it with a monarchy.

SAUL'S KINGSHIP

Human beings do not repudiate their histories or relinquish power easily, and even though there was certainly desire for reform, there was also the fear of oppression by the monarchy itself. The tribal elders would have a new king, but they also sought to limit his power. The only supratribal institution of the premonarchical period, the only one capable of furnishing an ideology of tribal unity and, therefore, the only social institution that could be effective in limiting the power of the king was the seer-priesthood.[47] An alliance between the tribal elders and the seer-priesthood could be very effective in hemming in the monarchy. As Cohen has observed, "It would have been too much to expect the old guard leaders to abdicate all their power . . . (even) as they were compelled to invest the monarchy with sufficient strength to carry out its primary mission . . . while at the same time retaining for themselves as much power as circumstances permitted."[48] These considerations help explain why Israel's first king was chosen from the tribe of Benjamin. Benjamin was the smallest and least influential of the tribes, making the risk of tyranny less likely in the eyes of the tribal leaders. Perhaps of more importance was the fact that Benjamin was already morally tainted because of its role in the Gibeah outrage that caused a civil war that almost tore Israel apart. No man of Benjamin could bring moral prestige to the new kingly office nor, one suspects, ever completely escape the suspicion of immorality. This latter circumstance was important for it weakened the prestige of the king should he be charged by the seer-priesthood with immorality or ritual sin. In a struggle for control, the seer-priests could hope to strip the monarchy of its legitimacy by pronouncing that Yahweh no longer supported the king, which was precisely what happened to Saul when he refused to submit to the will of Samuel and the tribal elders. Saul himself was a believer in his own ability to communicate with Yahweh[49]—"Is Saul among the prophets?"—so that when he could no longer do so he fell into deep periods of depression and despair that Samuel skillfully exploited until Saul's military judgment was compromised and he met his death on the field of battle at Mount Gilboa. By then he had been so skillfully outmaneuvered by Samuel that his successor, David, had already been chosen.

Once they had decided upon a king, the Israelites had two models from which to choose. The Egyptian model of a divine god-king possessed of absolute authority ran completely against the grain of Israelite values and history. The more Mesopotamian model, on the other hand, afforded a king that was surely mortal and whose authority had always been subject to two counterchecks, the assembly of elders and the gods themselves who could punish him directly or signal his loss of moral authority.[50] Under this system the law, while certainly a reflection of divine will, was essentially a man-made device to which all, king and peasant alike, were subject. The Mesopotamian model was one with which the Israelites were most familiar, for it was right before their eyes in the form of the monarchies of the Canaanite and Philistine states. Although the selection of Saul as king is portrayed entirely as an act of Yahweh's divine will made manifest in a lottery, in fact it is far more likely that he was selected by an assembly of tribal elders and then sanctified with the *mishpat* of Samuel. Once elected, the powers of the king apparently were formally codified when "Samuel declared the Law of the Kingdom to the people. He wrote it in a document and laid it up before Yahweh,"[51] but we do not know the details of the powers of the king or the structure of government. It is clear from later events, however, that the traditional power of the tribal elders to call the nation to arms was now vested in the king. Otherwise, we know little else of the king's powers.

This aside, however, it is clear that the powers and structure of kingship which eventually emerged under David and Solomon were replicas of the traditional Canaanite kingships, and there is some evidence that it was substantially the same under Saul. When Samuel opposed the institution of a monarchy, he listed a series of practices that were common to Canaanite kings which he warned would occur under an Israelite king.[52] These practices were familiar enough to the Israelite elders and still they voted to install a king. We might infer from this with some justification, then, that the list of practices was, in fact, what the Israelites expected and, drawing upon other evidence, what they seemed to have received under Saul. The list appears below:

I Samuel 8:11: "Your sons he will take and assign to his chariot and his cavalry, and they will run before his chariot." Saul was invested with the power to call men to military service when previously this power had been reserved to the tribal assembly.

I Samuel 8:12: "He will appoint for himself captains of thousands and captains of hundreds from them." The reference here is to *sarim*, a corps of officers drawn not from the tribal levy, but appointed by the king. The mention of chariot runners also implies a permanent corps of soldiers, for these soldiers typically served as the residential bodyguard of the king. We know, of course, that Saul did form the first corps of professional soldiers in Israelite military history.

I Samuel 8:12: "They [the professional retainers] will do his plowing, harvesting, and grape-gathering and make his weapons and the equipment of his chariotry." This speaks to a distinctly feudal arrangement of the Canaanite type, for it implies the creation of royal estates to support the king and his court.

I Samuel 8:14: "Your best fields and vineyards and olive groves he will take and give to his servants." The term servants, *ebed hammelek*, is to be understood as referring to the king's royal courtiers, and court functionaries, in short feudatories who hold grants of land confiscated from the people. Once again this speaks to the feudal arrangements typical of Canaanite and Philistine society of the time.

I Samuel 8:15: "Your seed crops and vine crops he will tithe to make gifts to his officers and servants." This tithe is to be understood as distinct from the tithe levied traditionally in Israel to support religious institutions, an arrangement that was itself based upon a feudal model with Yahweh as king. As used here, it is a reference to a tax levied on agricultural products to support the royal estates.[53] There is, then, some textual evidence to suggest that the monarchy established by Saul, including the establishment of royal residences, probably drew somewhat upon practices typical of the Canaanite and Philistine kings of the time. Of particular interest to the military historian, however, is how these practices shaped Saul's army.

The Philistine army of Saul's day was comprised of a core of professional military regulars, men doing feudal service, and mercenaries, often *apiru*, hired for specific campaigns. In shaping the Israelite army for war against the Philistines, Saul seems to have copied some of these institutions. As noted in chapter 2 and cited in I Samuel 13:2, Saul formed a corps of 3,000 professional soldiers to serve as the spine of the Israelite army. Typical of oriental armies of the day, Saul employed mercenary forces as well. In at least two places, the text testifies to the presence of mercenaries in Saul's army. In I Samuel 13:3 the word *ivrim* is used to mean *apiru* or mercenaries and again in I Samuel 14:11–12 when it is used to designate mercenaries who had previously fought with the Philistines before switching sides and joining the Israelites.[54] The third element of Saul's army was the general levy drawn from the tribes, equivalent in numbers if not in military sophistication to the Philistine feudatories. The levy, of course, had been traditional in Israel. During the period of the Judges, there is some evidence of mercenary units. Saul seems to have employed them on a somewhat more regular basis, however. What was completely new to the Israelite army was the corps of full-time professional soldiers. Given that most of the troops during wartime would be drawn from the general levy, it is likely that some of the professionals would be assigned command of militia units displacing their militia commanders. Saul's reference to his commanders as *sarim*, men appointed to command by the authority of the king, seems to imply such a practice.

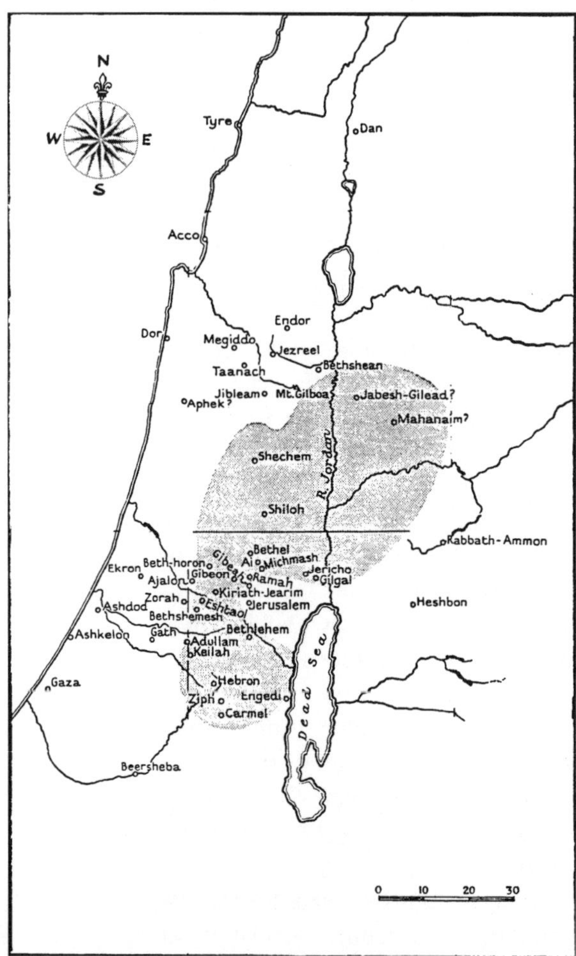

Figure 6.1 Saul's Kingdom

It is unlikely that Saul was able to institute all of the Canaanite practices discussed earlier, and there is evidence that his ability to command the loyalty of the tribes was less than complete even with regard to his ability to muster the army for war. In geographic terms, however, it is possible to be somewhat more certain in delineating the extent of Saul's kingdom. Figure 6.1 portrays the boundaries of Saul's kingdom at their greatest extent. It is likely that the kingdom included Gilead, Asher, Jezreel, Ephraim and Benjamin, and certainly the Galilee.[55] The fact that when David fled Saul's court he still did not feel safe in Judah suggests that the power of Saul's authority was felt there as well.

THE BATTLE OF JABESH-GILEAD

Saul was anointed king and returned to Gibeah sometime after the second battle of Ebenezer. During this time Nahash, king of the Ammonites, was oppressing the tribes of Gad and Reuben in the Transjordan, "gouging out the right eye of each man and allowing Israel no deliverer."[56] Some 7,000 men managed to escape the oppression and fled to the town of Jabesh-gilead across the Jordan. Nahash assembled his army and "went up and encamped against Jabesh-gilead,"[57] laying siege to the town. After some time, the people of Jabesh-gilead offered to come to terms with Nahash who rejected the offer, insisting that he would gouge out the right eye of the all the males. The townsmen asked for seven days to decide on accepting the terms. During the respite they sent messengers to all the Israelite tribes asking them to come and fight against Nahash. "When the messengers came to Gibeah of Saul and reported the news in the hearing of the people, all the people began to weep aloud. . . . When Saul heard this news . . . he became enraged."[58] Why were the *people* of Gibeah so upset at the news from Jabesh-gilead while none of the other tribes seems to have been concerned enough to take action?

The answer may be that the Benjaminites and the people of Jabesh-gilead were blood relatives, a circumstance resulting from the violence of the civil war prompted by the Gibeah outrage almost 100 years earlier. It will be recalled that all the Israelite tribes had fought a civil war against Benjamin, exterminating all but 600 of the Benjaminite males who took refuge at Rock Rimmon. The other tribes swore an oath not to provide their daughters as wives for the Benjaminite men, raising the prospect that the Benjaminite line would be completely extinguished. Having thought better of this policy, the Israelite tribes attacked the Israelite town of Jabesh-gilead because it had refused to fight in the war against Benjamin. The males were killed and 400 virgins carried off and given to the surviving Benjaminite males. Another 200 virgins were taken by force from Shiloh and given over to the Benjaminites. Thus it was that the tribe of Benjamin survived. What this means, of course, was that the people of Gibeah were blood relatives of the people of Jabesh-gilead, and that Saul's grandmother or great grandmother may have been among the virgins taken from Jabesh-gilead.[59] Saul became enraged because Nahash was killing his relatives, transforming the war from an act of state policy into a typical Israelite blood feud.

Saul may have been enraged as well that none of the other tribes had responded to the plea from Jabesh-gilead. In any case, his attempt to call the tribes to war was the first test of his new authority as king. His choice of such a dramatic method to call the muster suggests that he may have expected some resistance. Saul seized "a yoke of oxen dismembered them and sent them throughout the territory of Israel by messengers, saying, 'Whoever does not come out after Saul (and after Samuel), thus let it be done to his oxen.' "[60] The threat to slay the oxen barely concealed the even greater threat that bloody violence would be visited upon any *Israelites* who failed to heed Saul's call. Saul's method of rousing the army was the same one used by the Levite of the Gibeah outrage who cut up his concubine and sent a piece of her body to each of the tribes as a call to arms against Benjamin. Now a Benjaminite king was sending the same message to the Israelites, a not so subtle threat of blood vengeance should they fail to comply. The threat worked, for "the fear of Yahweh fell upon the people, and they gathered together as one man."[61]

The general muster turned out an army of significant size. The text relates that "Saul mustered them at Bezek: three hundred thousands of Israelites and thirty thousands of men of Judah,"[62] or 330 *alaphim*, approximately 23,000 troops. Taken as a proportion of the 25,000 to 30,000 men that was at least theoretically possible at maximum effort for a population of 150,000 or so, Saul's first attempt to muster the national army must be counted an unmitigated success. There is no mention of any shortage of weapons, suggesting that 20 years after the battle of Aphek-Ebenezer no attempt had yet been made by the Philistines to disarm the Israelites or prohibit their access to the iron smiths. Living beyond the Jordan, the Ammonites were beyond the reach of any Philistine attempt to control weapons, and we may assume that they were adequately armed. It is, of course, unthinkable that Saul would have taken an unarmed army into battle, so the Israelites must have been adequately armed. In the absence of a Philistine policy to disarm the Israelites or restrict access to the iron smiths, it is completely logical that the Israelites would have acquired and maintained arms after Aphek-Ebenezer. Iron weapons were relatively cheap compared with bronze, the ore being commonly available. Once in the possession of the Israelite soldier, responsibility for keeping the weapon in usable condition rested with him, a logistics arrangement far more efficient than a centralized weapons supply system like that used by the Canaanites and Egyptians.

One can only speculate as to the Philistine reaction when faced with a 23,000 man Israelite army sufficiently armed to engage the Ammonites across the Jordan, but the Israelite muster could hardly have gone unnoticed. In fact, there is no mention of the Philistine garrison at Gibeah, suggesting that it was either very small, perhaps only a customs post, or not yet established, for we do not hear of the garrison until the engagement at Michmash, 20 years later. This, along with the ban on iron also mentioned only at Michmash, supports the earlier suggestion that both may have been imposed in earnest only after Saul's wars had already established the Israelite kingdom by a number of victories over non-Philistine adversaries that may have occurred in the time between the battles of Jabesh-gilead and Michmash Pass (between 1031 and 1010 B.C.E.), and not, as the order of the text implies, between Michmash and the death of Saul at Gilboa in 1006. It may have been in reaction to this series of Saul's victories that the Philistines attempted to establish tighter control over the Israelites, and this might have precipitated the assault on the Gibeah garrison and Saul's wars against the Philistines.

Saul assembled his army at Bezek (probably modern Khirbet Ibziq) approximately 12 miles northeast of Shechem on the west slope of the Jordan, almost directly opposite Jabesh-gilead. The approach march from Gibeah to Bezek is about 41 miles while the distance between Bezek and Jabesh-gilead is a little less than ten miles with the Jordan River lying between the two towns. With the army assembled at Bezek, Saul sent word to the trapped garrison at Jabesh-gilead that he would attack sometime the next day "when the sun is hot." The phrase clearly implies that Saul intended to attack sometime around noon when, in fact, he was planning no such thing. Why, then, send a false message to the trapped garrison? The answer may lie in Saul's concern for operational security (OPSEC in modern staff argot) in case the messenger was taken prisoner, or to prevent the garrison from behaving expectantly during the morning and thus giving away the plan. Probably also at Saul's instruction, the commander of the garrison sent a message to Nahash the Ammonite that they were prepared to surrender the next day. "Tomorrow we shall come out to you, and you may do with us whatever seems good to you."[63]

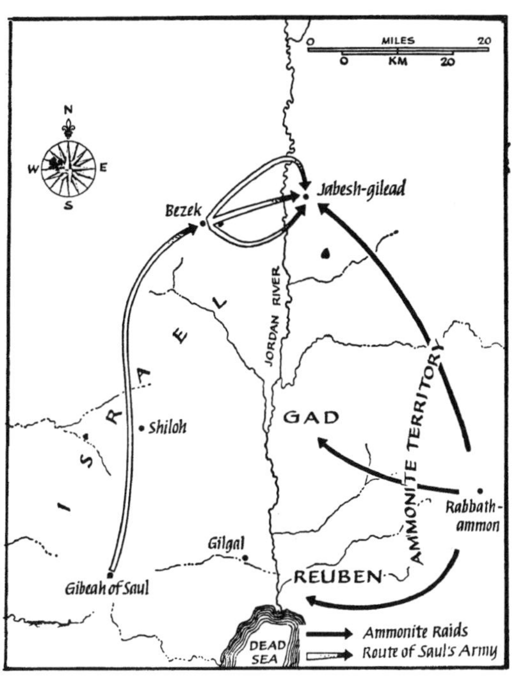

Figure 6.2 The Battle of Jabesh-gilead

The text describes the battle in the following manner. "The next day Saul positioned the army in three groups. They entered the camp during the morning watch and battered the Ammonites until the day had grown hot; those who survived were so scattered that no two of them remained together."[64] This was Saul's first battle, and his tactics and operational execution were brilliant. Having misled the garrison into thinking the attack would come at midday, Saul attacked at dawn. To attack the Ammonite camp "during the morning watch," Saul first had to move his army into position by covering the ten miles from Bezek to Jabesh-gilead. Jabesh-gilead is approximately three miles from the Jordan River. One imagines that sometime in the late afternoon of the previous day Saul moved his army from Bezek to the west bank of the Jordan River arriving sometime around dusk. The army rested and ate cold food, since campfires would not have been permitted, and prepared to cross the Jordan at night. Sometime around midnight, the army would have begun to cross, perhaps in three columns at three different fords, assembled on the opposite bank, and approached Jabesh-gilead where they took up positions on three sides of the Ammonite camp. With the Jordan River the main water source for the Ammonite army outside the walls of Jabesh-gilead, it is likely that the Ammonites were camped facing the city walls with their backs to the river. If so, then one column of Saul's attacking army would have taken them in the rear, most probably at sunrise or nautical twilight, while the two other columns swept around to seal off the flanks, trapping the Ammonite army in a three-sided pocket, crushing it against the walls of the city. Surprise must have been complete, and the strength of the assault overwhelming. Trapped inside the Israelite pocket, the Ammonites were "battered . . . until the day had grown hot," that is, until late morning or noon, and casualties must have been very heavy indeed, although the text tells us that some survived and were scattered along the floor of the Jordan Valley.

There may have been more to the battle than the text affords. Josephus, writing in his *Antiquities* sometime around 60 C.E., tells us that Saul, "not satisfied with merely having rescued Jabesh, made an expedition against the territory of the Ammonites, subdued it all, and having taken much booty, returned home a famous man."[65] Analysts of Josephus's histories suggest that he may have had access to far more complete material about events than has survived into modern times. If so, then Saul may have indeed pursued the Ammonites further, but we cannot be sure. Of interest, too, is Saul's visit to Gilgal after the battle at Samuel's suggestion "to renew the kingship." Gilgal was the first sanctuary of Yahweh in Canaan constructed by Joshua after crossing the Jordan. It became Joshua's logistical base and the location of the Kenite smiths who supplied the army with weapons. After the battle of Jabesh-gilead, Gilgal became the major assembly point for Saul's armies. It was sufficiently remote to be beyond the reach of the Philistines, close enough to the Jordan to effect a quick retreat if necessary, close enough to Saul's blood relatives in Jabesh-gilead, and, if we are correct that Saul fought his wars against Moab and Edom before his wars with the Philistines, strategically proximate to his enemies' homelands. Too, if the Kenite smiths had returned to Israel as Saul's warning to the Kenites suggests in I Samuel 15:6, the most logical place for them to employ their iron-making skills safe from Philistine eyes was at Gilgal. In short, Saul may have turned Gilgal into a major operational base for the same reasons Joshua did more than 100 years earlier.

THE BATTLE OF MICHMASH PASS

The battle of Michmash Pass circa 1010 B.C.E. marked the beginning of a series of wars against the Philistines that lasted until Saul met his death at Mount Gilboa circa 1006 B.C.E. Until now Saul had been a local king, similar to other Canaanite *melekim* of the time, who, if our chronology is correct, had spent the last 20 years establishing the boundaries of his kingdom by prosecuting a series of successful wars against non-Philistine peoples. Sometime during this time the Philistines seem to have increased their military presence in the Israelite territories, even at Gibeah itself, although the garrison may have been nothing more than a customs post, tax collector, or tribute official accompanied by his bodyguard, a practice similar to the Egyptian method of establishing their official presence in a town. The increased Philistine presence may have come about as a reaction to a Philistine concern about the military capability of the Israelites as demonstrated by Saul's victories. His establishment of a permanent corps of 3,000 military professionals, approximately 10 percent of the total 25,000 to 30,000 man strength of the Israelite army at full mobilization, may also have been cause for concern.[66]

The text gives no hint as to the motive for Jonathan's attack on the Philistine prefect "who was in Gibeah,"[67] only that the Philistines moved quickly to punish the perpetrators. The text tells us, "Jonathan struck down the Philistine prefect in Gibeah, and the Philistines heard about it. Saul had the ram's horn sounded throughout the land, saying 'Let the Hebrews hear.' When all Israel heard that Saul had struck down the Philistine prefect . . . all the people rallied to Saul at Gilgal."[68] Once again we encounter the term *ivrim* used to delineate "Hebrews" but whose meaning is really *apiru* in the present context.[69] Thus, Saul sounded the ram's horn to call his *apiru* mercenaries to his army as distinct from the general muster of the tribal levy, which had to be summoned separately. Saul then retired to Gilgal to assemble the army for war.

The Philistine response was quick and aggressive, "And they brought up three thousands of chariotry, six thousands of cavalry, and an army like the sands on the seashore in number against Israel, and came up and encamped at Michmash."[70] Three *alaphim* of chariots implies some 180 to 200 machines which, as is likely, were probably the special units of *hamashhith*, each machine carrying three or four men armed with javelins, spears, and swords, and each accompanied by 3 four-man squads of elite infantry runners, or some 1,600 men in the *hamashhith* units alone. The infantry force must have been considerably larger—"like the sand on the seashore"—perhaps twice as large as the mobile forces or some 3,000 men. Taken together, then, the Philistine army that marched against the Israelites was almost 5,000 men strong. We can safely discount the text's report of Philistine cavalry as being the intrusion of a later redactor writing during the period of Assyrian occupation. The speed and strength of the Philistine response threw fear into the Israelite population and "the people hid themselves in caves, among thorns [thickets], among rocks [fissures], in tunnels [dugouts], and in cisterns. Some Hebrews crossed the Jordan, to the territory of Gad and Gilead . . . and the rest of the people rallied to him [Saul] in alarm."[71] The text implies that only a small number successfully reached Gilgal to answer the tribal muster. In addition, the term "Hebrews" [*ivrim*] as used in this context tells us that it was Saul's *apiru* mercenaries who fled across the Jordan, not units of the militia.[72] Saul remained at Gilgal for seven days, attempting to rally the army and waiting for Samuel to arrive and give the *mishpat*, "with all the army trembling behind him . . . the army began to drift away from him."[73] Most of those who had answered the muster now lost their nerve and left Gilgal. With the mercenaries having deserted as well, "only the remnant of the army went up after Saul to meet the fighting force. . . . Saul mustered the people who were with him—some six hundred men."[74] Saul made his way to Gibeah and then to Geba where Jonathan had gathered the regulars under his command. Taken together, then, Saul's army at Michmash numbered some 4,000 men, 3,000 regulars and about 1,000 militia.

Michmash is located in the hill country of Bethel, about seven miles northeast of Jerusalem and four miles south of modern Beitlin, ancient Bethel. Geba is the ancient Benjaminite stronghold and modern village of Jeba about six miles north northeast of Jerusalem. The two cities are separated by a deep ravine (Wadi es-Suwenit). The Philistines advanced up from the plains through the Beth-horon pass to occupy Michmash itself, a risky but tactically brilliant positioning of their troops. Michmash is located on the *eastern* ascent of the Judean plateau controlling the eastern branch of the watershed road, in position to block Saul's army as it moved up the ascent from Gilgal toward Gibeah.[75] Saul's small force somehow eluded the Philistines and reached Jonathan and the regulars already at Geba, across from the Philistine main encampment on the hilltop at Michmash and overlooking the ravine from the north. Once in position, "the raiders came out of the Philistine camp in three columns: One column headed for the Ophrah road that leads to the district of Shaul, another column headed for Beth-horan, and the third column headed for

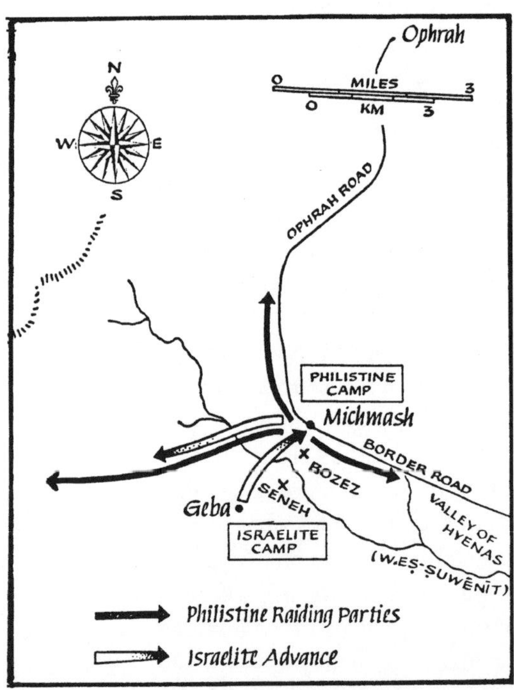

Figure 6.3 The Battle of Michmash Pass

the border road that overlooks the Valley of Zeboim [Valley of Hyenas, probably modern Wadi Abu Daba] toward the desert."[76] The mission of these flying columns is unclear. Gichon and Herzog suggest that they were laying waste the countryside in a punitive expedition, and this is certainly a reasonable explanation. It is unlikely, however, that the enemy commander would have divided his forces if he possessed a knowledge of Saul's whereabouts, that is, in Geba. More likely, the Philistine commander knew that Saul's regulars under Jonathan's command were at Geba (only a mile across the ravine), but was unaware of Saul and the militia levy's position. Even a rudimentary knowledge of the structure of the Israelite army would have led him to believe that the militia levy would be the largest element of Saul's army and that it, not the regulars at Geba, were the proper object of his concern. If so, then the flying columns might have been reconnaissance patrols in strength designed to locate and engage the main militia levy, and fix it in position until the Philistine main force could come up and engage it. So paltry was the muster of the Israelite militia that Saul was able to avoid the patrols and join Jonathan and the regulars at Geba.

If we are to believe the text, the condition of the Israelite army was terrible, for "at the time of the battle of Michmash neither sword nor spear was available to any of the soldiers who were with Saul and Jonathan—only Saul and his son Jonathan had them."[77] This condition, so the text tells us, was due to the Philistine embargo on iron working by the Israelites so as to prevent them from acquiring weapons.[78] But clearly this could not have been the case. Surely Saul's 3,000 man regular force would have already possessed weapons, despite the Philistine ban, otherwise they would have been no army at all! Military professionals do not engage in battle unarmed, and it is ludicrous to suggest that they did so at Michmash. The Philistines had been in Canaan for almost two centuries at the time of the engagement at Michmash, long enough for the secret of iron making to have made its way into the hands of the Israelite-Kenite smiths. Sufficiently long, too, to have established a black market in iron weapons. As noted earlier, it is possible that such a ban had been imposed only recently before Michmash and was probably in response to the fact of increased Israelite military capability as demonstrated in Saul's previous victories. If not, then why is it that we hear no more about the Philistine ban after Michmash? Somehow, perhaps as a consequence of the return of the Kenite smiths, Saul was able to supply his army with weapons without difficulty. More likely the text mentions the ban precisely because of its recent implementation and to exaggerate the military prowess of Jonathan and Saul.

Apparently the armies faced each other for a few days until the Philistines tried to push a troop unit through the ravine in the direction of the Israelite camp. The text tells us that, "Now the Philistine garrison had marched out to the pass of Michmash,"[79] which suggests a probe of some strength, perhaps even a main force advance with the intention of engaging the Israelites. Jonathan, supposedly accompanied only by his weapon-bearer, made his way around the ravine and came at the main Philistine camp from the rear. Both men scaled the cliff and gained the Philistine camp. "In the first engagement Jonathan and his weapons bearer struck down about twenty men within as it were a half furrow, an acre of field."[80] The surprise attack from the rear created panic in the Philistine camp whereupon Saul and his army "marched to the battle, where the swords [of the Philistines] were turned against each other in a very great panic. As for the Hebrews [*ivrim*] who had sided previously with the Philistines and gone up into the camp, they too turned to be with Israel under Saul and Jonathan; and when all the Israelites who had been hiding in the hill country of Ephraim heard that the Philistines had fled, they too pursued them in the fighting."[81] Taken as written, the story is probably a propagandistic account to emphasize Jonathan's courage and minimize Saul's contribution to the victory. However, several points are of interest.

First, while a surprise attack on the Philistine camp is certainly a possibility, especially so if the main force was attempting to push through the narrow ravine, it is highly improbable that it was convincingly executed by only two men, one of whom was armed with "crude flint weapons." A small elite force of say, 50 men, might have gained the enemy rear. The sudden appearance of this number of enemy soldiers within the camp would lend credibility to the claim that the Philistines panicked, especially so if the main force was already committed in the ravine. If the commander thought he was being attacked *in force* from the rear, he may have ordered a retreat that turned into a rout as the soldiers rushed to escape the narrow confines of the ravine. Or, it may have happened somewhat differently. The term used to describe the Philistine unit that Jonathan attacked is *hammassaba*, a unique usage meaning "outpost" and not "garrison."[82] Thus, the text can be interpreted to read, "[a] Philistine outpost had advanced into Michmash Pass,"[83] implying a much smaller Philistine probe, perhaps only a patrol. Under these circumstances, Jonathan and a small group of soldiers may have scaled the crag overlooking the ravine and fallen on the rear of the patrol blocking its retreat and slaughtering them. The text tells us that the engagement occurred within "a half furrow, an acre of field," an area consistent with the area required for an engagement of this size, lending topographical credibility to the account. What survivors there were might have fled back through the narrow opening and touched off a panic among the main camp.

It is interesting to note that "the Hebrews who had sided previously with the Philistines . . . turned to be with Israel under Saul and Jonathan."[84] The reference here is to the *ivrim* or *apiru* mercenaries in the hire of the Philistines. The Israelite mercenaries had fled before the battle had even begun! Those who insist on identifying *apiru* with Hebrews suggest that the *ivrim* who returned to Saul were, in fact, Israelites impressed into the Philistine army who, seeing their opportunity, deserted. Either way, the account suggests the basic problem of any mercenary force was their unreliability, and throughout antiquity part of the strategy of any successful army was its effort to entice the other fellow's mercenaries to change sides at some propitious moment.

The victory at Michmash may not have been as much a military achievement as a political one. I Samuel 14:23 tells us that, "As the fighting passed by Beth-aven, the entire army was with Saul—some ten thousands of men. But then the fighting scattered into every city in the hill country of Ephraim," suggesting that the Philistine rout at Michmash Pass may have touched off a general uprising throughout the hill country to eject the recently established Philistine outposts. Jonathan's ability to kill the Philistine prefect in Gibeah suggests that, following the Egyptian practice, the size of these outposts may have been quite small, making it possible that a popular rising of even moderate size could have succeeded. If so, this might explain why, after Michmash, there is no evidence of a renewed Philistine presence in the hill country until after Saul is killed at Mount Gilboa.

The pursuit of the Philistines down the Beth-horon road continued throughout the day. Saul issued an order forbidding anyone to eat. "Cursed be the man who eats food before evening has come and I have avenged myself upon my enemies."[85] Here we see the familiar problem of commanders of how to maintain the momentum of the attack once the enemy has quit the field and fled. It is well understood that the chariot added the new dimension of effective pursuit to ancient warfare,[86] wherein the chariot could overtake the fleeing enemy. Moreover, the endurance of the charioteer's horses could easily outlast the exhausted foot soldier. What was unique about the Israelite conduct of war, there being no chariots in the Israelite inventory, was the almost routine application of an effective pursuit on foot relying upon the discipline and endurance of the Israelite infantryman for success. Joshua's victory at the Aijalon Valley and his pursuit of the Canaanite kings, Gideon's pursuit of the Midianites, and Saul's pursuit of the enemy at Michmash are examples of Israelite armies conducting successful pursuits on foot. Pursuits are, for obvious reasons, almost always problematic. Either the troops become exhausted or they lose their discipline, as happened to Thutmose III's army at Megiddo when it stopped chasing the enemy and plundered its camp. Since ancient armies were commonly paid with captured booty, the chances that an army might choose booty over chasing the enemy were always high, particularly so for mercenary troops, although the habit was not unknown among Israelite militia levies. Saul's order prohibiting his exhausted troops from eating suggests an awareness of the problems associated with conducting a successful pursuit.

At the end of the day Saul's men were completely exhausted "and they pounced on the spoil" slaughtering the animals to satisfy their hunger. That same evening, after the men had rested, Saul suggested to Samuel, "Let us go down after the Philistines tonight! We shall plunder them until the light of morning and leave them not a man!"[87] The question was put to Yahweh for *mishpat*, but Yahweh did not answer and no action was taken. Nevertheless, Saul seems to have been suggesting a night attack against some Philistine garrison farther down the Beth-horon road or, perhaps, even against some outpost on the plain. This is remarkable, for no ancient army of this time could engage in battle at night. Saul was suggesting a night engagement that would last throughout the entire period of darkness, until "the light of morning." It is one thing to move an army into position under cover of darkness, as Joshua did more than once, or even to cross a river at night as Moses and Saul did, or even, as Gideon did, to carry out a small nighttime raid. But to conduct an all-night battle where large bodies of troops must be maneuvered and controlled in the dark is quite something else again. Saul's suggestion is, as far as I am aware, the only example in the period under study when an Israelite commander considered *fighting* in the dark utilizing units of considerable size. Indeed, it was only in modern times, and only with the aid of night-vision devices, that armies could routinely conduct night battles with some prospect of success. The fact that Saul would even consider it speaks to his faith in his officers and his own tactical imagination.

THE BATTLE OF THE VALE OF TEREBINTH

With the exception of Joshua's battle at Jericho, the most well-known battle of the Bible is the contest that took place at the Vale of Terebinth between David and Goliath. Despite the popular renown of the battle, the text offers only a few details of interest to the military historian. Of some interest is David's skill with the sling, a traditional weapon of the Israelite armies most often associated with the tribe of Benjamin whose slingers were either left-handed ("men restricted in the right hand") or ambidextrous. David, of course, is of the tribe of Judah and apparently right-handed. It is usually assumed that David's skill with the sling was obtained in his occupation as a shepherd. It is, however, possible that he was also trained as a slinger in the Israelite army.

The oldest textual tradition regarding David's arrival at Saul's court states that David was already a musician and a warrior of military age when he came to Saul's attention.[88] Saul was suffering from one of his bouts of depression when an attendant informed him that David's skill at the lyre might help Saul recover from his condition. "Then one of the attendants spoke up. 'I have noticed,' he said, 'that Jesse the Bethlehemite has a son who knows how to play, a powerful man, a warrior, skilled in speech, and handsome—and Yahweh is with him.' "[89] The term used to describe David is *ish milhama*, literally, "a man of war," but idiomatically "a trained soldier." The fact that David was immediately appointed as Saul's weapon-bearer implies as well that he was already a soldier. The weapon-bearer accompanied his master into the thick of battle, not exactly the place for a callow youth. Once David reached 20 years old he would have automatically been enlisted in the tribal militia, issued his weapons (assigning shepherds as slingers would have made good sense!), and been subject to muster. This was, too, the time of Saul's wars, so it is not beyond possibility that David may have already been called to service along with his militia unit sometime prior to coming to Saul's attention. Such service would have justified the claim that David was a trained soldier. Prior to David's battle with Goliath, Saul offered David his armor. David put the armor on but said, "I cannot walk in these, for I have not practiced."[90] David's military service as a light infantryman would have certainly made him familiar with the armor of other soldiers (perhaps Saul's regulars and mercenaries), but he would not have been issued armor himself. The text implies that David knows what armor is, but cannot use it properly because "I have not practiced," once more suggesting prior military experience. Taken together, then, the evidence supports the supposition that David was a young man with at least some military experience.

The battle took place at the Vale of Terebinth. "The Philistines had gathered their forces for battle, coming together at Sucoh of Judah, and encamped between Sucoh and Azekah at Ephes-dammim. So Saul and the men of Israel assembled, encamped in the valley of Terebinth, and deployed themselves to meet the Philistines in battle."[91] Sucoh of Judah (perhaps modern Khirbet Shuweikeh) was situated in the *shephelah* about 14 miles west of Bethlehem in the direction of Philistine territory. Azekah lay a few miles northwest of Sucoh and was a Philistine fortress that controlled the main road across the valley. The Vale of Terebinth is the Valley of Elah and lies immediately south of the Valley of Sorek, and is one of a series of strategically important valleys that lead from the plains up to the Judean ridge. Control of the valley's mouth was vital to the Israelite defense of the highlands while the Philistine's wanted it as a defense against Israelite incursions onto the open plain.

It would appear from the description in the text that the Philistines may have attempted to draw the Israelites into battle on the open plain rather than mount an attack up the valley to gain the Judean ridge. Otherwise it would have made no sense to permit the Israelites to concentrate at Sucoh, effectively blocking the route to the highlands. Most likely, the Israelites maintained a small garrison at the eastern end of the valley to act as a tripwire to any Philistine movement. Once "the Philistines gathered their forces for battle," the Israelites reenforced the garrison with a large body of troops. By this time the Israelites had developed the art of the military camp arranged in functional organizational areas and, perhaps, with some fortifications.[92] It is likely that the Philistine commander wished to entice Saul onto the open plain where his chariots and disciplined infantry could be brought to bear against the Israelite militia. Saul, entrenched at the bottom of the foothills, refused to take the bait. Both sides settled in waiting for something to happen.

It was at this time that the Philistine commander suggested the matter be settled by a duel between *is habbenayim* or champions of each side in single combat.[93] The rest, as they say, is history known to every schoolchild. David killed Goliath with a sling stone to the head, and the Philistines, seeing their champion dead, fled the field. The text tells us that "[t]he men of Israel and Judah rose up shouting and chased after them as far as the approaches to Gath and the gates of Ekron, and the Philistine wounded fell along the Shaaraim road all the way to Gath and Ekron."[94] The account is probably propaganda, for there is no evidence that Saul's influence ever extended into the plain of Philistia. Also, to pursue the Philistines in the manner described in the text would have exposed the Israelite army to a counterattack by Philistine chariots on the open plain. Most probably, then, after Goliath was slain both armies disengaged and retired to their original positions, neither commander being able to provoke the other into an action that would have given either a tactical advantage.

The description of Goliath's weapons and armor is of interest for what it does and does not tell us about warfare in this period. It is sometimes argued that the description of Goliath's weapons and armor is evidence of the Aegean origins of the Philistines,[95] or even that it reflects a prototype of the equipment worn by the Greek hoplite infantryman. What, then, does the description of Goliath tells us about war and weapons of the period? The text describes Goliath thus:

> And there marched forth from the ranks of the Philistines a certain infantryman from Gath whose name was Goliath. (His height was four cubits and a span!) A helmet was upon his head, and he was dressed in a plated cuirass. (The weight of the cuirass was five thousand bronze shekels!) Bronze greaves were upon his shins, and a bronze scimitar was slung between his shoulder blades. The shaft of his spear was like a weaver's heddle rod. (Its blade weighed six hundred iron shekels!) And a shield bearer preceded him.[96]

The name Goliath (*golyat*) is not Semitic but "Philistine" in that it is of Anatolian or Hittite origin[97] and, as such, is not evidence of the Aegean origins of the Philistines. Goliath's helmet is identified as a *koba*, probably derived from the Hittite *kupalis* for hat.[98] When the same word is used to describe Saul's helmet, it is qualified as *nochoshet* or "of bronze."[99] This is curious for the number of bronze helmets uncovered by archaeology in Palestine is very small, and they do not appear to be of Philistine or Judean origin. This suggests, then, that Goliath's helmet may have been of iron, but it was not until Assyrian times that the iron helmet came into common use. Indeed, while iron was used commonly for weapons, most armor and helmets remained made of bronze until Roman times.[100] What is important for the Aegean hypothesis, however, is that Goliath's helmet is clearly not a Philistine helmet of wrapped feathers or stiffened leather of the style that appears consistently on the reliefs.

Nor is it the horned helmet and chin strap of the Shardana portrayed on the same reliefs.

Goliath was equipped with scale armor or *siryon qash-qashim*, an unusual term probably of Hurrian origin.[101] Scale armor was made by sewing thin, individual, overlapping bronze plates to a leather jerkin in the manner of the overlapping scales of a fish.[102] Its weight was considerable, approximately 125 pounds.[103] Goliath's armor is typical of Egyptian and Canaanite armor used by charioteers and heavy spear infantry, and is clearly of Asiatic origin, not Aegean. The reliefs picture Philistine armor as a leather cuirass with padded shoulders. Goliath is also wearing *mitskha*, commonly translated as greaves, leg armor made of molded bronze encircling the entire calf and protecting the shin, much like the greaves of the later Greek hoplite. But the meaning of the term is uncertain, and could also mean "brow guard." None of the reliefs or paintings of Philistine warriors show them wearing greaves.[104] Greaves only came into common use during the Assyrian period and may have been an Assyrian innovation.

Goliath's weapons are also curious. He is armed with a *kidon* or bronze sickle-sword slung over his shoulders and not the straight iron sword characteristic of Philistine infantry with the usual scabbard or sword belt. This suggests that Goliath was not a typical Philistine infantryman at all, but a spear-bearing infantryman, a form of heavy infantry copied by the Philistines from the Canaanites. Further evidence of this lies in the fact that Goliath is not equipped with the typical Philistine round shield. Instead, he is accompanied by a shield-bearer, leaving both the warrior's hands free to wield his spear. The shaft of Goliath's spear "was like a weaver's heddle rod," and "its blade weighed six hundred iron shekels" or about 15 pounds! The use of the term *hanit* instead of the more common *romah* for spear implies, as Margowski suggests, that it was a javelin, that is, a thrown weapon.[105] The javelin was indeed introduced by the Philistines to Palestine, but its Aegean origin is uncertain. However, the text's description of Goliath's spear as *menor origim* or "like a weaver's heddle rod" suggests that the weapon was equipped with a thong and a slip-ring. With the thong spiraled around its shaft, a javelinier could rifle the javelin as he threw it, imparting a rotation to the weapon that added to its accuracy and range.[106] If the analysis is correct, then Goliath may have been equipped with the *ankyle* of the classical Greeks (the *amentum* of the later Romans)[107] and, perhaps, some indication of the weapon's Aegean origins.

On balance, however, Goliath is *not* armed like a Greek hoplite and most of his equipment is *not typical* of the Philistine soldier of the day. Plated armor and the sickle-sword are distinctly oriental in origin and certainly not Aegean, and the greaves and iron helmet are most likely Assyrian and of later introduction to Palestine. The absence of the round shield and its replacement with a shield-bearer suggests Canaanite influence, not Greek. Only the javelin's throwing ring is without a known Asiatic parallel and may, indeed, be a

Philistine innovation adopted from their Illyrian past. The text's description of Goliath is, then, a redactor's hodgepodge compilation of weapons and equipment, probably assembled during or shortly after the Assyrian occupation, including items which were held, in the common mind at least, to symbolize military prowess and power. As such, it tells us very little about the weapons and equipment of the Philistine soldier during the time of Saul.

THE BATTLE OF MOUNT GILBOA

The text tells us that "the fighting against the Philistines was severe all the days of Saul."[108] If the chronology offered earlier is correct, the period during which Saul fought against the Philistines began at Michmash and ended at Mount Gilboa, or about four years. Michmash had been a disaster for the Philistines, especially if it was followed by a popular uprising that ejected most of the Philistine outposts from the hill country. The attempt to gain the mouth of the Terebinth Valley with its access to the Judean ridge had ended in a standoff. We might imagine that between that time and the engagement at Mount Gilboa other Philistine efforts at frontal assaults through the valleys leading to the ridge were frustrated by Saul's control of the foothill ascents. The Philistine commanders eventually decided to abandon a frontal assault on the Judean ridge and make an end run around Israelite defenses. The plan was to move the Philistine army up the coast into the Jezreel and gain the northern spur of the central ridge where it debouches through gentle hills along the northwest side of Mount Gilboa. Once on the heights, the Philistine chariots could explode across the Shechem plain, attacking southward along the ridge threatening Gibeah itself.

The Philistines assembled their main army at Aphek near the coast, about 35 to 40 miles south of the foot of Mount Moreh where they planned to concentrate for battle. Moving parallel to the Judean ridge, the Philistines crossed from the plain into the Jezreel through one of the three passes through the Carmel mountains. The text is silent on which route was used. But it probably was the middle pass, the Wadi Ara, protected on the Jezreel Valley side by the fortress of Megiddo which had been in Philistine hands since after their victory at Aphek-Ebenezer along with Beth-shean on the eastern end of the valley plain. The southernmost route was across the plain of Dothan.[109] Although the shortest and easiest route, it was also closest to the Judean hills and offered the Israelites excellent opportunities for ambush. The northernmost route, the Wadi Melik, offered the greatest safety, but was also the longest and debouched near Yoq'neam, north of the assembly point. The Wadi Ara was bordered by steep and wooded hills, but was far enough from the Judean

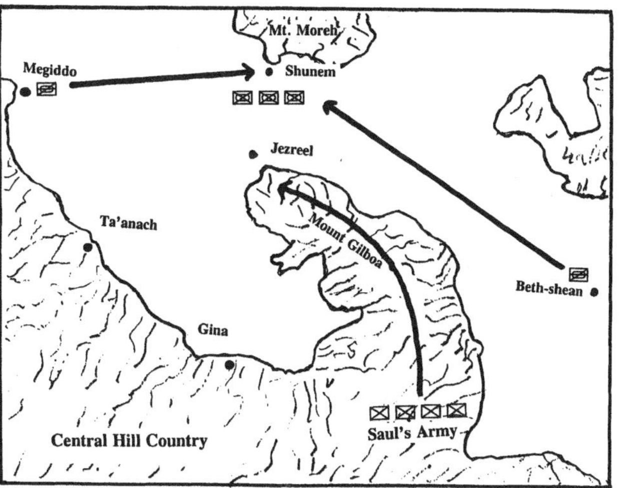

Figure 6.4 Philistine and Israelite Axes of Advance toward Mount Gilboa

ridge to reduce the chances of an Israelite ambush and sufficiently wide to permit the Philistine chariot and infantry teams room for maneuver if attacked.

After assembling the army at Aphek, the Philistines successfully negotiated the Wadi Ara and encamped at Shunem.[110] The exact location of Shunem is somewhat in dispute, but it's likely to be modern Solem located on the southern slope of Mount Moreh.[111] It is also likely, as Robinson suggests, that the Philistine garrison at Beth-shean also moved to assemble at Shunem[112] Saul's army probably moved parallel along the Judean ridge observing the Philistine army as it moved up the coast. Saul had the advantage of interior lines. As the Philistines moved through the Wadi Ara, Saul assembled his army on Mount Gilboa.[113] Once the Philistines began to concentrate at Shunem, the text says that "Israel encamped at the spring at Jezreel,"[114] probably the spring of Harod. It is certainly possible that Saul positioned a few units forward of the mountain slopes at the spring, but it defies tactical sense for Saul to have concentrated any part of his army there in strength. The slopes of Gilboa offered the Israelites good observation of the enemy, interior lines of communication and retreat, and favorable defensive terrain that forced the enemy to fight uphill. Depressed as he might have been that Yahweh had deserted him, it is difficult to believe that a warrior of Saul's hard experience would have squandered these advantages and deployed in the open terrain. In every previous battle between Saul and the Philistines, Saul always chose the terrain with a careful eye to neutralizing the Philistine advantage in chariots. It seems extremely unlikely, then, that he would have invited a battle on the open plain where the Philistine chariots could be employed with devastating effectiveness.

Another tactical question remains unanswered, however. Why did Saul permit the Philistines to pass through the Carmel pass unhindered? Gichon and Herzog suggest an intriguing answer. I Samuel 29:2–7 tells the tale of David's serving in the Philistine army as commander of a sizeable unit of mercenaries. David and his men had mustered at Aphek as ordered and were prepared to fight alongside the Philistines. Some of the Philistine commanders objected that David could not be trusted, however, and he was ordered to remain at Aphek and then return to his base at Ziklag. If one imagines that the Philistine camp at Aphek was under observation by Saul, he would have seen the main

Philistine army begin to move north even as David and his army of, perhaps, 1,000 men remained in the Aphek camp. If Saul knew, too, that David was in command of that force, he might have reckoned that its purpose was to attack up one of the valleys while Saul was engaged with the Philistine main body at Gilboa. To prevent this "stab in the back," Saul would have been forced to keep substantial forces on the ridge even as his advance elements moved toward Mount Gilboa. Thus deployed, Saul had few forces he could spare to harass the Philistine passage through the Wadi Ara. Once David's unit began to move south, Saul released the forces on the ridge and ordered them to join the main body at Gilboa.[115]

Figure 6.5 portrays the location and deployment of the Israelite and Philistine armies at Mount Gilboa. The text offers few details of the battle. Saul had moved his army along the parallel track of the Philistine axis of advance keeping to the ridge line until reaching the slopes of Mount Gilboa and facing the enemy across the valley at Shunem. The northern face of the mountain is very steep, and it is probable that Saul anchored his right wing on it, requiring only a small number of troops to make the terrain an effective defensive line. The defensive line (1) then ran in a semicircle downhill and to the western slope. The western slope is not as steep at the northern face, but is sufficiently steep to prevent chariots from advancing too far uphill before the terrain becomes unnegotiable. The Philistine infantry, too, once engaged would have been forced to fight uphill at the center of the line. Farther south, the terrain is merely hilly and only moderately difficult for chariots. Here Saul anchored his left wing, probably pulled back as tightly against the steeper terrain as tactical wisdom permitted. Saul's army was perfectly deployed to accomplish three things. First, to absorb the Philistine main attack in the center, gradually withdrawing up the steep slope until the chariots could no longer follow turning the battle into a purely infantry engagement. Second, to fight both a tactically and strategically defensive battle. Saul could never hope to overcome Philistine power with any degree of finality, a reality that dictated a defensive national military strategy. Third, if things went badly, Saul's army was positioned to break contact and execute a disciplined retrograde movement saving the army for another day.

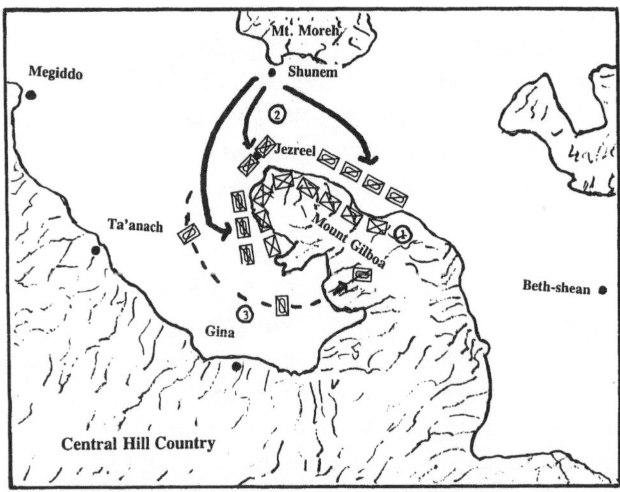

Figure 6.5 The Battle of Mount Gilboa

The text is lacking in details of the actual battle. I Samuel 31:1–2 records that "The Philistines fought with Israel, and as the men of Israel fled before them, falling wounded on Mount Gilboa, the Philistines overtook Saul and his sons. They cut down Jonathan, Abinadab, and Malchishua, Saul's sons." The Philistine attack (2) probably struck the Israelite defensive line with the greatest force in the center while other main force units engaged the left wing simultaneously. It seems clear from the text that the Philistine infantry pressed the Israelites hard all along the line, driving the Israelites further up the mountain slopes. The Philistine infantry probably gained the upper hand for the text tells us that "the men of Israel fled before them." Saul's sons were overtaken and "cut down," suggesting they were killed by the Philistine infantry.

One imagines that the left wing of Saul's army, already drawn tightly against the southwestern foothills of the mountain, was hard pressed as well. Here, the tactical objective of the Philistine attack was to pin the Israelites against the foothills, fixing them in place and restricting their range of maneuver. But where were the Philistine chariots? The text is silent, but it is likely that some chariot units accompanied the infantry attack against Saul's defensive line. Any Philistine commander worth his salt would have recognized that the steep terrain neutralized the power of his chariots to decisively influence the outcome of the battle. Their employment against the center-left of the line, therefore, must have had another purpose, perhaps to deceive Saul that the Philistine plan was to engage in strength along the center-left of the line when, in fact, the plan was to turn the Israelite position from the south and envelop it from the rear.

Saul's sons were probably slain by the Philistine infantry, but Saul himself committed suicide after being wounded by Philistine chariot archers. "The battle raged on against Saul. The archers found him with their bows, and he was wounded in the belly. So he said to his weapon-bearer, 'Draw your sword and run me through with it, lest these uncircumcised come and have their way with me!' But his weapon-bearer was unwilling, for he was greatly afraid; so Saul took the sword himself and fell upon it."[116] The reference to "archers" in the plural suggests that it was not a stray arrow that struck Saul, but an assault from a number of archers. Since the Philistines only used chariot-borne archers, the manner of Saul's wounding implies that Philistine chariots had gained a position on the mountain from where they could bring the Israelites under fire. An examination of Figure 6.5 shows that Saul's defensive arrangement on Mount Gilboa contained a fatal flaw, one that the Philistine commander discerned and turned to his advantage.

Saul's deployment on Mount Gilboa was tactically sound as far as it went. But the key to its defeat lay not in the strength of the Israelite center, but in the weakness of its left wing first deployed and then forced back tightly against the foothills. No more than a mile farther south of Saul's left wing, the terrain changes from steep foothills into a gentle slope easily navigable by chariots. The slope leads to the summit of Mount Gilboa. Any force reaching this position would have a clear field of fire against the Israelites below as well as being able to cut the main avenue of Israelite retreat. The only defensive position against a wide-sweeping Philistine chariot envelopment would have been an infantry force deployed in or around the village of Gina. Gina was on the very edge of the Israelite kingdom, and we do not know if it was an Israelite or Canaanite village at the time. In either case, it was the tactical key to the battle, and Saul, perhaps as a consequence of his depression resulting from the prediction of the witch of Endor, seems to have neglected to incorporate Gina into his defensive plan.

The results were catastrophic. Philistine chariot units swung wide around Saul's left wing (3) unhindered by any opposition at Gina, moved up the mountainside, and gained the heights above Saul and his army. From there they poured down murderous arrow fire upon the Israelites until, pressed from the front at the same time, their line broke and they fled back over the mountain toward the Shechem plain. Saul himself was mortally wounded, and killed himself to avoid being tortured.[117] If Saul's failure to occupy Gina cannot be attributed to incompetence or despair, what other factors may have played a role in Saul's neglect of so obviously important a tactical position? David Rohl thinks a clue lies in David's lament of Saul uttered upon his learning of the death of his king. Rohl points to II Samuel 1:19–27 and David's famous lament of Saul. David cursed the very mountains upon which Saul died. "You mountains of Gilboa, no dew, no rain fall upon you. Oh treacherous fields where the hero's shield lies dishonored!" What treachery was David referring to? Rohl suggests that Gina was an Israelite village and that Saul had indeed known of its importance and ordered the Israelites of Gina to defend the town against any Philistine attack. Given that the feud between David and Saul had long become public, and that Saul's behavior had alienated some elements of the population, Rohl suggests that the Israelites of Gina either deserted their positions or, worse, perhaps even went over to the Philistines as a way of settling some old score, exposing Saul and his army to the Philistine envelopment.[118]

SAUL'S OTHER WARS

I have argued that Saul's wars against his non-Philistine enemies—Zobah, Arameans, Ammonites, Moabites, Edomites, and the Amalekites—were probably fought in the period between the battles of Jabesh-gilead and Michmash Pass (1032 to 1010 B.C.E.) rather than, as implied from their placement in the text, after Michmash Pass and before the death of Saul on Mount Gilboa (1006 B.C.E.), a period of only four years or so. Of these non-Philistine wars, the text provides detail about only one, the war against the Amalekites. To ensure an adequate representation of all of Saul's wars within a strategic context,

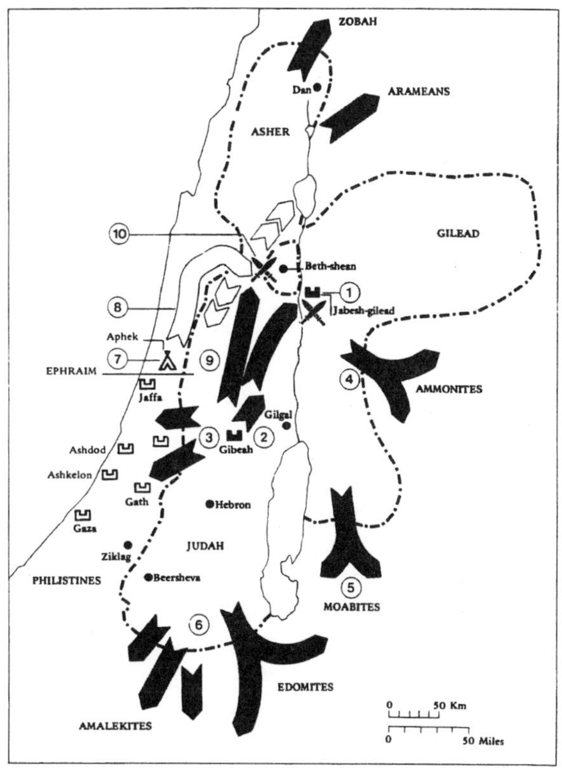

Figure 6.6 The Wars of Saul

1 Saul's first campaign to rescue besieged Jabesh-gilead; 2 The Michmash campaign; 3 The wars against the Philistines; 4 & 5 Wars against the eastern neighbours; 6 Campaigns to secure the southern borders; 7 Philistine concentration for the Gilboa campaign; 8 Philistine invasion of the Esdraelon; 9 Saul's last campaign: he moves to Mount Gilboa; 10 Saul is killed at the battle of Mount Gilboa.

Chaim Herzog and Mordechai Gichon, *Battles of the Bible* (Jerusalem: Steimatzky's Agency Ltd., 1978), 67. Reprinted with permission.

Figure 6.6 attempts to provide that context. I am indebted to Mordechai Gichon and Chaim Herzog for permission to use this illustration.[119]

There are only a few details of military interest offered by the text's account of Saul's war with the Amalekites. The first is the size of the army. "So Saul summoned the army and mustered it at Telaim—two hundred thousands of foot soldiers and ten thousands of the men of Judah."[120] Thus Saul mustered 210 *alaphim* or about 14,700 men, or roughly half the national levy. Of more interest is Saul's treatment of the Kenites who were living among the Amalekites. "Then Saul went to the city of Amalek and lay in wait in the Wadi. To the Kenites [he] said, 'Go! Get away from Amalek, lest I sweep you away with them.' "[121] Why did Saul warn the Kenites? The text says that Saul remembered that the Kenites "dealt kindly with the Israelites when they were coming up from Egypt."[122] But there may have been a more important reason to spare the Kenites. These were, of course, the metalsmiths, Joshua's weaponeers, some of whom once lived among the Israelites and returned among the Amalekites when the bronze industry collapsed. I have suggested that by Saul's time the Kenite smiths had acquired the knowledge of iron making and that some may have returned to Gilgal to manufacture weapons for Saul's army. If so, then the Kenites encountered among the Amalekites were clan relatives of those in Israel and, perhaps, even relatives of some Israelites as well.

Samuel had ordered Saul to put the city of the Amalekites under the ban, and Saul ordered the killing of much of the civilian populace. But, "Saul and the army spared not only Agag [the Amalekite king] but also the best of the flock and the herd—the fat ones and the young—and every good thing."[123] Samuel was furious and condemned Saul, inquiring of him, "Why did you not listen to Yahweh?" Saul replied like the pragmatic field commander he had become, "Because I listened to the soldiers!" Saul was hardly an irreligious man, but he ignored the ban because his army had to be paid, especially the mercenaries and his regulars. For militia soldiers, too, booty was one of the few ways they could increase their wealth, and one suspects that to destroy "every good thing" might have provoked the soldiers to anger, perhaps even to mutiny. Saul himself suggested exactly that when, later, he repented of his failure to carry out the ban and said to Samuel, "I have violated Yahweh's instructions and your [Samuel's] command, for I feared the soldiers and listened to them."[124] That Saul's fear of a mutiny was genuine is also clear from the compromise that was brokered to defuse the crisis. Some of the livestock was sacrificed, but not all, and the soldiers were permitted to keep the other valuables they had liberated.

Another aspect of Saul's wars with the non-Philistine peoples was his conquest and absorption of the remaining Canaanite enclaves that lay within the Israelite hill country. The textual evidence for Saul's actions is indirect, and addresses only two Canaanite cities, Beeroth and Gibeon. II Samuel 4:2–4, in discussing the struggle for power that resulted after Saul's death notes, "for Beeroth is reckoned to the Benjaminites." What had formerly been a Canaanite town, one of the daughter towns of Gibeon during Joshua's time, was now integrated into Benjaminite territory. When combined with the clue that the people of Beeroth were then living in Gittaim, it seems plausible that not only had Beeroth been incorporated into Saul's kingdom, but also its people had been driven away presumably so the Israelites could resettle the town.[125] With regard to Gibeon itself, the text tells us that after David was anointed king, the people of Gibeon came to him demanding vengeance against Saul's descendants. "Now the Gibeonites were not part of the people of Israel—they were part of the remnant of the Amorites [Canaanites], but the Israelites had sworn an oath to them—and Saul, in his zeal for the people of Israel and Judah, tried to exterminate them."[126] It will be recalled that Joshua had made a treaty with the Gibeonites guaranteeing them their safety in return for their support in his campaign against the Canaanite kings. The accusation before David is that Saul had violated that oath, and had attacked and "tried to exterminate" the Gibeonites. The accusation has the ring of truth to it. Both Beeroth and Gibeon were strategically located on the edge of Saul's western border and commanded strategic roads running along the central spine and, more importantly, vital approaches connecting the *shephelah* to the Judean ridge. Leaving these Canaanite towns to their own independence exposed Israel to a potential Gibeonite-Philistine alliance that would have cut Saul's kingdom strategically in half.[127] It seems reasonable, then, that Saul would have taken steps to bring these two Canaanite towns and, most likely, others as well, under his control. In agreeing to the Gibeonites request for justice in the matter, David appeared to give credence to the accusation of a massacre. On the other hand, it was very much to David's interest to agree even if the accusation was false. David gathered up all Saul's male heirs, his grandchildren, and, "[h]e handed them over to the Gibeonites, who crucified them on the mountain, seven of them lying prostrate together. They were put to death in the days of Ziv at the beginning of the barley harvest."[128] In this manner all of Saul's heirs except the lame Merribaal, son of Jonathan, were removed as rival claimants to the throne.

Saul's death on Mount Gilboa broke the back of Israelite power in the central hills and, although the text is silent, we might reasonably suppose that Philistine power was reimposed in the area much as it had been after Aphek-Ebenezer. The Philistines now controlled the entire Jezreel Valley and its precious caravan routes, but did not cross the Jordan River. It is almost certain that they controlled the river's fords, however, even though there is no evidence that they occupied Jericho. The later references to David having been king of Hebron suggest that the Philistines made little effort to occupy the south, and simply permitted their loyal vassal, David of Judah, to expand his holdings and become *melekh* over Hebron. This was a major strategic error, however, as it permitted David to retain his power base and gradually expand his holdings and standing among his Israelite countrymen until the day came when he was prepared to challenge the power of his feudal masters with consequences that shook Israel and the world.

NOTES

1. B. Mazer, "The Philistines and Their Wars with Israel," in *World History of the Jewish People* (Philadelphia, PA: Jewish Publications Society, 1979), 176.
2. I Samuel 13:19.
3. *The Cambridge Ancient History*, vol. 2, pt. 2 (Cambridge: Cambridge University Press, 1975), 570.
4. A.D.H. Mayes, "The Historical Context of the Battle against Sisera," *Vetus Testamentum* 19 (1951): 253–60.
5. I Samuel 4:2.
6. I Samuel 4:3.
7. I Samuel 4:4.
8. P. Kyle McCarter Jr., *I Samuel: The Anchor Bible* (New York: Doubleday, 1980), 109. From here on, this source will be cited as *Anchor Bible.*
9. I Samuel 4:9.
10. I Samuel 4:10.
11. *Anchor Bible*, 107.
12. See Richard A. Gabriel and Karen S. Metz, chap. 4 in *From Sumer to Rome: The Military Capabilities of Ancient Armies* (Westport, CT: Greenwood Press, 1991), for an analysis of death and wounding rates of ancient armies.
13. *The Cambridge Ancient History*, 571.
14. Mazer, 175. Sometimes the word is rendered in Hebrew as *hamashchit* whose derivative root in Hebrew is *sh-ch-t* or "butcher," a fitting name for an elite military unit.

15. Yehuda Margowsky, "War and Warfare," *Encyclopaedia Judaica*, vol. 16 (Jerusalem: Macmillan Company, 1971), 271–72.

16. Ibid.

17. *Anchor Bible*, 125; see also Delcor, Matthias, "Jahweh et Dagon ou le Jahwisme face a la religion des Philistins, apres I Samuel V," *Vetus Testamentum* 14 (1964): 136–54.

18. See Richard A. Gabriel, *Gods of Our Fathers: The Memory of Egypt in Judaism and Christianity* (Westport, CT: Greenwood Press, 2002), 87; see also Jan Assmann, *Moses the Egyptian* (Cambridge, MA: Harvard University Press, 1997), 3.

19. Gabriel, *Gods of Our Fathers*, 92; Assmann, 4.

20. I Samuel 5:6.

21. *Anchor Bible*, 123.

22. See *New American Bible* (New York: Catholic Book Publishers, 1992), 270.

23. Mazer, 166.

24. Norman K. Gottwald, *The Tribes of Yahweh* (Maryknoll, NY: Orbis Books, 1979), 414.

25. G. Bonfante, "Who Were the Philistines?" *American Journal of Archaeology* 50 (1946): 251–62, for the Aegean origins of the Philistines.

26. Gottwald, 414–15.

27. Ibid., 416.

28. W. F. Albright, "Syria, the Philistines, and Phoenicia," in *Cambridge Ancient History*, rev. ed. (1966), 32; see also Gottwald, 416.

29. Gottwald, 416; Mazer, 175.

30. Mazer, 175.

31. H. M. Orlinsky, "The Seer Priest," in *World History of the Jewish People*, vol. III, 269.

32. Ibid.

33. *Anchor Bible*, 182. *Halil* is often mistranslated as flute when it is in fact a reed instrument more like the clarinet in sound.

34. Orlinsky, 269.

35. *Anchor Bible*, 99; Orlinsky, 273.

36. I Samuel 7:6; see also Mazer, 177.

37. Theodore H. Robinson and W.O.E. Oesterley, *A History of Israel*, vol. 1 (Oxford, UK: Clarendon Press, 1948), 180; see also Mazer, 177.

38. I Samuel 7:5.

39. *Anchor Bible*, 144.

40. I Samuel 7:7.

41. I Samuel 7:9.

42. I Samuel 7:10–11.

43. The original Hebrew, *eben ha'ezer*, translates as "stone of help," implying that where the stone was erected was the place where Yahweh helped the Israelites. Used as a cultic designation, it means "Stone of the Helper" or even "Stone of the Divine Warrior." See *Anchor Bible*, 146.

44. *Anchor Bible*, 145.

45. Ibid., 146.

46. I Samuel 7:13–14.

47. Orlinsky, 277; see also M. A. Cohen, "The Role of the Shilonite Priesthood

in the United Monarchy of Ancient Israel," *Hebrew Union College Annual* 36 (1965): 59–98.

48. Ibid.

49. Robinson, 180.

50. E. A. Speiser, "The Manner of the King," in *World History of the Jewish People*, vol. III, 283.

51. I Samuel 10:25.

52. I Samuel 8:11–17.

53. For all of the textual references cited in this section, see *Anchor Bible*, 158.

54. For the detailed argument that the term *ivrim* has two meanings depending upon context, see Gottwald, 419–22.

55. *The Cambridge Ancient History*, 575.

56. I Samuel 10:27.

57. I Samuel 11:1.

58. I Samuel 11:5–6.

59. Kenneth I. Cohen, "King Saul: A Bungler from the Beginning," *Bible Review* 10 (October 1994): 37.

60. I Samuel 11:7.

61. I Samuel 11:7.

62. I Samuel 11:8.

63. I Samuel 11:10.

64. I Samuel 11:11.

65. Josephus, *Antiquities* 6:80, in *Anchor Bible*, 204.

66. I Samuel 13:2, for the textual reference to Saul's regulars.

67. Gibeah is used interchangeably in some places as synonymous with Geba, although the two cities are indeed distinct.

68. I Samuel 13:3–4.

69. See David M. Rohl, *Pharoahs and Kings: A Biblical Quest* (New York: Crown Publishers, 1995), 210–12, and Gottwald, 417–23, for the argument that *ivrim* are really the *apiru* in some textual contexts.

70. I Samuel 13:5.

71. I Samuel 13:6–7.

72. Rohl, 210.

73. I Samuel 13:8.

74. I Samuel 13:15.

75. Chaim Herzog and Mordechai Gichon, *Battles of the Bible* (Jerusalem: Steimatzky's Agency Ltd., 1978), 68.

76. I Samuel 13:17–18.

77. I Samuel 13:22.

78. I Samuel 13:19.

79. I Samuel 13:23.

80. I Samuel 14:1–13; see also *Anchor Bible*, 236.

81. I Samuel 14:20–22.

82. *Anchor Bible*, 236.

83. Ibid., 233.

84. I Samuel 14:21.

85. I Samuel 14:24.

86. Gabriel and Metz, 31–32.
87. I Samuel 14:36.
88. *Anchor Bible*, 282, for the argument regarding which textual tradition is older.
89. I Samuel 16:18.
90. I Samuel 17:39.
91. I Samuel 17:1–2.
92. Herzog and Gichon, 72.
93. For an examination of the derivation of the term as "champions," see Roland de Vaux, "Single Combat in the Old Testament," in *The Bible and the Ancient Near East* (Garden City, NY: Doubleday, 1971), 122–35, especially 124–25.
94. I Samuel 17:52.
95. Robert Drews, *The End of the Bronze Age: Changes in Warfare and the Catastrophe, ca. 1200 B.C.E.* (Princeton, NJ: Princeton University Press, 1993), 175–87.
96. I Samuel 17:4–7.
97. *Anchor Bible*, 291.
98. Ibid., 292; see also E. Sapir, "Hebrew Helmet: A Loanword, and Its Bearing on Indo-European Phonology," *Journal of the American Oriental Society* 57 (1937): 73–77.
99. T. R. Hobbs, *A Time for War* (Wilmington, DE: Michael Glazier, 1989), 128.
100. *Anchor Bible*, 293.
101. Ibid., 292; see also E. A. Speiser, "On Some Articles of Armor and Their Names," *Journal of the American Oriental Society* 70 (1950): 47–49.
102. Gabriel and Metz, 51–58.
103. Hobbs, 131; *Anchor Bible*, 292.
104. Hobbs, 132.
105. Margowsky, 266.
106. See Yigael Yadin, "Goliath's Javelin and the *menor origim*," *Palestine Exploration Quarterly* 86 (1955): 58–69.
107. Drews, 185.
108. I Samuel 14:52.
109. Robinson, 189.
110. I Samuel 28:4.
111. *Anchor Bible*, 420.
112. Robinson, 190–191; *The Cambridge Ancient History*, 578.
113. I Samuel 28:4.
114. I Samuel 29:1.
115. Herzog and Gichon, 73.
116. I Samuel 31:3–4.
117. *Anchor Bible*, 443.
118. Rohl, 217. The argument swings on the translation of some key phrases of David's lament. Unfortunately, there exists no consensus regarding the translation. Compare, for example, the differences in the text of II Samuel 6:8 as they appear in the *Anchor* version and in *Tanakh: The New JPS Translation According to the Traditional Hebrew Text.*

119. My thanks to Chaim Herzog and Mordechai Gichon for permission to cite this illustration from *Battles of the Bible*.

120. I Samuel 15:4.

121. I Samuel 15:6.

122. Ibid.

123. I Samuel 15:9.

124. I Samuel 15:24.

125. *The Cambridge Ancient History*, 576.

126. II Samuel 21:2.

127. A. Malamat, "Doctrines of Causality in Biblical and Hittite Historiography: A Parallel," *Vetus Testamentum* 5 (1955): 1–12, for the argument of Saul's strategy with regard to Beeroth and Gibeon.

128. II Samuel 21:9.

7

David and the Israelite Empire

Except for Moses, King David is the most familiar character in the Bible. His achievements are the stuff of national myth and legend, and it is David that modern Israelis regard as the founder of the first Israelite national state, even though Saul may have laid the foundations for that state. John Bright is correct when he suggests that the first Israelite national state, and the empire that followed, was the creation of David alone.[1] Before David the Israelites were a sacral union of tribes that possessed no central government in the proper sense of the word. Saul's authority had encompassed only some of the tribes, and he had made no effort to change the tribal organization or to establish a centralized bureaucracy to address national concerns. Even the army, except for a small corps of military regulars, remained a tribal levy whose political reliability was always in doubt.[2] David's reign from Hebron for seven and a half years and later from Jerusalem for 33 years, beginning in 1004,[3] brought into being a genuine Israelite national state. David was to Israel what Sargon I was to Sumer, Ahmose I to Egypt, Philip II to Greece, and Augustus to Rome, that is, a great national leader whose vision and military exploits brought into being a form of national existence for his people that they had never before possessed. Once that was achieved, David expanded the Israelite state into a genuine imperial realm, which he bequeathed to his son.

The basis of David's claim to kingship was very different from Saul's, a fact that made its institutional expression different as well. Unlike Saul, David laid no claim to divine selection as king. Rather, David's military successes and the creation of a powerful band of professional soldiers loyal only to his person presented the elders of Israel, especially those of the northern tribes, with the dilemma of a single alternative. With Saul's son and successor, Ish-baal, dead and the Philistine threat to the northern tribes as strong as ever, the elders of the northern tribes had either to rally around the one person with sufficient power and prestige to deal with the Philistines or succumb to further occupation. It is often overlooked that the support of the northern tribes for David's claim to the throne centered upon the promise that David would deal militarily with the Philistine threat.[4] David's claim to kingship was formalized by the consent of the tribal elders speaking for the people as part of a larger political agreement, one that recognized the political and military power that David had achieved by himself with no reference to the divine authority of Yahweh's *mishpat*. One indication of this was that when David captured Jerusalem the city remained David's personal possession and outside the union of Israel and Judah. Later, as David's long reign took root, the myth grew that Yahweh had somehow concluded an eternal covenant with David assuring him of the perpetuity of his dynasty.[5] But this, too, was an afterthought. David was anointed king because he was the only person in Israel who possessed the necessary means to be king.

The Davidic monarchy was far more institutionalized than it had been under Saul, and was organized along a division of labor that included the king, priesthood, civil service, military, and judiciary.[6] I Chronicles 27:25–31 provides an extensive list of the king's functionaries required to manage the royal estates, and it was the income from these estates as well as war booty and tribute from conquered nations that financed public functions. There is no evidence that taxation was used as a source of public funds under David. It is likely, however, that David introduced corvee labor to carry out public works, for there are scattered references to public works, agricultural projects, and fortifications that could only have been undertaken in this manner.[7] It has sometimes been argued that David modeled his court after the Egyptian court or, at least, after what might be regarded as a "typical" Near Eastern model.[8] Yeivin, on the other hand, suggests that the Davidic court was copied from the more familiar Canaanite system.[9] Yeivin suggests that David's experience with the Jebusites after he captured Jerusalem led him to employ these experienced officials from the beginning. Thus, "First and foremost among these, the Jebusite state in Jerusalem, which fell to David in the eighth year of his reign, and the senior officials of which he could reemploy in organizing his centralized rule, and apparently did so."[10] Saul, too, had been assisted by foreigners, but on a much smaller scale. David institutionalized the practice, and the employment of foreigners in the state bureaucracy became a common practice. Indeed, only the military leadership and the priesthood remained almost exclusively Israelite while the rest of the administration was comprised largely of experienced Canaanite officials.[11] The use of foreigners in this manner was commonplace in the ancient world whenever the cultural level of the conquered was higher than that of the conquerors as, for example, it was when Rome conquered Greece.[12]

Once anointed king, David spent nearly the next 20 years ridding his country of the Philistine occupiers and engaging in wars of conquest against the states on Israel's border, eventually projecting Israelite military power as far as the Euphrates River to the northeast. These wars resulted in the militarization of the Israelite people who were required to endure frequent periods of military service. In addition, the style of warfare changed from defensive to offensive, a change that required a new ideological justification for war. This was achieved by portraying Israel's current enemies as extensions of its ancient enemies. Thus it was that the Amalek were almost exterminated because they had resisted Israel's passage from Egypt. Edom was destroyed because he was the jealous half brother of Israel, as were Moab and Ammon because both had sought to stop Israel from reaching the promised land.[13] This aside, however, there were more practical reasons for David's wars.

During Saul's time Israel could hardly guarantee its own existence. Although Saul successfully fought a number of tribal wars along Israel's borders, the fact that Philistine power was supreme meant that Saul's strategy of national survival was of necessity defensive with little hope of permanently displacing Philistine power. To his great credit Saul was able for a time to prevent a renewed Philistine occupation of the Israelite hill country, and the Israelite army acquired some degree of combat sophistication, equipment, training, and logistics capabilities. Despite the disaster at Gilboa, it must be said that Saul was successful in fighting the Philistines to a draw, no small feat in itself. Moreover, Saul had little choice in responding to the Philistine movement into the Jezreel. The Philistine maneuver was designed to encircle the hill country and to sever the northern territories from the south. The tribes of Asher, Zebulun, Issachar, and Naftali were its strategic targets. Failure to confront the Philistines at Gilboa was to concede victory by default, a disaster for Israel.

As long as Israel remained militarily weak, it could only deal with threats to its interests defensively. Under David, however, an Israelite national entity was finally created and its new political institutions—the monarchy and a professional army—were for the first time able to give military effect to a national political will. For the first time Israel possessed sufficient political and military resources to develop a grand strategy aimed at controlling its own national destiny. Under these conditions it was to be expected that David would behave like any near eastern monarch of the day and implement a grand strategy based on the pursuit of security first, then the power to protect the national existence, and, finally, conquest leading to empire.[14]

David's dream of empire could be reasonably entertained because there was no great power to oppose the Israelite expansion. For centuries Palestine had been caught between the bipolar world of Egypt to the south and the Mitanni and then the Hittites to the north. By David's time, these great powers had collapsed. The Hittites disappeared entirely while Egypt suffered under severe domestic problems. Babylonia was conquered by the Arameans, and Assyria had been pressed back to her old borders. The collapse of these great powers created a power vacuum in which three new nations—Israel, the Arameans, and Phoenicia—maneuvered for dominance.[15] David's military success raised Israel to the status of an intermediate power between Anatolia and Mesopotamia in the north and Egypt in the south, something that no power had ever been able to achieve. David's conquests established a sphere of influence in Palestine for Israel whose proportions exceeded anything before established by any great power there. In the same manner that the Philistines considered themselves the natural heirs to the Egyptians in Palestine, David thought of Palestine as the passage of the entire land of Canaan into Israelite hands.[16]

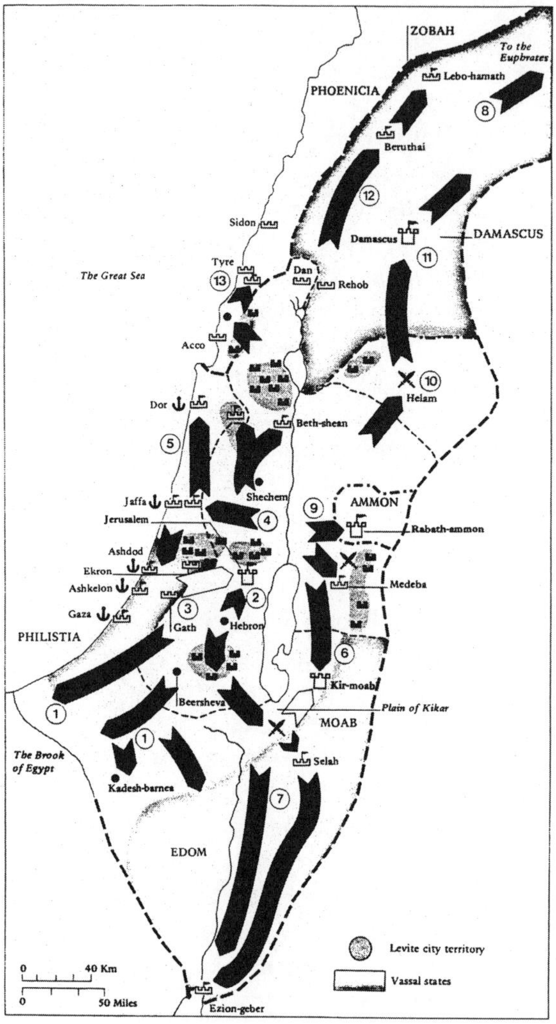

Figure 7.1 The Wars of David

1. Subjugation of the Negev tribes 2. The conquest of Jerusalem 3. Philistine attempts to oust David in the Rephaim Valley 4. Subjugation of Philistia 5. Conquest of the Sharon Plain and Valley of Jezreel 6. The war against Moab 7. Subjugation of Edom 8. Trade with the Euphrates region 9. The war against the Arameans and Ammonites 10. The defeat of the Arameans in the Edrei gap 11. Subjugation of Damascus 12. Extension of the empire to the borders of Hamath and the Euphrates 13. Establishment of Israelite sovereignty in western Galilee, as far as the Phoenician border.

In Chaim Herzog and Mordechai Gichon, *Battles of the Bible* (Jerusalem: Steimatzky's Agency Ltd., 1978), 76. Reprinted with permission.

Malamat has identified five stages through which Israelite grand strategy progressed. The first was the establishment of the Israelite tribal kingdom to replace the now destroyed kingdom of Saul. Establishing himself at Hebron in the south, David used his position as king of Hebron as a springboard to become king of all Israel. During this time David captured Jerusalem, out maneuvered Saul's son for the loyalty of the Israelite elders, and established a mercenary army loyal to himself. In addition, he married the daughter of the king of Geshur, and cultivated close ties with the kings of Ammon and Moab, politically outflanking the territories of the northern Israelite tribes.[17] The second stage followed upon David forging an alliance with the northern tribes to recognize him as king of all Israel, a union that found expression in the establishment of a powerful monarchy, the creation of a national army, and the pursuit of a single foreign policy as regards Israelite national security. This development threatened the power of the Philistines who reacted militarily by attacking David in Hebron. These circumstances forced the emergence of the third stage, the consolidation of an Israelite national state, which required the removal of all other competing centers of power.[18] As we shall see, this required the defeat, but not destruction, of Philistine power and, equally important, the integration of the Canaanite kingdoms into the Israelite national state. Once this was achieved, Israel took on the character of a multinational state, the fourth stage, in which the resources of the Israelites, the Canaanite city-states, and the Philistines could be marshaled in support of reducing the threat posed by the belt of potentially hostile states surrounding Israel. The actual order in which these states, Moab, Edom, and Ammon, were attacked and reduced is unclear, but that they were either annexed outright or garrisoned with troops and military governors is evident from the text.[19] Figure 7.1 shows David's wars as they occurred within the context of the new Israelite grand strategy.

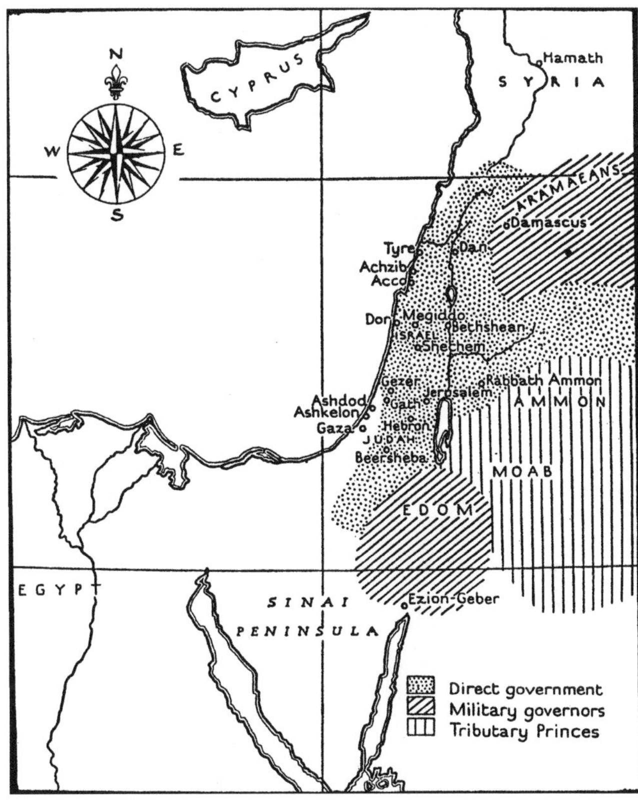

Figure 7.2 The Kingdom of David

While David was forging the Israelite state in the crucible of military action, the Arameans were establishing a powerful state of their own to the north. Here we encounter an important Aramean kingdom in southern Syria known as Aram-Zobah, ruled by the Beth-rehob dynasty. The kingdom was actually a federation of Aramean and non-Aramean kingdoms in Syria and the northern Transjordan. The Zobah kingdom itself was probably in the northern part of the Lebanon Valley where we find the three major cities of Tebah, Cun, and Berothai mentioned in the text as belonging to Hadadezer ben Rehob, king of Aram-Zobah. The region around Damascus was under Aram-Zobah control, and the kingdoms of Maachah and Tob in the northern Transjordan and the kingdom of Ammon were allies and satellites of Aram-Zobah.[20]

As Israelite power expanded northward, it collided head-on with the Aramean bloc headed by Hadadezer seeking to extend its control into the Jordan Valley. The result was a series of battles in which David defeated the Arameans and gained mastery over the kingdom of Aram-Zobah, as well as its vassals and allied territories reaching all the way to the Euphrates River. In the kingdom of Aram-Damascus, "David put governors in Aram of Damascus, and the Arameans became servants to David and brought tribute,"[21] in short, military occupation. David turned the other states of the region into Israelite satellites, leaving their kings in power. Thus II Samuel 10:19 informs us that "when all the kings who were servants of Hadadezer saw that they had been defeated by Israel they made peace with Israel and became subject to them."

With these victories David created an Israelite empire that ran from the River of Egypt (Wadi Arish) to Lebo in the Lebanon Valley. Figure 7.2 shows the boundaries of the Davidic empire. This was the empire bequeathed by David to Solomon who, as the text tells us, "ruled over all the kingdoms from the River Euphrates to the land of the Philistines and to the border of Egypt."[22] That the imperial status of Israel was recognized by the other powers of the region is implied by the use of the Akkadian tutelary, *sarru rabu*, as Solomon's official form of address. The term means *imperatore* or emperor.[23]

DAVID'S RISE TO POWER

David's rise to power began when he was summoned to Saul's court to apply his skill at music to lift Saul from his depression. The story of Saul's depression as portrayed in I Samuel is probably a propaganda device used by the text's author to discredit Saul and ought to give us pause in accepting it as history. Saul's suspicion of David, for example, is ostensibly explained by Saul's insanity when, in fact, it is more reasonably explained by Saul's concern for the future of his dynasty. The ambitious David had worked his way up so that next to Jonathan he was the most powerful person in the court and perfectly positioned to seize the crown should anything happen to Saul or Jonathan. Saul may also have seen that Jonathan's affection for David blinded him to the threat David posed to the future of the dynasty in which case Saul moved to remove David as a function of the natural distrust any ruler must feel against those around him who grow too powerful.[24] Samuel's purpose was to legitimize David's claim to the throne, which was otherwise quite illegitimate, and to relieve David of any responsibility for the disasters that overtook Saul's family. Thus we might be somewhat wary of the account of Saul's insanity as history.

Forced to flee Saul's court, David lived a life on the run as the leader of a small outlaw band of *apiru* who lived by robbery and pillage. Without a secure base of operations, however, David was almost captured several times when citizens revealed his hiding place to Saul's soldiers. David was not safe even in his native Judah and was forced to flee to the land of the Philistines where he and his men sought employment in the service of the Philistine prince of Gath. It is important to note that the text makes no pretense of explaining David's decision to join the enemy as anything but a pragmatic one taken by David alone. Unlike elsewhere in the text where David's questionable decisions are explained away as ordered by Yahweh, here it is clear that David had gone over to the Philistines of his own choosing. David remained in the service of Achish of Gath for more than two years during which time he undertook border raids against the nomadic tribes. Oesterley and Robinson suggest that for much of this time David was based in Gath itself and not

Ziklag, which was only later granted him as a fief. The reason is that David would not have been granted the fief until he had completely proven his loyalty to the Philistines, a condition that puts the lie to the claim that David only undertook raids against non-Israelite tribes.[25] It would have been impossible for David to earn Achish's trust without at least some attacks against Israelite settlements.[26] It was only after this that David was established as a Philistine vassal in Ziklag and granted the right to dispose of the spoils of his raids.

David's time in Ziklag is of great importance, for it was from there that he mounted his campaign to become king of Judah, most probably with the aid of the Philistines. Gath was located on the border of Judah and the Philistines had an acute security interest in keeping it out of the hands of the Saulid monarchy. How better to achieve this than to install one of their own "cat's-paws" as its ruler? David may have sensed this possibility, for soon after being installed in Ziklag he began currying the favor of the elders of Judah. The main security problem for Judah was the raids of the desert nomads, most particularly the Amalek. The tribe of Judah had not really achieved cohesion until recently, making it very difficult for them to respond effectively to the Amalekite raids.[27] Saul had fought against the Amalek, but had never attempted to eradicate the threat. Perhaps realizing the importance of the problem to the elders of Judah, David struck hard at the Amalek finally exterminating them, for they are mentioned no more in the texts as a coherent people.[28] Having gained the attention of the elders of Judah, David set out to gain their support through systematic bribery by sharing the spoils of his raids with them. The text tells us that "when David came to Ziklag, he sent of the spoil unto the elders of Judah, even to his friends, saying, 'Behold a present for you of the spoil of the enemies of the Lord.' "[29] Some sense of how extensive David's bribery was can be gained from a list of the towns in Judah that received the spoils. The towns listed in the text are Beth-el, Ramoth, Siphmoth, Eshtemoa, Racal, Hormah, Borashan, Athach, and Hebron. Also listed are the Kenite tribes who had attached themselves to Israel.[30]

David's success against the Amalek where Saul had failed coupled with substantial bribes to the elders of the tribe of Judah established the groundwork for David's "election" as king of Judah. But why would the Judeans elect David, or anyone, king at all? There is no evidence of any House of David in Judah prior to this time, nor is there any indication that his family was of any importance. Moreover, as we have seen, the institution of the Saulid monarchy was an untested innovation, one not yet widely accepted by the tribes, especially so in the case of Judah, which had only recently obtained the degree of social cohesion and identification that had previously been achieved by the other Israelite tribes. There was no tradition of monarchy among the Israelites let alone among the Judeans. Although the text tells us that David was elected by the elders of Judah, in fact it is far more likely that the "election" simply recognized a fait accompli, that the Philistines had decided to create a puppet

Israelite kingdom in Judah to weaken the Israelite nation led by Saul's heirs. Saul himself had been killed at Gilboa, and his son, Ishbaal, had been installed by the Israelite military across the Jordan as Saul's legitimate successor. With the creation of a second Israelite king in Judah, the Philistines hoped to weaken the Saulid claim to leadership and to prevent any further unification of the country under a single Israelite monarch. It was sound strategic thinking and David, the loyal vassal of Achish of Gath, was just the man to do the Philistine's bidding. It was against this background that David and his men "took up residence in Hebron. Then the men of Judah came and anointed David king over the house of Judah."[31]

That the Philistines sought to create a rival Israelite king also seems clear from the account of Saul's death at Gilboa in II Samuel 1:10. A soldier claiming to have been at the battle visited David and told him that "I took the diadem from his [Saul's] head and the bracelet from his arm and brought them here to my lord." Here was David, Achish's loyal vassal, in possession of Saul's crown and other symbols of office immediately after Saul's death. The story was probably fabricated to explain how David came to possess Saul's symbols of royal authority, and, although speculation, David may have worn them as king of Hebron. We know from the textual accounts of Saul's death that Saul's body fell into the hands of the Philistines who stripped it of its armor, beheaded it, and hung the body from the walls of Beth-shean even as Saul's head made the rounds from city to city. It was the Philistines, then, who last had possession of Saul's symbols of royal authority, and it was likely that it was they who gave the crown and bracelet to David as a means of symbolizing that David was the legitimate heir while Ishbaal had to make do without his father's royal equipment. The geographic proximity of Philistia to Judah, the important security interests that the Philistines had in Judah, and the overwhelming military power of the Philistine states, especially Gath, the closest to Judah itself, gave the Philistines powerful influence over events in Judah. It is unlikely that David could have become king of Judah without at least Philistine acquiescence and, most probably, support.

Once installed, David moved immediately to strengthen his hold on power by settling his old outlaw comrades, the *gedud*,[32] in the cities and towns of Judah. These experienced warriors formed the nucleus of the self-defense force of Judah and became the local commanders of the tribal militia raising its overall military competence for use by David later on.[33] These old comrades also served as a base of loyal supporters within the population, something David lacked even as he held the support of the Judean tribal elders. Later, David used the same technique to increase his control of the conquered Canaanite areas and border towns by settling large numbers of landless Levites among the Canaanite towns and appointing them to government posts.[34] From the original *gedud* David chose a unit of 30 picked men, the *gibborim*, a cadre of specially trusted and talented officers who served as his high command and military advisors. This special palace guard was separate from a corps of Philistine mercenaries that included the Cherethites and Pelethites which became David's *mishma'ath* or personal bodyguard, and a special unit from Gath.[35] Interestingly, there is some evidence that David might have employed Philistine mercenaries as early as during his stay in Ziklag. Psalm 57, entitled *A Mikhtam of David . . . when he fled from Saul, in the cave*, speaks of mercenaries called *leba'im* who are described as "fiery men; their teeth are a spear and arrow and their tongue a sharp sword," and whose military emblem was the lion goddess.[36] David was surely clever enough to realize that his newly acquired crown was as yet insecure upon his head. Without an army of his own, the Philistines might choose to replace him at any moment should he try to slip the Philistine leash. Moreover, Ishbaal was alive and forming his own rump government across the Jordan and would have to be dealt with sooner or later. It is, then, no surprise that David set immediately about creating a military force that he could use to defend himself if it came to that, as, indeed, it quickly did.

After Saul's death, Abiner, Saul's commander in chief, installed Ishbaal as king and moved the capital from Gibeah to Mahanaim, a city located across the Jordan on the banks of the Jabbok River in Gilead which, as we have seen earlier, had strong blood ties to Saul and his family.[37] After Saul's death at Gilboa, it is likely that the Philistines reoccupied their garrisons in the hill country leaving Gibeah vulnerable to Philistine attack. The remote forests of Gilead and the barrier of the Jordan offered more refuge and security than the old capital. Judah abutted the land of Benjamin and the clashes of the rival armies of David and Ishbaal turned the borderland of Benjamin into a bloody battlefield that put the old capital at great risk. Abiner, Israel's greatest general of the day, was quick to see the risks and moved Ishbaal and his court out of harm's way.

The war between David and Ishbaal must have begun fairly quickly after David became king, for we know that Ishbaal ruled only two years before his death while David ruled seven years and six months over Hebron.[38] The war would have been impossible without Philistine acquiescence, for the Philistines occupied the key roads and towns of the hill country and could easily have prevented the movement of both armies through the area. The fact that they did not suggests once more that the Philistines supported David's campaign against Ishbaal as a way of furthering their own strategic and security interests. One also imagines that Philistine garrisons could have provided logistical support to David's armies.

THE BATTLE OF GIBEON'S POOL

We do not know if the clash between the armies that occurred at Gibeon's Pool was the first battle in the two-year long civil war or whether it occurred after hostilities had already broken out. It is portrayed in II Samuel 2:12–13 as being the first encounter. That both sides were spoiling for a fight is clear enough as "Abiner . . . and the servants of Ishbaal son of Saul marched out of Mahanaim towards Gibeon . . . and Joab . . . and the servants of David also marched out, and they met each other at the Pool of Gibeon, one group drawing up beside the pool on one side and the other group beside it on the other." The commanders agreed to field 12 men each to do battle, the outcome being agreed upon by both sides. "They took hold of each other's heads, their swords at each others' sides, and fell dead together."[39] All the warriors were killed and both armies took up arms and a great battle ensued between the main forces: "the fighting was very fierce that day, and Abiner and the men of Israel were driven back by the onslaught of the servants of David."[40]

The idea of having two small units decide the outcome of a battle strikes the modern commander as madness. Yet, as Eisefeldt argues convincingly, it is likely that the battle at Gibeon's Pool happened much as the text describes it.[41] First, battles between individual combatants occurred frequently in the Bible, David and Goliath being but one example. The list of victories of David's champions given in II Samuel 23:8–39 are all victories of individual combatants. Second, it was commonly believed in all armies that the gods took a hand in victory and defeat. Small units of combatants could be used to decide the larger issue of victory or defeat because it was the gods who were guiding the outcome. When all the young men fell dead at Gibeon's Pool, the larger armies took up arms and continued the fight precisely because the gods had chosen no clear victor. Third, the manner of combat described in the text is known. Each man attempted to gain an advantage by seizing the head of his opponent with one hand, leaving his sword hand free to plunge his weapon into his opponent's side. A relief from biblical Gozan (modern Tel Halaf) derived from a time contemporary with the battle shows soldiers portrayed in just such a posture as described by the text.[42] The practice of individual combat is found in Ugarit and elsewhere and it is probable that the Philistines adopted it from the Canaanites. Here we see it has been adopted by the Israelites as well. It is interesting, however, that the term used to describe the weapons of the warriors at Gibeon's Pool is *helqat hassurim* which seems to mean a flint knife of some sort.[43] This is puzzling in light of the fact that the iron sword and long iron dagger were in common use at the time.

Once the two armies clashed, the army of Ishbaal suffered the worst of it and attempted to retreat. Joab's army pursued cautiously, but Asael, Joab's younger brother, struck out alone after Abiner, overtaking him, and bringing him to combat. "So Abiner struck him [Asael] in the belly with the butt of his spear, which came out his back. He fell down and died there in his tracks."[44] The armies caught up with one another, but both commanders agreed to break off the fighting and permit both sides to withdraw so that Joab called off the army and let Abiner and his men retreat. Abiner marched on to his base at Mahanaim, and Joab marched all night back to Hebron.[45] Joab assembled his army to make an account of the battle. It was clear that Abiner's army had been badly mauled. "Joab, when he had returned from the pursuit of Abiner, assembled the entire army. Nineteen men in addition to Asael were found missing from the servants of David, who, however, had slain three hundred and sixty of the Benjaminites, Abiner's men."[46] It is worth noting, too, that the army of Ishbaal is referred to as "the men of Israel," a term that implies the militia levy,[47] while David's men are called "the servants of David," which connotes non-militia troops, perhaps his old comrades, his bodyguard, some Judean professionals, and the new corps of Philistine mercenaries. David was already building a professional army upon which he would rely completely as time passed relegating the militia levy to a secondary role in his military adventures.

THE MURDERS OF ABINER AND ISHBAAL

The text tells us that after the clash at Gibeon's Pool, "the fighting between the house of Saul and the house of David dragged out, with David growing stronger and stronger and the house of Saul growing weaker and weaker."[48] David maneuvered strategically to outflank Ishbaal's position in Gilead by marrying Maachah, the daughter of Talmai, king of Geshur, a kingdom that bordered upon Gilead. For almost two years, the war had been going badly for Ishbaal, something that could not have escaped the attention of Abiner. Although the text suggests a falling out between the two men over Abiner's attempt to possess one of Ishbaal's concubines, which in the Near East might be taken as an attempt to establish a rival claim to the throne, it is hardly likely that such a pragmatist as Abiner would be motivated to risk all he possessed over a personal insult. More likely he had concluded that the war was going to be lost in any event, and if he remained loyal to Ishbaal, he had only his own execution to look forward to. Thus Abiner decided to defect while he still had something of value to offer David. The text tells us that "Abiner sent messengers to David as his representatives to say, "Make a pact with me, and my influence will be on your side, bringing all Israel [the army] over to you."[49] David shrewdly accepted the offer, and Abiner journeyed to Hebron and made an agreement to change sides. What he was promised in return is not recorded, but it may have been command of David's army once the war was over.

The terms of the agreement were quickly rendered irrelevant when Abiner was murdered by Joab. Samuel attempts to relieve David of any guilt in the treachery by suggesting that Joab killed Abiner as a *go'el haddam* or "redeemer of blood," that is, a man who owes a blood debt because Abiner had slain Asael, Joab's younger brother.[50] But Joab himself tells us that his reason for killing Abiner was purely military, that is that Abiner had come to David's court "to learn your going out and your coming in and to learn everything else you do,"[51] using the term *yasa uba*, a term usually used to refer to military maneuvers.[52] In short, Joab suspected Abiner of seeking military intelligence to reverse the course of the war. Josephus, himself a general, suggests in Antiquities 7.31, 36 that Joab suspected that Abiner had been promised command of the army and killed him to forestall his own replacement.[53]

Whoever acted for what motive, the truth is that Abiner could not have been permitted to live under any circumstances. With Saul dead and Ishbaal on the verge of defeat, Abiner was the most famous soldier in Israel. As far as we know, the army was loyal to him, and, most important from David's perspective, Abiner was a relative of Saul and had a claim to thc throne by virtue of blood, something David did not possess. It would have been a fatal foolishness to permit Abiner to live under any circumstances. Later David moved to have the entire remaining Saulid bloodline exterminated. Only the crippled son of Jonathan, whom David kept a prisoner at court, was permitted to live. The removal of Abiner was a bold strategic stroke in another sense: it struck at the morale of the Israelite army. Abiner's death was demoralizing as II Samuel 4:1 tells us, "When Ishbaal son of Saul heard that Abiner had died in Hebron, his courage flagged, and all Israel was dismayed." That David knew that Abiner's soldiers would blame him for the murder of their chief seems evident from the unusual funeral arrangements he ordered for Abiner. The text tells us that "[t]hen David said to Joab and all the people who were with him, 'Tear your clothes, put on sackcloth, and wail in Abiner's path!' King David himself followed behind the bier."[54] This was unusual for it was Joab and not David who led the funeral procession with a substantial part of the army in attendance. It is unlikely that Abiner traveled to Hebron without a substantial bodyguard of his own. With their chief murdered, it was not unlikely that Abiner's bodyguard would try to avenge their commander by killing Joab or even David himself. Never one to take chances, David arranged to protect himself against assassination.[55]

It is intriguing that Joab was not punished for Abiner's killing, nor was he punished for the later slaying of Abshalom, David's son, nor later for the murder of Amasa. If, as the text suggests, these murders were carried out without any complicity on David's part, then why was Joab not punished? The obvious suspicion is that, the text aside, Joab was acting on David's orders. Another answer is that Joab was David's blood relative. I Chronicles 2:13–16 informs us that Joab, David's field general, Abishai, his commander of the Thirty, and Asahel were David's nephews by his sister Zeruiah. Amasa, who led the army in Abshalom's revolt, was also a blood relative, the son of David's sister Abigail.[56] David not only forgave Amasa his sedition, but also made him commander of his army. It appears that when all was said and done, blood was thicker than water in David's court. Or, as has been suggested,

David's relatives were not punished because they were acting in David's interests, even if without direct orders.

With Abiner out of the way and the military tide flowing against Ishbaal, it was only a matter of time before he, too, was killed. Ishbaal was the legitimate blood heir to the Saulid dynasty, and David's claim to the throne would always be in doubt as long as Ishbaal lived. David had a very compelling interest in Ishbaal's death. The text tells us that two of Ishbaal's captains, Baanah and Rekhab, plotted to kill Ishbaal although no motive is offered. The two assassins approached Ishbaal's house during the heat of the day as Ishbaal was taking a midday rest. "The portress of the house had been gathering wheat; she had nodded and fallen asleep. So Rekhab and Baanah, his brother, slipped by and went into the house, where Ishbaal was lying upon a couch in his bedchamber. They struck him and killed him cutting off his head, took it and travelled the Arabah road all night."[57] With Ishbaal's head in their possession, the assassins hurried to David's court where they expected to be rewarded for their deed. Instead David had them executed which the text suggests was sufficient proof of David's noncomplicity in regicide.

The tale is suspicious from the outset. Ishbaal's house was not an ordinary house but an armed and fortified stronghold after the manner of Saul's residence at Gibeah, and there is every reason to suppose that Saul's bodyguard, or some similar unit, protected Ishbaal. Its absence is unexplained. The text tells us that the doorway to the king's residence was guarded by a single old woman who had fallen asleep. Even if this were usually the case, one would have thought that with Abiner recently murdered, the king's residence would have been the subject of heightened security. The ease with which the murderers escaped is also suspicious, since the text tells of no attempt at pursuit by Ishbaal's bodyguard. Finally, their arrival in David's court speaks for itself. The whole drama suggests an elaborate plot which, at the very least, had to involve the captain of the king's bodyguard, for only he was in a position to "security strip" the target, that is, to remove or reduce the guard around the king. Whoever killed Ishbaal, it was very unlikely that they acted alone. Once more, however, the primary beneficiary of the assassination was David.

With Ishbaal's death the hopes of the northern Israelite tribes to remain free of Philistine control came crashing down. The Philistine presence in the Jezreel after Gilboa, their renewed occupation of the high country, and the political and military defeat of the Israelite army of the northern tribes by David, whom, we might surmise, was viewed by the northerners as a Philistine vassal carrying out their strategic design, combined to threaten their very existence. Under these circumstances their approach to David to accept Ishbaal's throne and become king over all Israel must have been a desperate act. David was the only Israelite military or political leader who could protect the independence of the northern tribes against Philistine influence. Their alignment with David was not a consequence of any claim or loyalty to the throne, but of desperate necessity.[58] And so "they came to the king at Hebron. King David made a pact with them at Hebron before Yahweh, and they anointed David king over Israel."[59] David was 30 years old when he became king of Israel, and he ruled for 40 years.

THE PHILISTINE WARS

The questions of when David's battles against the Philistines occurred and when he captured Jerusalem have been debated over and over again. The capture of Jerusalem has been placed before the battles with the Philistines, between them, and after them.[60] The II Samuel text portrays the capture of Jerusalem as having occurred shortly after David was anointed king at Hebron and before the Philistine wars. However, given that the arrangement of the textual material is more thematic than historical and was organized later, the problem of the order in which the events occurred remains insoluble. The military historian is forced to arrange the chronology on some other grounds in order to make political and military sense of the events recorded in the text. The following chronology is suggested for ordering the events described in this section. (1) After Ishbaal's death, David became king of Israel uniting Israel and Judah under one king. It is probable that the killing of the Saulids occurred during this period as well. (2) The unified Israelite monarchy represented a defeat for Philistine national security strategy and the Philistines moved with military force to crush the new regime by attacking David in Hebron. (3) David engaged the Philistines in a series of battles defeating them and gaining control of the hill country. (4) With the hill country secure, David attacked and captured Jerusalem and later made it his new capital. He also transferred the Ark of the Covenant to Jerusalem replacing Shiloh as the most important seat of national worship. A short time later David defeated the Philistines in a major campaign that finally brought them under Israelite control if not occupation. (5) With the new Israelite nation united, David undertook a series of wars leading ultimately to the establishment of an imperial state which David bequeathed to his son, Solomon.[61] The text tells us that David ruled in Hebron for seven and a half years while Ishbaal ruled in Mahanaim for two years. This suggests that the civil war raged for two years until Ishbaal's death and that the Philistine wars probably occurred over a four-year period prior to David's capture of Jerusalem. One final battle with the Philistines occurred sometime after the capture of Jerusalem.

Philistine support for David had always sought to weaken the Israelites by the old practice of divide and conquer. The strategic goal was to prevent the emergence of a single unified Israelite state. To this end the Philistines supported David against Ishbaal and interposed themselves between the two camps in the hill country. With the anointing of David as king of all Israel, Philistine policy collapsed in shambles and they took immediate steps to destroy the new regime. The text tells us that "[w]hen the Philistines heard that David had been anointed king over Israel, they came up in search of him, but when David heard of this, he went down to the stronghold,"[62] suggesting that the Philistine motives were to kill or capture David and dismantle the monarchy and its army. The Philistines moved directly up the Elah Valley moving toward its northern head at Rephaim.[63] The "lowlands of Rephaim" mentioned in the text as the place of the Philistine deployment is southeast of Jerusalem. Its occupation by the Philistines permitted them to drive a wedge between the two Israelite kingdoms blocking any attempt at reenforcement by the militia forces of the northern tribes. The Philistines already had access to the hill country and the Jebusite city of Jerusalem was on friendly terms permitting them free movement under the city's walls. The Philistines moved up the valley toward the central spine and camped close to the city itself in preparation for further operations against David's army.

I Chronicles 11:15–16 offers us an insight into Philistine tactical thinking when it tells us that "[t]hree of the thirty chiefs went down among the crags to David, to the cave of Adullam, while a division of Philistines was encamped in the Valley of Rephaim. At the time David was in the fortress and a Philistine garrison was stationed at Bethlehem." If the Philistines expected to find David in or near Hebron, the seat of his government, why did they deploy their forces around the southern slope of Jerusalem? The Chronicles text suggests the answer when it tells us that a Philistine garrison had taken up positions in Bethlehem. Hebron was now facing two Philistine armies positioned to prevent David's escape or to prevent reenforcement of the city. These forces were deployed to attack from Jerusalem whose approaches to Hebron were less steep than from the south and permitted the Philistines the advantage of attacking downhill. The Philistine plan was tactically sound. They moved up the Valley of Elah, which was already under their control, into the Rephaim Valley, which was close to Jerusalem and controlled by the friendly Jebusites. At the same time Philistine units moved into Bethlehem to act as a blocking force, perhaps to trap David between the two cities. Once in position, the Philistines could attack Hebron from the north to trap David and his army in the city or else force him to flee southward into the open desert.

The Philistine troops "spread out in the lowlands of Rephaim" as they moved into position. Tidwell argues that the term *nts*, to "spread out," is a military term usually associated with a specific type of military operation, namely, a small-scale raid using small numbers of troops to strike swiftly and then withdraw.[64] He suggests that the first battle with the Philistines was little more than a skirmish. However, the use of small units screening the advance of a larger force was certainly not unknown in Philistine tactics and the reference could as easily apply to them. As we have seen, the Philistines had become adept at the use of mobile chariot-infantry teams to clear the main force route of advance or to scavenge the countryside as they did at Michmash. The Philistine tactical plan suggests that they expected to find David in Hebron, and the use of tactical screens either to protect the main force advance or to cast a wide net in their search for David would not have been unexpected.

David, himself a talented tactician and, perhaps, because of his pathological fear of being trapped in a walled city, which he probably acquired in his outlaw days,[65] abandoned Hebron and "went down to the stronghold" that I Chronicles 11:16 identifies as *mesudat adullam*, the stronghold of Adullam, a refuge in the *shephelah*, some 16 miles southwest of Jerusalem, which David had used during his outlaw days.[66] The decision not to defend Hebron was sound. David's army was too small, perhaps no more than 2,000 men, to defend the city's walls. Nor were his troops trained in defensive siege tactics. Their forte was mobile hit-and-run warfare, making maximum tactical use of the terrain, skills that could not be brought to bear in the defense.[67] To defend Hebron would have permitted the Philistines to ravage the countryside and towns of the new state at will which surely would have weakened support for the new king. At Adullam, David's army was out from the confines of Hebron where it could make maximum use of its tactical abilities and was positioned to observe the Philistine advance as it maneuvered along a parallel track up the valley and into position around Rephaim.

The text is sparse concerning the details of the battle, telling us only that David inquired of Yahweh, " 'Shall I go up against the Philistines? Will you hand them over to me?' 'Go up!' Yahweh told him. 'For I shall indeed hand them over to you!' So David entered Baal-perazim and defeated them there."[68] The phrase "go up" suggests an attack near the front[69] but not necessarily a frontal attack. One can only speculate that in typical Israelite tactical tradition David observed the movement of the enemy army even as his own position remained unknown to the Philistine reconnaissance teams. Moving along a parallel track to the Philistine route of advance, he would have been able to observe and locate any terrain that afforded him a tactical advantage. The sense of the text is that the Philistines were not yet deployed but were still "spread out" as they moved toward Rephaim, for the battle is not recorded as having been fought in the Rephaim. This implies that David might have struck the Philistine army while it was still in column of march having first penetrated its reconnaissance screen to move into position or, equally likely, struck the column's head as it was moving into its assembly area to encamp. In either case, the attack came as a surprise and may have panicked the Philistines who fled back down the valley as they had in previous battles. The defeat was tactically but not strategically decisive, and David and the Philistines were now openly at arms.

Although the text places David's second battle with the Philistines right after the first, we cannot be certain that the two battles actually occurred in so short a time. The fact that the Philistines advanced along the same route into the same valley—the lowlands of Rephaim—seems to suggest, however, that the Philistine commander, having been surprised and driven off the first time, may have assembled a larger force and attacked a few days later. If so, then David and his army were already in position on the heights where they could observe the Philistine route of advance. Watching the Philistines advance, David inquired of Yahweh for tactical advice as he had done before. This time Yahweh advised against a frontal assault saying, " 'You must not go up!' said Yahweh. 'Circle around them and approach them in front of Bachaim. Then, when you hear the sound of the wind in the asherahs of Bachaim, look sharp, for Yahweh will have marched out ahead of you to attack the Philistine camp!' David did as Yahweh had instructed him, and he defeated the Philistines from Geba to Gezer."[70]

The text leaves the location of Bachaim unclear, implying only that it was either a town or a region, probably somewhere north of Jerusalem.[71] The mention of *asherahs* is puzzling because they were wooden pedestals that served as cult objects, which might suggest that the location of the battle was near a shrine of some kind.[72] *Asherahs* are also thought to be a row of trees somehow associated with the worship of the goddess Ashtarte. The description of the battle in I Chronicles 14:14–15 tells us nothing of *asherahs*, suggesting instead that the sound of the wind was in the Baka-bushes. Further, Yahweh's tactical advice is somewhat clearer. "God said to him [David], 'Do not attack them directly, but turn away from them and come at them in front of the Baka-bushes; and when you hear the sound of the steps in the tops of the Baka-bushes, then proceed to do battle for God has gone out before you to destroy the Philistine army.' " Gichon and Herzog are probably correct that David set a small force before the Philistines as bait that retreated, drawing the Philistines after them[73] to set the trap.

The Philistine troops would have been marching since morning and were approaching an area of thick woods sometime shortly before noon, just as the heat of the day was making itself felt. The text tells us that David attacked the Philistine *camp*. It was too early in the day for the Philistines to stop their march and go into an overnight encampment. One imagines, then, that the Philistine main body, following its lead elements who had been chasing some of David's men up the ridge, called a halt and set the men to rest just before midday somewhere near a thick wood. David's main army must have been hidden in the woods, perhaps some distance back from the wood line. A superb tactician, he not only took advantage of the terrain but the weather as well. Each day the sea breeze from the Mediterranean reaches Jerusalem around noontime, arriving quite suddenly and sometimes with strong gusts. This, then, was "the sound of [Yahweh's] steps in the tops of the Baka-bushes," of which the text speaks. The sound of the wind in the trees and bushes would have permitted David's army to move from their positions deep in the woods to the tree line next to the Philistine assembly area without being detected, catching the Philistines by complete surprise and unformed for battle. Under these conditions the battle could easily have turned into a slaughter

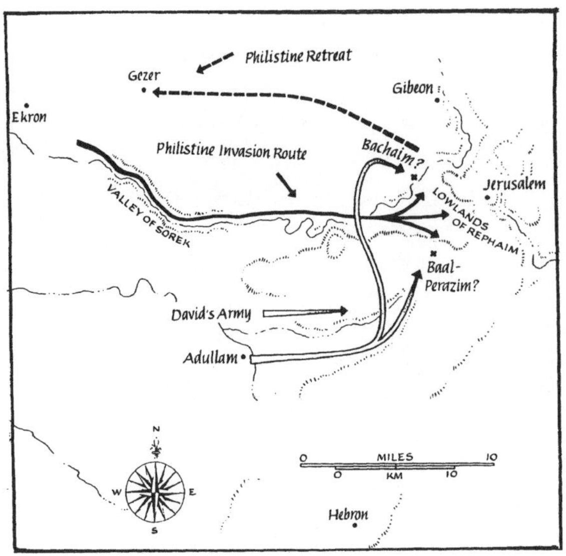

Figure 7.3 David's Philistine Wars

with the Philistine army coming completely apart and running for their lives. Figure 7.3 portrays the two battles. A defeat of such magnitude would explain the text's claim that "David . . . defeated the Philistines from Gibeon all the way to Gezer."[74] Whereas the first encounter had resulted in a tactical victory for the Israelites, the second battle seems to have produced a defeat of strategic proportions for the Philistines, driving them completely from the hill country once and for all. Never again do we hear of Philistine troops or garrisons in the hill country.

It is likely that there were other skirmishes between the two sides before David finally settled the issue by winning a major victory over the Philistines and occupying some of their territory. II Samuel 21:15–22 records the heroic feats of David's warriors and mentions three additional battlefields where their great deeds were accomplished: Gob, Nob, and Gath. Gob is probably Gibbethon, a city close to Gezer, while Gath is not the well-known Philistine capital of Achish—other texts note that Achish was still king of Gath in the first three years of Solomon's rule—but probably a northern Philistine town whose location is to be sought in the vicinity of Gezer.[75] These battles, then, were fought on the edge of the territory of the Philistines, and it is unlikely that David penetrated deeply into Philistia or occupied its primary cities. Moreover, although David "defeated the Philistines from Gibeon all the way to Gezer," by no means did he capture Gezer, which remained a Canaanite town closely tied to the Egyptians until Pharaoh Siamun transferred the town to Solomon as part of his daughter's wedding dowry.

It seems probable that the series of clashes ultimately resulted in a major battle in which David finally brought the Philistines to heel. II Samuel 8:1 tells us that "[a]fter this David defeated the Philistines and subjugated them, taking the common land out of Philistine control."[76] The Anchor Bible emphasizes the use of the word *hammigras* to designated the rural "common land" between Israelite cities that was often occupied or frequently raided by the Philistines. Malamat, citing the original Hebrew, translates the same verse as follows: "After this David defeated the Philistines and subdued them, and David took the maetaeq haammah out of the hands of the Philistines," which he suggests means that David took some Philistine borderlands from them after the defeat.[77] The text employs the term "Methegh-ammah out of the hand of the Philistines." The term *Methegh-ammah* literally means "Bridle of the Mother," which has been understood by some scholars to mean the capital city of the Philistines.[78] I Chronicles 18:1 interprets this to mean Gath, although as noted earlier, it is not the Gath of Achish but a smaller town somewhere near Gezer. Taken together the texts suggest that David defeated the Philistines in a major engagement and that, perhaps, some Philistine borderlands and towns were absorbed by Israel into its territory. Mazar notes, for example, that in at least one instance a Philistine town near the mouth of the Yarkon River (modern Tel Qasileh) shows strong evidence of having been destroyed and resettled by Israelites during this time.[79] Beyond this, there is no evidence of military conquest among the other Philistine towns or other Canaanite cities on the coastal plain or in the Jezreel Valley, although it is likely that Israelite garrisons would have been posted along the coast from Joppa to Mount Carmel if only as a precaution.[80] More likely the Philistine defeat was of such drastic proportions that they ultimately came to terms with the Israelites and devised an arrangement that guaranteed Philistia's continued existence but diminished its military power.

Two sound strategic reasons influenced David's decision to come to terms with the Philistines rather than occupy their territories and govern them directly as he did later in other border states. First, although Egyptian power had been seriously weakened on the land-bridge as a consequence of domestic upheaval within Egypt itself, Egypt still retained close relations with Gaza and Gezer and undoubtedly still saw itself as the chief power and claimant in southern Palestine.[81] Any Israelite attempt to destroy Philistia and annex its territory would have amounted to a serious shift in the power balance and would have been viewed with great alarm in Egypt. David had to reckon with the possibility of an Egyptian invasion to preserve the territorial integrity of Philistia if he chose to attempt annexation. Some indication of the degree of Egyptian strategic interest in the area can be gained by noting that as soon as Egypt had settled her domestic difficulties, Pharaoh Siamun of the Twenty-first Dynasty conducted a military expedition into southern Palestine precisely to reaffirm Egypt's claim to the area.[82] The expedition was diplomatically rebuffed by Solomon and resulted in the transfer of the important garrison city of Gezer from Egypt to Israel.

A second strategic reason was that Israel's economic survival depended on keeping the trade routes across the land-bridge open and secure. Sidon and Tyre had already established themselves as the primary naval powers in the area and had cooperated successfully with the Philistines who, as a land power, had done an excellent job of keeping the coastal routes open to trade. Israel had neither the manpower nor the inclination (Israel has never been a naval power) to dismantle and then attempt to reconstruct this already efficient set of circumstances. It was much easier and far less expensive to come to a diplomatic accommodation with all concerned to preserve the status quo. One can easily imagine that Israel may have collected some share of the trade tariffs that had previously gone to the Philistines, or that Israelite merchants were given economic concessions. These details aside, however, a stable peace served the interests of all parties. And Aharaoni is probably correct in asserting that some Palestinian cities and towns submitted peacefully to the new Israelite regime.[83]

There is not a word in the text about what happened to the Canaanite city-states once the Philistines came under Israelite influence. Later we learn that Solomon divided the country into 12 administrative districts, and that districts 2, 3, 4, and 5 were in territory controlled by the Canaanites.[84] This would imply that these districts were acquired some time previously, and since there is no evidence that Solomon himself conquered them, it is a reasonable suggestion that these areas were integrated into the Israelite state by David. Moreover, the Canaanite states were too economically valuable and strategically placed—and their military establishments too strong—to permit them to remain independent under the new Israelite order. The only question is whether David had to use force to bring the Canaanite city-states under control. There is evidence from archaeology that some of the more important Canaanite fortifications were demolished during this time.[85] Perhaps it was necessary for David to demonstrate his willingness to use force in a few instances before the Canaanite rulers came to realize that a peaceful incorporation into the Israelite new order was the wisest course of action. Once annexation was achieved, of course, the military establishments of both the Philistine and Canaanite states would have fallen into David's hands for use in pursuing his imperial ambitions.

An important question for military historians is why David succeeded against the Philistines where Saul failed. Despite the disaster at Mount Gilboa, Saul had shown himself an excellent field commander and good tactician, defeating the Philistines in a number of important battles. It is common to cite Saul's depression for his failure at Gilboa. Even if true, this could hardly account for his earlier successes as well. David, of course, had spent years in the service of the Philistines and was more familiar with Philistine tactical thinking and execution than Saul. Moreover, David's years as an outlaw on the run probably conditioned his own thinking to the use of speed, deception, and surprise, all tactical devices he used at one time or another against his adversaries. If Saul was a "muddy boots general" in the mold of U. S. Grant, David was more the guerrilla fighter in the image of John Singleton Mosby, the famous Gray Ghost of the Confederacy. History, especially military history, never reveals its alternatives. Had David been in command at Gilboa, would he have succeeded where Saul failed? Would Saul have failed where David succeeded at Baal-perazim or the Bachaim wood? There are, of course, no answers; only the eternal debate among soldiers seeking to measure their own mettle against history's great generals.

THE CAPTURE OF JERUSALEM

The questions of when and how David captured Jerusalem have been debated by historians for decades. The difficulty arises from the text, which seems to suggest that David's attack on the city occurred right after he was anointed king of Judah.[86] This has led some scholars to suggest that David moved quickly to establish a new capital as a rallying point for the new nation, moving the Ark of the Covenant to the city to establish it as the national religious center as well.[87] Under these circumstances, the capture of the city would have been the reason for the Philistine attack so that the Philistine wars were fought after the city was captured even though David did not make it his capital for five more years.[88] While intriguing, this chronology is not convincing.

First, in the same chapter, II Samuel 5:17, the text tells us that the attack occurred "when the Philistines heard that David had been anointed king over Israel, they came up in search of him," making it clear that it was David's anointing per se and not an attack on Jerusalem that prompted the Philistine attack. Second, while Jerusalem was a difficult nut to crack militarily, in fact the security of the city had been for centuries guaranteed more by diplomatic and strategic considerations than by military ones. Jerusalem's strategic location guarding the north-south and east-west roads across the central spine made it extremely valuable to the great powers who controlled the southern coastal plain. In order to ensure freedom of movement across the spine, first the Egyptians and then the Philistines seem to have guaranteed the independence of the city to prevent it from falling into hostile hands. So it was that when Joshua defeated the five Canaanite kings he did not attack Jerusalem even though Adonizedek, its king, had led the coalition against him. The Egyptians maintained garrisons on the southern coastal plain and would have viewed such an attack with alarm and moved to prevent it from succeeding. Saul, too, never attacked Jerusalem even as he attempted to control the outlets to the central spine from the valleys below. While the text is silent on the subject, it is a reasonable assumption that the Philistines, who saw themselves as the heirs to the Egyptians in Palestine, would have viewed an attack on the city with similar alarm. The strategic key to David having any chance to capture Jerusalem, then, lay in first driving the Philistines from the hill country so that they could not come to the aid of the city during the attack. The removal of the Philistines, who had reoccupied key places in the hill country after Saul's defeat at Gilboa, could only have been achieved by the Philistine defeats recorded in the text and described earlier, even though the wars are presented in the text as having occurred after David captured Jerusalem. It is probable that the text is out of order.

That David cleared the high country of Philistine garrisons can be reasonably inferred from the story of the transfer of the Ark to Jerusalem told in II Samuel 6:1–18. The last previous textual mention of the Ark is in I Samuel 7:1 when, after the Philistines returned it, it came to rest in the town of Kiriath-jearim, literally, "city of forests." This town was part of the Gibeonite tetrapolis located eight miles west of Jerusalem and commanded the road from the central spine down to the Beth-horon pass and the *shephelah*. Its possession was paramount to the security of the central ridge, so much so that Saul broke the oath of peace that Joshua had made with the Gibeonites attacking the town and forcibly removing its population and resettling it with Israelites.[89] The location of the town was militarily so important that it is inconceivable that the Philistines did not reoccupy it after Saul's death. This would have made it impossible for David to move the Ark as long as the Philistines occupied the town. The transfer of the Ark to Jerusalem, then, could only have been accomplished *after* David had driven the Philistines from the hill country.

From the perspective of tactical necessity, then, it seems more reasonable to conclude that David first fought a series of engagements with the Philistines that resulted in their being driven from the hill country around Jerusalem which then opened up the opportunity for an attack against Jerusalem itself. For the first time in memory the city was left without the protection, if only temporarily, of some great power to guarantee its independence. And while it is common to assume that David attacked the city in order to make it his new capital, there were other sound reasons for attempting to occupy Jerusalem. It was the strongest remaining foreign outpost on the central spine controlling military movement and economic transit in all directions. Controlling the city would give the new Israelite state an important fortress from which to defend against future Philistine attempts to reoccupy the ridge. Moreover, if David were to control all Israel, the Jebusite outpost would have to be taken sooner or later. David's defeat of the Philistines and their evacuation of the hill country presented an opportunity that David exploited fully by attacking the city. It is a good commander who can recognize when the tide of circumstance has turned to his favor and move quickly to take advantage of it. While the significance of David's capture of Jerusalem is often expressed in religious terms, in fact David's success must be seen as a military achievement of the first magnitude. In the long history of the city, only two other generals, Nebuchadnrezzar of Assyria and Titus of Rome, have ever taken the city by direct attack.[90] There can be no clearer evidence of David's brilliance as a field commander than his success in capturing Jerusalem.

And Jerusalem was no soft target, its walls being among the finest examples in all antiquity of defensive military fortifications.[91] The City of David stood on the southeastern spur of the Temple Mount protected by steep slopes on three sides, the Kidron Valley to the east, the Hinnom Valley to the south, and the Tyropoeon Valley to the west.[92] To the east, south, and west, the ground fell steeply away so that even minor defensive fortifications were sufficient to give an attacker a difficult time of it. To the north there is a saddle between the citadel and the main ridge, and it was here that the strongest defenses were found. The Jebusite walls were constructed of rough-hewn, ill-fitting blocks of stone with the spaces between the stones filled with rubble. Every six courses of stone the wall was slightly recessed so as to form a series of steps several feet in height and six inches deep. Two of these walls stood on the north side of the ridge forming a double line of defense.[93] Even the large and well-equipped armies of Assyria and Rome found the city no easy objective to overcome. For an army presumed to be the size of David's with no siege capability at all, the task might have appeared impossible.

The old Jebusite stronghold was well equipped to weather a siege. It had an abundant virgin spring, the Gihon, located under the Ophel, that supplied its water directly through a vertical tunnel. The city itself enclosed an area of about 16 acres.[94] Using Yadin's method of calculating the populations of ancient cities employed earlier, the population of Jebusite Jerusalem during David's time can be estimated to have been approximately 3,840 people, or 240 persons per square urban acre multiplied by 16 acres. Approximately 25 percent of the population, or approximately 1,000 men, would have been available for defense. Sixteen acres of enclosed land requires a wall of approximately 1,540 yards long to encompass. Given their population, the Jebusites could have deployed one defender for every 1.5 yards of wall, a formidable defensive force against an army with no siege train. How, then, did David capture Jerusalem?

The text explains the victory this way. "Then the king and his men went to Jerusalem, to the Jebusites, the inhabitants of the region; but they told David, 'You shall not come in here!' . . . So David seized the stronghold of Zion, which is now the City of David, and he said at that time, 'Whoever smites a Jebusite, let him strike at the windpipe, for David hates the lame and the blind!' David occupied the stronghold and called it the City of David. He built a city around it from the Milo inward."[95] The text is lacking in details and even presents additional puzzles. What, for example, was the size of David's army arrayed against the substantial defensive force of the Jebusites? The text suggest that the army consisted of "the king and his men," or the men that David had attracted from his outlaw days and the Ziklag period prior to his being anointed king. Mazar suggests that at this time that force could not have numbered more than 600 men, larger than the 400 men the text noted were with David in his early outlaw days, probably divided into three 200-man combat battalions, each under the command of one of David's "Three" mentioned later in the text.[96] While all these troops were *ozre milhamah*, that is experienced combat warriors, their numbers were too few to successfully carry out an assault upon Jerusalem.

The small size of David's army, as inferred from the text, has led some to suggest that the only way David could have captured the city was through a ruse. This explanation has focused upon the use of the term *sinnor* or *tsinor* which usually means throat or windpipe, but which some scholars have interpreted to mean "watercourse" or "water channel."[97] In this view, then, when David shouted to his men, "Whoever smites a Jebusite, let him strike at the windpipe," he was really ordering an attack on the "watercourse" or "water channel." But what is the watercourse? Some have suggested that it was a tunnel, "a rock hewn partly subterranean passage" that led from the town down to the eastern slope of the ridge to the Gihon spring[98] accessing the city's water supply. In this view, David first struck at the "stronghold of Zion" located on the northern section of the narrow ridge of the Temple Mount and captured it by a *coup de main*. Because the stronghold was separated from the city itself, David next had to find a way to gain entrance to the city. Having discovered (or been told of) the *sinnor*, David's men, led by Joab, moved through the tunnel, gained access to the city, and attacked the city from within, probably at some point gaining control of the gate and throwing it open to the rest of David's men, although this is speculation. In this manner, then, David and his small force of warriors could have captured the city.[99]

While intriguing, the explanation for David's success at Jerusalem is open to doubt on two counts: (1) that the size of David's army inferred from the Samuel text is incorrect, and (2) that the watercourse could not have played the important role attributed to it. As to the size of David's army, I Chronicles 11:4 suggests that David's army was considerably larger than implied by the Samuel text when it says, "Then David and all Israel went to Jerusalem." The term "all Israel" is usually taken to mean the militia army, or sometimes the army and the elders.[100] The army referred to in the Chronicles text is the militia levy led by tribal officers and not David's corps of professional soldiers, "the king's men," noted in the Samuel text. Moreover, it was unlikely that David had recruited the three Philistine mercenary corps, the Cherethites, Pelethites, and the unit from Gath, by the time of the assault on Jerusalem.[101] The Philistines, after all, were still at war with David at the time and were unlikely to permit Philistine professionals to serve in the army of their enemy. The text can reasonably be interpreted to mean that shortly after his anointing as King of Judah and, perhaps, even before the initial battles with the Philistines and certainly before the attack on Jerusalem, the militia armies of the northern tribes had sent units to serve under David at Hebron. If so, then the force available to David to attack Jerusalem was much larger than has usually been understood.

The text offers some support for this view in I Chronicles 12:24, where we are presented with a list of tribal militia units that joined David at Hebron "to deliver the kingdom of Saul to him in accordance with the word of Yahweh." Then again in verse 39 we are told that "[a]ll these men were warriors in battle array who came to David at Hebron with singleness of purpose, to make David king over all Israel; also all the rest of Israel was unanimous in wanting to make David king." It seems reasonable that the negotiations between David and the representatives of the northern tribes as to the terms of their support for his kingship involved, of necessity, the most important elements of the tribal union, that is, not only the elders (as noted in II Samuel where there is no mention of the presence of the army at Hebron) but also the men with the weapons and the greatest ability to resist any agreement, namely, the army. Moreover, the tribal militia commanders often saw themselves as representing the people as much as the elders, for it was the commanders who led the clans of the people in war. As events later revealed, the army played a much larger role in the selection of northern kings than had been the case of the southern tribes.[102] This tradition made itself evident when the army supported the attempt by Abshalom to remove David by military force. Having agreed to the terms that, no doubt, included a promise from David to remove the Philistine threat to the Jezreel and the northern tribes, the text implies that the militia commanders of the northern tribes made their units available to David, who, we may surmise, may even have had them at his disposal in the initial battles against the Philistines. The composition and size of the militia units that came to Hebron is clearly recorded in I Chronicles 12:24–41. Employing Mendenhall's method of calculating the size of the *alaphim* along with our earlier estimates of the size of the Israelite population, the size of the militia force that joined David at Hebron could have numbered approximately 20,000 men.[103] If the analysis is correct, then, the force at David's disposal with which to drive the Philistines off the central ridge and attack Jerusalem was much larger than has been heretofore supposed.

There is also some evidence to suggest that the tale of the watercourse is not correct. The watercourse is known in archaeological circles as Warren's Shaft. Discovered by Charles Warren in 1867, it seemed at the time to lend support to the implications of the text.[104] More recent archaeological excavations by K. Kenyon, however, cast some doubt on the role that the tunnel could have played in David's capture of the city.[105] It is well known that Jerusalem had two water supply systems for use during a siege. One is the famous Siloam tunnel constructed during the time of Hezekiah and is, therefore, of no relevance to the time of David.[106] The other older system is Warren's Shaft and consists of a sloping tunnel and vertical connecting shaft. Until Kenyon's recent work, it was believed that the entry from the town into the water shaft system lay outside the city walls, which, of course, would have completely nullified its use as a water system during a siege, but would have been consistent with the theory that David's men gained entrance to the city via the watercourse.[107] But Kenyon's work makes it clear that the entrance to the water system lay *within* the fortified area, not outside it, making the Jebusite system congruent with the water supply systems known from other fortified sites.[108] It seems unlikely, then, that David could have captured Jerusalem by means of the watercourse. More probably, David's command to strike at the windpipes and throats of the Jebusites was just that, sound advice from an experienced commander to his troops, especially so if many of them were militia recruits and not David's usual professionals.

How, then, did David capture Jerusalem? The answer may be the same way that Joshua and Saul captured other cities, by violent storm. It is interesting that the description of the attack on Jerusalem contained in I Chronicles 9:4–9 makes no mention at all of the watercourse or any role it may have played in the attack. Instead, it offers a description that is much more consistent with the events associated with the storming of a city. Thus, the text says that David issued a challenge to his men saying, "whoever kills a Jebusite first will be chief and commander." Joab the son of Zeruiah went up first and so he became chief." The description is similar to one found in earlier Egyptian texts praising the courage of the first soldier to breach the wall in an attack by storm. Here is a parallel example from Thutmose III's chronicle of his attack on Kadesh as spoken by a brave Egyptian soldier. "His majesty sent forth every valiant man of his army, to breach the new wall which Kadesh had made. I was the one who breached it, being the first of every valiant man."[109] The Egyptians often rewarded the bravest men with their highest military decoration, *The Fly of Valor*, a small golden fly on a gold chain. It was not unusual, then, that Joab was rewarded with a promotion as a consequence of his bravery. The fact that he was also David's nephew probably played some part as well.

If, as we have suggested earlier, David's army was considerably larger than usually assumed, then capturing Jerusalem by storm would have been well within the military capability of David's force. The key, as it had been for Joshua and Saul, was numbers, the ability to place more attackers at shifting points along the wall than the defenders could successfully engage at any one point. The Jebusites could deploy about one man every 1.5 yards of wall in the defense. If David used only half the 20,000 or so men mentioned in the I Chronicles text as joining him at Hebron, the rest deployed in various positions along the approaches to the city to intercept any Philistine effort at relieving the city, then David could have deployed almost seven men per yard of wall in the attack, or about the same ratio that favored Joshua in his attack on Jericho. We might reasonably conclude then, if the Chronicles text is in fact describing an attack by storm against the city, and if the description of militia units as being at Hebron prior to the attack by the same text is also correct, that David may have taken Jerusalem in the same way previous Israelite commanders took other cities, by storm.

It is often noted that David took Jerusalem with the intention of making it the capital of the new united Israelite state. To be sure the city had much to recommend it. As a Jebusite city, it was untainted by the tribal rivalries that often plagued the Israelite tribal union. The violence that accompanied the civil war between Ishbaal and David, as well as the murders and treachery, probably made it impossible to restore Gibeah as the leading city of Israel. Hebron, David's capital, was too far south and far removed from the northern tribes to be acceptable.[110] Jerusalem had never been an Israelite city and in this sense, like Washington and Canberra, was neutral ground. The special status of Jerusalem as an entity separate from the tribal union was evident in the fact that it remained the personal possession of the king in much the same way that Roman Egypt remained the personal possession of Augustus.

But if David made Jerusalem his new capital, it is not clear that he intended to do so from the beginning. As suggested earlier, there were sufficient strategic and tactical reasons for capturing the city. The texts tell us that David ruled over Hebron for seven and a half years before taking up residence in Jerusalem. No matter when David captured the city, either right after his anointing or during the early Philistine wars, it appears that Hebron remained David's capital and base of operations for at least three years before he took up residence in Jerusalem. This delay suggests that David's attack on Jerusalem was probably motivated more by military considerations than political objectives.

The texts lend some support to this view. II Samuel 5:9 tells us that "David occupied the stronghold and called it the City of David. He built a city around it from the Milo inward." I Chronicles 11:7–8 provides more detail. "Because David took up residence in the fortress they called it the City of David. He built the city from around the Milo to the surrounding wall, while Joab restored the remainder of the city." The texts appear to suggest that the city's fortifications had been somehow destroyed so that later, when David finally occupied the stronghold, they needed significant rebuilding. Whether David took the city by ruse or storm, neither method would have usually caused widespread destruction to the city's walls. That the destruction was of some magnitude is implied by the I Chronicle use of the word *yehayyeh*, literally "salvaged" or "revitalized" to describe Joab's efforts to "salvage the remainder of the city."[111] It might be reasonably conjectured, then, that once David captured Jerusalem he set about reducing its fortifications by destroying some of its defensive walls probably in an effort to reduce its military value to any future enemy. This would suggest that David had no intention, at least not at this early date, to make Jerusalem his capital. Only later, the text tells us, after he had taken up residence in the citadel did the city become known as the City of David[112] and only then, having decided to make Jerusalem his new capital, did David begin to rebuild the city and its fortifications. Oesterley and Robinson note that even then David made no great effort to rebuild the old fortifications, but only strengthened the northeast corner of the outer wall, the Milo, from which he constructed a thin wall to close the breach that he had created earlier.[113] David seems to have left the task of "salvaging the remainder of the city" to Joab.

David's disinterest in the fixed fortifications of Jerusalem even after it had become his new capital is completely understandable given his own military experience as a commander of mobile forces who preferred to fight in the open to maximize the advantages of mobility, maneuver, and surprise. He readily abandoned Hebron when the Philistines first attacked him so that he could maneuver over difficult ground to take the enemy by surprise attack.

Later, when Absalom mounted a coup against him and was preparing to attack Jerusalem, David abandoned the city without hesitation, preferring to fight later in the forests of Gilead, terrain that afforded him the tactical advantage.[114] Like some other great commanders—Thutmose III, Philip of Macedon, Alexander the Great, Napoleon Bonaparte, George Patton, Heinz Guderian, and Avigdor Kahalani—David may have regarded the construction of fixed fortifications as "testimony to the colossal stupidity of generals."[115]

THE BORDER WARS: MOAB AND EDOM

Although David now controlled the hill country and Jerusalem, most Philistine and Canaanite cities remained outside Israelite control. David moved to reduce these potential centers of resistance, first by military force and then by diplomatic accommodation. It was at this time that the last phase of the wars with the Philistines occurred, resulting in the annexation of some Philistine lands and an eventual accommodation with the Canaanites as well. As a matter of strategic application, David had no choice but to subdue the Philistines and reduce their military forces for their armies were still formidable. Unless they were destroyed or rendered loyal diplomatically, David's back would have been exposed and his wars of conquest impossible.[116] Although no mention is made of the Canaanite city-states in the text, the previous analysis suggests that they were eventually brought into the Israelite orbit and their military establishments reduced.

This set of circumstances permitted David to acquire Philistine and Canaanite military units for use in his wars, for it was a long-established practice that a vassal owed military service to his king. David's service as Achish of Gath's vassal had made him thoroughly familiar with Philistine military capabilities, and it may have been around this time that David assembled his corps of Philistine mercenaries, the Cherethites, Pelethites, and Gittites, to serve as his personal bodyguard. The use of Philistine and Canaanite troops in the Davidic army raises the question of whether David employed chariots in his armies. Horses, of course, had been known in Israel and Canaan long before the Exodus. The Egyptian words for horse (*ssm.t*) and (*ibr*) as well as the word for chariot (*mrkbt*) are both Semitic loan words, that is Hebrew *soob* for horse and *merkaba* for chariot.[117] Contrary to what some have suggested, the Israelite resistance to the chariot was not a consequence of ignorance or low levels of military sophistication. The primary obstacles to the use of the chariot by the Israelites were the great expense of purchasing or manufacturing the vehicles, the lack of adequate grasslands or grain land that could be used to feed the animals, the lack of sufficient craftsmen to construct and maintain the machines, and the fact that until Davidic times the Israelites were more or less confined to the rugged hill country where chariots were not particularly militarily effective. Under David's new order, his Canaanite and Philistine "allies" could provide and maintain chariot units for David's army. Once the Israelites had gained access to the Jezreel and Transjordan, Israel became a net exporter of grain, evidence that there was sufficient surplus to supply the needs of a large number of chariot horses as well.[118] Moreover, once the Israelite state encompassed the Jezreel and the Transjordan and ran from Dan to Beersheba, chariot units became valuable military assets in long-range patrolling and fighting in open country, especially so given the Aramean menace to the north, an army that was highly "mechanized." Still, the use of chariots by David's army is not directly attested to by the text.[119] This may reflect a reluctance on the part of the author to credit Israel's former enemies with any role at all in David's victories or, perhaps, reflects David's preference for infantry while using chariots in only limited roles. It would be a prejudice that we would not find unusual in an old infantry general forced by events to adjust to new equipment.

Once all of Canaan had been brought under Israelite control, David ordered a census of the country. While the text places the census near the end of David's life, it is the preponderance of scholarly opinion that the census was actually carried out much earlier.[120] Having created an Israelite state, the problem for David was how to preserve it, and to do so required the establishment of a national army which required a knowledge of Israel's potential manpower strength. The military purpose of the census can be reasonably implied from the fact that David chose Joab, the commander of the army, to conduct it. I Chronicles 21:2 tells us that "David said to Joab and the princes of the people, 'Go, count Israel from Beersheba to Dan and bring the results to me so that I may know their number.' " The census seems to have encompassed greater Canaan but did not include Edom or Moab, which suggests that it was carried out sometime after the Philistine wars but before the attacks on Moab, Ammon, and Edom.

The results of the census are given in II Samuel 24:9. "And Joab gave the sum of the numbering of the people to the king: in Israel there were eight hundred thousand fighting men who could handle the sword, and the men of Judah were five hundred thousand." Using the method for calculating the size of the *alaphim* that we have used throughout this work, the figures noted earlier amount to 1,100 *alaphim* or about 66,000 men of military age which, using Yadin's method again, suggests a total Israelite population of some 200,000 to 240,000 people. Our earlier estimate of the Israelite population during the time of Saul was between 100,000 to 150,000, but included only those tribes in the hill country and Transjordan and did not include the northern tribes or Judah. With all of Canaan included, a general population of 200,000 to 240,000 is well within a reasonable range achieved by growth, accretion, assimilation, and adding the figures from the excluded tribes.

A manpower pool of 66,000 males of military age does not mean, of course, that all were called to or were fit for military service. One suspects that however many Philistine and Canaanite troops were attached to the Israelite army they would have reduced the number drawn from the general manpower pool. I Chronicles 27:1–23 provides an indication of the number of men available from the manpower pool that were actually called to active service. The text tells us that, "This is the roster of the sons of Israel by family heads, captains of thousands and hundreds together with their official agents who served the king in every matter pertaining to the divisions on duty in monthly relays throughout all the months of the year; each division consisted of 24 thousand men." The text goes on to list each tribal division. Using the same methods once more, the levy from each tribe comes to about 1,500 men, or an overall force of about 18,000 men ready for active duty by general mobilization, an effective levy of approximately one-third the general population of military age, a proportion found among other conscript armies of the period. Although the estimate must be taken cautiously (as should all previous estimates of manpower strength), the number is consistent with the 20,000 armed men that the text tells us descended on Hebron to anoint David king of all Israel.

This, then, was the military instrument that David had at his disposal to undertake his wars of conquest. A substantial part of David's army must have been comprised of professionals, including his old comrades from his outlaw days, the Thirty, who acted as advisors and special commanders, at least three corps of Philistine mercenaries numbering, perhaps, 600 men each,[121] and selected units of Canaanite and Philistine professionals gazetted to David by his vassals as required for which no strength estimates are possible. One imagines these units to have included chariots, archers, and heavy infantry, all Philistine and Canaanite military specialties, the mix dictated by the nature of the tactical situation at the time of deployment. Filling out the ranks were the conscript militia units of the tribal levy, the number called to service varying with each campaign and tactical situation. David was a professional soldier, and like many professionals then and since may have harbored doubts about the war-fighting quality of conscript troops. David surely understood the *political* dimension of the Israelite levy and that its loyalty could not always be assured. It was against these very tribal commanders, after all, that David had fought in his war with Ishbaal. He had witnessed firsthand the willingness of tribal commanders to change sides when Abiner had offered to betray his king. Nor could the lesson of their political influence have been lost on David when the militia commanders and their troops (which, if we can trust the text, greatly outnumbered David's own army) descended on Hebron to make a deal with their former enemy. In short, the militia levy was politically unreliable and this may have made it militarily unreliable in David's eyes as well. If so, David probably used militia troops very carefully in his wars, relying more on his professionals. Events proved David's distrust justified when some militia commanders and their soldiers joined Absalom's conspiracy to remove David from the throne.

The order of David's wars as presented in the biblical text is almost certainly not the order in which the conflicts actually occurred.[122] For reasons already noted, we may be relatively certain that the defeat marking the end of the Philistine wars occurred where the text places it, that is, before David's other wars. The war against Moab is recorded as occurring next,[123] followed by the war against the Arameans and then Edom. Later in II Samuel 10 the text describes the war against the Ammonites as part of the larger campaign against the Aramean coalition. A glance at a map of Israel suggests that the war against Edom probably occurred before the war against Moab for basic considerations of geography. Moab was a small kingdom located directly across the Dead Sea, itself a formidable barrier to military movement from Israel. To the north Moab bordered on the kingdom of Ammon while to the south it bordered Edom. Any Israelite attack against Moab would have had to pass through one or both of these countries, something not recorded in the text. Nor would it have been likely that Ammon would have granted the Israelites passage through their country only to watch their southern border occupied by their most powerful regional competitor. An attack on Edom, on the other hand, made geostrategic sense. Edom shared a long border with Judah providing David with the advantage of interior lines and short distances for supply. The conquest of Edom would have given Israel control of the southern part of the King's Highway and access to the Red Sea, cutting off the southern terminus of this important trade route from Ammon. Israelite occupation of Edom would also have given Israel control of the iron and copper mines in the area, guaranteeing its supply of important metals for weapons and agricultural implements.[124] With Edom in hand, David would have been able to attack Moab from the south by gaining control of the route of land invasion that led around the Dead Sea encroaching on Ammon from the south. This was an important consideration, for although Gilead acted as a geographic buffer between Ammon and the military forces of the Aramean coalition to the north, its ability to stop the transit of Aramean troops through its lands to support the Ammonites was minimal, as it later proved to be when Aramean forces came to the aid of Ammon without resistance from the Israelites in Gilead.

Given that the arrangement of the wars in the text is thematic and not historical,[125] we are probably justified in suggesting that geostrategic considerations may have shaped David's decisions concerning when and how to conduct his wars. If so, then after the Philistine wars were over, David may have attacked Edom first and then attacked Moab. With his forces now almost surrounding Ammon from the south and in Gilead to the north, David used the pretext of a diplomatic insult to attack Ammon. Watching its border buffer states fall to the Israelites one after another, the Ammonites must have known that war with Israel was inevitable and moved to engage the aid of the Arameans. It was the conflict between Israel and Ammon over control of the King's Highway and the agricultural lands of the Transjordan that drew the Arameans into war with the Israelites.

Regardless of the order in which the wars occurred historically, the text provides only sketchy accounts of them that curiously seem to emphasize the cruelty with which David's army treated the captured populations. With regard to Edom, the text tells us that, "Abishai son of Zeruiah defeated the Edomites in the Valley of Salt—eighteen thousands. David stationed a prefect in Edom, and all the Edomites became servants of the king."[126] Having defeated the Edomites in the field, David ordered his army to exterminate the male population. I Kings 11:16 tells us that "Joab and all Israel remained there six months until he [Joab] had cut off every male in Edom." In short, the Israelite army ravaged the country killing most of the males of military age, reducing the country's military manpower base to nothing.[127] Edom ceased to exist as a separate country and was annexed to Israel,[128] for the text tells us that, "[h]e [David] stationed garrisons in Edom and all Edom became subjects of David."[129] Given the geographical continuity of Edom with Judah, annexation of Edom into the Israelite state was sound policy.

David's treatment of the Moabites was particularly cruel given that during his outlaw days he had found refuge among the Moabites. But reasons of state are always more important than personal gratitude, and David set about destroying the Moabite army so that it could not rise against Israel again. II Samuel 8:2 tells us that after David had defeated the Moabites, "he made them [the POW] lie down on the ground, measured them off by line—two lines were to be put to death and one full line was to be spared. So the Moabites became tribute-bearing servants of David." The survivors presumably were condemned to slave labor and sent to the iron mines of Moab. The method of execution described in the text is not repeated anywhere else in the Bible.[130] It is, however, curiously similar to the decimation of some of Ramses II's chariot units who broke and ran at the battle of Kadesh. He had the units assembled before him and made them lie down in the dust as pharaoh's officers walked among the lines killing the cowardly soldiers as they went. Moab was probably garrisoned with Israelite troops and ruled by a military governor. It is interesting to note that the text offers no *causus belli* for either war, from which we may reasonably infer that David attacked both countries for security reasons, that is, to remove any threat to Israel's geographic integrity from its immediate border. This policy quickly brought Israel into conflict with Ammon, the most important of the eastern border states, and an historical competitor for influence in the region.

THE ARAMEAN CAMPAIGN

David seized on a diplomatic insult to undertake the war with Ammon, which might suggest that the conflict with Ammon may well have been regarded as inevitable in any case and contemplated from the very beginning once David had decided to remove the threat that Israel's border states presented. Ammon had always been the major competitor of Israel for regional dominance and had supported Saul against the Philistines as a way of preserving the regional power balance. David's victories over the Philistines and the southern states could hardly have gone unnoticed in Rabbah, the Ammonite capital located on the site of modern Amman, and it is likely that the Ammonites had already begun to explore closer relations with the Aramean coalition led by Hadadezer, the king of Zobah. Hadadezer's interest lay in any policy that served to contain Israelite power, which had grown to threatening proportions. An alliance with Hanun, king of Ammon, also opened the door to greater Aramean influence in the Transjordan and access to the King's Highway. Under these circumstances, it is likely that all parties were prepared to go to war to achieve their objectives. Figure 7.4 portrays the main battles of the Aramean campaign: (1) Joab's first engagement with the Aramean-Ammonite coalition forces, (2) the final attack on Rabbah, (3) the battle at Helam, and (4) Hadadezer's defeat.

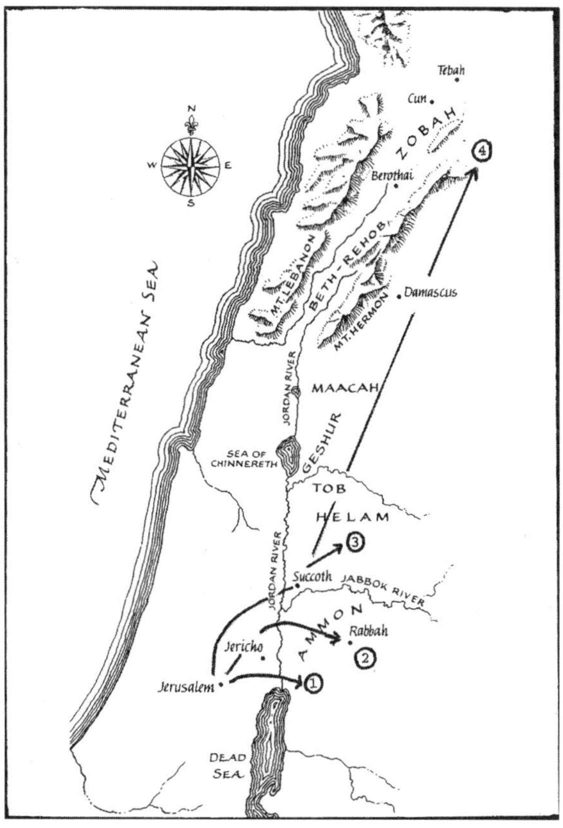

Figure 7.4 David's Battles with the Ammonites and Arameans

The text tells us that "[w]hen the Ammonites saw that they had offended David, they sent away and hired the Arameans of Beth-rob and the Arameans of Zobah—twenty thousands of foot soldiers—and the king of Maccah and the men of Tob—twelve thousands of men. When David heard, he dispatched Joab with all the soldiers."[131] The text implies that David was reacting to an Ammonite mobilization which included the arrival of a large body of Aramean troops provided by at least four states—Beth-rob, Zobah, Maccah and Tob—of the coalition led by Hadadezer. In response, he dispatched Joab with "all the soldiers," a phrase that suggests a full-scale mobilization to counter the coalition's numerical advantage. David immediately went over to the offensive, a fact that suggests that he was hardly surprised by the arrival of the Arameans, and ordered Joab to strike directly at Rabbah, the Ammonite capitol.

The most direct road from Jerusalem to Rabbah crossed the Jordan just north of the Dead Sea and proceeded east via Heshbon,[132] and later events suggest that it was this route that Joab took to advance quickly on his objective. Once across the Jordan, whose crossing, interestingly, was unopposed, Joab and the Israelite army had to travel 25 miles across flat open country to reach their objective, a dangerous maneuver indeed given that the Arameans possessed a highly "mechanized" army with significantly large numbers of chariot units organic to their force structure.[133] At a rate of march of, say, ten miles a day, Joab's army would have been vulnerable to a chariot attack in open country for at least two days. For whatever reasons the enemy chariot forces did not attack, but, as later events showed, their reconnaissance units must have located and kept Joab's army under observation, for when he reached Rabbah, the enemy was waiting for him.

The coalition commander had deployed his troops to trap Joab's army against the walls of Rabbah itself by using his Ammonite troops and then crush it from behind using the Aramean chariot units. The text describes the deployment, a classic "hammer and anvil" trap, in detail. "The Ammonites marched out and drew up for battle at the entrance to the [Rabbah] gate,"[134] deploying with their backs to the city walls for a quick retreat and creating a strong defensive position or "anvil" while inviting the Israelite attack. The "hammer" comprised the Aramean units positioned nearby, but out of sight of the advancing Israelites, "the Arameans of Zobah and Rehob, then men of Tob, and Maccah remaining apart in open country."[135] Although the text makes no mention at all of Aramean chariot units, it is almost inconceivable that they were not present. First, they were organic to the usual force structure; second, the flat open terrain around Rabbah was ideal chariot country; and third, the tactical deployment seems to have required that the Aramean units remain out of sight until the moment to strike, which would have required that they be some distance away. Only chariot units could react quickly if deployed in this manner.

Joab seems not to have detected the Ammonite trap until it was too late and his army was already deployed against the Rabbah anvil. When he finally discovered the Aramean units, they were already behind him. The text tells us that "Joab, seeing that battlefronts were set against him both before and behind,"[136] began to maneuver to escape the trap.[137] The Israelite army had stumbled into a tactical ambush and, given the relative size of the forces, risked being annihilated in a single battle. But Joab was an experienced field commander and he did not compound his mistake by losing his head. Instead, he redeployed his troops to deal with the perilous situation. Joab "made a selection from all the elite troops in Israel and drew up to meet the Arameans. The rest of the army he put under the command of his brother Abishai, who drew up to meet the Ammonites."[138] Here we see Joab in his finest hour as a field commander.

It is a maxim of modern military thinking that one ought never to divide one's forces for to do so increases the problems of command and control and risks destruction piecemeal. Yet, as we have seen, Israelite military history is full of examples from the very beginning of commanders who divided their forces and carried the day. The key to success, of course, was to make certain that one's unit commanders were competent and that the division of forces correctly addressed the tactical problem confronted. In both cases Joab performed superbly. Abishai was an experienced field commander and could be relied upon to carry out his orders without fail. The manner in which Joab divided the army was brilliant. He selected the elite units and placed them under his own command to do battle with the more experienced and better equipped Aramean troops who posed the greatest threat. To Abishai he left the conscript militia units, perhaps leavened with a few experienced commanders. The less experienced militia was given the simpler tactical task of a straightforward frontal attack against an enemy whose own deployment deprived it of any tactical maneuver save a retreat inside the city's walls. Although the text is silent, it is likely that Joab's units had to meet an Aramean chariot attack in the open, no small feat, but one, as we have seen earlier, that was possible to accomplish and had been done before by well-trained Israelite elite troops.[139] Still, the Israelites were in a difficult situation and the desperation was evident in Joab's order to his brother that "if the Arameans are too strong for me, you must give me help, and if the Ammonites are too strong for you, I'll come to help you. Take courage . . . [and] may Yahweh do what seems good to him!"[140] Tactically, the order required that once the enemy was engaged and driven to retreat, neither commander was to pursue. Rather, he was to turn and use his forces in support of those units still hard pressed by the fighting. It was, to say the least, a bold and dangerous gamble with the stakes being nothing less than the death or survival of the army of Israel.

The audacious gamble paid off handsomely when Joab's elite troops received the Aramean attack in open country, stopped it, and beat it back. "When Joab and the force that was with him closed in to fight with the Arameans, they fled from him."[141] Either the battle occurred within sight of the Ammonites or Joab, having turned away the Aramean assault, now marched on the Ammonite position to join Abishai's attack already underway. However it happened, when the Ammonites saw that the Arameans had been defeated, they "also fled from Abishai and went into the city."[142] The text tells us nothing about the remnants of the Aramean force. The Ammonites retreated safely to their city to fight another day. It is probable that Joab's forces took heavy casualties in stopping a chariot attack in open field only with infantry. The casualty rate was sufficiently severe to force Joab to abandon any attempt at obtaining his original objective of capturing Rabbah or defeating the Ammonite armies, for the text tells us that "Joab returned to Jerusalem from the Ammonite campaign" without undertaking any other military operations. Perhaps, too, the Arameans, though driven from the field, retained substantial combat power, in which case Joab would have faced the prospect of having to fight them again in the open field. If discretion is indeed the better part of valor, Joab decided rightly to relinquish the field and live to fight another day. The Israelite army limped home. Rabbah had been a near run thing indeed, and Joab was fortunate to escape with much of his army intact.

Although the Arameans had been driven from the field, the Israelite failure to take Rabbah and their subsequent withdrawal permitted the Arameans to remain in the northern Transjordan. Hadadezer reassembled his forces and reinforced his army with other coalition units from across the Euphrates and moved south to engage the Israelites.[143] The army advanced on Helam under the command of Hadadezer's general, Shobach.[144] The location of Helam is unknown, but it is not possible that the town mentioned by Ezekiel as lying between Damascus and Hamath is the same town.[145] Mazer suggests that Helam lay somewhere in the northern Gilead or the Bashan,[146] where the hilly and uneven terrain would have prevented the decisive use of chariots by the Arameans. Gichon and Herzog argue that Helam is modern Aalma located in southern Syria, and that David engaged the Arameans in the Edrei Gap, 12 miles of traversable ground between the deep gorge of the Yarmuk River and the natural barrier called the Trachona, a field of petrified lava blocks. This, they argue, is the only reasonable location for a battle this size. It was here, too, that in 334 and 336 C.E. the Byzantine armies withstood the assaults of the Arab armies.[147] The ground in the Edrei Gap is rough and uneven and would have worked against the effective employment of the Aramean chariots.

Israelite intelligence probably detected the massing of Aramean troops, and David, realizing the strategic nature of the deployment, moved to deal with the threat. "When David was told, he gathered all Israel, crossed the Jordan, and came to Helam, where the Arameans drew up in front of him."[148] Once more we witness David's sound tactical sense. Rabbah and the area around the city were still in the hands of the Ammonites, and, we may suppose, at least some Aramean military contingents. Had David crossed the Jordan where Joab crossed, thereby taking the most direct route to the battlefield, he would have had to make the march north with his right flank exposed to an Ammonite/Aramean attack. Instead, David's route of march paralleled the Jordan's course using it as an obstacle to protect his flank. Yadin suggests that David crossed the river at Adamah, modern Tel ed-Damiyeh, at the southern end of the valley of Succoth;[149] thereby gaining access to the main road heading north in the Transjordan without opposition. As it moved north, David's army was between the Ammonites and their Aramean allies at Helam. The fact that the text makes no mention of Ammonite troops at the battle suggests that David's route of advance had rendered the Ammonites incapable of reaching the battlefield. Once across the Jordan, perhaps David positioned some units as a blocking force to intercept any Ammonite movement toward Helam or, perhaps, he sent some small units southward toward Rabbah in a feint to convince the Ammonites that he was about to attack Rabbah once more. The text mentions neither of these actions, but either would have achieved the tactical objective of keeping the Ammonites out of the fight.

The text records David's victory at Helam as follows: "the Arameans drew up in front of him [David], fought with him, and fled before the advance of Israel. David killed seven hundred of the Aramean charioteers and forty thousands of their cavalrymen, and also struck down Shobach, the commander of their army, so that he died there."[150] The battle must have been of considerable size. David had "all Israel" with him, a phrase that implies a full mobilization of the Israelite army, a force of around 20,000 men. Gichon and Herzog suggest that the combined manpower strength of the Aramean coalition could have reached 40,000 troops, although it is clear from later events that the Aramean army at Helam was only a portion of that. The fact that Shobach, the Aramean commander, was killed seems to imply that the Arameans suffered substantial casualties. Adjusting the numbers for the Aramean casualty figures in the usual way, we find that 420 charioteers and 2,400 soldiers were killed. Analyses of kill rates suffered in ancient battles by the defeated compared with those suffered by the victor suggest that *on average* the vanquished lost 37.3 percent of its force compared with 5.5 percent for the victor.[151] The casualties suffered by the Arameans at Helam suggest that their army numbered between 9,000 and 10,000 men. If in fact David had the entire Israelite army of 20,000 men with him, then he would have held a significant numerical advantage over the Arameans. Moreover, if David's army suffered the usual 5.5 percent of casualties usually incurred by the victor or about 1,100 men, the victory at Helam left David with plenty of combat strength to take the war northward into the territory of the Aramean king. Once more recognizing the strategic nature of the conflict with the Arameans, David did exactly that.

The Aramean defeat at Helam had important political consequences that greatly altered the military equation. The text tells us that "when all the vassals of Hadadezer saw that they had been defeated by Israel, they sued Israel for peace and became its vassals."[152] The states of the Aramean coalition had been held in line by practical calculations of self-interest. David's victory changed those calculations, and some of the coalition states seized the opportunity to free themselves from Hadadezer's control. Of great importance was the fact that some of the coalition states north of the Euphrates had also broken away, forcing Hadadezer to mount a military campaign against them to bring them into line. The texts seem to document these events. II Samuel 8:3 tells us that when David attacked Hadadezer, he "was then on his way to restore his monument at the Euphrates River." The reference is to Hadadezer's stela or monument, which was a symbol of his dominion or rule over the coalition states. I Chronicles 18:3 is clearer in noting that the purpose of Hadadezer's march to the Euphrates was "to reestablish his dominion on the Euphrates River." Once more the primacy of politics over military considerations in war revealed itself. David's victory at Helam had weakened the Aramean coalition politically forcing Hadadezer to deal with the revolt by force. In so doing, Hadadezer had left his back exposed to an Israelite attack. David moved quickly to seize the tide at its height.

The text presents the battle against Hadadezer as occurring before the battle against the Arameans of Damascus, when geography tells us the battles must have taken place in reverse order. David could not have engaged Hadadezer's army on the Euphrates without first having to march across Aram Damascus, the vassal state to the south of the river that lay between the two armies. Moreover, any competent general would have taken care to ensure that some force was protecting the border while the main force was away on campaign across the Euphrates. The army of Aram Damascus was probably deployed to perform this mission. I Samuel 8:3 tells us that David was "on his way to leave his stela at the River [Euphrates]" when, as Malamat interprets it, David was in hot pursuit of Hadadezer and slammed into the army of Aram Damascus protecting Hadadezer's rear.[153] The text provides no details of the battle, only the enemy's casualty figures. Thus, "David slew twenty-two thousands of them,"[154] or about 1,300 of an army of 4,000.

Having defeated the Aram Arameans of Damascus, David continued his advance toward the Euphrates in search of Hadadezer's army. The text does not record where the battle between the two armies occurred, once more listing only the enemy casualties. "David defeated Hadadezer . . . capturing from him a thousand of chariots, seven thousands of cavalrymen, and twenty thousands of foot soldiers. He [David] hamstrung all the chariot horses, except for a hundred of them which he retained."[155] In adjusted figures, Hadadezer's army lost some 60 charioteers, 420 "cavalrymen," and about 1,200 foot soldiers, or about 2,000 men altogether. This implies an Aramean force of about 6,000 men at the beginning of the battle. If so, then once more David's army of some 18,000 men (adjusted for losses at 5.5 percent in the first two battles) had a sound numerical advantage. Hadadezer's coalition army of 40,000 had already suffered 14,000 casualties in the two previous battles. Making allowances for the fog and friction of war, that is, wounded, desertions, disease, and so forth, it would appear that some of Hadadezer's coalition allies, sensing the dawn of Israelite power in their region, may have abandoned Hadadezer to his fate leaving him to engage David with only a remnant force.

David moved to establish Israelite influence in the area of the former Aramean coalition. Many of the coalition states were permitted to keep their kings who swore allegiance to David as his vassals. Only in Aram Damascus did David impose a prefect and garrisons and military government to oversee Israelite interests there. David occupied Damascus the way the Philistines had occupied Palestine, with officers and small garrisons in the important towns.[156] A military occupation of Aram Damascus made sound strategic sense, for it permitted the deployment of an Israelite force in an area that not only protected the northern border but that could also be used as a strategic platform to react rapidly to any of the other vassal states should events require it.

With the Arameans defeated, the Ammonites were left without a protector, and David moved to bring them to heel. The text tells us that "[w]hen the time of year at which the kings marched out came round again, David sent Joab with his servants and all Israel to ravage the Ammonites and lay siege to Rabbah."[157] A literal translation of the opening clause of the text, "and it was at the return of the year (*litshubat hashana*), at the time of the marching out of the kings,"[158] establishes that David's attack against Rabbah occurred a year after his campaign and victory over the Arameans. Most likely both campaigns began in the springtime, the dry season and the traditional time "kings went forth" to war on one another. It was during the siege of Rabbah that the infamous incident with Bathsheba occurred, which might explain why it was that Joab was in command of the army while David remained in Jerusalem! We learn, from Uriah the Hittite's conversation that "the ark and Israel and Judah are staying in Succoth . . . while my lord Joab and my lord's [David's] servants are encamped on the battlefield,"[159] that is, the bulk of the conscript army was stationed in readiness at the forward base of Succoth while Joab and the professionals were dug in around Rabbah attempting to subdue the city. Here is evidence that Succoth, located 25 miles northwest of Ammon and about a mile north of the Jabbok River, may have become a major staging base for future Israelite operations. Its strategic value as a forward platform for military operations to the north and east is obvious.

David's command to Joab to send Uriah, Bathsheba's husband, "where there is hard fighting . . . so that he will be struck down and die" is well known. But the manner in which Uriah was killed and the difficulties Joab encountered against Rabbah suggests that the old method of overcoming walled defenses was still being used by the Israelite army during David's time. There is evidence not of a siege train or equipment or its employment in the classic sense of a siege, but rather as with Joshua and Saul, of the usual attack by storm. Uriah's death occurred when "the men of the city came out to fight with Joab, some of the army of the servants of David fell, and Uriah the Hittite also died."[160] The Ammonites were apparently not penned up in their city, but capable of conducting offensive forays to disrupt Israelite preparations for an assault. Uriah was killed in one of these forays. The text tells us that in some of the skirmishes, the Israelites fared badly. "The men [Ammonites] overpowered us," Joab's messenger reports to David. "They marched out against us in the field, and we drove them back to the entrance of the gate, the arrows rained heavily on your servants from the wall, and some eighteen of the king's servants died."[161] David recognized a failed assault when told of it and replied with the obvious question, "Why did you go close to the wall?"[162] That David expected the city to be taken by storm is clear from his order to Joab: "Intensify your assault on the city and raze it!"[163] It was at this point, one surmises, that the elite forces under Joab's command ("the servants of David") that had been trying to take the city were reinforced by the conscript army ("all Israel") that had been bivouacked at Succoth and the city finally taken.

Shortly thereafter, Joab and his men broke through Rabbah's defenses and captured the Royal Citadel (*ir hammelukha*) which Joab described as the "citadel of the waters," most probably meaning that he had captured the city's central cistern or main spring fed by the Jabbok.[164] With the citadel in Israelite hands, the rest of the assault was easily accomplished. Joab sent a message to David telling him that he had captured the citadel and to "muster the rest of the army, encamp against the city, and capture it yourself; otherwise I'll be the one to capture it, and my name will be called there."[165] With the outcome no longer in doubt, David arrived at Succoth, gathered up what was left of the Israelite forces there, and marched against Rabbah to take credit for the victory. With Rabbah occupied, David "brought out the people who were in it, ripped it with saws and iron cutting tools, and set them to work with the brick mold. Then, after he had done the same to all the cities of the Ammonites, David and the entire army returned to Jerusalem."[166] Rabbah's defenses were dismantled, a common practice to prevent them from being used again against the conqueror, and the city's population set to labor. The use of the phrase *weheebid malben*, literally, "to cause them to work with the brick mold,"[167] is curiously reminiscent of Pharaoh forcing the Israelites to make bricks for his new city. Perhaps David set the Ammonites to work as corvee labor as well. The text also suggests that after Rabbah had fallen, the Israelite army went on to capture and dismantle the fortifications of other Ammonite cities, perhaps also forcing their populations into public labor.

The tale of Uriah the Hittite, Bathsheba's husband whom David sent to the front to be killed, is of interest to the military historian for what it reveals about the psychology of the Israelite soldier. Uriah was not an Israelite in the ethnic sense of the term, but a Hittite whose family had arrived in Palestine sometime after the collapse of the Hittite Empire in the north. He was one of David's mercenary elite and not a conscript soldier. It is curious, then, also to find Uriah a follower of Yahweh and a strict observer of the ritual purity of the military camp described in Leviticus and Deuteronomy. It suggests that at least some of the growth in the "Israelite" population of Palestine was due to conversions among the native and immigrant populations of the country. In an attempt to disguise the paternity of Bathsheba's pregnancy, David brought Uriah back from the battlefield and ordered him to go to his house and visit his wife. "But when Uriah took leave of the king, he marched out with the weapons bearers and slept at the king's door; he did not go down to his house."[168] When David discovered this, he asked Uriah why he did not go down to his wife. Uriah replied, "[M]y lord's servants [Uriah's comrades] are encamped on the battlefield . . . how can I go to my house to eat and drink and lie with my wife! By our very life, I won't do such a thing."[169] Uriah was still observing the ritual purity of the battle camp even though he was on furlough. His sense of unit identification and the social cohesion that results from being part of an elite unit governed his behavior, an early example of the codes of personal behavior still common among elite units today and the high levels of cohesion these units typically demonstrate.

THE REVOLT OF THE ARMY

Having established Israel as the predominant power in the region, David and the army returned to Jerusalem where he took up governance of the new imperial realm. Sometime during this time David's son, Absholom, was exiled for the murder of his brother, Amnon, who had raped their sister Tamar.[170] Amnon's murder occurred two years after the rape, and Abshalom returned after an exile of three years, suggesting that the events in the text occurred perhaps six years or so after David's capture of Rabbah. In short order Abshalom began to maneuver against his father, setting himself up as a judge because the press of David's duties caused him to neglect this important function. The text tells us that "[a]t a later time Abshalom began to make use of a chariot with horses and fifty men to run before him."[171] The text is of interest to the military historian for here is the first mention of any Israelite actually using a chariot, if only for personal transportation. Abshalom had outfitted himself in the equipment of the traditional Canaanite *maryannu*, complete with runners to protect him in battle. It was also the equipment of the Canaanite and Philistine kings. Everywhere else in the text only the mule is mentioned as the royal mount. Thus, when David fled Jerusalem he rode on saddled asses which the text tells us "are for the royal household to ride."[172] When Abshalom struck down Amnon, he fled on a mule. When Abshalom fled from David's army after the battle in the Ephraim Forest, he did so on a mule. The royal mount, then, was still the mule during Davidic times and not the horse,[173] and, we may surmise, it was the primary animal for use by the military as well. It is curious that even at this late date the Israelite army and its commanders are still not utilizing the horse to any great degree even though it had become the principal animal of other armies of the region long before.

Abshalom's use of the horse and chariot typical of Canaanite and Philistine royalty was probably intended as a public display of his intentions to replace his father as king. In short order some of the militia army and its commanders went over to Abshalom, and, as the text notes, "the conspiracy was strong, and the army with Abshalom grew larger and larger."[174] The Israelite militia was always as much a political as a military institution, and David was wise not to trust it. Now the army had turned openly against him. There were several reasons for the military's discontent. First, the growth of state governmental and religious institutions was intruding into traditional areas of tribal power and control. Second, David's wars subjected the militia levy to long periods of military service with no real reward. The growth of David's professional corps and the financial needs of the state probably required that much of the war booty traditionally used to pay the militia be diverted elsewhere. Military service in David's wars took many men away from their farms and trades for long periods, often causing the economic fortunes of their families to suffer. Third, David's preference for his professionals must have been obvious, and although the militia levies played an important part in the wars, one suspects that they were often used as cannon fodder to reduce the risk to the highly trained and expensive professionals. Militias, as Rome learned later, have no interest in imperial military service.[175] One suspects, although the text is silent, that many of the tribal elders went over to Abshalom as well. The army marched on Jerusalem and David fled from the city accompanied by his Philistine praetorians who remained loyal to their king.

David's retreat from Jerusalem toward the Jordan suggests that the number of units supporting the revolt was substantial, too substantial for David to deal with militarily at the moment. David's tactics in dealing with the revolt are a textbook demonstration of his understanding of the maxim, later formulated by Clausewitz, that politics control military affairs and not the reverse. David understood that his praetorian guard was too small to immediately engage the army and that he needed time to make good his escape and increase his forces before drawing Abshalom's army into a fight. A smart commander would have immediately set after David and his men while they were tired, under strength, and on the run, caught them, and forced them to battle. If Abshalom's army moved quickly against him, David was doomed. When David was informed that his former counselor, Ahithophel, had gone over to the rebels, his concern increased, for he knew Ahithophel to be a competent advisor who would urge Abshalom to immediately assemble the army and pursue after David. David sent one of his other advisors, Hushai the Archite, back to the court with instructions to pretend to join the rebels and to "frustrate Ahithophel's counsel for me."[176] David used Hushai the Archite to block the counsel of Ahithophel. Here is a classic example of the primacy of political decisions in determining the direction of military operations, and David, a proto-Clausewitzian at his core, intended to save his army on the battlefield by influencing the political process at its center.

The text tells us that "Abshalom and all the men of Israel had arrived in Jerusalem, and Ahithophel was among them."[177] Tadmor suggests that this was an important event for it demonstrated that the elders of the tribes and the military were acting together as a consultative body to Abshalom as to what to do about David.[178] Never before, Tadmor asserts, do we find the people at arms and the elders acting as a consultative body to the king. The presence of such a body suggests the extent of support for the revolt and the preeminent role played by the militia commanders in the rebellion. It also suggests that David had made few inroads into strengthening his control of the militia despite his victories on the battlefield.

David knew Ahithophel well and had accurately taken his measure so it must have come as no surprise when Ahithophel recommended the immediate pursuit of David. Ahithophel advised Abshalom to "Let me choose twelve thousands of men and go in pursuit of David tonight. I'll come upon him when he is weary and his guard is down. I'll surprise him, so that the entire army that is with him will desert and I can attack the king alone. Then the entire army will come back to you as a bride comes back to her husband. You seek the life of only one man, so that the entire army can be at peace."[179] The advice was sound. Strike at David immediately (literally, "tonight") while he was exhausted. Interestingly, this implies either a night approach march to contact or, more interestingly, a night attack in force, both very difficult maneuvers to execute successfully. Offer to permit David's army to return to the country without punishment, thereby separating their loyalty from David. David, of course, must be killed.

Hushai the Archite, acting as David's cat's-paw, argued against an immediate attack, that David was too wily a soldier to be taken by surprise with the rest of the army. Moreover, the loyalty of the praetorian guard was absolute and could not be shaken by the mere promise of a pardon for "they are embittered, like a bear bereft in the wild or a sow snared in the wild."[180] Better, Hushai advised, to wait and gather the entire militia army about you, "like sands of the sea, so that you may personally travel among them," that is, to lead them as their new king against David. Then, with the advantage of numbers, "We'll come upon David . . . and descend upon him as a fog descends over the ground; and of him and the men with him not even one will be spared."[181] David's army was to be put to death, removing once and for all the competitor to the influence of the old militia leaders. It was a course of action that, although militarily unwise, appealed to the political interests of the parties involved. The army was to be given the advantage of numbers and the opportunity to remove David's praetorian army for good while Abshalom was to be the leader of the operation, his debut before the people as Israel's new king. As best we know, Abshalom was not an experienced field general like his father, and there is no textual reference to any military experience he may have had or whether he had ever accompanied his father on campaign, a relatively common experience for royal sons in the Near East. If Abshalom possessed any military sense, it may have deserted him for he chose to follow Hushai's advice and wait. It was the wrong decision at the wrong time, and it made all the difference to the outcome of events.

Once informed of Abshalom's decision not to pursue, David no longer needed to be concerned about an attack at the rear, and he moved quickly. "So David and the entire army that was with him arose and crossed the Jordan, so that by the morning light there was not a straggler who had not crossed the Jordan."[182] Here is another example of a successful night crossing of a water obstacle that seems to have become a routine maneuver for the Israelites. David made straight for Mahanaim where he was met by the city's leaders, who welcomed him and brought field provisions for his army.[183] It was curious that David should find support in the town that was the seat of Ishbaal's government and a hotbed of Benjaminite loyalties, suggesting that since the civil war David may have taken steps to regain the loyalty of Saul and Ishbaal's supporters. The Ammonites, too, offered provisions to David and his army, "for they thought the army would have become famished, exhausted, and parched in the wilderness."[184] After his victory at Rabbah, David had permitted Shobi, son of his old ally Nahash who supported David in his war against Ishbaal, to ascend the throne of the Ammonites. In gratitude perhaps, or because the Ammonites were up to their old tricks of supporting any opposition to the Israelite throne to weaken Israelite influence in the region, they resupplied David's army. It is not beyond the realm of possibility, although there is no support in the text, that some Ammonite military units may have been given over to David's use against Abshalom. Using Mahanaim as a base of operations, David rested his army and, we might reasonably assume, gathered to him those tribal militias in the Transjordan states that remained loyal. Sometime later, we do not know how long, Abshalom and the army of Israel crossed the Jordan to bring David to battle.

The text tells us that David mustered his army at Mahanaim and divided it into three elements under the commands of Joab, Abishai, and Ittai the Gittite, his best, most experienced, and loyal field commanders.[185] The decentralization of command was brilliant and determined by David's choice of a battlefield environment that most suited the tactical capabilities of his army. To maximize these capabilities, moreover, required not forces massed for battle in set-piece fashion, but highly maneuverable and quickly moving elements, tactical capabilities best achieved by smaller units. David had originally planned to lead the army himself, but his field commanders objected on the grounds that his death, even in victory, would be devastating to Israel. If the army were to face defeat that day, David himself would survive to fight another time. David agreed to remain behind in Mahanaim and, of great interest, no overall field commander was appointed in his place. All three elements, each under the command of a trusted officer, would fight as independent units, their missions orchestrated and coordinated by the nature of the battle itself. This was remarkable and an example of what the staff officers of the German General Staff of the nineteenth century would call *auftragstaktik*. The same "mission order" doctrine remains at the core of the tactical operations of the modern Israeli Defense Force.

BATTLE OF THE EPHRAIM FOREST

David chose the Ephraim Forest to engage Abshalom and the militia army. The forest probably lay in the wooded hill country east of the Jordan and south of the Jabbok River, a region originally settled by the tribe of Ephraim long ago, thus accounting for its name.[186] Its location to the south of Mahanaim and across the Jabbok suggests that David had moved his army in anticipation of intercepting the northern movement of Abshalom's army as it marched toward David's stronghold at Mahanaim. The forest was not, as Ackroyd reminds us, "an orderly tree-planted area, but rough country with trees and scrub and uneven ground, dangerous terrain for both battle and flight."[187] Jeremiah 22:6 compares the forests of Ephraim with the forests of Lebanon in their depth and density. The battlefield afforded David's army with its experience in speed, maneuver, surprise, and endurance great advantages, especially so against Abshalom's army comprised almost totally of conscript militia led by tribal commanders. Its field general, Amasa, David's nephew by his wife's sister, as events proved, was hardly an imaginative and daring commander. Abshalom's army could be expected to perform reasonably well on open and level ground where the tactical demands upon it were minimal. If forced to fight against an enemy whose army possessed the tactical sophistication of David's professionals, it would have a very hard time indeed.

The text tells us that "the army marched out into the field to confront Israel, and there was a battle in the Ephraim Forest. The army of Israel was routed there before the advance of the servants of David, and the slaughter that day was great . . . twenty thousands!"[188] The sense of the text is that the casualties were high, at least to the militia elements, giving the impression that the conflict between David and Abshalom had taken on the dimension of a fratricidal civil war. This same sense of civil war in which too much death among countrymen could endanger the nation's future is also gained from Joab's actions on the battlefield. Once the Israelite army had broken, the slaughter of the pursuit began and would have gone on unabated were it not for Joab. With Machiavellian cleverness, Joab realized that a wholesale slaughter of the Israelite army would leave Israel defenseless against its enemies and engender hatred for David. As such, "Joab blew on the shofar, and the army turned back from its pursuit of Israel, for Joab held it in check . . . and all Israel fled, each man to his tent."[189] David had chosen the battlefield with a keen eye for the tactical advantages of terrain, and the text testifies to the impact of the terrain on the battle. The text says, "The fighting was scattered over the surface of the whole region, and the forest consumed more troops that day than the sword."[190] The influence of the terrain at Ephraim was similar to what the Union Army endured during the Peninsula Campaign of 1862 where the thick forests and uneven ground forced large units to break apart and maneuver piecemeal. Stumbling through the forests, small units of combatants clashed and died over and over again, all beyond the tactical control of their officers. The hit-and-run battle went on for weeks until finally, with staggering casualties, the Union Army withdrew.

With the army in retreat, Absalom attempted to flee but was overtaken and killed by Joab's order. Before the battle David had ordered Joab and his officers to "protect young Absalom for me." Joab, ever the pragmatist, understood that Absalom would remain a rallying point for future opposition if permitted to live. As with so many others around David who had to die for reasons of state, Joab was once more present at the death of an important person whose life had to be sacrificed. When David learned of Absalom's death, he went into deep mourning and refused to receive the victorious army in the usual public ceremony. David's refusal greatly angered Joab who reminded David of his debt to his soldiers in the strongest terms. One imagines Joab almost screaming at David. "Indeed you have made it clear today that officers and servants [soldiers] are nothing to you—for you know that if Absalom were alive today, we'd all be dead! Then things would seem right to you! Now then, get up, go out there, and placate your servants! For, by Yahweh, I swear that if you don't go out there, not a man will stay with you tonight."[191] War may, indeed, be too important a business to be left to generals. It is wise, however, for political leaders whose policies so often cause the deaths of soldiers never to forget the human dimension of the sacrifice for which they so frequently seem to ask.

Joab's order to stop the slaughter of Absalom's defeated army paid quick dividends when David turned his attention to healing the breach with the rebel tribal and military leaders. David apparently pardoned the rebel commanders as the story of Shimci's pardon implies.[192] In what must have seemed an almost too magnanimous act of reconciliation, David appointed Amasa, the commander of Absalom's army, to replace the loyal Joab as commander of David's army.[193] These acts of reconciliation appear to have been accomplished shortly after the battle while the army was still in the field and had not yet crossed the Jordan River on its return to Jerusalem,[194] demonstrating once again David's shrewd perception of the primacy of political considerations in handling military affairs. Some of the defeated rebel units came over to David immediately, for the text tells us that "[t]he entire army of Judah was marching along with the king, and also half the army of Israel."[195] At this point dissention broke out in the ranks with the leaders of the northern tribes complaining that David favored the southern tribes in his handling of matters while neglecting the interests of the north. The text is unclear as to who rendered the complaint, but surely it could not have been those northern commanders whom David had just defeated and pardoned. More likely, it was the commanders of those northern contingents who had remained loyal and fought with David. David's forgiveness of the rebel officers and appointing Amasa commander of the army must have struck them as ingratitude for their loyal service and caused them to question whether they had benefited at all from their loyalty to the king. At some point in the altercation one Sheba son of Bichri, a Benjaminite, gave voice to the loyalist complaint. "We have no share in David and no estate in the son of Jesse! Every man to his tent, Israel. So all Israel left David to follow Sheba son of Bichri."[196] David faced another revolt by his military commanders.

It is unlikely that Sheba's rebellion was widespread, and the claim that "all Israel" left David seems an exaggeration. Even so, David moved to put down the rebels. He ordered Amasa to mobilize "the men of Judah for me in three days."[197] Given that much of the army of Judah had supported Abshalom with Amasa as its commander, David's order to mobilize the Judean militia seems to have been designed to test the loyalty of Amasa and the Judeans. Having been given three days to mobilize his forces, the text says that "Amasa went to call up Judah, but was late for the appointment,"[198] which, in David's mind, probably suggested that the Judean militia had refused to respond to the call of the king, once more calling their loyalty into question. David moved quickly to control events. He summoned Abishai and ordered him and Joab to assemble the professional army and track down and capture Sheba, "and they marched out of Jerusalem in pursuit of Sheba son of Bichri."[199]

The treacherous and ungrateful Amasa remained to be dealt with. Once more it was Joab who acted to remove the danger to his king. Apparently Amasa had been summoned to the field, for the events described in the text occurred "near the big rock that is in Gibeon." Here Joab waited in ambush. "Joab was dressed in his tunic, and over it he was girded with a sword strapped to his hip in its sheath."[200] As Amasa approached, probably mounted on a mule, Joab stepped into the road and signaled for him to halt. Joab approached Amasa calling out, "Are you well brother?" As Amasa leaned down to receive the traditional kiss of greeting, Joab reached up "grasping Amasa's beard with his right hand to kiss him. Amasa was not on guard against the sword that was in Joab's hand. He struck him with it in the belly, so that his entrails spilled out on the ground; and though he did not strike him a second time, he died."[201] Joab's temperament was revealed in the use to which he put Amasa's body. He posted a soldier to guard the disemboweled corpse and left it in the middle of the road so that "Amasa was weltering in gore in the middle of the highway." Those who, in war, have seen corpses rotting in the heat will recognize the sight as truly impressive. The text tells us that as the soldiers marching on the road came upon Amasa's corpse, Joab's sentry cried out, "Whoever favors Joab and whoever is on David's side, after [follow] Joab!"[202] But who were these soldiers coming down the highway? Joab's men, the professionals, were already ahead of him as he waited in ambush for Amasa. The soldiers must have been the late contingents of the Judean militia attempting to catch up. Joab's message to these men was clear. Look upon the corpse of your commander who betrayed David and choose which side you are on. The grisly tactic seems to have worked, "for all the men went on by after Joab in pursuit of Sheba son of Bichri."[203] Once more Joab had served his king well. Joab and Abishai trapped Sheba in the town of Abel of Beth-maacah where they convinced the town leaders to turn Sheba over to them in return for not attacking the town, "and they [the townspeople] cut off Sheba son of Bichri's head and threw it to Joab."[204] The ease with which Sheba was caught suggests that whatever support he might have had was not widespread.

The two revolts revealed the fragility of David's control over the tribal kingdoms and especially their militia units and commanders who seemed to have shown little hesitation in openly opposing their king when they thought it warranted. Once the northern tribes had seen the Philistines as the main threat to their independence. Now it was the king himself who was seen as the main threat. The monarchy was still a new institution, and it is clear from the revolts against Saul and David that its legitimacy was still very much in question. The old tribal order was struggling to survive, and was not above using military force to that end. None of this, of course, was likely to reduce David's distrust of the militia, and may explain why, as time passed, he relied more and more upon the professional army and mercenaries to execute his will.[205] Abshalom's rebellion had been rooted in the ambition of one man and had threatened the king. Sheba's revolt, small as it was, was a more ominous sign that threatened the institution of the monarchy itself. The tension between the northern tribes and southern-based monarchy was never fully resolved during David's lifetime. The Sheba incident foreshadowed the final withdrawal of the loyalty of the northern tribes from the monarchy that came to pass upon the death of Solomon. It was not incidental that when the northern tribes rose in revolt once again, the battle cry was the same as that used by Sheba. "We have no share in David and no estate in the son of Jesse! To your tents, Oh Israel! Now look to your own House, Oh David!"[206]

NOTES

1. John Bright, "The Organization and Administration of the Israelite Empire," in *Magnalia Dei: The Mighty Acts of God*, ed. Frank Moore Cross, Werner E. Lemke, and Patrick D. Miler Jr. (New York: Doubleday and Company, 1975), 195.

2. Ibid.

3. *The Cambridge Ancient History*, vol. 2, pt. 2 (Cambridge, England: Cambridge University Press, 1975), 580; see *The Westminster Historical Atlas to the Bible* (Philadelphia, PA: Westminster Press, 1945), 47, for the dates and length of David's reign.

4. Brian Peckham, "Israel and Phoenicia," in Cross et al., *Magnalia Dei*, 230; see also p. 243 where Peckham argues that the conquest of the Philistines as a condition of the treaty is explicit in Abiner's negotiations with Israel (II Samuel 3:18),

and implicit in the introduction to the treaty (II Samuel 5:2), which refers to I Samuel 18:16 and to David's victories over the Philistines (I Samuel 18:30).

5. *The Cambridge Ancient History*, vol. 2, pt. 2, 580; see also II Samuel 7:23.

6. I Samuel 15:18; T. R. Hobbs, *A Time for War* (Wilmington, DE: Michael Glazier, 1989), 55.

7. Hobbs, 59.

8. Ibid.

9. Sh. Yeivin, "Administration: Chapter 6," in *The World History of the Jewish People*, vol. 4, pt. 2, ed. Benjamin Mazar (Jerusalem: Massada Press Ltd., 1979), 150.

10. Ibid.

11. Ibid.

12. H. Reviv, "The Structure of Society: Chapter 5," in *The World History of the Jewish People*, vol. 4, pt. 2, 139.

13. Hobbs, 67.

14. Ibid., 144.

15. Abraham Malamat, "A Political Look at the Kingdom of David and Solomon and Its Relations with Egypt," in *Studies in the Period of David and Solomon*, ed. Tomoo Ishida (Tokyo: International Symposium for Biblical Studies, 1979), 192.

16. Abraham Malamat, "The Kingdom of David and Solomon in Its Contact with Egypt and Aram Naharaim," *Biblical Archaeologist* 21 (1958): 100.

17. Malamat, "A Political Look at the Kingdom of David and Solomon," 192.

18. Ibid.

19. II Samuel 8:2, 12:30.

20. Benjamin Mazar, "The Aramean Empire and Its Relations with Israel," *Biblical Archaeologist* 25 (1962): 102–3.

21. II Samuel 8:6.

22. I Kings 5:1.

23. Malamat, "A Political Look at the Kingdom of David and Solomon," 197.

24. Niels Peter Lemche, "David's Rise," *Journal for the Study of the Old Testament* 10 (1978): 7–8.

25. W.O.E. Oesterley and Theodore H. Robinson, *A History of Israel* (Oxford: Clarendon Press, 1948), 207.

26. Lemche, 10–11.

27. Peckham, 230.

28. Oesterley and Robinson, 203.

29. I Samuel 30:26–31.

30. Reviv, 135.

31. II Samuel 2:4.

32. Benjamin Mazar, "The Era of David and Solomon," in *World History of the Jewish People*, vol. 4, pt. 1, 84; see also by the same author, "The Military Elite of King David," in *Vetus Testamentum*, vol. 13 (1963), 310.

33. Chaim Herzog and Mordechai Gichon, *Battles of the Bible* (Jerusalem: Steimatzky's Agency Ltd., 1978), 77.

34. Reviv, 140.

35. Mazar, *World History of the Jewish People*, 82.

36. Mazar, "The Military Elite of King David," 311–12.

37. P. Kyle McCarter Jr., *II Samuel: The Anchor Bible* (New York: Doubleday, 1984), 87. The precise location of Mahanaim is uncertain. From here on, this source will be cited as *Anchor Bible.*

38. II Samuel 2:10–11.

39. II Samuel 2:16.

40. II Samuel 2:17.

41. O. Eissfeldt, "Noch einmal: Ein gescheiterter Versuch der Wiedervereinigung Israels," *Nouvelle Clio* (1952): 55–59; see also F. C. Fensham, "The Battle between the Men of Joab and Abiner as a Possible Ordeal by Battle," in *Vetus Testamentum* (1970); 356–57.

42. Eissfeldt, 59; E. L. Sukenik and Yigael Yadin, "Let the Young Men, I Pray Thee, Arise and Play Before Us," *Journal of Palestine Oriental Studies* (1948): 110–16.

43. *Anchor Bible*, 96.

44. II Samuel 2:17.

45. II Samuel 2:28–32.

46. II Samuel 2:30–31.

47. Hayim Tadmor, "Traditional Institutions and the Monarchy: Social and Political Tensions in the Time of David and Solomon," in *Studies in the Period of David and Solomon*, ed. Tomoo Ishida (Tokyo: International Symposium for Biblical Studies, 1979), 240.

48. II Samuel 3:1.

49. II Samuel 3:12.

50. II Samuel 3:30; see also *Anchor Bible*, 117.

51. II Samuel 3:24–25.

52. *Anchor Bible*, 117.

53. Ibid., 122.

54. II Samuel 3:31.

55. *Anchor Bible*, 118.

56. D. N. Freedman, "The Age of David and Solomon," in *World History of the Jewish People*, 110.

57. II Samuel 4:6–7.

58. Lemche, 17.

59. II Samuel 5:3.

60. C. E. Hauer, "Jerusalem, the Stronghold, and Rephaim," *Catholic Biblical Quarterly* 32 (1970): 571–78; N. L. Tidwell, "The Philistine Incursions into the Valley of Rephaim," in *Studies in the Historical Books of the Old Testament* (Leiden: E. Brill, 1979), 190–212; and Benjamin Mazar, "The Ancient City: Jerusalem in the Biblical Period," in *Jerusalem Revealed* (New Haven, CT: Yale University Press, 1976), 1–8, for discussions of the three positions.

61. This chronology is adopted from *Anchor Bible*, 175.

62. II Samuel 5:17.

63. Herzog and Gichon, 79.

64. Tidwell, 195.

65. Hauer, citing II Samuel 15:13–18, makes the argument that David had a "pathological fear" of being trapped in a city; in Hauer, 577.

66. *Anchor Bible*, 153, for probable location of Adullam.
67. Hauer, 577.
68. II Samuel 5:19–20.
69. Oesterley and Robinson, 213.
70. II Samuel 5:23–25.
71. *Anchor Bible*, 156; see also Mazar, *World History of the Jewish People*, 78, which suggests the battle might have been fought at the classic battleground of Beth-horan.
72. *Anchor Bible*, 156.
73. Herzog and Gichon, 79–80.
74. II Samuel 5:25.
75. Abraham Malamat, "Aspects of the Foreign Policies of David and Solomon," *Journal of Near Eastern Studies* 22 (January 1963): 15.
76. This is the *Anchor Bible* translation.
77. Malamat, "Aspects of the Foreign Policies of David and Solomon," 14; see also Yigael Yadin, "Hazor, Gezer, and Megiddo in Solomon's Times," in *The Kingdoms of Israel and Judah*, ed. A. Malamat (Jerusalem: Massada Press, 1961), 77.
78. Hobbs, 148.
79. Mazar, *World History of the Jewish People*, 80.
80. Ibid.
81. Bright, 197.
82. Ibid.
83. Herzog and Gichon, 84.
84. *The Cambridge Ancient History*, vol. 2, pt. 2, 584.
85. Mazar, *World History of the Jewish People*, 80.
86. II Samuel 5:6.
87. See Hauer, 573, for the chronology of wars used here.
88. Ibid.
89. The Gibeonites went to David and demanded that as recompense for Saul's breaking of the oath, that David have all of Saul's surviving male bloodline, his grandchildren, killed. David agreed and had them executed.
90. Oesterley and Robinson, 217. Although the city surrendered many times to other conquerors, it was only taken by force three times.
91. Ibid.
92. Ibid., 214; see also Benjamin Mazar, *The Mountain of the Lord* (Garden City, NY: Doubleday, 1975), 170.
93. Oesterley and Robinson, 214; Mazar 171.
94. Mazar, *Mountain of the Lord*, 171.
95. II Samuel 5:6–9.
96. Mazar, *The Military Elite of King David*, 314.
97. *Anchor Bible*, 137.
98. Herzog and Gichon, 78–79.
99. Ibid.
100. Tadmor, 244.
101. A. van Selms, "The Armed Forces in Israel under Saul and David," in *Ou Testamentiese Werkgemeenskap* (1960), 63.

102. Tadmor, 244.

103. For Mendenhall's conversion of the unit strength of the troops at Hebron, see Jacob M. Myers, *I Chronicles: The Anchor Bible* (New York: Doubleday, 1965), 98.

104. *Anchor Bible*, 139.

105. Benjamin Mazar, *World History of the Jewish People*, vol. 4, pt. 2, 209.

106. Ibid.

107. Ibid., 210.

108. Ibid.

109. Yigael Yadin, *The Art of Warfare in Biblical Lands in Light of Archaeology*, vol. 1 (New York: McGraw-Hill, 1963), 97.

110. Hauer, 573.

111. *Anchor Bible*, 141.

112. King's naming cities after themselves was a common occurrence in antiquity. One thinks immediately of Ramses, Sargon, and Alexander, to name but three.

113. Oesterley and Robinson, 216.

114. II Samuel 15:14.

115. The quote is from the movie *Patton*.

116. Bright, 196.

117. Yutaka Ikeda, "Solomon's Trade in Horses and Chariots and Its International Setting," in *Studies in the Period of David and Solomon*, ed. Tomoo Ishida (Tokyo: International Symposium for Biblical Studies, 1979), 216–17.

118. Mazar, *World History of the Jewish People*, vol. 4, pt. 2, 252.

119. For a list of the citations in the biblical texts referring to chariots and horses, see Ikeda, 217.

120. Hobbs, 56.

121. Mazar, "The Military Elite of King David," 314; see also van Selms, 63.

122. *Anchor Bible*, 251.

123. II Samuel 8:2.

124. Mazar, *World History of the Jewish People*, vol. 2, pt. 2, 252.

125. *Anchor Bible*, 251.

126. II Samuel 8:13.

127. Hobbs, 149.

128. Mazar, *World History of the Jewish People*, vol. 4, pt. 1, 83.

129. I Chronicles 27:13.

130. *Anchor Bible*, 249.

131. II Samuel 10:6–7.

132. *Anchor Bible*, 271; see also Yigael Yadin, "Some Aspects of the Strategy of Ahab and David," *Biblica* 36 (1955): 347.

133. Mazar, *World History of the Jewish People*, vol. 4, part. 1, 82.

134. II Samuel 10:8.

135. Ibid.

136. II Samuel 10:9.

137. Herzog and Gichon, 83, argue that Joab avoided the trap by the use of reconnaissance patrols to screen the advance of his army.

138. II Samuel 10:9–10.

139. See chapter 2 of this work for the Israelite tactics for stopping a chariot attack in the open.

140. II Samuel 10:11–12.
141. II Samuel 10:13.
142. II Samuel 10:14.
143. II Samuel 10:15–16.
144. Ibid.
145. *Anchor Bible*, 273.
146. Mazar, *World History of the Jewish People*, vol. 4, pt. 1, 82.
147. Herzog and Gichon, 83.
148. II Samuel 10:17.
149. *Anchor Bible*, 273; Yadin, "Some Aspects of the Strategy of Ahab and David," 347–351.
150. II Samuel 10:17–18.
151. Richard A. Gabriel and Karen S. Metz, *From Sumer to Rome: The Military Capabilities of Ancient Armies* (Westport, CT: Greenwood Press, 1991), 86, for the methodology of calculating average casualty rates for victor and vanquished in antiquity.
152. II Samuel 10:19.
153. Malamat, "Aspects of the Foreign Policies of David and Solomon," 4; both Thutmose II and Thutmose III erected victory stela on the Euphrates.
154. II Samuel 8:5.
155. II Samuel 8:4.
156. Oesterley and Robinson, 221.
157. II Samuel 11:1.
158. *Anchor Bible*, 284.
159. II Samuel 11:11.
160. II Samuel 11:17.
161. II Samuel 11:23–24.
162. Ibid.
163. II Samuel 11:25.
164. *Anchor Bible*, 310.
165. II Samuel 12:28.
166. II Samuel 12:31.
167. *Anchor Bible*, 313.
168. II Samuel 11:8–9.
169. II Samuel 11:11.
170. The siblings are probably half-relatives.
171. II Samuel 15:1.
172. II Samuel 16:2.
173. *Anchor Bible*, 406; see also C. C. Conroy, "Absalom Absalom! Narrative and Language in II Samuel 13–20," *Analecta Biblica* 81 (1978): 59–71.
174. II Samuel 15:12.
175. *Anchor Bible*, 358–59; Bright, 203–4.
176. II Samuel 15:34.
177. II Samuel 16:15.
178. Tadmor, 247.
179. II Samuel 17:1–4.
180. II Samuel 17:8.

181. II Samuel 17:12.
182. II Samuel 17:22.
183. II Samuel 17:27–28.
184. Ibid.
185. II Samuel 18:2.
186. *Anchor Bible*, 405; see also M. Noth, *The History of Israel* (New York: Harper and Row, 1960), 201.
187. *Anchor Bible*, 405; see also P. R. Ackroyd, *The Second Book of Samuel* (London: Cambridge Bible Commentary, 1977), 134.
188. II Samuel 18:6–7.
189. II Samuel 18:16–17.
190. II Samuel 18:8.
191. II Samuel 19:7–8.
192. II Samuel 19:20–24.
193. II Samuel 19:14.
194. II Samuel 19:40.
195. II Samuel 19:41.
196. II Samuel 20:1–2.
197. II Samuel 20:4.
198. II Samuel 20:5.
199. II Samuel 20:7.
200. II Samuel 20:8.
201. II Samuel 20:9–10.
202. II Samuel 20:11.
203. II Samuel 20:13.
204. II Samuel 20:22.
205. *Anchor Bible*, 431; see also Bright, 205.
206. I Kings 12:16.

8

Solomon

History remembers Solomon for his construction of the Temple, his wisdom in practical matters, and his success as a merchant prince that made his wealth as legendary as Croesus, none of which would justify attention by the military historian. And yet, although often overlooked, Solomon's achievements in the area of military affairs were of considerable import for Israel and the history of the Near East. Solomon was the last king of the United Monarchy, and the evidence is clear that he made great efforts to secure the defense of his country by providing it with a military machine the equal of any potential adversary. Unlike Saul and David, Solomon was not a warrior. As D. N. Freedman has put it poetically, "he had never seen lamb, lion, or bear . . . and had never guarded a flock or fought off a wild beast."[1] As far as we know, Solomon was not possessed of any military experience whatsoever. Unlike the kings of Egypt and Assyria who saw to the military training and even combat exposure of their heirs, the sons of Israelite kings, Jonathan excepted, do not seem to have been provided with this experience by their fathers, although it is likely that royal princes may have received at least some instruction in the martial arts.[2] And so it is curious that Solomon, born to the comforts of the court, without the disposition or experience of a soldier, turned out to be the greatest reformer of the Israelite military establishment, transforming it from a tribal militia into a modern, fully equipped, combined arms army typical of the other oriental states of the day.

Solomon is credited with creating a national Israelite army under a single unified command authority completely loyal to the king. The old divided command structure that often set the king's mercenary guard against the tribal levy, a situation that also encouraged the rebellion of local contingent commanders against national commanders, was replaced by a unified national command. To carry out his plans for civic construction and military fortification, Solomon reorganized the state into twelve administrative districts, an innovation that also made troop conscription more efficient and reliable. The new administrative organization also made possible the establishment of a new military logistics system. Solomon developed a new national defense doctrine closely integrating economic resources with military power directed by national political authorities to safeguard the new Israelite state, affording it a new flexibility and enhanced position in international affairs. It was Solomon, too, who modernized the Israelite army into a genuine combined arms force complete with a powerful chariot arm. He constructed new fortifications in the Jezreel Valley, in the Transjordan, in the Negev and, perhaps, even in Philistia, arranged in the same manner as the old Canaanite system for mobile strategic defense in depth. To protect Israel's routes of commerce and supply, Solomon constructed "store cities" and other armed garrisons at strategic points. Although no wars are recorded as having occurred during Solomon's reign, in two important confrontations with Egypt Solomon showed all the strategic ability of a brilliant general. In both cases Solomon was successful, and in both cases Israel's strategic position significantly improved. There is, then, much about Solomon's role in the history of ancient Israel to interest the military historian.

There was nothing in the early history of this man who became king of Israel to indicate that he would one day occupy the throne. He had no legitimate genealogical claim to the throne in terms of primogeniture.[3] Adonijah probably pressed his own claim on the grounds of being the senior son after the death of Abshalom. In fact, the senior son was David's second born of Abigail, named Chileab/Daniel.[4] II Samuel 12:24 says that Solomon was the first of Bathsheba's children by David to survive while I Chronicles 3:1–9 tells us that Solomon was the fourth and last of Bathsheba's sons after Shimea, Shobab, and Nathan. II Samuel 5:15 lists Solomon as the fourth of the children born to David in Jerusalem after his six sons and one daughter born in Hebron. The Uriah and Bathsheba episode tells us that Solomon's birth occurred immediately after David's Ammonite war, which Professor Yeivin suggests occurred during the first decade of the tenth century B.C.E.[5] and would have made Solomon between 18 and 20 years old when the rose to power circa 970 B.C.E. Why, then, was Solomon successful? He was, after all, a man with no popular support, of no military competence, no demonstrated ability, and no prophetic election. Malamat suggests simply that he was David's choice even before the harem conspiracy was set in motion. Malamat argues that David had already selected Solomon for the throne early in the succession crisis when he ordered Solomon to marry the Ammonite princess, Naama, thereby implying to the world that Solomon was his heir. The marriage, an act of international diplomacy, would have been of no value to the Ammonites or Israel had Solomon not already been presented as the legitimate heir.[6] This aside, it must be said that if Solomon was David's choice, it was hardly clear to others for it eventually required military force and, ultimately, the murder of his rivals to enforce his claim to the throne.

Buber is correct when he asserts that "Solomon was an oriental king" and brought to the Israelite monarchy a conception of kingship far different from that of David or Saul. Solomon imposed upon the Israelites a typical oriental kingship, complete with corvee labor, conscription, taxation, and absolute despotism.[7] He seems to have had nothing but contempt for Israelite democratic traditions and the role of tribal elders in governance. Having come to power by harem conspiracy, he took no oath nor accepted any covenant with Israelite traditions or other institutions. The traditional restraints that bound David and Saul were absent.[8] As such, Solomon paid little attention to the need to maintain the legitimacy of the crown in the eyes of the northern tribes who had always seen their loyalty to the throne as conditional and based on a voluntary covenant. Solomon did little to reconcile the outstanding grievances with the north until these grievances broke into open revolt. By then it was already too late, and the United Monarchy was eventually destroyed by the rebellion of the northern tribes.

COUP D'ETAT AND REFORM

The details of the harem conspiracy and the coup d'etat that brought Solomon to the throne are interesting for what they tell us about the role of the military in Israelite court politics under David and Solomon. Although probably unforeseen at the outset of events, the support of the military for Solomon in the coup produced one of the major reforms of the army, the establishment of a single unified military command authority to replace the traditional mercenary/tribal levy system that had existed under David and Saul. That military commanders should have become important political figures in Israelite politics is not surprising. David himself was a rebellious military commander as was Abiner who betrayed his sovereign in the civil war with David. It was the army's support of Abshalom that encouraged him to try to remove his father, and it was Amasa, the commander of the army of Judah, who supported him in open revolt. Joab, too, David's army commander, had been responsible for a number of political murders in the service of David's and his own political ambitions. It was not without some reason, then, that those who supported Solomon's ambitions would suspect the generals of harboring dangerous political ambitions of their own. In this regard, the two key players were Joab, commander of the tribal levy, and Benaiah, the commander of the palace guard.

I Kings 1:1 tells us that "David was now old, advanced in years," implying that the question of succession was on everyone's lips. Adonijah, David's third son, "provided himself with chariots and horses, and an escort of fifty outrunners,"[9] the traditional Canaanite/Philistine (and by now Israelite!) trappings of royal status, and boasted "I will be king!" Within a short time, the court split into two factions. "Adonijah conferred with Joab son of Zeruiah and with the priest Abiathar, and they supported Adonijah; but the priest Zadok, the prophet Nathan, Shimei, and Rei, and David's own fighting men did not side with Adonijah."[10] As events progressed, news reached Nathan and the Solomonic faction that Adonijah was holding a great feast at Gihon for his supporters to which "he invited all of the king's sons and the army officers."[11] It may have been this gathering of military men that led Nathan to suspect that Joab was preparing to install Adonijah as king soon. To preclude this, Nathan and Bathsheba went to David and convinced him that Adonijah had already proclaimed himself king without David's approval. The text implies that David was very old, suggesting that he may have been easily convinced of the danger by the conspirators. "Then King David said, 'Summon to me the priest Zadok, the prophet Nathan, and Benaiah son of Jehoiada' [the commander of the king's mercenary bodyguard]. When they came before the king, the king said to them, 'Take my loyal soldiers, and have my son Solomon ride on my mule [interestingly David still clung to the old Israelite symbol of royalty, the mule] and bring him down to Gihon. Let the priest Zadok and the prophet Nathan anoint him there over Israel, whereupon you shall sound the horn and shout, "Long live King Solomon!" ' "[12] That the conspirators meant business was clear from the presence of the king's armed bodyguard. When they arrived and carried out David's orders, "all of Adonijah's guests [presumably Joab as well] rose in alarm and each went his own way."[13] The nature of the coup and the threat of violence were evident in that Adonijah fled for his life and ran to the Tent of Meeting, the sanctuary of the Ark at Gibeon, "and grasped the horns of the altar." As long as he remained on the altar, he could not be slain for it was a grievous sin to kill in the sanctuary of Yahweh. In one bold stroke made effective by the threat of violence posed by the presence of the mercenary bodyguard, the conspirators had seized the throne of Israel. A short time later, David "slept with his fathers and was buried in the City of David," and "the kingdom was secured in Solomon's hands."[14]

But Adonijah and Joab were still alive, and both presented threats to the new king. Adonijah was, of course, the older son who had been supported by the army. To forestall any attempt at a counterrevolution, Adonijah was murdered on the flimsy pretext of having requested to marry one of Solomon's concubines. Not surprisingly, it was Benaiah and his palace guard who carried out the killing. The more serious threat, however, was Joab. As commander of the national army, Joab was the only rival in a position to muster sufficient armed force to defeat the mercenary bodyguard. Joab had been the most famous soldier in Israel for years, the man who had distinguished himself at Rabbah, again in the war with the Arameans, commanded the troops in the Forest of Gilead, and had captured and put Sheba the rebel to death. Presumably he had a following among the people and a strong base of support among the tribal military units of which he was commander in chief. Ever since the Bathsheba affair when David did not take the field, it had been Joab, not David, who was really the driving force behind Israel's military victories.

It was probably Joab, not Solomon, who was responsible for beginning many of the reforms of the army that later were accredited to Solomon, for only Joab had the military expertise and experience to foresee what was needed while Solomon had no military knowledge or experience at all. Although portrayed as a contemporary of David, Joab was still a relatively young man at the time of the coup in contrast to David who is portrayed as almost senile. Joab was David's nephew by the latter's sister Zeruiah and, as such, was considerably younger than David. Assuming an average age of the first pregnancy of Zeruiah to be 14 or so years, Joab was *at least* 15 years younger than David. If David was 65 years old or so, then Joab was only 50, still energetic and healthy. Given his age and military reputation, moreover, Joab may have already become the de facto leader of Israel as David grew older. Under these circumstances Joab's support for Adonijah was understandable. Joab may have intended to rule Israel with Adonijah as a puppet. The parallel with Abiner and Ishbaal is striking indeed. Finally, of course, Solomon could not overlook Joab's expertise and success in past court struggles in which rival loyalties came to a head. Here Solomon could not help but recall Joab's proclivity for settling such disputes by murder. It had been Joab who had murdered Abiner, Abshalom, Amasa, and Sheba in pursuit of his own ambitions or those of his king. As long as Joab breathed, Solomon had good reason not to sleep soundly.

It was, perhaps, Joab's reputation as Israel's leading general and David's growing weakness that explains Benaiah's support for the Solomonic faction. From the early days the leader of the palace guard had been Abishai, Joab's younger brother, and it was Joab and Abishai who had run Sheba to ground and delivered his head to the king. After the Abshalom affair and the Sheba incident, Abishai was replaced by Benaiah, who, II Samuel 23:18–23 tells us, was one of David's best warriors. We do not hear of Abishai again nor do we know what happened to him. It is certain, however, that Joab now had to regard the new commander with some suspicion, a suspicion that quickly became mutual. And this may indeed have been David's intention all along. It will be recalled that after the Abshalom revolt, David removed Joab from his position as commander in chief of the army and appointed Amasa the commander of the rebels in his place. Although this was ostensibly done to placate the hostile feelings of the Judean rebel commanders, in fact David might have already concluded that Joab had become too powerful and had to be removed. Certainly Joab's reaction to his removal suggests exactly that. Instead of going quietly, Joab murdered Amasa and joined with his brother and elements of the bodyguard to pursue Sheba and bring him to book. In the face of these events, David may well have been compelled to reappoint Joab as commander in chief. II Samuel 20:23 tells us that "Joab was in charge of the whole army of Israel. Benaiah son of Jehoiada was in charge of the Cherethites and Pelethites." The price of Joab's reappointment may have been the removal of his brother as commander of the bodyguard and his replacement by a man of unquestioned loyalty to the king. Perhaps fearing the power of Joab, David sought to use Benaiah and his praetorian guard as a counterweight to Joab.[15] At least this is the conclusion Ishida draws from the fact that in the second list of high officials in David's court that appears in II Samuel 20:23–26, placed in the text right after the Sheba incident, David's name as ruler of the land is omitted suggesting, in Ishida's view, that Joab had already become the de facto ruler of Israel. If so, Solomon and Benaiah had much to fear from Joab.

Benaiah's early support of Solomon was probably rooted in the fact that Joab's reputation and authority had already done much to undermine the prestige and influence of the palace guard. Indeed, Benaiah may have feared that the influence and even existence of the praetorians might have been eclipsed altogether if Joab succeeded in becoming Adonijah's Abiner. And so it was that Benaiah murdered Joab on Solomon's order, even as he clung to the horns of the altar and sought safety in the sanctuary of Yahweh and "in his [Joab's] place, the king appointed Benaiah son of Jehoiada over the army."[16] There is no mention of the appointment of a new commander for the praetorian guard. No longer do we hear of one commander over the mercenaries and one commander over the tribal levy. The old divided military command structure that often set the king's mercenary guard against the commander of the tribal levy was replaced by a single commander in chief of all Israelite military forces. The old system had encouraged too great an independence on the part of tribal unit commanders often forcing the king to acquiesce in their demands or even deal with outright rebellions. The new command structure was designed to prevent these shortcomings from limiting the king's authority. Solomon's new administrative and logistics structure deliberately cut across clan and tribal lines further reducing the authority and power of tribal officials to resist the will of the king on such key issues as corvee labor recruitment, conscription, taxation, and the provision of military stores. An oriental king at heart, Solomon was already on his way to reorganizing the Israelite monarchy and reforming it in the image of other oriental kings.

As part of his centralization of power, Solomon may have carried out a sweeping reorganization of the administrative structure of the nation. "Solomon had twelve prefects governing all Israel, who provided food for the king, and his household; each had to provide food for one month in the year."[17] "All those prefects, each during his month, would furnish provisions for King Solomon and all who were admitted to King Solomon's table [the extended household and court]. They would also, each in his turn, deliver barley and straw for the horses and the swift steeds to the places where they were stationed."[18] The reorganization seems to have taken place very early in Solomon's reign, surely prior to beginning construction on the Temple in his fourth year, leading some to suggest that it was not undertaken by Solomon at all but had been mostly completed before David died. Mazar suggests that the text implies exactly this in I Kings 2:12 when it tells us that, "Solomon sat on the throne of David his father; and his kingdom was established very firmly."[19] If so, then it may have been that Joab, who carried it out for the new administrative system, also rationalized the logistical base of the army, assuring it a stable and adequate source of supply, an achievement that would probably have been beyond the technical expertise of the militarily inexperienced king.

The administrative reorganization sought to achieve three objectives. First, the system was designed to organize the population for use as corvee labor to construct public works and military fortifications. At the same time, of course, the system could be used to rationalize the conscription of troops. With governors and overseers in charge of each of the 12 districts armed with lists of military age males, large groups of men could be called to military service quickly. Second, the system created artificial districts drawn with a view toward making them somewhat equal in economic productivity and wealth so that the burden of supplying the court and the army with taxes in kind would not fall too heavily upon any one district.[20] This required that the district lines be drawn across traditional tribal boundaries and include lands that were heretofore Canaanite and, perhaps, Philistine. The objective was to hasten the incorporation of these Canaanite and Philistine territories into the new Israelite state. The settlement of Levite communities in these areas was designed to accomplish the same thing. Third, drawing the district lines across tribal boundaries effectively gerrymandering the old bases of power seems to have been deliberately intended to weaken the power of the traditional tribal elites, including their ability to control their troop contingents and the loyalty of their unit commanders.[21] This, of course, would have made sense given Solomon's establishment of a single national military command authority that could be relied upon to see to it that no local tribal commanders presented significant challenges to the royal will. Solomon's reforms set the Israelite military and its relations with the monarchy for the first time on a sound rational foundation based on centralized authority and national defense needs. In doing so, Solomon transformed Israelite military and political institutions into structures identical to those that characterized Canaanite and Philistine kingdoms and were typical of the oriental monarchies of the day.

CONFRONTATION WITH EGYPT

Solomon had not been king more than a year or so after David's death when he was forced to deal with a threat to Israel's security. As so many times before, the threat came from Egypt and its perpetrator was probably Siamun, the penultimate pharaoh of the Twenty-first Dynasty (1075–945 B.C.E.).[22] The Twenty-first Dynasty, with its capital at Tanis in the Nile Delta, ruled only northern Egypt while the south, with its capital at Thebes, was in the firm grip of the theocratic regime of the priesthood of Amun. While Egyptian power was always formidable, the power of Egypt under the Twenty-first Dynasty was not as great as had been the case under the warrior pharaohs of, say, the Eighteenth Dynasty. This being said, it is likely that Siamun sought to take advantage of the new king's inexperience as well as the instability and uncertainty of the Israelite court as Solomon sought to deal with his rivals. In this regard, it is unlikely that the murder of Joab, Israel's most competent general, went unnoticed in the Egyptian capital.

The immediate cause of the crisis was an Egyptian attack on the city of Gezer sometime around 967–966 B.C.E.[23] I Kings 9:16 tells us that "Pharaoh king of Egypt had gone up and captured Gezer and burnt it with fire, and had slain the Canaanites who dwelt in the city." Archaeological evidence supports the account. It was during this time that the Egyptian outpost at Sharuhen seems to have been refurbished and reoccupied by Egyptian troops. Sharuhen had been the forward staging base for Egyptian incursions into Palestine for more than 500 years, and the archeological evidence suggests strongly that it was used again by Siamun. Further, the town of Tel Mor, six miles to the northwest of Ashdod, was apparently destroyed in the first half of the tenth century B.C.E. Since there is no account of David having destroyed the town, it seems reasonable that Siamun destroyed it during his campaign against Gezer.[24] The town is located near Ashdod and is in the heart of Philistia.

The issue, then, was Philistia and not Gezer. It will be recalled that David had refrained from directly attacking Philistia even though it is probable that he possessed the military capability to do so successfully. Instead, only some of the border areas of Philistia were incorporated into the new Israelite state. The reason for David's restraint was the strong relationship between the Philistines and Egypt. For centuries Egypt had regarded Philistia as an Egyptian satellite and had long exercised suzerainty over the territory.[25] Gezer had been the last Egyptian stronghold to fall more than a century before. Siamun's attack on Gezer was probably designed to reestablish Egyptian influence in southern Palestine and Philistia. The Egyptian incursion was serious insofar as it threatened to reduce Israelite influence in Philistia, which, as we have noted earlier, may have been the source of some chariot units provided by Philistine vassals to the Israelite army, and it is likely that at the time of the crisis Israel was still somewhat dependent on its Canaanite and Philistine vassals for chariot units. But there may have been an even more serious strategic reason for Jerusalem to be concerned. Siamun's march through Philistia had terminated at Gezer which controlled the access to two valleys leading to the central Judean ridge and had been the historical bridgehead for past Canaanite and Philistine assaults on Israel. Given Gezer's strategic position and

David's policy, it is also likely that the Canaanites there had become vassals of David and, like the Philistines, provided military assistance to Israel. Siamun's destruction of the city struck at an important Israelite politico-military asset with the result that Egyptian power was ensconced on the border of Israel directly astride a traditional route of invasion.

Solomon reacted strongly to reverse the Egyptian threat. Despite the domestic turmoil following David's death and the murder of Israel's chief military commander, the army itself was still strong and sufficiently capable of acquitting itself against the forces of Egypt, themselves weakened by domestic problems. The text is silent on Solomon's actions, but Malamat makes a convincing case that at the very least they involved a credible threat of force that convinced the Egyptians to abandon their hold on Gezer and transfer it to Israel.[26] To reduce the injury to Egyptian prestige, Solomon agreed to marry pharaoh's daughter and to accept Gezer, now in ruins, as her dowry. It was a diplomatic solution to a strategic crisis and strongly favored Israel. In this regard, not only did Israel incorporate Gezer into its territory, but there is some evidence that Israel may have incorporated most of Ekron, too, of which Gezer was a part.[27] The evidence is indirect, however. Later, when Solomon fortified Israel against another Egyptian threat, the text tells us that among the cities he fortified were Gezer and Baalith,[28] both located in Philistia. Baalith is mentioned in Joshua 19:44 as part of the original territory of Dan located some eight miles west of Ekron.[29] This implies that Solomon was in control of a good part of Philistia.

It is conceivable that Solomon pressed Israelite control even farther south, although not as far as Gaza, for without some Israelite fortifications farther south Solomon's extensive fortifications in the Negev would have been pointless since they could have easily been flanked by an army moving along the coastal road. Israelite fortifications in southern Philistia would have been required to make the Negev fortifications an effective barrier against Egyptian invasion. Some evidence is afforded by II Chronicles 11:8, which provides a list of the fortifications constructed by Rehoboam after Solomon's death. The list includes Gath, the old capital of the Philistine king, Achish. While we are uncertain as to when or how, gradually or suddenly, Israel incorporated most of Philistia, that it did so seems reasonable. It is with this in mind that the words of I Kings 5:1 that "Solomon's rule extended over the kingdoms from the Euphrates to the land of the Philistines and the boundary of Egypt" are to be understood. Earlier Israelite hesitancy regarding an occupation of Philistia was premised on the reality of Egyptian power to enforce its claims to suzerainty over the area. Solomon had called the Egyptian bluff and revealed the weakness of that power. In so doing he created a territorial vacuum which Israel filled.[30] The Kings text is clear in suggesting that the "land of the Philistines" was a distinct area under Israelite control. If the analysis is correct, then "the United Monarchy arrived at its fullest extent—not under David but as a result of Solomon's own political achievements."[31]

The suggestion that Solomon was able to force the Egyptians to abandon their objectives in Philistia finds support in the rest of the passage in I Kings 9:17 which describes Siamun's destruction of Gezer. Having destroyed the city, Siamun then "gave it as dowry to his daughter, Solomon's wife." It is well documented that, like David, Solomon used marriage as a tool of international diplomacy even to the extent of incorporating the deities of his foreign wives into the Israelite pantheon. The marriage of Solomon to pharaoh's daughter is noted in no fewer than five places in the biblical text.[32] The importance of an event, treaty, or agreement can be measured by the status of the woman involved in the marital agreement. The Egyptian-Israelite agreement regarding Gezer must have been of great import because apart from Solomon, there is no evidence that a daughter of pharaoh was ever given to a foreigner as a wife.[33] When the king of Babylon requested the hand of Amenhotep III's daughter in marriage, he was rebuffed with the following words: "From of old a daughter of the king of Egypt has not been given to anyone."[34] The Egyptian reticence is remarkable as marrying off royal daughters for political reasons was common everywhere else in the Near East. The reason for the Egyptian refusal was that unlike other countries where only male lineage was important, in Egypt legitimate royal lineage passed through the *female* and not the male line.[35] Anyone married to an Egyptian royal daughter could put forth a legitimate claim to the throne, as sometimes happened in the selection of pharaohs themselves throughout Egyptian history. When, for example, Tutankhamen died, his wife made an overture to the Hittite king to send one of his sons for her to marry with the offer that he would then become king of Egypt. The plot was neutralized when the groom was assassinated and the royal wife disappeared.[36] It might well be argued, then, that the marriage of pharaoh's daughter to Solomon was an act of great diplomatic significance, and surely one that implied that Israel had reached the status of a great regional power.

REVOLT

For the next 20 years, Solomon occupied himself with civic building projects, including the construction of the Temple, and in establishing profitable commercial relationships with Tyre (Phoenicia) and Mesopotamia. The Tyre-Jerusalem commercial axis depended on Tyrian naval superiority and her large fleet of commercial ships while Israel, for its part, assumed the role of controlling the commercial overland routes in all directions. In this manner both countries controlled the trade of the entire region, from Gaza to Byblos, and Mesopotamia to Ezion Geber.[37] The big loser in this arrangement was Egypt whose access to the region's markets had been severely curtailed. As the Twenty-first Dynasty lumbered to its demise, there was little Egypt could do to reverse the course of events. But the expenditures for Solomon's public works almost bankrupted the treasury, forcing Solomon to cede twenty towns in the Galilee to the king of Tyre to cover his debts. Solomon's extensive and prolonged use of corvee labor brought the Israelite population to the edge of revolt and, finally, into open rebellion.[38]

Events in Egypt now began to move against Israel. A new dynasty of warrior kings had replaced the weak Twenty-first Dynasty. Its leaders were descended from the Libyan people who had infiltrated and settled in the Nile Delta over the previous two centuries. One of these kings, Shishak, established the Twenty-second Dynasty sometime around 945 B.C.E., or about the twenty-fourth year of Solomon's reign. Shishak, like his father and grandfather, bore the title Great Chief of the Me, a reference to the Meshwesh people of Libya, and was a competent general. Shishak initiated a more aggressive policy toward Israel and embarked upon a course to reestablish Egyptian influence not only in Philistia, but also in all Palestine as well.[39] For 16 years the kings of Israel and Egypt maneuvered against each other in pursuit of their national interests until, after Solomon died, the Egyptian pharaoh settled matters once and for all when "in the fifth year of King Rehoboam, King Shishak of Egypt marched against Jerusalem."[40]

Solomon also was forced to deal with domestic unrest and the revolt of two subject peoples, Edom and Aram Damascus. I Kings 11:14–22 tells the story of Hadad of Edom, a prince of the royal family that escaped the slaughter of Edomite males that Joab inflicted upon the country after David's conquest. Hadad and some followers fled to Egypt where he was welcomed by pharaoh and grew to adulthood. When news of the deaths of David and Joab reached Egypt, Hadad, with Egyptian support, returned to Edom and led a revolt against the Israelites. The text is silent on its outcome, but it almost certainly required Solomon to send troops and suppress the local population to protect the important line of communication with the vital port of Ezion-Geber. A second and more serious revolt occurred in the Aramean state of Aram Damascus led by Rezon, a general in the army of Hadadezer of Zobah. II Samuel 8:6 tells us that when David conquered the Arameans, "David put governors in Aram of Damascus." The importance of the area to Israelite security and its trade to Mesopotamia can be assumed from the fact that of all the districts of Syria and the northern Transjordan only Damascus was placed under Israelite governors.[41] Following the Egyptian/Philistine model, Israelite troop garrisons were also placed in Aram Damascus. I Kings 11:24–25 tells us that Rezon escaped the slaughter by David's army and "gathered men about him and became captain over a troop; they went to Damascus and settled there, and they established a kingdom in Damascus. He was an adversary of Israel all the days of Solomon, adding to the trouble caused by Hadad; he repudiated [the authority of] Israel and reigned over Aram." There can be no doubt that this was a full-scale revolt involving the destruction or ejection of the Israelite garrisons and authorities by armed force and the reoccupation of the district by a powerful enemy. There is no evidence from the text or elsewhere that Solomon attempted to reverse the situation through military force.

Solomon also had to put down a revolt among his own people, probably provoked by the prolonged use of harsh forced labor over a period of 20 years. Jeroboam was an Ephraimite who served with the king's crews working on the construction of the Millo and the walls of Jerusalem.[42] Somehow Jeroboam came to the king's attention and was promoted to the overseer of recruiting the labor gangs "in Joseph," that is, in the area of Mount Ephraim, his native territory. Perhaps as a consequence of the harsh treatment of his fellow tribesmen, Jeroboam came to lead a group of malcontents in some sort of protest against the king.[43] The text tells us that "he raised his hand against the king," but no details are provided. The *Septuagint* informs us, however, that Jeroboam fortified a town called Sareida, perhaps modern Ain Seredah, located in the hills of the western slope of the central range in Ephraim. It also says that he raised a force of 300 chariots, but this is uncertain, and rebelled against the king.[44] In response, "Solomon sought to put Jeroboam to death, but Jeroboam promptly fled to King Shishak of Egypt; and he remained in Egypt until the death of Solomon."[45] Of all Solomon's difficulties, Jeroboam would prove to be the most dangerous, for the day would come when he would return to Israel with consequences that were devastating to the country.

FORTIFICATIONS

It is against this backdrop of domestic and foreign threats that one must understand Solomon's policies beginning in his twenty-fourth year when the construction of the Temple, the Jerusalem palace, and the Millo was already complete. Solomon correctly assessed the Egyptian threat to Israel's security and moved to bolster the country's defenses. I Kings 9:15–19 describes Solomon's defensive plan. "This was the purpose of the forced labor which Solomon imposed: It was to build the House of the Lord, his own palace, the Millo, and the wall of Jerusalem, and to fortify Hazor, Megiddo, and Gezer . . . Solomon fortified Gezer, lower Beth-horan, Baalith, and Tamar in the wilderness . . . and all of Solomon's garrison towns, chariot towns, and cavalry towns . . . throughout the territory that he ruled." The number of major forts makes clear that they do not form a continuous line of defense, much less a borderline defended in depth. Taken as part of a larger integrated system, however, Solomon's fortifications reveal themselves to be links in a schematic of strong points serving at one and the same time as pivots for defense and as bases for mobile force (chariots) reaction and proaction. The fortresses noted earlier (and others extant but not mentioned in the text) were the major stationary bases for the deployment and staging of Solomon's national field army. The entire scheme is strongly reminiscent of the old Canaanite system (see chapters 1 and 2 of this work) premised on the assumption that the best defense is an elastic mobile-force offensive centered around strong-points arraigned in depth.[46]

The locations of the fortifications make sound strategic and tactical sense for defending the nation against Egypt in the south and Syria-Babylonia in the north. Thus *Hazor* guarded the main highway from Israel to Syria at the point where it branched off into two strategic roads: the first passing along the Jordan Valley, past Ijon and then on to Hamath or Damascus, and the second ascending the Syrian plateau and running straight to Damascus. *Megiddo* controlled the major west-to-east axis of northern Palestine, that branch of the Via Maris that passed through the Jezreel Valley and the "Iron Pass," the Carmel's main north-to-south route of traverse.[47] *Gezer* was the key border fortress that guarded the entry into the Judean ridge through either the Aijalon Valley or the Valley of Sorek, as well as guarding all the approaches to Jerusalem from the general direction of Jaffa. The location of *Tamar* is unclear, but is thought to be a small village southwest of the Dead Sea, perhaps modern Qurnub, about 24 miles east of Beer-sheba.[48] Others have identified it in the general area of Gasar Gehainije or Ein Hosob.[49] All these locations are on the major communications artery between central Palestine and Ezion-Geber and the southern Transjordan highlands of Moab and Edom. An Israelite garrison here would have been in position to block the King's Highway, a logical route for an Egyptian strike into the Transjordan. The fortification of *Lower Beth-horan* protected the main western approach to Jerusalem and towered above the plain of Lod permitting attack or defense against the roads leading toward Jaffa and the north, as well as those leading past Aijalon to Gezer and Beth-shemesh. An enemy attempting to penetrate the mountains along the more southern route was vulnerable to a flanking attack from this position. II Chronicles 7:5 notes that the defenses of *Upper Beth-horan* were also improved. Upper and Lower Beth-horon are only 2.5 miles apart, and taken together they command the most difficult defile along the road to Jerusalem. The location of *Baalith* is uncertain, but I am inclined to agree with Gichon that, as noted previously, it is the Baalath mentioned in Joshua 19:44 if we agree to its identification with Mughar, 4.5 miles southeast of Jabneh.[50] Baalath-Mughar lies on the southern leg of the Via Maris on a small hill commanding the surrounding plain. From here an Israelite garrison could intercept Egyptian invaders moving north. Moreover, its position blocks any attempt from the south to circumvent the Negev forts while its location deep in Philistia permits military action against Philistine cities, perhaps evidence that following Siamun's failed attempt on Philistia, Solomon moved to occupy and fortify Baalath-Mughar. Its tactical importance is further testified to by the fact that it was at the hill of Baalath-Mughar that one of the last mounted operations of World War II was carried out by the British against the Turks strongly entrenched upon the hill.[51]

All the major fortified cities are located near strategic roads, and all command large areas of terrain that are particularly well suited to offensive chariot attack. As with Hazor, Megiddo, and Gezer, we may presume the other major cities contained large chariot garrisons with which Israelite commanders could defend their positions by taking the offensive in the open field. Like Canaanite commanders before them, Israelite commanders would employ a static defense of the cities themselves only as a last resort. The fortifications of Jerusalem were also improved with the construction of a tower at the northeast corner called the Millo and the repair and addition of new defensive walls.[52] David had done little to strengthen the city's defenses, and Solomon's new city encompassed far more territory than the original Jebusite town and seems to have spread across the valley of Tyropoeon to the western hill and northward to include the Temple.[53]

The text tells of the building of "garrison towns, chariot towns, and cavalry towns . . . throughout the territory he [Solomon] ruled." These were military garrisons for horses and chariots, walled and fortified arms depots, and supply centers for use by army units stationed throughout the land. Presumably, these fortresses and garrisons filled in the gaps between the major fortified cities and controlled key roads and avenues of advance. That the network of these fortifications was extensive is clearly implied by the text.[54] The Kings texts do not tell us much about these garrisons, but II Chronicles 11:12 describes the fortresses of Rehoboam which most likely were identical. The text tells us that in the fortified places Rehoboam "put commanders and supplies of food, oil, and wine in them. In every single city he also put large shields and spears and strengthened them very much," in short, arms, men, and supplies to sustain a prolonged siege. One suspects reasonably that the garrisons of several forts could be quickly assembled to form a combined force capable of undertaking operations in the open field. The "store cities" were probably major depots colocated in the provincial capitals. Under the watchful eye of the governor, who reported directly to the king, they were mostly located on major highways facilitating their role as centers of provincial administration, collection points for taxes and corvee recruitment and assembly, and supply links in the overall fortification system of the kingdom.[55] Of some curiosity is the use of the term "cavalry towns" and "cavalry" itself. Cavalry, properly understood, did not make its appearance in the ancient world until Assurnasirpal II (883–859 B.C.E.) introduced this new combat arm to the army of Assyria,[56] a century after Solomon. The text employs the word *parashim*, which lends itself to two meanings. The first is charioteer. The second is infantry surrounding the king, which might imply that the infantry runners accompanying the chariots were regarded as cavalrymen. Whatever its intended meaning, however, it cannot be reasonably construed to mean cavalry in the most commonly understood sense of fighting men doing battle from horseback.

Not mentioned in the texts, but certainly a critical part of Solomon's overall defensive system of fortifications, were the 40 or so fortresses and strongpoints which he constructed in the southern Negev around the same time.[57] The traditional southern border of Judah ran along the edge of the Beer-sheba basin and did not extend to the southern Negev. Solomon seems to have extended the border of Judah considerably southward and fortified it against an anticipated Egyptian attack.[58] Although uncertain, it is probable that if the fortifications in southern Philistia had not yet already been constructed, as suggested earlier, they were constructed at this time. The two sets of fortifications reinforced one another in that each prevented the other from being flanked by an Egyptian advance into Palestine. The Negev fortresses were of several shapes—ovals, rectangles, and squares—and some were outfitted with towers at the corners. All were constructed with casement walls. Casement walls are light, cheap, and can be constructed quickly, and appear to have been first employed by the Israelites during Solomon's time, copied from and, perhaps, constructed by Phoenician/Canaanite engineers.[59] The story of Solomon's temple makes clear that Israel lacked any architectural tradition in public buildings and fortifications so that its models were drawn from outside Israel, most commonly from Phoenicia, the repository of the old Canaanite culture.[60] Archaeology suggests, however, that there was a local Canaanite tradition of casement construction reaching back at least to the seventeenth century B.C.E.[61] Archaeological evidence also suggests that the site plan and casement construction of the fortifications of Hazor, Megiddo, and Gezer were nearly identical.[62] As with the Temple, Solomon may have relied upon Phoenician engineers to construct his defensive fortifications. The pattern of the Negev fortifications suggests that they may have had a secondary role as well, to protect against raids by nomads. A large number of small forts arrayed in-depth and in mutually protective fashion could trap nomadic raiders in the depth of the defensive zone forcing them to engage the garrisons nearest to their line of advance. Once engaged, troops from other nearby garrisons could join the fight, often taking the enemy in the flank or rear.[63] The student of history will recognize the concept as similar to that later employed by the Romans in the *limes*. The Negev and coastal defense barrier ultimately proved ineffective against the army of Shishak who, sometime around 924 B.C.E., attacked Israel. The campaign was devastating, and the Negev fortresses were completely destroyed forcing the southern border of Judah northward. The central Negev was virtually abandoned, and no serious attempt at resettlement was undertaken for many years.[64]

THE CHARIOT CORPS

To transform Israel into a modern state required the establishment of a national army, a process that had already begun under David and accelerated under Solomon with his creation of rational manpower and logistics systems and a unified national command authority. A modern army also required modern weaponry, and it is to Solomon that credit is due for the establishment of an Israelite chariot corps. When this corps was established is a matter of some uncertainty. II Chronicles 1:14 places the establishment of the corps early in Solomon's reign, while I Kings 10:26 suggests that the corps was established after Solomon's construction projects were finished, that is, sometime in his twenty-fourth year. That David's wars against the chariot-borne Arameans could not have been successful without chariots suggests that the *employment* of chariots by the Israelites probably began prior to Solomon. However, these units were most likely provided and commanded by Canaanite and Philistine vassals, not Israelites themselves. As the Israelites gradually integrated the Canaanite enclaves into the state—as well as "annihilating" their populations and impressing the rest into forced labor[65]—control of their chariot units gradually passed to the Israelites. The same was likely true for the Philistines. As Solomon encroached on Philistine lands, it is likely that the military units of Israel's former vassals were disbanded and their equipment transferred to Israelite commanders. Most likely, then, the process of building a genuine Israelite chariot arm occurred gradually reaching its peak under Solomon around the time that the Egyptian threat from Shishak was growing. The first mention of Israelites in command of chariot units does not appear until this time when I Kings 9:22 tells us that Solomon "did not reduce any Israelites to slavery [corvee labor]; they served, rather, as warriors and his attendants, officials, and officers, and as commanders of his chariotry and cavalry."

The strength of the chariot corps under Solomon is put at "1,400 chariots and 12,000 horses which he stationed in the chariot towns and with the king in Jerusalem [the strategic reserve]."[66] II Chronicles 9:25 says that "Solomon also had 4,000 stalls for horses and chariots." We may take these figures as a realistic description of the strength of the Israelite chariot corps. Calculations made by archaeologists at Megiddo suggest that there was room there for about 450 horses and 150 chariots along with exercise grounds, water tanks, billets for grooms, and so on. Given that there were stables of similar type at Tell el-Hesy, Gezer, Ta'anach, and, perhaps, Hazor and other cities, the figure of 4,000 horse stalls in the country does not seem unlikely.[67] A century later (835 B.C.E.) at the battle of Karkar against the Assyrian king Shalmaneser III the Israelites put 2,000 chariots in the field as part of the allied effort, a number congruent with the estimates of the strength of Solomon's corps a century earlier.

It has sometimes been thought that the Israelites lacked the technical expertise to construct chariots of their own[68] and were dependent on Egypt for their machines. I Kings 10:29 seems to imply that this was the case when it tells us that "a chariot imported from Mizraim [Egypt] cost 600 shekels of silver, and horse 150; these in turn were exported by them to all the kings of the Hittites and the kings of the Arameans." It is not to be believed that the Israelites would somehow have failed, at the least, to press the Canaanite and Philistine chariot makers into service even as they served as apprentices to learn the art of construction themselves. Moreover, if Solomon relied upon Egyptian sources for his chariots, the cost of the machines and their horses would have been impossible to sustain, to say nothing of the danger of relying upon foreign sources of supply for such strategic materials. The cost of a single chariot, 600 shekels, was 15.1 pounds of silver. There being no coinage prices were paid in weight, or 21,000 pounds of silver to purchase 1,400 vehicles.[69] At 150 shekels each, a horse would have cost 3.75 pounds of silver, or 45,000 pounds of silver for the 12,000 horses noted in the text. The astronomical sum of 33 tons of silver would have been required just to purchase the horses and machines, to say nothing of the cost of stalls, grooms, feed, repairs, and so on, well beyond the ability of the Israelite economy to sustain it.

What, then, was Solomon importing from Egypt and selling to the Hittites and Arameans? A clue lies in the text's use of two distinct terms for chariot. Both in Exodus and in discussing Solomon's chariots in I Kings, the text uses the term *rekeb* for chariot. Its use in Exodus 14:6–7 denotes the Egyptian military chariot. But when describing the chariot trade with Egypt, the text uses the term *merkaba* for chariot.[70] The same term is used to describe Absalom's chariot in II Samuel 8:11 and Adonijah's chariot in I Kings 1:5. The *merkaba* was not a military chariot but an expensive display vehicle commonly possessed by kings, princes, and other members of the Near East nobility, including Israel, equipped with expensive steeds to transport their owners from place to place.[71] So it was these expensive vehicles with their fine horse teams, not military chariots, that Solomon imported from Egypt and resold to his own nobility and to the nobility of other countries.

The Egyptian military chariot, however, was much cheaper and easily affordable. It is often assumed that the scarcity of wood in Egypt required it to import wood for the construction of the chariots, thereby greatly increasing their cost.[72] In fact, Egyptian wood imports were mostly strong wooden beams for use in constructing major buildings and cedar planking for use as decorative wall covering in temples.[73] Egypt had long used indigenous wood to manufacture chariots for her armies. The Nubian acacia is an excellent indigenous hardwood and had been used for centuries in the manufacture of ships, coffins, and chariots. Queen Hapshepsut's chariot was made of Nubian acacia.[74] Egypt had always possessed an adequate supply of most woods used in the manufacture of chariots.[75] The Egyptian military chariot, therefore, was much cheaper than the display vehicle. According to the Papyrus Anastasi III

(6:7–8), an Egyptian military chariot in the thirteenth century B.C.E. cost 8 *deben* or about 64 shekels of silver and the cost of a horse between 30 and 35 shekels.[76] At these prices Solomon could well have purchased sufficient chariots and horses to outfit his entire chariot arm for 12,740 pounds of silver, still expensive, but well within the economic capability of the Israelite economy. More likely, however, Israelite chariots were manufactured in Israel.

It has long been assumed that Solomon obtained the horses for his chariot arm from Cilicia. The text commonly cited in support of this proposition is I Kings 10:28 which tells us that "Solomon's horses were procured from Mizraim and Kue." The word "Mizraim," however, denotes Egypt, as understood by most scholars in the very next phrase that says, "a chariot imported from Mizraim [Egypt] cost 600 shekels of silver," that is, Solomon's chariots were imported from Egypt. Mazar notes that Kue cannot be understood to mean Anatolia, for Kue was not horse-breeding country but a location near the Mediterranean coast where horses were brought from northern Anatolia for transshipment, presumably by sea, to Israel.[77] Unless we are willing to permit the word *Mizraim* to mean Egypt in one phrase and Anatolia in the very next phrase of the same sentence, the notion that Solomon's horses came from Anatolia and not Egypt cannot be sustained by the text. However, so strongly embedded is the idea that Solomon controlled the horse trade across the Palestinian land-bridge that some scholars have suggested that even the Egyptian army was dependent on Israel for its supply of horses,[78] even as the Israelites shipped the animals to Egypt to be trained for the chariot yoke "since Israel had neither the expertise nor the conditions for training horses to work with chariots and charioteers."[79] Both propositions strain credulity but follow from the assumption that Egypt did not breed horses and therefore had to import them from Israel.[80] The corollary is, of course, that Egypt did not export horses.

But the evidence suggests the contrary. The Hyksos introduced the horse to Egypt circa seventeenth century B.C.E., and the first kings of the Eighteenth Dynasty obtained their horses through booty or purchase abroad. Within a century, however, the horse had become acclimatized in Egypt so that Egypt became a horse-breeding country, easily providing its own large chariot army with sufficient mounts and exporting the rest. The land of the Nile Delta, particularly the region of Pithom, afforded vast grassy pasturage suitable for raising large herds of horses[81] just as it had afforded pasture for the cattle herds of the Israelites once settled there. Exodus 1:11 notes that Par Ramesses, mentioned along with Pithom as one of pharaoh's "store cities," was one of the royal Delta residences where Ramses II constructed "great stables" necessary for breeding and training horses. There is ample evidence from other texts to suggest that Egypt exported a particular breed of fine large horses, perhaps for use with the display chariots of the nobility, and that Nubian horses were especially valued by the Assyrians for their size, stamina, and the ease with which they could be broken to the chariot yoke.[82] An Egyptian chariot horse cost the equivalent of 32 shekels of silver. The evidence suggests, then, that while Solomon may well have sold display chariots and horse teams to the nobility of the Hittites and the Arameans, it is unlikely that Solomon sold chariot horses to them as well since these kingdoms were already much closer to the Anatolian horse-breeding grasslands than Israel was. The most logical and cost-effective place for Solomon to obtain horses for his chariot corps was right next door, in *Mizraim* or Egypt, just as the text says he did. Relations with Egypt were generally friendly, and Solomon's father-in-law was pharaoh. Under these circumstances, a brisk trade in horses would have been quite likely.

The purchase of horses from Egypt does not preclude the possibility, implied by the text, that Solomon also purchased chariot mounts from Anatolian sources as well. Indeed, having two sources for such an important military item as horses would have made logistical and strategic sense. The most efficient and reliable route for obtaining horses from this area would have been an overland route along inland Syria, generally following the course of the Orontes River, a route with abundant pasturage, cornfields, and water to sustain the animals along a string of relay stations equipped with corrals to hold the animals. The route was controlled by and passed through the kingdom of Hamath, long known for raising and selling horses.[83] Hamath had been a satellite of Hadadezer until David had taken it in the war with the Arameans. David did not occupy Hamath, however, but signed a treaty with its king that included military and commercial relationships. Hamath was left as a buffer between Aram Damascus and Israel. Under these conditions, it is certainly possible that Hamath became another source of horses for Solomon's chariot corps.

It is against this background that we might makes sense of the information missing from Kings but extant in II Chronicles 8:3–4 that "Solomon went to Hamath-Zobah and took it, and built Tadmor (Palmyra) in the desert and all the store cities which he built in Hamath." Once more, the timing of the event is important. If Egypt was a major supplier of horses for Israel, the establishment of the Twenty-second Dynasty and the ascent of Pharaoh Shishak to the throne at about this time might have imperiled this source of supply. To the north Rezon and his guerrilla army had wrested control of Aram Damascus from Israel and driven out her occupying troops, a development that placed Hamath, Israel's other supplier of horses, at risk. Given the geographic proximity of Aram Damascus to Hamath, a resurgent Damascus might have already begun to force Hamath to loosen its Israelite connections. The text can be read to imply that Solomon responded with military force, perhaps with Hamath's approval, to shore up Israelite defenses in the north by fortifying Tadmor. Tadmor was an important city east of Zobah on the caravan route to Mesopotamia and located within Hamath. In Israelite eyes, Tadmor was a strategic point for trade and an advanced garrison to check any Aramean military initiatives toward Israel.[84] The "store cities" are, of course, the relay and holding stations where horses could be kept and reared until requisitioned by the central administration in Israel.[85] With Solomon's primary source of horses disrupted by the rise of Shishak in Egypt, he moved to secure his only remaining source in Hamath, using military force to seize and occupy the district, albeit with the probable connivance of Hamath itself. The stratagem must have worked, for we do not hear of any problems related to the supply of horses again. A century later Israel was still well equipped with a large chariot corps, and sent 2,000 vehicles and crews to support the allied coalition at Karkar.

DECLINE AND DESTRUCTION

For the remaining 16 years of his reign, Solomon managed to maintain Israel's domestic prosperity and avoid any wars with its neighbors. Presumably his program of civic construction and military fortifications continued, for immediately after Solomon's death we hear of the Israelite tribal elders pleading with Rehoboam to remove the heavy yoke of forced labor.[86] It is also possible that the improved fortifications of Judah attributed to Rehoboam were actually begun under Solomon. The army, too, must have been maintained at a substantial level of military capability, for when Rehoboam took the field against Jeroboam he was able to utilize the professional army immediately and effectively. The text says that Rehoboam mustered 180,000 men against Jeroboam, no doubt an exaggeration but which nonetheless suggests that a very substantial force could be quickly mobilized for battle.[87] Foreign relations were more problematical, however. Presumably Aram Damascus was never recovered, for we hear nothing of it again. Edom, too, may have eventually struggled free of Israelite control weakening the Israelite trade monopoly over the King's Highway and Ebion-Gezer.

To achieve his ends Solomon had transformed Israel into an oriental-style monarchy in which royal authority was exercised without restraint with little consideration given to the traditional rights and values associated with the Israelite notion of kingship. When power passed from Solomon to Rehoboam, this orientalism was maintained by the new king with disastrous consequences. Having grown weary of the forced labor imposed by Solomon's oriental style of rule, the tribal elders petitioned the new king to undo the heavy burden. The northern tribes had always regarded their support of the Judean monarchy as conditional so that when Rehoboam refused, the tribes went over to revolt.[88] Shishak had given Jeroboam refuge when he fled from Solomon, and now used him to Egypt's advantage. In a maneuver reminiscent of German intelligence inserting Lenin into Russia during World War I to foster domestic unrest and weaken Russia from within, Shishak sent Jeroboam back to Israel sometime after Solomon's death to exploit the break between the new king and the tribal leaders. As with Lenin, the stratagem was successful for "When all Israel heard that Jeroboam had returned, they sent him messengers and summoned him to the assembly and made him king over all Israel."[89] The result was civil war.

Rehoboam was still in command of the professional army, which he quickly mobilized and used to take the war to the north.[90] Over a period of five years, Rehoboam seems to have succeeded in driving Jeroboam and his rebels from most of the major northern cities and towns forcing them to take to the hills and conduct guerilla operations.[91] Just when Rehoboam seemed on the edge of victory, Shishak undertook a major invasion of Israel. "In the fifth year of King Rehoboam [circa 918 B.C.E.], Shishak the king of Egypt came up against Jerusalem . . . with 1,200 chariots and 60,000 horsemen; the people who came with him from Egypt were innumerable—Libyans, Sukkim, and Ethiopians. They captured the fortified places belonging to Judah and came as far as Jerusalem."[92] The Egyptian army crossed the border and advanced along the Via Maris capturing Gaza and moving quickly up the coast subduing one objective after another. Turning east, Shishak's army crossed into the Jezreel Valley via the Aruna road subduing all the major cities of the valley and those to its immediate north, though Hazor was not attacked. Turning south, the Egyptians took Beth-shean and the Jordan Valley towns before moving up the east ridge of the central spine subduing Shechem before surrounding Jerusalem. A list of the towns captured by Shishak during the invasion is preserved on the great wall at Karnak and includes most the major fortified towns of Israel. Thus, the list includes Gaza, Aijalon, Beth-horon, Gibeon, Beth-shean, Shunem, Ta'anach, Adar, Aruna, Megiddo, Succoth, and Shechem.[93]

Many of the cities and towns Shishak captured were in the north, and, as Peckham notes, it is hardly credible that all these northern towns were destroyed.[94] The goal of Shishak's invasion was to reestablish Egyptian suzerainty over the coastal plain and to break the stranglehold over the commercial routes that Israel had maintained for more than 40 years. Shishak sought to sever the commercial relationship between Tyre and Israel that had shut Egypt out of the important northern trade.[95] To this end, the city and towns of Israel would have been of no use at all if they were destroyed. Oesterley offers a credible explanation of Shishak's route of attack through the north by suggesting that Jeroboam had already been driven from these cities by Rehoboam's army, which occupied them as a means of keeping the northern tribes under control.[96] Shishak's armies liberated the northern towns from Rehoboam's occupying army of Judah and turned them over to Jeroboam. This done, Shishak surrounded Jerusalem trapping Rehoboam and his commanders within its walls.[97] With an Egyptian army outside Jerusalem's gates, Israel's northern towns occupied by the rebels, and the cities of Judah taken by storm and its lands ravaged, Rehoboam had little choice but to surrender Jerusalem to the Egyptians who then "carried off the treasures of the House of the Lord and the treasures of the royal palace. [They] carried off everything; even the golden shields that Solomon had made."[98] On their way out of the country, the Egyptians destroyed Solomon's Negev forts. The kingdom of David and Solomon was brought to its knees.

In the north, Jeroboam's fortunes were reversed and he set about organizing his kingdom. He rebuilt Shechem and constructed new fortifications on the Judean border. Having organized the military into a standing force, Jeroboam then dismantled the old Judean-based religious establishment by appointing non-Levites to the priesthood and establishing new shrines where the populace could worship. It was these acts, perhaps even more than the military defeat of Rehoboam at the hands of the Egyptians, that marked the real end of the United Monarchy. The severance of the two kingdoms was now complete. The north had a political, military, and religious establishment of its own while "only the tribe of Judah remained loyal to the House of David." Wars broke out between the two kingdoms off and on for the next two centuries, but Israel was never again a united political entity under its own governance until the War of Independence of 1948 reestablished it.

From the time of Saul to Solomon, the kingdom of Israel had lasted little more than 100 years.

NOTES

1. D. N. Freedman, "The Age of David and Solomon," in *World History of the Jewish People* (Israel: Jewish History Publications Ltd., 1961), 120.

2. For an account of the military training experienced by the sons of Egyptian pharaohs, see Richard A. Gabriel, *Warrior Pharaoh* (New York: Iuniverse Press, 2001).

3. Israelite practice regarding primogeniture gradually incorporated the Near Eastern practice of male lineage in contrast to the Egyptian practice of legitimizing heirs to the throne only through female lineage.

4. Freedman, 120.

5. Abraham Malamat, "Organs of Statecraft in the Israelite Monarchy," *Biblical Archaeologist* 28 (1965): 59.

6. Ibid.

7. Freedman, 120, citing Buber.

8. Theodore Robinson and W.O.E. Oesterley, *A History of Israel*, vol. 1 (Oxford: Clarendon Press, 1948), 240.

9. I Kings 1:5.

10. I Kings 1:7–8.

11. I Kings 1:25.

12. I Kings 1:32–34.

13. I Kings 1:49.

14. I Kings 2:46.

15. Tomoo Ishida, "Solomon's Succession to the Throne of David—A Political Analysis," in *Studies in the Period of David and Solomon*, ed. Tomoo Ishida (Tokyo: International Symposium for Biblical Studies, 1979), 185.

16. I Kings 2:35. Affording sanctuary in the Tent of Meeting seems to have been an Israelite practice since Exodus 21:14. The practice probably was adopted from the Egyptians who recognized that anyone taking refuge in a religious temple was beyond the reach of civil authorities as long as he remained in the temple. For more on this and other Israelite practices with Egyptian origins, see Richard A. Gabriel, *Gods of Our Fathers: The Memory of Egypt in Judaism and Christianity* (Westport, CT: Greenwood Press, 2002); see also M. Rostovtzeff, "The Foundations of Social and Economic Life in Hellenistic Times," *Journal of Egyptian Archaeology* 6 (1920): 170.

17. I Kings 4:7.

18. I Kings 5:7.

19. Benjamin Mazar, "The Era of David and Solomon," in *World History of the Jewish People*, 4, 1 (Jerusalem: Massada Press, 1979), 92.

20. *Cambridge Ancient History* (Cambridge: Cambridge University Press, 1973), 2, 1, 588.

21. Freedman, 122; see also John Bright, "The Organization and Administration of the Israelite Empire," in *Magnalia Dei: The Mighty Acts of God*, ed. Frank Moore Cross, Werner E. Lemke, and Patrick D. Miller Jr. (New York: Doubleday and Company, 1975), 198.

22. Abraham Malamat, "A Political Look at the Kingdom of David and Solomon and Its Relations with Egypt," in *Studies in the Period of David and Solomon*, ed. Tomoo Ishida (Tokyo: Symposium for Biblical Studies, 1979), 198.

23. Ibid.

24. Abraham Malamat, "Aspects of the Foreign Policies of David and Solomon," *Journal of Near Eastern Studies* 12, no. 1 (January 1963): 12. The author offers the possibility that the pharaoh whose daughter married Solomon was not Siamun, but Psusennes II.

25. Bright, 197.

26. Malamat, "Aspects of the Foreign Policies of David and Solomon," 16.

27. Ibid.

28. I Kings 9:17–18.

29. Malamat, "Aspects of the Foreign Policies of David and Solomon," 16–17.

30. Bright, 197.

31. Malamat, "A Political Look at the Kingdoms of David and Solomon," 199.

32. I Kings 3:1, 7:8, 9:16, 9:24, and 11:1.

33. Malamat, "Aspects of the Foreign Policies of David and Solomon," 10.

34. Ibid. See the citation in footnote 40 from S.A.B. Mercer, *The Tell El-Amarna Tablets*, I (1939), 12–13.

35. While the Israelites did not adopt female lineage as determinate in the selection of their kings, they did adopt the female lineage as determinate of ethno-religious identification. To this day, the Orthodox maintain that only the offspring of a Jewish female can be considered genuinely Jewish. The paternity of the child is of no consequence in this regard.

36. The wife of Tutankhamen, Ankhesenamun, made to offer to Suppiluliumas the Great, king of the Hittites. See Gabriel, *Gods of Our Fathers*, 58–59.

37. Brian Peckham, "Israel and Phoenicia," in *Magnalia Dei: The Mighty Acts of God*, 232.

38. I Kings 9:20–22. The argument that Solomon did not employ Israelites as enforced laborers is hardly convincing in light of the fact that it was precisely the harsh conditions of the enforced labor under Solomon that led the tribal leaders later to petition Rehoboam to lighten the yoke.

39. Malamat, "A Political Look at the Kingdoms of David and Solomon," 200; see also Robinson and Oesterley, 260.

40. I Kings 14:25.

41. Malamat, "Aspects of the Foreign Policies of David and Solomon," 5.

42. I Kings 11:26–27.

43. Robinson and Oesterley, 272.

44. Ibid.

45. I Kings, 11:40.

46. Mordechai Gichon, "The Defenses of the Solomonic Kingdom," *Palestine Exploration Quarterly* (July–December 1963): 114.

47. Ibid., 116.

48. Jacob M. Myers, *II Chronicles: The Anchor Bible* (New York: Doubleday, 1965), 48. From here on this source will be cited as *Anchor Bible*.

49. Gichon, 116.

50. Ibid., 121.

51. Ibid.

52. Robinson and Oesterley, 247.

53. Ibid.

54. Mazar, 96.

55. Gichon, 124.

56. Richard A. Gabriel, *The Culture of War: Invention and Early Development* (Westport, CT: Greenwood Press, 1990), 61.

57. Rudolph Cohen, "The Fortresses King Solomon Built to Protect His Southern Border," *Biblical Archeology Review* 11 (May–June, 1985): 58; see also by the same author, "Solomon's Negev Defense Line Contained Three Fewer Fortresses," *Biblical Archaeology Review* 12 (July–August, 1986): 40–45.

58. Cohen, 70.

59. William G. Dever, "Monumental Architecture in Ancient Israel in the Period of the United Monarchy," in *Studies in the Period of David and Solomon*, ed. Tomoo Ishida (Tokyo: Symposium for Biblical Studies, 1979), 293.

60. Ibid.

61. Ibid., 289.

62. Mazar, 97.

63. Gichon, 125.

64. Cohen, 70.

65. I Kings 9:21.

66. I Kings 9:26.

67. *Anchor Bible*, 59.

68. Mazar, 96.

69. For the conversion data used here, see *Anchor Bible*, 5.

70. Yutaka Ikeda, "Solomon's Trade in Horses and Chariots in Its International

Setting," in *Studies in the Period of David and Solomon*, ed. Tomoo Ishida (Tokyo: International Symposium for Biblical Studies, December, 1979), 223.

71. Ibid., 221.
72. Ibid., 225; see also W. F. Albright, *Archaeology and the Religion of Israel*, 5th ed. (Baltimore, MD: Johns Hopkins Press, 1969), 213.
73. Ibid.
74. Ibid.
75. Ibid., 225; see also Albright, 213.
76. Ikeda, 230.
77. Mazar, 95.
78. Ibid., 96.
79. Ibid.
80. *Anchor Bible*, 5; see also Albright, 135.
81. Ikeda, 227.
82. Ibid., 229.
83. Ibid., 236.
84. *Anchor Bible*, 48.
85. Ikeda, 238.
86. I Kings 12:3–5.
87. I Kings 12:21.
88. I Kings 12:16–17.
89. I Kings 12:20.
90. I Kings 12:21.
91. Robinson and Oesterley, 275.
92. II Chronicles 12:2–4; also I Kings 14:25.
93. David M. Rohl, *Pharaohs and Kings: A Biblical Quest* (New York: Crown Publishers, 1995), 306–7, for the list of cities conquered by Shishak listed on the wall at Karnak as well as a helpful map of Shishak's route.
94. Peckham, 233.
95. Ibid.
96. Robinson and Oesterley, 275.
97. II Chronicles 12:5.
98. I Kings 14:26.

Selected Bibliography

Ackroyd, P. R. *The Second Book of Samuel*. London: Cambridge Bible Commentary, 1977.

Albright, W. F. *Archaeology and the Religion of Israel*, 5th ed. Baltimore, MD: Johns Hopkins Press, 1969.

Albright, W. F. "The Song of Deborah in Light of Archaeology." *Bulletin of the American Schools of Oriental Research* 62 (1936): 26–31.

Aldred, Cyril. *Akhenaten: King of Egypt*. London: Thames and Hudson, 1988.

Armstrong, Karen. *A History of God*. New York: Ballantine Books, 1993.

Assmann, Jan. *Moses the Egyptian*. Cambridge, MA: Harvard University Press, 1997.

Bell, H. Idris. "Hellenic Culture in Egypt." *Journal of Egyptian Archaeology* 8 (1922): 139–55.

Boling, Robert G. *Judges: The Anchor Bible*. New York: Doubleday, 1975.

Boling, Robert G. and G. Ernest Wright. *Joshua: The Anchor Bible*. New York: Doubleday, 1982.

Bonfante, G. "Who Were the Philistines?" *American Journal of Archaeology* 50 (1946): 251–62.

Borowski, Oded. "The Negev: The Southern Stage for Biblical History." *Bible Review* 4 (1989): 40–43.

Borowski, Oded. "The Sharon: Symbol of God's Abundance." *Bible Review* 4 (1988): 40–43.

Breasted, James H. *The Dawn of Conscience*. New York: Charles Scribner, 1947.

Bright, John. "The Organization and Administration of the Israelite Empire." In *Magnalia Dei: The Mighty Acts of God*, edited by Frank Cross Moore, Werner E. Lemke, and Patrick D. Miller. New York: Doubleday, 1975, 193–208.

Brodsky, Harold. "The Shelpelah: Guardian of Judea." *Bible Review* 3 (1987): 48–52.

Buber, Martin. *The Revelation and the Covenant*. Amherst, NY: Humanity Books, 1998.

Budge, E. A. Wallis. *Osiris and the Egyptian Resurrection*. 2 vols. New York: Dover Press, 1973.

Cambridge Ancient History. Cambridge: Cambridge University Press, 1973.

Campbell, Edward F. Jr. "The Amarna Letters and the Amarna Period." *Biblical Archaeologist* 23 (1960): 2–22.

Clayton, Peter A. *Chronicle of the Pharaohs*. London: Thames and Hudson, 1994.

Cohen, Kenneth I. "King Saul: Bungler from the Beginning." *Bible Review* 10 (1994): 34–39, 56–57.

Cohen, Rudolph. "The Fortresses King Solomon Built to Protect His Southern Border." *Biblical Archaeological Review* 11 (1985): 56–70.

Cohen, Rudolph. "Solomon's Negev Defense Line Contained Three Fewer Fortresses." *Biblical Archaeology Review* 12 (1986): 40–45.

Conteneau, Georges. *Everyday Life in Babylon and Assyria*. London: Edward Arnold, 1954.

Cottrell, Leonard. *The Warrior Pharaohs*. New York: Dutton, 1969.

Craige, P. C. "War, Religion, and Scripture." *Bulletin of the Canadian Society of Biblical Literature* 46 (1986): 2–13.

Cross, Frank Moore, Werner E. Lemke, and Patrick D. Miller Jr., eds. *Magnalia Dei: The Mighty Acts of God*. New York: Doubleday, 1975.

Curtius, Qunitus. *History of Alexander*. Translated by John C. Rolfe. Cambridge, MA: Harvard University Press, 1946.

de Vaux, Roland. *The Bible and the Ancient Near East*. Garden City, NY: Doubleday, 1971.

Dever, William G. "Monumental Architecture in Ancient Israel in the Period of the United Monarchy." In *Studies in the Period of David and Solomon*, edited by Tomoo Ishida, 269–306. Tokyo: International Symposium for Biblical Studies, 1979.

Dever, William G. "The Peoples of Palestine in the Middle Bronze I Period." *Harvard Theological Review* 64 (1971): 197–226.

Dowley, T., ed. *Discovering the Bible*. Grand Rapids, MI: Erdmans, 1986.

Drews, Robert. "The Chariots of Iron of Joshua and Judges." *Journal for the Study of the Old Testament* 45 (1989): 15–23.

Drews, Robert. *The End of the Bronze Age*. Princeton, NJ: Princeton University Press, 1993.

Dupuy, T. N. *The Evolution of Weapons and Warfare*. New York: Bobbs-Merrill, 1980.

Encyclopedia Judaica. Jerusalem: Macmillan Company, 1975.

Fensham, F. C. "The Battle between the Men of Joab and Abner as a Possible Ordeal by Battle." *Vetus Testamentum* 20 (1970): 356–57.

Ferrill, Arther. *The Origins of War*. London: Thames and Hudson, 1985.

Forbes, R. J. *Studies in Ancient Technology*. Leiden: E. J. Brill, 1964.

Freedman, D. N. "The Age of David and Solomon." In *World History of the Jewish People*. Vol. 3. Philadelphia: Jewish Publications Ltd., 1979, 101–25.

Gabriel, Richard A. *The Culture of War: Invention and Early Development*. Westport, CT: Greenwood Press, 1990.

Gabriel, Richard A. *Gods of Our Fathers: The Memory of Egypt in Judaism and Christianity*. Westport, CT: Greenwood Press, 2002.
Gabriel, Richard A. *Great Captains of Antiquity*. Westport, CT: Greenwood Press, 2000.
Gabriel, Richard A. *No More Heroes: Madness and Psychiatry in War*. New York: Hill and Wang, 1987.
Gabriel, Richard A. *Warrior Pharaoh*. New York: Iuniverse Press, 2001.
Gabriel, Richard A. and Donald Boose Jr. *The Great Battles of Antiquity*. Westport, CT: Greenwood Press, 1994.
Gabriel, Richard A. and Karen S. Metz. *From Sumer to Rome: The Military Capabilities of Ancient Armies*. Westport, CT: Greenwood Press, 1991.
Gabriel, Richard A. and Karen S. Metz. *A History of Military Medicine*. 2 vols. Westport, CT: Greenwood Press, 1992.
Gal, Reuven. *A Portrait of the Israeli Soldier*. Westport, CT: Greenwood Press, 1986.
Gale, General Sir Richard. *Great Battles of Bible History*. New York: John Day Company, 1970.
Gardiner, Sir Alan. *Egypt of the Pharaohs*. London: Oxford University Press, 1961.
Gichon, Mordechai. "The Defense of the Solomonic Kingdom." *Palestine Exploration Quarterly* (1963): 113–26.
Gottwald, Norman K. *The Tribes of Yahweh*. New York: Orbis Books, 1979.
Graetz, Heinrich. *History of the Jews*. 2 vols. Philadelphia: Jewish Publication Society of America, 1956.
Grant, Michael. *The History of Ancient Israel*. New York: Charles Scribner, 1984.
Grimal, Nicolas. *History of Ancient Egypt*. London: Blackwell Publishers, 1992.
Hanson, P. D. "War, Peace, and Justice in Early Israel." *Biblical Archaeological Society* 3 (1987): 32–45.
Hauer, C. E. "Jerusalem, the Stronghold, and Rephaim." *Catholic Biblical Quarterly* 32 (1970): 571–78.
Hawk, L. Daniel. "Saul as Sacrifice: The Tragedy of Israel's First Monarch." *Bible Review* 12 (1996): 20–25.
Hays, J. Daniel. "Moses: The Private Man behind the Public Leader." *Bible Review* 26 (200): 17–26, 60–63.
Herzog, Chaim and Mordechai Gichon. *Battles of the Bible*. Jerusalem: Steimatzky's Agency Ltd., 1978.
Hobbs, T. R. *A Time for War*. Wilmington, DE: Michael Glazier, 1989.
Homan, Michael M. "The Divine Warrior in His Tent: A Military Model for Yahweh's Tabernacle." *Bible Review* 16 (2000): 22–33.
Hulse, E. V. "Joshua's Curse and the Abandonment of Ancient Jericho: Schistosomiasis as a Possible Medical Explanation." *Medical History* 15 (1971): 376–86.
Hurowitz, Victor. "Inside Solomon's Temple." *Bible Review* 10 (1994): 25–37, 50.
Ikeda, Yutaka. "Solomon's Trade in Horses and Chariots in Its International Setting." In *Studies in the Period of David and Solomon*, edited by Tomoo Ishida, 215–38. Tokyo: International Symposium for Biblical Studies, 1979.
Ishida, Tomoo. "Solomon's Succession to the Throne of David: A Political Analysis." In *Studies in the Period of David and Solomon*, edited by Tomoo Ishida, 175–87. Tokyo: International Symposium for Biblical Studies, 1979.

Ishida, Tomoo, ed. *Studies in the Period of David and Solomon*. Tokyo: International Symposium for Biblical Studies, 1979.

Isserlin, B.S.J. "The Israelite Conquest of Canaan: A Comparative Review of the Arguments Applicable." *Palestine Exploration Quarterly* 115 (1983): 85–94.

Isserlin, B.S.J. *The Israelites*. London: Thames and Hudson, 1998.

Kirsch, Jonathan. *Moses: A Life*. New York: Ballantine Books, 1998.

Kitchen, Kenneth A. "The Desert Tabernacle." *Bible Review* 16 (2000): 14–21.

Klein, Joel. *Through the Name of God*. Westport, CT: Greenwood Press, 2001.

Kuhn, Thomas. *The Structure of Scientific Revolution*. Chicago: University of Chicago Press, 1962.

Laffont, Robert. *The Ancient Art of Warfare*. 2 vols. New York: Time-Life Books, 1966.

Lapp, Paul W. "Ta'anach by the Waters of Megiddo." *Biblical Archaeologist* 30 (1967): 2–27.

Lemche, Niels Peter. "David's Rise." *Journal for the Study of the Old Testament* 10 (1978): 2–25.

L'Heureux, P. "The *yelide harapa*—A Cultic Association of Warriors." *Bulletin of the American Schools of Oriental Research* 221 (1976): 83–85.

Liver, Jacob, ed. *The Military History of the Land of Israel in Biblical Times* (in Hebrew). Jerusalem: Israel Defense Force Publishing House, 1964.

Luccas, A. "The Number of Israelites at the Exodus." *Palestine Exploration Quarterly* (1944): 164–68.

Machlin, Milton. *Joshua's Altar: The Dig at Mount Ebal*. New York: William Morrow, 1991.

Malamat, Abraham. "Aspects of the Foreign Policies of David and Solomon." *Journal of Near Eastern Studies* 22 (1963): 1–17.

Malamat, Abraham. "Cushan Rishathaim and the Decline of the Near East around 1200 B.C.E." *Journal of Near Eastern Studies* 13 (1954): 231–242.

Malamat, Abraham. "The Danite Migration and the Pan-Israelite Exodus-Conquest: A Biblical Narrative Pattern." *Biblica* 51 (1970): 1–16.

Malamat, Abraham. "The Egyptian Decline in Canaan and the Sea Peoples." In *World History of the Jewish People*, Vol. 3, 1979, 23–38.

Malamat, Abraham. "Hazor, the Head of All Those Kingdoms." *Journal of Biblical Literature* 79 (1960): 12–19.

Malamat, Abraham. "Israelite Conduct of War in the Conquest of Canaan According to Biblical Tradition." In *Symposia Celebrating the 75th Anniversary of the American Schools of Oriental Research*. Chicago: University of Chicago Press, 1979, 35–56.

Malamat, Abraham. "The Kingdom of David and Solomon in Its Contact with Egypt and Aram Naharaim." *Biblical Archaeologist* 21 (1958): 103–12.

Malamat, Abraham. "Organs of Statecraft in the Israelite Monarchy." *Biblical Archaeologist* 28 (1965): 35–63.

Malamat, Abraham. "The Period of the Judges." In *World History of the Jewish People*, Vol. 3, 1979, 129–163.

Malamat, Abraham. "A Political Look at the Kingdom of David and Solomon and Its Relations with Egypt." In *Studies in the Period of David and Solomon*, edited by Tomoo Ishida, 189–204. Tokyo: International Symposium for Biblical Studies, 1979.

Malamat, Abraham. "The War of Gideon and Midian: A Military Approach." *Palestine Exploration Quarterly* 85 (1953): 61–65.

Margoswky, Yehuda. "War and Warfare." *Encyclopedia Judaica*, Vol. 1. New York: Macmillan, 1971, 266–81.

Mayes, A.D.H. "The Historical Context of the Battle against Sisera." *Vetus Testamentum* 19 (1969): 352–60.

Mazar, Benjamin. "The Aramean Empire and Its Relations with Israel." *Biblical Archaeologist* 25 (1962): 98–120.

Mazar, Benjamin. "The Era of David and Solomon." In *World History of the Jewish People*, Vol. 4, 1979, 76–99.

Mazar, Benjamin. "Jerusalem in the Biblical Period." In *Jerusalem Revealed: Archaeology in the Holy City*. New Haven, CT: Yale University Press, 1976, 1–8.

Mazar, Benjamin. "The Military Elite of King David." *Vetus Testamentum* 13 (1963): 310–20.

Mazar, Benjamin. *The Mountain of the Lord*. Garden City, NY: Doubleday, 1975.

Mazar, Benjamin. "The Philistines and Their Wars with Israel." In *World History of the Jewish People*, Vol. 3, 1979, 164–79.

McCarter, P. Kyle. *I Samuel: The Anchor Bible*. New York: Doubleday, 1980.

McCarter, P. Kyle. *II Samuel: The Anchor Bible*. New York: Doubleday, 1984.

Mercer, S.A.A. *The Tell El-Amarna Tablets*, Toronto: Macmillan Co. of Canada, 1939.

Mendenhall, George E. "The Census Lists of Number 1 and 26." *Journal of Biblical Literature* 77 (1958): 52–66.

Mendenhall, George E. "The Hebrew Conquest of Palestine." *Biblical Archaeologist* 25 (1962): 66–87.

Millard, A. R. "Saul's Shield Not Anointed with Oil." *Bulletin of the American Schools of Oriental Research* 230 (1978): 77–78.

Miller, J. Maxwell. "Archaeology and the Israelite Conquest of Canaan: Some Methodological Observations." *Palestine Exploration Quarterly* 109 (1977): 87–93.

Moyer, J. "Weapons and Warfare in the Book of Judges." In *Discovering the Bible*, edited by T. Dowley, 42–50. Grand Rapids, MI: Erdmans, 1986.

Myers, Jacob M. *II Chronicles: The Anchor Bible*. New York: Doubleday, 1965.

Naville, Edouard. "The Geography of the Exodus." *Journal of Egyptian Archaeology* 10 (1924): 18–39.

New American Bible. New York: Catholic Book Publishers, 1992.

Noth, A. *The History of Israel*. New York: Harper and Row, 1960.

Oesterley, W.O.E, and Theodore Robinson. *A History of Israel*. 2 vols. Oxford: Clarendon Press, 1948.

Olmstead, A. T. *The History of Assyria*. Chicago: University of Chicago Press, 1951.

Orlinsky. H. M. "The Seer Priest." In *World History of the Jewish People*, Vol. 3, 1979, 268–79.

Peckham, Brian. "Israel and Phoenicia." In *Magnalia Dei: The Mighty Acts of God*, edited by Frank Moore Cross et al., 1979, 224–48.

Postgate, J. N. *Taxation and Conscription in the Assyrian Empire*. Rome: Biblical Institute Press, 1974.

Pritchard, James B. *Ancient Near Eastern Texts Relating to the Old Testament*. Princeton, NJ: Princeton University Press, 1955.

Propp, William H. C. *Exodus 1–18: The Anchor Bible*. New York: Doubleday, 1998.

Redford, Donald B. *Akhenaten: The Heretic King*. Princeton, NJ: Princeton University Press, 1984.

Redford, Donald B. *Egypt, Canaan, and Israel in Ancient Times*. Princeton, NJ: Princeton University Press, 1992.

Reviv, H. "The Structure of Society." In *World History of the Jewish People*, Vol. 4, 1979, 125–46.

Robinson, Theodore H. and W.O.E. Oesterley. *A History of Israel*. 2 vols. Oxford: Clarendon Press, 1948.

Rohl, David M. *Pharaohs and Kings: A Biblical Quest*. New York: Crown Publishers, 1995.

Rosen, Stephen A. "The Canaanean Blade and the Early Bronze Age." *Israel Exploration Journal* 33 (1983): 15–29.

Rostovtzeff, M. "The Foundations of Social and Economic Life in Egypt in Hellenistic Times." *Journal of Egyptian Archaeology* 6 (1920): 161–78.

Rowley, H. H. *From Joseph to Joshua*. London: Oxford University Press, 1948.

Saggs, H.W.F. *The Might That Was Assyria*. London: Sidgwick and Jackson, 1984.

Schulman, Alan R. "Some Observations on the Military Background of the Amarna Period." *Journal of the American Research Center in Egypt* 3 (1964): 51–70.

Schulman, Alan Richard. *Military Rank, Title, and Organization in the Egyptian New Kingdom*. Berlin: Bruno Hessling Verlag, 1964.

Singer, Itamar. "Merneptah's Campaign to Canaan and the Egyptian Occupation of the Southern Coastal Plain of Palestine in the Ramesside Period." *Bulletin of the American Schools of Oriental Research* 269 (1988): 1–10.

Smith, Morton. *Jesus the Magician*. New York: Barnes and Noble, 1997.

Soggin, J. Alberto. "Compulsory Labor under David and Solomon." In *Studies in the Period of David and Solomon*, edited by Tomoo Ishida, 1979, 259–67.

Speiser, E. A. "The Manner of the King." In *World History of the Jewish People*, Vol. 3, 1979, 280–87.

Stager, Lawrence E. "The Archaeology of the Family in Ancient Israel." *Bulletin of the American Schools of Oriental Research* 260 (1985): 1–35.

Stiebing, William H. Jr., "Did Weather Make Israel's Emergence Possible?" *Bible Review* 10 (1994): 19–27, 54.

Stillman, Nigel and Nigel Tallis. *Armies of the Ancient Near East*. Sussex, UK: Flexiprint Ltd., 1984.

Strange, John. "The Transition from the Bronze Age to the Iron Age in the Eastern Mediterranean and the Emergence of the Israelite State." *Scandinavian Journal of the Old Testament* (1987): 1–19.

Tadmor, Hayim. "Traditional Institutions and the Monarchy: Social and Political Tensions in the Time of David and Solomon." In *Studies in the Period of David and Solomon*, edited by Tomoo Ishida, 1979, 239–57.

Tanakh: The Holy Scriptures. New York: Jewish Publication Society, 1985.

Thomson, H. C. "Shopet and Mishpat in the Book of Judges." In *Transactions of the Glascow Oriental Society*, 74–85. Leiden: E. S. Brill, 1963.

Tidwell, N. L. "The Philistine Incursions in the Valley of Rephaim." In *Studies in the Historical Books of the Old Testament*, 190–212. Leiden: E. S. Brill, 1979.

Van Creveld, Martin. *Technology and War from 2000 B.C. to the Present*. New York: Free Press, 1989.

Wainwright, G. A. "Some Sea Peoples." *Journal of Egyptian Archaeology* 47 (1961): 71–90.

Wees, H. "Leaders of Men: Military Organization in the Iliad." *Classical Quarterly* 36 (1986): 285–303.

Westminster Historical Atlas to the Bible. Philadelphia, PA: Westminster Press, 1945.

Wiesel, Elie. "Joshua: Silent at the Tent Door." *Bible Review* 14 (1998): 20–21.

Willeson, F. "The Philistine Corps of the Scimitar From Gath." *Journal of Semitic Studies* 3 (1958): 327–35.

Wilson, J. V. Kinnier. "Medicine in the Land and Times of the Old Testament." In *Studies in the Period of David and Solomon*, edited by Tomoo Ishida, 337–65, 1979.

World History of the Jewish People. Philadelphia, PA: Jewish Publications Ltd., 1979.

Yadin, Yigael. *The Art of Warfare in Biblical Lands in Light of Archaeology*. 2 vols. New York: McGraw-Hill, 1964.

Yeivin, Saul. "Administration." In *World History of the Jewish People*. Vol. 4. 1979, 147–71.

Yurco, Frank. "Merneptah's Canaanite Campaign." *Journal of the American Research Center in Egypt* 23 (1986): 189–215.

Index

About the Author

RICHARD A. GABRIEL is Professor of Ethics and Humanities, Daniel Webster College. He is the author of 34 books, many of them in the area of ancient military history. He was Director of Advanced Courses at the U.S. Army War College and a professor at St. Anselm College.